Praise for Peter Annin's *The Great Lakes Water Wars*

"If you are one of the many people who care about the Great Lakes, you must read this book. Annin is undisputedly the preeminent journalist writing about the most significant freshwater resource on the planet."

—**Todd L. Ambs**, Director, Healing Our Waters–Great Lakes Coalition

"The Great Lakes are far more than five arcs of blue on the map in the heart of North America—they are the motivating force behind 150 years of human dreams, schemes, growth, and maneuvering. Peter Annin's *The Great Lakes Water Wars* brings to life the rapscallions, the politicians, the environmentalists, and also brings to life the five lakes themselves. Every tale is a reminder that just when the Great Lakes seem secure, someone is quietly plotting a freshwater grab."

—**Charles Fishman**, best-selling author of *The Big Thirst*

"Annin's *The Great Lakes Water Wars* is one of those rare books that weaves together current events, policy, science, and law, using the most important force of all: great storytelling. You have to force yourself to remember that you're actually reading about policy, science, and law."

—**Cameron Davis**, Great Lakes "Czar" under the Obama administration

"The Great Lakes have been central to the lives of people in Michigan since before recorded history. We must protect the treasure that these magnificent lakes represent. In this updated edition of *The Great Lakes Water Wars*, Peter Annin looks at the policy challenges facing our Great Lakes, laying a critical foundation for sound management as we make the decisions today that will impact the Lakes tomorrow and beyond."

—**Candice S. Miller**, Public Works Commissioner, Macomb County; member, Great Lakes Commission, and former Michigan Congresswoman (R)

"A deeply researched history of interstate and cross-border cooperation addressing the vulnerability of an essential resource. This fascinating read is a thorough analysis in policy making that will be a source of facts and wisdom when Great Lakes diversion projects reemerge."

—**Pierre Marc Johnson**, former Premier of Québec, international trade negotiator, and adviser to sustainable development organizations

"Impressive—the first word that came to mind after reading this thoroughly researched and eminently readable account of the Great Lakes water wars. Annin's historical narrative, based on hundreds of interviews and documents, includes tensions caused by water diversions from the Great Lakes spanning three centuries, as well as the twenty-first century's regional cooperation effort aimed at permanently protecting this precious resource."

—**Jim Nicholas**, former Director, Michigan Water Science Center, US Geological Survey

"By capturing the amazing story of our struggles to manage the Great Lakes, Peter Annin demonstrates how water challenges in this region will become more complex and unpredictable than anyone imagined. All who live near and depend on these waters will find new insights into the binational sociopolitical system we must transform to sustain our Great Lakes for future generations."

—**Michael Reuter**, Midwest Division Director, The Nature Conservancy

"*The Great Lakes Water Wars* provides essential context for the region's ongoing discussions about the sustainable use of Great Lakes water resources. The book offers a thorough, informative, and insightful recounting of how the region's struggle to manage Great Lakes water resources has informed the way future uses will be reviewed and evaluated. The book is especially important now, as the region works to balance its commitment to protecting water resources with the widespread acknowledgment that the 'Blue Economy' is the key to the region's future health and prosperity."

—**Kathryn A. Buckner**, President, Council of Great Lakes Industries

"This book oozes power, from the awe-inspiring crash of waves on Lake Superior to the visceral conflict over water diversion fights, the audacity of pumping schemes, and the big idea that the Great Lakes region should have control over its own destiny. Never boring, the writing zooms along at a pleasant pace that allows the reader to absorb the issues and a quest for resolution."

—**Tim Eder**, Program Officer, C.S. Mott Foundation, former Executive Director, Great Lakes Commission

"This extensively revised edition of *The Great Lakes Water Wars* places the Great Lakes in the context of water wars across the globe. Annin's meticulous research and historical backstories mesmerize Great Lakes nerds like me and present a captivating story for general readers. It is a vitally important book by a master storyteller for anybody who relies on fresh water for life. Yes, that's all of us."

—**Andy Buchsbaum**, Vice President, National Wildlife Federation

"Not mere water, the Great Lakes are a spirit, ecology, economy, brand, political movement, and human right that millions will defend like family. Annin deftly draws these competing forces into his narrative of a 'century of water' that alternately points this saturated region toward vibrant renewal or a spiral of conflict. Essential for anyone who believes Great Lakes water is the next grand idea."

—**Joel Brammeier**, President and CEO, Alliance for the Great Lakes

About Island Press

Since 1984, the nonprofit organization Island Press has been stimulating, shaping, and communicating ideas that are essential for solving environmental problems worldwide. With more than 1,000 titles in print and some 30 new releases each year, we are the nation's leading publisher on environmental issues. We identify innovative thinkers and emerging trends in the environmental field. We work with world-renowned experts and authors to develop cross-disciplinary solutions to environmental challenges.

Island Press designs and executes educational campaigns, in conjunction with our authors, to communicate their critical messages in print, in person, and online using the latest technologies, innovative programs, and the media. Our goal is to reach targeted audiences—scientists, policy makers, environmental advocates, urban planners, the media, and concerned citizens—with information that can be used to create the framework for long-term ecological health and human well-being.

Island Press gratefully acknowledges major support from The Bobolink Foundation, Caldera Foundation, The Curtis and Edith Munson Foundation, The Forrest C. and Frances H. Lattner Foundation, The JPB Foundation, The Kresge Foundation, The Summit Charitable Foundation, Inc., and many other generous organizations and individuals.

The opinions expressed in this book are those of the author(s) and do not necessarily reflect the views of our supporters.

The Great Lakes Water Wars

The Great Lakes Water Wars

Revised Edition

Peter Annin

Washington | Covelo | London

Library of Congress Control Number: 2018941939

All Island Press books are printed on environmentally responsible materials.

Manufactured in the United States of America
10 9 8 7 6 5 4 3 2 1

Keywords: Aral Sea, Asian carp, Brandon Road Lock and Dam, CAWS,
Chicago diversion, Chicago Sanitary and Ship Canal, Foxconn,
Georgian Bay, GLMRIS, GRAND Canal, Great Lakes, Great Lakes Charter,
Great Lakes climate change, Great Lakes Compact, Great Lakes water levels,
Long Lac, Lowell, Ogallala Aquifer, NAWAPA, New Berlin,
Nova Group, Ogoki, Pleasant Prairie, St. Clair River, water diversion,
Water Resources Development Act, Waukesha

Precipitation that falls inside the Basin boundary eventually finds its way to the Great Lakes. Precipitation outside the Basin boundary ends up in the Mississippi River, Hudson Bay, or other watersheds.

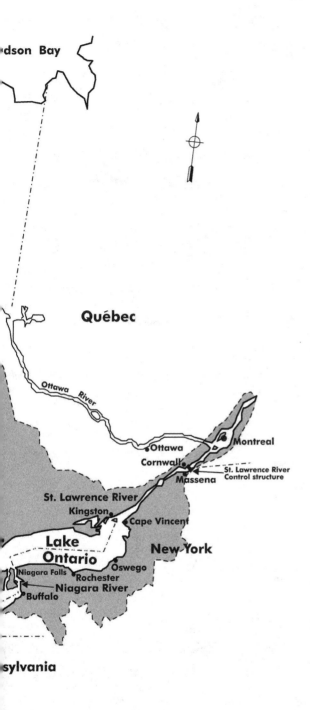

dson Bay

Québec

Ottawa River

•Ottawa
Cornwall•
Massena

Montreal•

St. Lawrence River
Control structure

St. Lawrence River
Kingston•
Cape Vincent

Lake
Ontario

New York

Oswego•

Niagara Falls•Rochester
Niagara River
•Buffalo

sylvania

U.S. Army Corps of Engineers, Detroit District

Contents

Acronyms

ACRCC	Asian Carp Regional Coordinating Committee
CAWS	Chicago Area Waterway System
CELA	Canadian Environmental Law Association
cfs	cubic feet per second
cms	cubic meters per second
CGLI	Council of Great Lakes Industries
DNR	Department of Natural Resources
EPA	Environmental Protection Agency
GATT	General Agreement on Tariffs and Trade
GLMRIS	Great Lakes and Mississippi River Interbasin Study
GRAND Canal	Great Recycling and Northern Development Canal
IJC	International Joint Commission
JEDD	Joint Economic Development District
mgd	millions of gallons per day
mld	millions of liters per day
MOU	Memorandum of Understanding
NAWAPA	North American Water and Power Alliance
NOAA	National Oceanic and Atmospheric Administration
NWF	National Wildlife Federation
OPG	Ontario Power Generation
PRPI	Powder River Pipeline Inc.
SNWA	Southern Nevada Water Authority
WRDA	Water Resources Development Act

But wherever the truth may lie, this much is crystal clear: our bigger-and-better society is now like a hypochondriac, so obsessed with its own economic health as to have lost the capacity to remain healthy. The whole world is so greedy for more bathtubs that it has lost the stability necessary to build them, or even to turn off the tap. Nothing could be more salutary at this stage than a little healthy contempt for a plethora of material blessings.

— Aldo Leopold, *A Sand County Almanac* (1949)

To Meri, Nick, and Reid

Author's Note

It has been more than a decade since the first edition of this book was published. During that time, many readers have reached out, wondering if a new edition was in the offing. Several were impatient for an update, given that so much Great Lakes water history had transpired. The Great Lakes Compact was adopted by all eight Great Lakes legislatures, as well as the US Congress, and it was signed by President George W. Bush in 2008. Ontario and Québec passed similar water-diversion legislation in 2007 and 2009. Wisconsin officials approved a water diversion in New Berlin, and Waukesha was due to submit a diversion application next.

Given that the first edition of this book included a chapter on Waukesha, I decided to wait until Waukesha's application was voted on before forging ahead with an update. No one expected Waukesha's application to drag on for seven interminable years. The verdict finally came on June 21, 2016, but an appeal delayed a final resolution until the summer of 2017.

During the wait, the Great Lakes made history in other ways. Climate change continued to impact the Basin; water levels set record lows *and* record highs; and Asian carp pressed closer to Lake Michigan, prompting several Great Lakes states to ask the US Supreme Court to reopen the infamous Chicago diversion decree. The lakes were aboil with water news, and the author of this book was sitting on his hands waiting for Waukesha.

So, here we are, more than a decade later with the much-anticipated second edition of *The Great Lakes Water Wars*. It is a very different book. Three new chapters and an epilogue have been added: a second chapter on Waukesha, a second chapter on the Chicago diversion, and a chapter on the New Berlin diversion. The controversial Foxconn diversion is included as well. Four chapters have been so thoroughly overhauled that they may seem entirely new. Every chapter has been updated and revised.

What hasn't changed in the last decade is the visceral nature of the water diversion controversy. This new edition only reinforces the primary take-home message of the last: water diversion remains one of the most fought-over environmental issues in the Great Lakes, which hold roughly 20 percent of all the fresh surface water on earth. In many ways, the Great Lakes Compact, and its controversial exception clauses, have made the water-diversion issue even more complex. This book is designed to cut through those complexities. It is intentionally crafted as a nontechnical read. The first edition, which won the Great Lakes Book Award for nonfiction, has been called the definitive work on the Great Lakes water-diversion controversy. I hope this new edition will live up to that high standard.

Peter Annin
Co-Director
Mary Griggs Burke Center for Freshwater Innovation
Northland College
Ashland, Wisconsin

Prologue

Today I stand on the shores of Lake Superior and I see an intimidating, mercurial freshwater ocean. I see a lake the Ojibway called Gitchee Gumee—"Big Sea"—and revered like no other. I see a lake whose average annual temperature is just 40 degrees Fahrenheit. Forty degrees. A shipwrecked person floating in such water would be dead in just a few hours. I see a lake whose violent temper sank the *Edmund Fitzgerald,* a 729-foot freighter that disappeared in 1975 in hurricane-force winds and twenty-five-foot waves, sending twenty-nine humbled men to a watery grave. I see a lake so large that she creates her own weather—often changing without warning, catching even the most seasoned sailor off guard. I see a lake that is no place for charlatans—where there are old sailors, and there are brazen sailors, but there are no old, brazen sailors.

Today I stand on the shores of Lake Superior and I see a unique, fragile, cold-water ecosystem. I see the largest surface area of delicious fresh water in the world. I see a lake so deep (more than 1,300 feet) that her steepest underwater canyon is the lowest spot on the North American continent. I see a lake so large that she could swallow all four of the other Great Lakes and still have room to spare. I see the mother of all lakes, the headwaters of a great basin that holds one-fifth of all the fresh surface water on the planet. I see a five-lake ecosystem that contains enough water to cover the lower forty-eight states—every American acre south of the Canadian border—with 9.5 feet of Great Lakes water. I see an ecosystem that quenches the thirst of billions of creatures and 35 million people in eight U.S. states and two Canadian provinces.

Today I stand on the shores of Lake Superior and I see a naïve innocent, a voluptuous bounty on the verge of violation. I see millions of angry, parched people from far-flung venues who view "undeveloped water" as a wasted opportunity. I see dryland farmers clamoring with sharp spigots, claiming they can't feed the world without more irrigation. I see thousands of massive supertankers lining up on behalf of

The shore of Lake Superior on Stockton Island, Apostle Islands National Lake-shore. (Photo by Bob Jauch)

millions of thirsty Asians. I see endless Romanesque canals carrying water to manicured lawns in a burgeoning, unsustainable Sunbelt. I see anxious scientists who worry about the transformations that climate change could bring. I see Great Lakes politicians destructively bickering among themselves, ultimately threatening the lakes they hope to save. I see urban voters—with no connection to land, water, or wildlife—who elect their dilettante peers to public office, affecting water policy everywhere. I see countless people inexplicably bypassing cold, refreshing water from the tap, so they can spend more money on water in a bottle. I see international entrepreneurs rubbing their hands at the thought of getting rich from something that comes out of the ground for free. I see wasteful water practices, throughout the Great Lakes Basin, that historians will look back upon with scorn. I see water—clear, cold, luscious water—that many people see the value in taking, and few see the value in leaving. I see millions upon millions of Great Lakes residents who underestimate the struggle that awaits them.

Today, when I stand on the shores of Lake Superior, I don't see a lake. I see a sprawling, deep blue battleground that stretches from Duluth, Minnesota, to Trois-Rivières, Québec—and I wonder, *Who will win the war?*

Part I

Hope and Hopelessness

Chapter 1

To Have and Have Not

We have left the century of oil and entered the century of water. That's not to say that automobiles will be powered by water soon, but rather that, increasingly, water will supplant oil as the defining natural resource of the next one hundred years. While it's true that nearly three-quarters of the earth's surface is made up of water, all that blue space on the grade-school globe can be deceiving: 97 percent of the world's water is seawater—loaded with salt and unfit for drinking. The rest is drinkable, but two-thirds of that is locked up in the polar ice caps and is thus unavailable. That means less than 1 percent of all the surface water on earth is accessible, potable fresh water.[1]

Every day much of the world is reminded of just what a precious resource fresh water can be. Approximately 780 million people around the world today do not have access to clean drinking water, and the United Nations estimates that 1,000 children die *daily* due to unhealthy water conditions.[2] The UN adds that by 2025, two-thirds of the world's population could be "water stressed"—the vast majority of them in the developing world.[3] Much of the world's population growth is occurring in areas where water is far from abundant, and sanitation is abysmal. Five countries—India, Indonesia, Nigeria, Ethiopia and Pakistan—account for 75 percent of the world's population that practices what the UN refers to as "open defecation."[4] Yet when people finally do obtain traditional flush toilets, their water consumption can skyrocket, prompting international foundations to invest in new toilet technologies for the developing world.[5] During the next one hundred years, the globe will be increasingly divided into the water "haves" and

3

"have-nots.""Unless the balance between demand and finite supplies is restored, the world will face an increasingly severe global water deficit," warns the UN. "By 2050, global water demand is projected to increase by 55 percent."[6]

In 2015, São Paulo, Brazil—the largest city in the Western Hemisphere—was hammered by a severe drought that attracted global attention and raised the prospect of a major water crisis in one of the world's largest cities. By 2016, the city of 12 million people had rebounded, but questions remain about the sustainability of its water supply. As São Paulo was cycling out of the water headlines, Cape Town, South Africa, cycled into them. In 2018, the city of 4 million people announced that it had only a few months' water left in its reservoirs and began referring to the time when the water would run out as "Day Zero"—when water service to homes and businesses would stop. The announcement created hoarding, water lines, and a ration of thirteen gallons of water per person per day. Cities like Cape Town use a lot of water, but farms use much more. Agriculture is the single largest consumer of water in the world, by far.[7] That trend is expected to continue as the world works overtime to feed its burgeoning population. A key question during this century will be whether water-efficiency technologies will be able to offset any increases in agricultural water consumption. Regardless, it's hard to imagine any solution to the global water crisis without agriculture at the table.

As water scarcity becomes an increasingly divisive political issue, water tension will inevitably rise. Many experts believe that water scarcity and drought played a major role in the recent Syrian civil war, helping to destabilize the entire region and creating a new breeding ground for terror groups like the Islamic State. The Syrian drought pushed more than a million desperate farmers and their families into urban areas, contributing to the eventual chaos. "The combination of very severe drought, persistent multiyear crop failures, and the related economic deterioration led to very significant dislocation and migration of rural communities to the cities," reports Peter Gleick, a global water expert at the Pacific Institute in Oakland, California. "These factors further contributed to urban unemployment and economic dislocations and social unrest."[8]

As global water friction grows, unprecedented domestic and inter-national pressure is expected to be directed at water-rich regions, lead-ing to political, economic, social, and environmental stress. In particular, many of these water-abundant areas worry that they will be pressured to divert water from major lakes and rivers in order to subsidize un-sustainable water practices elsewhere, possibly at great cost to local water-dependent ecosystems. As a result, water diversion—artificially transporting water from its native basin to some other place—has be-come increasingly controversial. This is an enormously important issue for areas like the Great Lakes region of North America. The Great Lakes hold roughly 20 percent of all the fresh surface water on earth—more than half of that is in Lake Superior alone. Large lakes everywhere could face increased pressure, because—from a global water-quantity standpoint—they are where the action is. Robert Sterner, director of the Large Lakes Observatory at the University of Minnesota Duluth, estimates that the five largest lakes in the world hold more than half of the globe's available fresh surface-water supply.

During this era of increased water scarcity, some water-stressed communities in wealthy countries will be forced to consider serious conservation measures for the first time. People elsewhere will demand that water-rich regions "share" their resource with the rest of the world. Increased pleas for humanitarian water assistance are expected as well. All of these factors are bound to contribute to heightened global water anxiety. "In an increasingly large number of places, scarcity of water resources is a problem—where populations and economic demand are really coming up against limited natural supplies," says Mr. Gleick. "I don't like the term 'water wars'. . . But water is increasingly a factor in conflict, and there's a long history of violence over water, and I think it's going to get worse."⁹

Just how much fighting there has been over water is a matter of wide debate. But Mr. Gleick keeps a running list of water tension around the world in what is perhaps the most comprehensive water-conflict chronology ever compiled. The list, available on line, goes on and on for pages, citing numerous incidents between 3000 BC and today in which water either was used as a military tool, was targeted by military op-ponents, or otherwise became a source of tension. The water conflicts

Lake Rankings

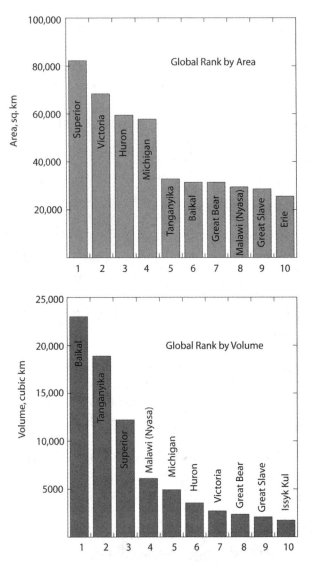

Four of the Great Lakes rank among the world's top ten by surface area. Three rank among the top ten by volume. The five largest lakes in the world hold more than half of the world's available fresh surface-water supply. (Provided by Large Lakes Observatory, University of Minnesota Duluth)

highlighted on Mr. Gleick's list range from California to China. Here's a quick snapshot of some noteworthy examples:

- A series of bombings in California between 1907 and 1913 were designed to prevent the diversion of water from the Owens Valley to Los Angeles.
- The Arizona National Guard was mobilized in 1935 during a dispute with California over water in the Colorado River.
- Riots broke out in 2016 in northern KwaZulu-Natal in South Africa after a severe drought sparked a dispute over water access.
- That same year, two people died and others were injured during water riots in Bangalore, India, after the nation's Supreme Court ordered water released from dams on the Cauvery River.[10]

Asia, a continent that holds 60 percent of the world's population but only 36 percent of the world's water, has many of the most volatile global water hotspots.[11] The Aral Sea, in the Central Asian nations of Uzbekistan and Kazakhstan, is one of the most overtapped water systems in the world and is now one-tenth its original size. "This is a serious problem in a lot of different places, many of them in Asia where you have the biggest disparity in population and available water," says Sandra Postel, director of the Global Water Policy Project. "That's translating into a fair amount of rivers running dry during long stretches of the year." China has responded to its significant water woes by embarking on a massive $63-billion scheme known as the South-to-North Water Diversion Project, which is designed to move trillions of gallons per year through hundreds of miles of canals and tunnels from the Yangtze River in the south to thirsty sections of northern China, including Beijing.[12]

Massive water-transfer projects are nothing new of course; the Romans turned them into an art form. So has California. But one of the most unique methods of water transportation to emerge has been the giant multimillion-gallon, PVC-coated fabric bags that are towed through the sea to transport fresh water from places like Suriname in South America to more-parched venues like Barbados and Curaçao.[13] The bags can hold as much water as an Olympic swimming pool, and they are towed behind tugs to water-stressed communities, where they are then emptied, and the water is distributed to customers. Scarcity drives up prices, and it's the growing preciousness of clean, reliable fresh water that is ramping up its value to the point where these kinds of speculative adventures can even be considered. Large multinational corporations have increased their presence in the municipal water-supply business, a move that has become controversial in the developing world because water supplies provided by for-profit corporations have sometimes resulted in rates that are beyond the reach of many customers.[14] The growing role of international corporations in the delivery of bottled, bulk, and municipal water has spawned a heated debate about whether water in its natural state is an economic commodity or something that is held in the public trust that people have a "human right" to access. There is concern among some experts that international trade protocols could interpret water in its natural state as a "good," which could complicate efforts by some communities to protect their local water resources from international exploitation. The divergent views on this issue regularly flare up at global water gatherings like the World Water Forum, a triennial event that is one of the world's largest gatherings of water aficionados of all stripes. Many international legal experts say that the global debate about whether water is a public resource or a private good remains unresolved.

~

While water scarcity is a serious problem in the developing world, it's a growing concern in North America as well. In fact, the Great Lakes Basin is literally surrounded on three sides by a wide variety of water scarcity and conflict. To the west, farmers in Montana have been arguing, off and on, with their colleagues in Alberta over water rights to the Milk and St. Mary Rivers for a century. Farther west, in the Klamath River Basin of southern Oregon and northern California, farmers, tribes, environmentalists, and state and federal officials have been fighting over water since 2001 after an endangered-species issue curtailed water access and threatened livelihoods.[15] California experienced a drought of biblical proportions from 2011 through 2017. The first four years of the drought were the driest in recorded history.[16] Years before the drought hit, the federal government was forced to wrest Colorado River water away from regional farmers so that their water could be redistributed piecemeal to sprawling metropolitan areas like San Diego.[17] In south-central Arizona, an overdrawn aquifer has created a cone of depression near the town of Eloy, where the soil has slumped more than twelve feet, creating mile-long cracks that have split the interstate highway and sliced deep into the earth.[18] In the Rio Grande Valley of Texas, Mexicans and Americans are arguing over the particulars of a 1944 treaty that sets strict limits on each nation's water rights.[19] In the Southeast, in the Apalachicola–Flint River Basin, the states of Alabama, Georgia, and Florida have been suing each other in federal court for a quarter century over water issues that affect millions from Atlanta to the Gulf of Mexico.[20] Water became so scarce there in 2007 that Georgia governor Sonny Perdue held a prayer vigil for rain on the state capitol steps, drawing national attention.[21] Farther up the Eastern Seaboard, the US Supreme Court intervened in a 2003 dispute between Virginia and Maryland over water in the storied Potomac River, and that was followed by a similar legal dispute over the Potomac more than a decade later that pitted Maryland against West Virginia.[22] And in Massachusetts, the overtapped Ipswich River outside Boston repeatedly runs dry, when excessive withdrawals of the regional groundwater supply rob the waterway of its crucial base flow.[23]

These hotspots have created an arc of water tension on the west, south, and east sides of the Great Lakes Basin. It is this arc of water tension that tends to drive the Great Lakes water-diversion debate—sometimes accurately and sometimes inaccurately. In virtually all of these problem areas populations are rising, which means that water stress is likely to get worse. Serious water shortages will be exacerbated by the drought cycle. "The United States is heading toward a water-scarcity crisis," predicts Robert Glennon, a law professor at the University of Arizona. "Our current water-use practices are unsustainable, and environmental factors threaten a water supply heavily burdened by increased demand."[24] One of the most sobering prognostications comes from the US Department of the Interior, which has published a map entitled "Potential Water Supply Crises by 2025." The map shows the western half of the continental United States and highlights a large number of areas where the department predicts the likelihood of future water conflict as either "highly likely," "substantial," or "moderate." Every state on the map except South Dakota has some sort of a water

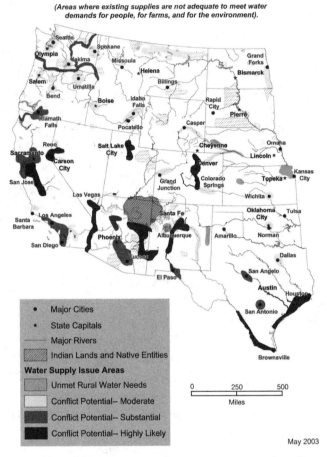

Potential Water Supply Crises by 2025

(Areas where existing supplies are not adequate to meet water demands for people, for farms, and for the environment).

Legend:
- Major Cities
- State Capitals
- Major Rivers
- Indian Lands and Native Entities

Water Supply Issue Areas
- Unmet Rural Water Needs
- Conflict Potential-- Moderate
- Conflict Potential-- Substantial
- Conflict Potential-- Highly Likely

0   250   500
Miles

May 2003

The western United States is expected to experience a number of water supply conflicts in coming years. (US Department of Interior)

trouble spot, with the most serious areas of concern being in Arizona, Texas, California, New Mexico, Colorado, Utah, and Nevada.

When it comes to water scarcity and usage, Las Vegas is in a category all its own. While Americans in general have some of the highest per capita water use in the world,[25] Las Vegas residents consume more than twice as much as the average American—205 gallons per day—and more than half of that water ends up on their lawns. (According to the US Environmental Protection Agency, 70 percent of the city's household water consumption goes to "landscaping."[26]) Yet the desert city remains one of the fastest growing in the nation and it is well known for its opulent water fountains and lush, irrigated golf courses—traits that make the city seem like a hard sell for some future interbasin water transfer.[27] But in Vegas people aren't shy about suggesting such things. "Water is a commodity," says Hal Rothman, author of *Neon Metropolis: How Las Vegas Started the Twenty-First Century.* "It's a lot like oil. We use oil to heat Boston, but that oil doesn't come from Boston. It comes from Saudi Arabia."[28] Talk like that makes people nervous in the Great Lakes region—which some have referred to as the Saudi Arabia of water. Why? Because it implies that people in places like Las Vegas can continue to live beyond their ecological means simply by importing water from someplace else.

The problem is that water is not like oil. Ecosystems don't depend on oil for their survival; they count on water for that. If all the oil on earth disappeared tomorrow, the world would be a very different place, but it would survive. If all the water on earth disappeared, however, life itself would come to a screeching halt.

Truth be told, the boom in Las Vegas—and in a lot of other Southwestern cities—has come at a severe environmental cost: the decimation of the once-mighty Colorado River. Since the early 1900s, Southwestern officials have treated the Colorado more like a workhorse than an ecosystem. It is now one of the most oversubscribed rivers in North America, and regularly no longer flows to the sea. "To some conservationists, the Colorado River is the preeminent symbol of everything mankind has done wrong," wrote Marc Reisner back in 1986 in his seminal book *Cadillac Desert.* "Even as hydrologists amuse themselves by speculating about how many times each molecule of water has passed through pairs of kidneys—[the Colorado] is still unable to satisfy all the demands on it . . . [and though there are] plans to import water from as far away as Alaska, the 20 million people in the Colorado Basin will probably find themselves facing chronic shortages, if not some kind of catastrophe, before any of these grandiose schemes is built."[29] (The Colorado River now supplies water to 30 million people.[30])

Outside the American Southwest, there is very little sympathy for the unsustainable water problems faced by that region. Great Lakes

Canadians are perhaps the least sympathetic of all. "Knowledgeable Canadians understand that there is no water shortage in the US," says Ralph Pentland, a Canadian water expert. The problem, Mr. Pentland says, is not a shortage of good water, but a shortage of good water management. "If you look at the Colorado Basin . . . they have problems caused by eight decades of subsidization of dumb projects, plus a water law that doesn't make sense." That sentiment comes from a country with some of the most abundant renewable per-capita water resources on the planet.[31]

~

For decades, Canadians and Americans in the Great Lakes Basin have feared that the thirsty will come calling. The question has always been: Will the Great Lakes be ready for them? The topic has been complicated by a wide debate within water circles about how much diversionary pressure the Great Lakes could realistically face as global water stress mounts. "I think the era of big, federal, subsidized water projects is over," declares Daniel Injerd, former director of the Office of Water Resources at the Illinois Department of Natural Resources. "I don't see a significant threat out there for Great Lakes water, probably not in my lifetime." Mr. Injerd's point is that diverting water over long distances is very, very expensive—so expensive that it's difficult to do without significant federal support. He, and many other water experts, argue that an environmentally conscious America would never tolerate an enormously subsidized, multibillion-dollar diversion plan that ships water from one end of the nation to the other, especially during tight budgetary times. His analysis is consistent with that of the International Joint Commission (IJC). The IJC was created by the Boundary Waters Treaty of 1909 to help resolve water disputes between Canada and the United States. In a report released in 2000, the IJC acknowledged the water-diversion anxiety in the Great Lakes region, but after extensive study it too declared that "the era of major diversions and water transfers in the United States and Canada has ended."[32]

Despite these assurances, regional residents on both sides of the border remain worried about outsiders taking Great Lakes water. These fears are driven, in part, by a general lack of faith that government institutions will protect the environment. But such worries can also be attributed to the almost spiritual connection that millions of people have with the Great Lakes. For many Native Americans in the United States, and First Nations indigenous people in Canada, it *is* a spiritual connection. In other parts of North America, mountains, oceans, and old-growth forests serve as the ecological talismans of the people. But for Canadians and Americans living in the Great Lakes region, nothing defines their relationship with the environment more than an abundance of fresh water—especially their sacred "Sweetwater Seas."

There are those who take issue with the IJC's position regarding the threat of Great Lakes diversions. These observers argue that the diversion threat is not gone, but merely dormant. All one needs to do, they say, is follow the population and water-scarcity trend lines into the future, and where the two lines intersect sometime later this century, water will become valuable enough to make a whole slew of wild diversion schemes a political reality again. "I don't think the era of water diversions is over by any means," argues Noah Hall, a professor at Wayne State University Law School in Michigan. "To me it's not even a question, it's an inevitability. You look at what's happening to water supplies in almost every other part of the country—it used to be just the Southwest and California, but now you are seeing it in the Southeast, and the Northeast—the economics are fluid. It's a simple supply-and-demand model."

Water experts from outside the Great Lakes region are not prepared to write off the diversion threat either. "Never say never," says Sandra Postel. "Climate change is a huge wild card in this entire thing. If there's evidence that the agricultural heartland in this country is starting to dry up and needs irrigation, well, then I think that changes the whole dynamic." Other experts say that future diversion schemes will have to meet a strict economic litmus test—something that was often not required of the large-scale diversions of the past. "There'll be increased calls for new projects to move water from one place to another," predicts Peter Gleick. "But you don't have to move water very far before really expensive desalination starts to look economic. Water conservation and efficiency is far more cost-effective right now than most sources of new supply."

If the Great Lakes water-diversion idea is so far-fetched, why do so many smart, influential people keep proposing it? In 2007, when New Mexico governor Bill Richardson was running for the Democratic presidential nomination against Barack Obama, he created quite a stir by proposing a "national water policy" whereby water-rich states would share their aqua wealth with dry states like his. In an interview with the *Las Vegas Sun* he said, "I believe that Western states and Eastern states have not been talking to each other when it comes to proper use of our water resources. . . . I want a national water policy. We need a dialogue between states to deal with issues like water conservation, water-reuse technology, water delivery, and water production. States like Wisconsin are awash in water."[33]

The following year, a leading Québec think tank released a white paper promoting bulk water exports from throughout Canada. "Large-scale exports of fresh water would be a wealth-creating idea for Québec and for Canada as a whole," declared the Montréal Economic Institute. "It is urgent to look seriously at developing our blue gold."[34] And in 2017, James Famiglietti, senior water scientist with NASA's Jet Propulsion Laboratory in California, sparked controversy by predicting that by midcentury climate change and population growth could force the nation to build a pipeline from the Great Lakes to the Southwest. "You can imagine that fifty years from now—well, we're already talking about this—but fifty years from now there might actually be a pipeline that brings water from the Great Lakes to Phoenix. I think that's part of our future." He added that Great Lakes water-diversion regulations would need to change for that to happen, possibly through "national intervention." "As the population grows, and as climate continues to change, we probably will have to move water from where it is, to where it is not, and that will require some rethinking of some of these policies and laws."[35]

Perhaps because of these recurring flirtations with the idea of Great Lakes water diversions, in 2015 the IJC backed off, somewhat, from its definitive declaration fifteen years earlier that the diversion era was over. "The mega-diversion era ended in the United States with the Central Arizona Project in the 1970s and in Canada with the La Grande Project in the early 1990s," the IJC said in a 2015 report. "But the possibility remains that climate change or other unforeseen circumstances could conceivably change that calculus. The Great Lakes

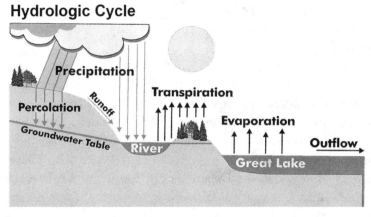

Less than 1 percent of the Great Lakes' water is renewed annually through rainfall, snowfall, and groundwater recharge. (US Army Corps of Engineers, Detroit District)

Region needs to continue to be vigilant and precautionary in its approach to diversions."[36] Many seasoned Great Lakes politicos are not surprised that the controversy is so persistent. "Diversion is the hydra-headed monster in this story," says former Wisconsin governor Tony Earl. "It's always been out there [and] keeps popping back to life. . . . It never goes away."

~

For many water managers in the Great Lakes region, this debate is purely academic—they say the Great Lakes don't have any water to spare. Yes, the lakes represent one of the largest collections of fresh surface water on earth—6 quadrillion gallons, or 5,439 cubic miles.[37] But less than 1 percent of that water is renewed by rainfall, snowfall, and groundwater recharge every year. The other 99 percent was deposited by glaciers during the last ice age. Think of the Great Lakes as a giant water bank account, deposited in the heart of the North American continent more than ten thousand years ago, that earns less than 1 percent of water interest per year. If you start pulling water from the principal, you may need another ice age to get it back. "The Great Lakes are . . . more than just a resource to be consumed; they are also home to a great diversity of plants, animals, and other biota," says the

IJC. "If all interests in the Basin are considered, there is never a 'surplus' of water in the Great Lakes system; every drop of water has several potential uses."[38]

In many ways, the glaciers defined the shape of the Great Lakes Basin. They advanced and receded repeatedly over hundreds of thousands of years, scraping, eroding, rescraping, re-eroding the landscape, sanding down hills, and creating huge cavities in the softer areas of Earth's surface. "We're talking a kilometer or so thick of ice going out in lobes and eroding through several of these basins," explains John Johnston, assistant professor in the Department of Earth and Environmental Sciences at the University of Waterloo in Ontario. The last glacier receded roughly ten thousand years ago, and as it melted and water levels settled, it left behind the geologic footprint of the contemporary Great Lakes Basin. The result is a large, water-rich ecosystem spanning more than 750 miles end to end.[39]

While the Basin is considered to be one ecosystem, the individual lakes have unique characteristics that distinguish them from each other. Lake Superior is the largest, deepest, cleanest, and coldest lake in the system, with the least-populated shoreline—the lake is so large that it could swallow all the other lakes, plus three additional Lake Eries. Lake Michigan is the second largest lake by volume, though it comes in third in surface area. Its southern shoreline is one of the most heavily populated and industrialized in the region, home to 9.5 million people in the Chicago metropolitan area alone.[40] Lake Huron is the second largest lake by surface area, but the third largest by volume; and while much of the shoreline is heavily forested, it hosts more agriculture than Lake Superior, but less population than Lake Michigan. Lake Erie is the shallowest in the Basin and the smallest by volume, and it hosts one of the most bountiful freshwater fisheries in the world. With an average depth of just sixty-two feet, it's the warmest lake and has traditionally struggled the most with water-quality issues. Lake Ontario, at the tail end of the system, is the smallest lake by surface area, but it's deep—with a maximum depth of 802 feet, it's deeper than Lake Huron.[41] Several of the Great Lakes rank among the largest in the world.

Water from the Great Lakes nourishes 35 million people in cities like Chicago, Cleveland, Detroit, and Toronto, and it's the lifeblood

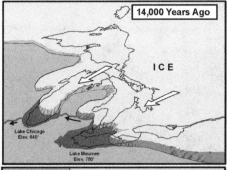

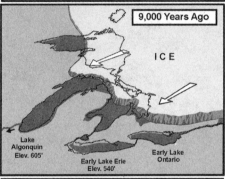

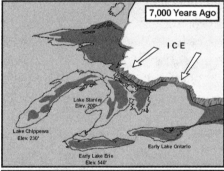

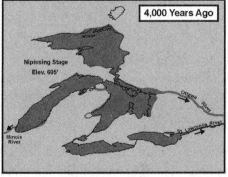

In many ways, the glaciers defined the shape of the Great Lakes, advancing and receding repeatedly over hundreds of thousands of years. (US Army Corps of Engineers, Detroit District)

Great Lakes Profile

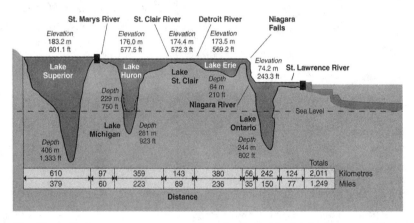

The Great Lakes are one ecosystem, but the individual lakes vary widely in depth and surface area. (Michigan Sea Grant)

of many industries, power plants, hydroelectric power facilities, and farms. Agriculture remains one of the largest consumers of Great Lakes water and it is the largest consumer of water globally as well.[42] Great Lakes water also supports a vibrant multibillion-dollar regional tourism industry and a $7-billion fishery, and it floats the thousand-foot freighters that ply the lakes during the $35-billion Great Lakes shipping season. During low-water periods, for every one-inch drop in Great Lakes water levels, those thousand-foot freighters must shave 270 tons of cargo from their holds to ensure that they don't scrape bottom as they slip from one lake to another. That makes shipping more expensive, which influences the cost of everything from coal to steel—and the electric bills and automobiles that go with them. While it's true that less than 1 percent of the water in the lakes is renewed every year, many industrialists argue that that statistic can be deceiving. While much of that 1 percent is being "used," they say it's not all being "consumed." When hydroelectric power plants cycle water through their turbines, they are using the water temporarily and returning it to the system. Water consumption (what is often called "consumptive use"), however, refers to water that is *not* returned to the lakes, whether lost through evaporation at a power plant or enclosed in a can of beer.

"I think water is one of the region's competitive advantages. We don't have the sun of Arizona; we don't have the mountains of the West. We have water," says Jon Allan, director of the Michigan Office of the Great Lakes. "[But] we have to be very careful not to overregulate . . . to strike that balance for our water future but not do it in a way that really disadvantages us." According to Jim Nicholas, former director of the US Geological Survey's Water Science Center in Lansing, Michigan, the renewable supply in the Great Lakes Basin is equivalent to 161.6 billion gallons per day. Of that, he says, only 1.5 percent is actually being consumed, or lost from the system because of human use.

Some corporate officials cite those low consumption rates as proof that cities, farms, and industries in the Great Lakes Basin have not come close to using up all of the region's renewable water supply—suggesting that there's plenty of water left for humans to consume without affecting the ecosystem. This, however, is not a conclusion that Mr. Nicholas is willing to make. The problem with such claims, he says, is that they ignore the fact that the water in the Great Lakes region is already being used by the ecosystem, and it's not clear how increased water consumption might affect the region's unique water-dependent environment. "We have a lot more water than Arizona," he says. "[But] just having more water doesn't mean that there's more water available."

It's clear that the Great Lakes region, the North American continent, and the entire world are all moving deeper into a period of expanding water tension. Those tensions are expected to put increased pressure on water-rich regions of the world, like the North American Great Lakes. Consequently, there has been a collective agreement among the water intelligentsia in the Great Lakes that the region needs a modern, binding world-class water-management system that protects these globally significant water bodies as we enter an era of increasing international water insecurity. Since the 1980s, officials have implemented a wide variety of policies to control Great Lakes water withdrawals and diversions. But most of those measures have proven to be awkward and dysfunctional. By the year 2000, the IJC and the US Congress were encouraging the region's governors and premiers to come up with a new regional water-management paradigm. After years and years of closed-door meetings, dozens of hearings, and thousands of public comments, on December 13, 2005, the Council of Great Lakes Governors—along with the premiers of Ontario and Québec—released the final version of its much-anticipated Great Lakes–St. Lawrence River Basin Sustainable Water Resources Agreement (the "International Agreement") and the companion Great Lakes–St. Lawrence Basin Water Resources Compact (the "Compact"). The Agreement was a nonbinding international commitment between the eight Great Lakes states and two Canadian provinces to coordinate the sustainable management of the regional water supply. The Compact was designed to become a legally binding document that implements the terms of the International Agreement on the US side of the border, which is where most of the regulatory weaknesses lay and the future demand for Great Lakes water was expected to be greatest.

The Compact became law in 2008, changing Great Lakes water-management history forever, but not before clearing some remarkable technical, legal, political, and legislative hurdles. More than once, it seemed as if the Compact might not complete the journey. Throughout modern history, the Great Lakes have been the target of a whole host of sometimes far-fetched diversion proposals—fueling regional paranoia and prompting Great Lakes experts to point to desiccated water bodies like the Aral Sea as ominous touchstones (chapter 2). As potable fresh water becomes more precious, wild-eyed Great Lakes diversion schemes will continue to be proposed, even though the Compact makes them much less likely. Water tensions and legal challenges are bound to follow.

This book delves into the deep, convoluted, and emotional history of the Great Lakes water-diversion controversy, which stretches back more than one hundred years and has seen schemes to send Great Lakes water everywhere from Akron to Asia. The colorful case studies in the following pages help illustrate the weaknesses of prior Great Lakes water-management systems, the remarkable controversies that surrounded them, and the unprecedented drive to implement new laws to protect the lakes in perpetuity. That new water system has already been tested more than once, and the emotional rancor over Great Lakes water diversions—and the precedent that they could set—is as fierce as ever. This book is the story of that controversy, how it started, where it stands today, and what it means for the future of one of the most important freshwater ecosystems on earth.

Chapter 2

The Aral Experiment

In the far northwest corner of arid Uzbekistan, in the sandy village of Muynak, stands a memorial to local soldiers who died in World War II. Here in the heart of Central Asia, once part of the sprawling Soviet empire, in the early 1940s men boarded trains for the Russian front to help their Soviet comrades beat back the German invasion. Many of those soldiers, of course, did not return home alive. In Muynak, hundreds of names are listed at the base of the memorial. When it was built, the memorial was perched at the edge of the sapphire Aral Sea, once the fourth-largest inland body of water in the world. The monument made for a picturesque setting where relatives could pay their respects and leave a bouquet of flowers in the fresh sea air, while waterfowl flew overhead, shorebirds probed the water's edge, and cormorants dove for minnows in the shallows.

The war memorial at Muynak has since become a less inspiring place. The towering monument sits atop a dry, thirty-foot cliff overlooking a sprawling scrub-brush desert that stretches for miles beyond the horizon. The cool sea breeze has been supplanted by a hot desert wind; the crashing waves have been replaced by aimless drifts of desert sand. At the base of the cliff, cattle wander through the sparsely vegetated landscape, and off in the distance one can see the remnants of a ship graveyard, where Muynak's once-mighty fishing fleet was left to die after the waters of the Aral Sea faded away. At one time there were more than one hundred old fishing boats in this nautical cemetery—surreal rusting hulks beached awkwardly in the desert sand—but barely a dozen remain. Local officials had most of the boats

The Aral Sea has receded so far that it is no longer visible from the war memorial at Muynak, Uzbekistan. (Photo by Peter Annin)

dismantled for scrap—partly for money, and partly to remove these sad reminders that Muynak was once one of the most productive fishing villages in all of the Soviet Union.

What happened to the Aral? In the 1950s, ambitious Soviet planners embarked on a massive water-diversion program designed to make the desert bloom. Engineers redirected much of the river flow that fed the sea, diverting the water to a vast complex of agricultural fields. The Soviets succeeded in their crusade; Central Asia became a booming marketplace—particularly for cotton, and even rice. But this economic conquest came at a severe ecological cost. In just a few decades, the water diversions left the Aral in ruins. Cut off from its freshwater feeder streams, the sea began shrinking. Decades later, the disastrous ecological effects of this grand plan have left tens of thousands in shock. In less than half a century, water levels in the Aral have fallen more than ninety-three vertical feet.[1] Since 1960, the sea has lost 90 percent of its surface area and 96 percent of its volume.[2] The farmer's gain was the fisherman's loss—jobs dried up with the water, leaving chronic

*Once there were more than one hundred old fishing boats at the "ship graveyard"
in Muynak, Uzbekistan. Now only a handful remain. The rest were dismantled
for scrap metal. (Photo by Peter Annin)*

unemployment and social paralysis. The climate is different, too. Like
the North American Great Lakes, the old Aral moderated temperature
extremes near the shoreline. Now Muynak's summers are hotter, winters colder, and regional precipitation patterns have changed.

Over the years, the Aral Sea disaster has been invoked repeatedly
by Great Lakes environmentalists as an ecological rallying cry: an example of what not to become. Scientists, water managers, and politicians frequently refer to it as well. Since the Aral Sea has become this
ominous touchstone in the Great Lakes water-diversion debate—and
because the vast majority of the Great Lakes residents who refer to it
have never actually been there—the author of this book traveled to the
Aral Sea with a delegation from the Russian Academy of Sciences. The
idea was to write the story of this tormented water body in one short
chapter, in order to help Great Lakes residents decide for themselves
what lessons are to be learned from the Aral Sea disaster. The purpose of this chapter is not to allege that an Aral-like draining of the

Great Lakes is in the offing, or even remotely likely. Rather, the idea is to shed light on a place that is often referred to in the Great Lakes water-diversion debate, but is little understood beyond a superficial level. That said, the Aral Sea's demise does show that, despite their magnitude, large lakes are much more vulnerable than their massive size might suggest.

~

Standing in the middle of the dry seafloor in a place where the water was once forty-five feet deep, the magnitude of the Aral Sea disaster can be difficult to grasp—nothing but salty sand stretches off to the horizon in all directions. Photos cannot capture the true extent of this ecological calamity; it even challenges the bounds of the written word. The Aral has receded so far that it takes more than five hours of driving on the old seabed in a four-wheel-drive vehicle to get from Muynak, on the old south shore, to the edge of what's left of the shrunken Aral—a distance of more than sixty miles. Yes, there is still water in the Aral, but since 1960 the sea has shrunk to one-tenth of its original surface area, and the water continues to fall by 1.3 vertical feet each year.[3] Islands have become peninsulas, peninsulas have become dry hills, and former sunken islands have emerged from the surface to split the old Aral into two much smaller bodies of water—the Southern Aral and the Northern Aral, each of which now has its own story to tell.

The dry seabed of the Southern or Large Aral is a bizarre and otherworldly place. Some areas are a flat, barren, brine-crunchy moonscape that stretches to the horizon. When one stands in the middle of this great salt flat, it's hard to imagine that just a short half century ago fish-filled waters would have been high overhead. The old seabed's fine, talc-like soil is easily stirred up by a vehicle's tires, and the dust rises like a great billowing sandstorm behind the rear bumper. Once airborne, the dust finds its way into everything—the hair, eyes, nose, and mouth—even with windows closed. But there are also incongruent oases in some isolated spots. In these areas, where the aquifer lies just below the surface, a new rich ecosystem has taken over. Lush fields of reeds and grasses stand more than six feet high, dwarfing human and vehicle alike. Honeybees pick over colorful wildflowers, and songbirds flit among the stems. Wildlife is plentiful in this fertile cover.

Located in the heart of Central Asia, the Aral Sea straddles the boundary between Uzbekistan and Kazakhstan. (Randy Yeip of the Knight Center for Environmental Journalism at Michigan State University)

The dry bed of the Aral Sea. In 1960, the water was perhaps forty-five feet deep
at this spot, which is now nearly sixty miles from the water's edge. (Photo by
Peter Annin)

After hours and hours of dusty driving, the Aral Sea becomes visible off in the distance. (Photo by Peter Annin)

Pheasants and wild hares seem to be everywhere. Foxes, jackals, wild boars—even wolves—are present, too. Raptors such as harriers and eagles are notably abundant. Though no surface water is visible, these oases provide a fleeting glimpse of what the Aral's ecosystem must have been like.

After hours and hours of dusty driving, the blue hues of the Southern Aral finally become visible off in the distance—a view that warrants stopping for a look. Here one begins to feel the microclimate that disappeared from Muynak decades ago. Out in the middle of the baking desert, the cooler air by the sea provides a welcome respite. When the vehicle finally reaches the water's edge, the sea smell is tangible, the briny whiteness of the soil even brighter. Boats are noticeably absent, and it seems eerily tranquil. A few wayward ducks fly overhead, as do some herons. A handful of small gulls sits in the water fifty yards from shore. "They are here for the brine shrimp," says Professor Nikolay Aladin, an Aral Sea expert with the Brackish Water Hydrobiology Lab in St. Petersburg. The shrimp are believed to have arrived in 2001, their eggs possibly transported by birds from the Caspian Sea, three hundred miles to the west.

The sea is clear, cool, and extraordinarily salty. Like the Dead Sea in the Middle East, the Southern Aral's high salinity makes the water dense, increasing the buoyancy of things floating in it. It's possible for a grown person, even without a lifejacket, to float high in the water. After a dip in the Aral, there's no need for a towel. The desert's evaporative powers quickly slurp droplets from the skin. In a few tingling minutes, small salt clusters stain the body at every spot where a drop once rested. Surveying the scene from the Aral's sad shoreline, one finds it hard to imagine anyone allowing a wholesale ecological disaster like this to happen ever again.

~

The Aral Sea's demise is one of the greatest environmental crimes ever committed, and it's a depressing example of water arrogance run amuck. It shows the damaging effects that shortsighted water policies can have on people, the economy, and the environment. To residents of the Great Lakes region, and of other water-rich parts of the world, the Aral Sea disaster serves as a reminder that the largest bodies of water on earth are vulnerable to overexploitation. "The Aral Sea is a dramatic example of what happens when you take abundant water for granted and suck, and suck, and suck, and eventually it goes dry," says Noah Hall, a law professor at Wayne State University. "It's everyone's worst nightmare." The Aral's woes show that if humans put their minds to it, a great body of water can be decimated in decades. "The Aral Sea is a biblical disaster," says Professor Aladin. "It is really unbelievable what has happened here."

It's hard to imagine that the Aral once hosted a thriving ecosystem chock-full of birds, fish, and other fauna. Much of the original shoreline was surrounded by thick reed beds teeming with life. "The coastal zone around the Aral Sea was a paradise for wildlife," explains Professor Ilia Joldasova, a fish biologist with the Uzbekistan Academy of Sciences. "A lot of people came to the Aral to fish and hunt. It was a tourist mecca. It was a thriving area—an oasis in the middle of the desert." What was remarkable about the Aral, she says, was not its

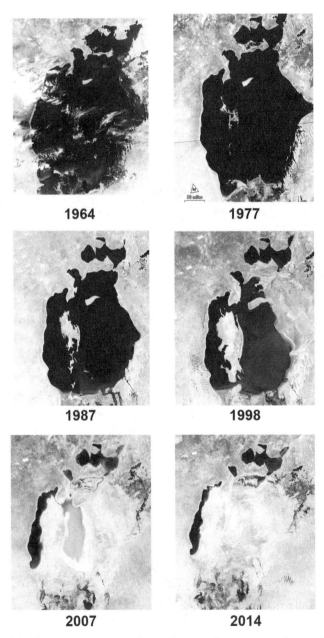

1964   **1977**

1987   **1998**

2007   **2014**

The Aral Sea has lost 96 percent of its volume and 90 percent of its surface area since 1960. (Satellite photos courtesy of the US Department of the Interior, US Geological Survey, and the National Aeronautics and Space Administration) biodiversity, but the productivity of the ecosystem, particularly along the south shore. "The southern bays were like a kindergarten for fish," she says. "In the spring, the bays held so many spawning fish that the water looked like it was boiling."

It's no surprise then that the fishing village of Muynak, located on the sea's original southern shore, was a thriving hub of commercial activity. At all hours of the day and night, fishermen crowded the local wharves, transporting their catch to the Muynak cannery—one of the Soviet Union's largest. Uzabkay Irmuhanov first started working at the cannery in the 1960s. Eventually he worked his way up to become chief mechanic at the facility, which once employed fifteen hundred people on three shifts, churning out 16 million cans of fish per year. But as the sea shrank, Mr. Irmuhanov says, the output at the plant dropped at first to 12 million cans, and then 6 million cans. Activity at the plant dwindled from three shifts down to one, and then none. "Officially, it's not closed," he says with a straight face, gesturing to the mothballed plant over his shoulder. "If we got some fish, we could be processing again."

Kirbay Utaganov knows a thing or two about fish. An affable, friendly man with a deeply creased face that smiles easily behind thick glasses, Mr. Utaganov spent decades working as a set-net fisherman on the Aral Sea. In his later years he oversaw a crew of six as the captain of a boat called *854 Muynak*. When the Aral's waters began to recede, he and his fellow fishermen became more and more alarmed. "I began to worry about how I would feed and clothe my children," he says. By the late 1970s Mr. Utaganov gave up on the Aral and went to Turkmenistan to work. Eventually he retired, but he remains fond of sharing stories with old fishing comrades on a street corner near the fisherman's collective in Muynak. When asked if he thinks the sea will ever come back, he chuckles. "I don't think it's possible to bring the Aral back," he says. "Before, the water [seemed] unlimited, but now, if we want to or not, we need to conserve."

~

Back in the 1950s, Joseph Stalin, the ruthless Soviet dictator, was the first leader to recognize the Aral as something other than a fish factory. Because the sea's waters were slightly brackish, Mr. Stalin and his bureaucratic planners did not see opportunity in the sea itself, but in the freshwater rivers that fed it. The Amu Darya and Syr Darya are like the twin Niles of Central Asia, and they played a key role in the grand Soviet vision to make the desert bloom. But reworking a region's hydrology takes time, and Mr. Stalin, who died in 1953, didn't live to see the transformation. It wasn't until 1960, under the reign of Nikita Khrushchev, that large-scale diversions of the Amu Darya and Syr Darya turned the Central Asian desert into a sea of green.

As harvests ballooned, on the sea's south shore the Amu Darya's broad delta began to shrivel. Within a few years, the sea's water level fell so far that the southern shore's spawning grounds dried up, devastating the fishing industry. Professor Joldasova says that Muynak's catch rates dropped from 25,000 metric tons per year in 1959 to 7,500 tons in 1968. By the mid 1970s, the sea's edge had receded so far that fishermen had to dig a canal connecting Muynak to the receding water. And as the water level fell, native fish (some of which resembled North American species like walleye, yellow perch, northern pike, and catfish) could no longer tolerate the ever-increasing salinity, and died off. By the early 1980s, the annual Muynak harvest had fallen to 3,500 metric tons. "Then, in 1983, the fishing industry collapsed," Professor Joldasova says. "The government halted the catch." By that time, many fishermen had already left the region to work elsewhere. "By the mid-1980s, the amount of Amu Darya water reaching the Aral Sea fell to zero," Professor Joldasova says. There was a time during the mid-1980s when the Amu Darya's water only made it as far as the city of Nukus, Uzbekistan, ninety miles upstream. The Muynak fishermen's boats end up becoming stranded in what eventually became the ship graveyard. By 1988, the water level had fallen so far that the sea separated into the Southern Aral and the Northern Aral with only a small stream connecting the two. In 1989 a simple earthen dike was built that severed the stream, permanently altering what was once one of the world's great bodies of water.

After the breakup of the Soviet Union in 1991, international aid poured in as fast as news of the disaster poured out. Much of that early money was wasted on misguided projects with few lasting results other than allegations of incompetence and graft. "All this money was spent on conferences and training and to rewrite the old projects and call them new projects," says Ubbiniyaz Ashirbekov, former head

Muynak, Uzbekistan, was once one of the most productive fishing villages in the former Soviet Union. (Photo by Peter Annin)

of the International Fund for Saving the Aral Sea's office in Nukus, Uzbekistan. Regional squabbling and allegations of corruption left international organizations frustrated, while local leaders, in turn, became disenchanted with the international community. "All these people promised to help us and we believed them," Mr. Ashirbekov says. "We were promised mountains of support, but . . . not even a hill has materialized." The Aral Sea region was once managed as a geographic unit by Soviet bureaucrats in Moscow, but after the USSR's collapse in 1991, control transferred to five separate independent republics. During Soviet times it was easy to get the Central Asian republics—Uzbekistan, Kazakhstan, Turkmenistan, Tajikistan, and Kyrgyzstan (they are often referred to as the "Five Stans")—to work together. That's because the Five Stans simply did what Moscow told them to do. But regional efforts to resolve water issues have since become marked by national chauvinism and border disputes. "The World Bank went in there in 1992 [and said], 'We're going to use money to bring the five countries together,'" remembers Michael Glantz, an Aral Sea expert at the Consortium for Capacity Building at the University of Colorado. "After a couple years they abandoned that. They couldn't get them to work together."

For the most part, the Five Stans are poor nations, economically addicted to the irrigated agriculture that has led to the Aral Sea's demise. There are costs to adopting more-efficient irrigation systems, taking crops out of production to conserve water, and educating farmers on water efficiency. These are expenses that the local republics are unwilling or unable to spare. Flood irrigation is by far the most common method used to water crops, and it's a highly inefficient means of water delivery. Not only does it waste water through extensive evaporation, but it also leads to salinized soils. As flood irrigation drains off the fields, it takes some of the salts and other minerals with it. That, in turn, washes back into the river, so downstream irrigators end up watering their fields with salt deposits from upstream farms. This situation is repeated throughout the watershed, resulting in higher and higher salinity farther downstream. Throughout the lower Amu Darya drainage basin, salt is visible on the soil everywhere. Agricultural fields are tinged white between row crops, irrigation canals are rimmed like a margarita glass. Over time, salt accumulates in the soil and groundwater, leading to declines in crop yields, and ultimately, to land that can no longer be farmed at all. Agricultural chemical use has dropped substantially from Soviet days, but regular chemical applications are still common. When farmers flush their fields, the cocktail of salt and pesticides is washed back into the river system, or down into the groundwater. In many parts of the Aral's watershed, well water has extremely high salinity levels, and some believe that chemicals are a serious problem in the groundwater as well.

Many scientists and health workers argue that these agricultural practices, in combination with the receding waters, have led to serious health effects on the local population in places like Karakalpakstan, a semiautonomous republic in northwest Uzbekistan. Karakalpakstan borders what was once the southern edge of the Aral Sea and also encompasses the lower reaches of the Amu Darya. Chemical contamination, which once was underwater, is now whipped up by fierce winds—particularly in winter. The winds lift the soft, dry seabed—and the chemicals in it—forming contaminated dust storms that spread for hundreds of miles. One study estimated that 43 million metric tons of regional salt and dust are blown into the air annually.[4] Researchers have detected dioxins and "dioxinlike" chemicals in Karakalpakstan food samples at levels almost three times higher than those recommended as allowable by the World Health Organization.[5] Salt-laced Aral Sea dust storms have become more frequent and intense, sometimes covering more than 38,000 square miles and extending downwind more than 300 miles.[6]

Not everyone agrees that the health problems in Karakalpakstan can be linked solely to the Aral Sea disaster. Sarah O'Hara, a professor of geography at the University of Nottingham in the United Kingdom, has done research on the health implications of dust in Central Asia. She says that while dust is definitely a concern, poor nutrition looms as an even greater danger for many local residents. The cause of the regional cluster of ailments needs further study, she says. "The situation is extremely complicated." Professor Nick Aladin from St. Petersburg says chemical contamination has diminished since Soviet times, if only because local farmers can't afford to purchase as much fertilizer or pesticide. "The idea that there's horrible chemical contamination in everything," he says, "is one of the myths of the Aral Sea."

∼

Can anything be done to revive the Aral Sea ecosystem? Because of the sheer magnitude of the problem, local officials in Uzbekistan have practically given up hope of fully restoring the Southern Aral. The Amu Darya's delta is so far from the shrunken Aral's edge that it would be impossible to bring the sea back without spending billions and billions of dollars. "It would be good to restore all of the Aral Sea—give us the money and we will do it," says Ubbiniyaz Ashirbekov at the International Fund for Saving the Aral Sea. "Our pocket is empty." Instead, Mr. Ashirbekov and his colleagues have built a series of delta-area shallow reservoirs that have helped bring back a smidgen of the old fishing culture. "These reservoirs have an economic and a social impact," says Professor Aladin, who endorses the reservoir program. "People here are so homesick for the sea that these reservoirs serve as a kind of compensation." The reservoir-expansion program has also brought wildlife back to the Amu Darya delta. The reservoirs are sprinkled with cormorants, gulls, terns, herons, waterfowl, and shorebirds—a vibrant contrast to the desert and old seabed that surround them.

Another glimmer of hope can be found in Kazakhstan, where the troubled earthen dike separating the Northern Aral from the Southern Aral was replaced in 2005 with a 13-kilometer modern dike and dam system, thanks to financial assistance from the World Bank. Keeping the Northern Aral separate has allowed the Kazakh government to use the diminished flows from the Syr Darya to partially restore the Northern Aral's water level.[7] The transformation of the Northern Aral since 2005 has been truly remarkable. Water levels have rebounded by more than six feet, and salinity levels have dropped to where they were before the desiccation began. "The Northern Aral has recovered spectacularly," says Aral Sea expert Philip Micklin, emeritus professor at Western Michigan University. What's more, because fish populations were never extirpated from the Syr Darya, native fish have rebounded extensively, allowing people to make a living off of fishing once again, including export markets of pike-perch to Europe. (Pike-perch resemble the North American walleye or pickerel.) "Nobody could believe how soon the fish moved back in," Professor Micklin says. There is so much water in the smaller Northern Aral now that sometimes water needs to be released into the expansive and heavily desiccated Southern Aral, creating a large shallow wetland lobe that disappears and reappears, depending on the year. "It's what they call an ephemeral lake now that it fills and then dries," Professor Micklin says.

The intermittent spillover effect has prompted a debate in Kazakhstan about whether to raise the level of the dike by another six meters or more, allowing waters of the Northern Aral to once again rise close to 1960 levels, reaching old ports that remain miles from the water's edge today. But that option is very expensive, prompting competing proposals to install a smaller dam on one bay in the Northern Aral, bifurcating the ecosystem again. That multiple-reservoir option is cheaper, but less appealing to scientists. Despite the restoration success in Kazakhstan, the dam separating the Northern and Southern Arals has been met with mixed emotions in some sectors, because it is seen as a sign that the Kazakh government has given up on the wider Aral ecosystem. "It is an extreme intervention," Professor O'Hara says. "It is helping to stabilize that part of the sea, but it is small."

"The small sea will be saved by Kazakhstan," predicts Michael Glantz, "and the western part of the big sea will probably be saved only because it's so deep. But to save [the rest of the] big sea . . . that's not going to happen." Professor Micklin says that, from an engineering perspective, saving the Southern Aral is theoretically possible—based on his calculations it could recover in about a century—but he admits that it would require unrealistic transformations of the region's agricultural economy, and a multibillion-dollar international aid effort.[8] "Irrigation efficiency could be substantially improved but at great cost and requiring a long period for implementation," he wrote in a recent journal article. "The area irrigated could also be significantly reduced, but would do great economic harm."[9] But Professor Aladin from the Russian Academy of Sciences says it is important not to lose all hope. "Disaster created by the hand of man could be repaired by the hand of man," he says. "We mustn't be hopeless, because when you are hopeless you are a victim, but when you believe in a better future, you are not a loser."

~

What lessons can Great Lakes residents learn from the Aral Sea's demise? Environmental advocates regularly point to the Aral Sea as a symbol of doom. Websites and even peer-reviewed academic articles about the Great Lakes reference the Aral's desiccation. No serious observer believes that an Aral-like disaster will ever happen in the Great Lakes. Central Asia's desert climate contrasts sharply with that of the wet weather of the North American Great Lakes region. More importantly, now that modern anti-diversion laws are in place, industrial-scale water-diversion proposals in the Great Lakes would be dead on arrival. But the Aral Sea's mythology continues to reverberate in the region—perhaps because it serves as a reminder that massive bodies of water are more vulnerable than they appear. "People see how vast the Great Lakes are and mistake that vastness for invincibility," warns Cameron Davis, who served as President Barack Obama's Great Lakes "czar" from 2009 to 2017.

Professor Micklin is one of the few Aral Sea experts who lives in the Great Lakes Basin. He says the lessons of the Aral Sea are not complex. Like many other experts, he does not see the Aral's desiccation ever being repeated in the Great Lakes region. "The era of big, large-scale diversions is over," he declares. But he says the region should learn from the Aral's history. "You can do a heck of a lot of damage, even to huge water bodies, in a pretty short period of time. . . . We need to be very careful." Before the sea was drained, some Soviet scientists warned of environmental calamity, but they were ignored. "The problem is that once you make a commitment to give somebody water, you can't take it back, because they become dependent on it." The Aral's experience shows that humans do have the power and the ability to destroy natural wonders like the Great Lakes, and long before that, to inflict substantial harm on the regional ecosystem and economy. What's more, with the unpredictable advent of climate change (discussed in the next chapter) water managers in the Great Lakes region need to ensure that they don't inadvertently take steps today that could lead to unintended consequences tomorrow. Large lakes have limits. The sad people of Muynak, Uzbekistan, can testify to that as well as anyone on earth.

Chapter 3

Climate Change and Water Levels— Going to Extremes?

Ontario's Wasaga Beach is one of the finest swimming destinations in all of North America. Nestled into the southeast corner of Lake Huron's expansive Georgian Bay, Wasaga boasts nine miles of white-sand beach that slants out into Lake Huron's waters at such a gradual slope that a hundred yards from shore the water barely reaches a swimmer's waistline. A provincial park since 1962, Wasaga is just eighty miles from cosmopolitan Toronto, which helps explain why it is one of the most popular day-use tourist destinations in Canada. "On a busy weekend, we can have 60,000 to 120,000 people," says former park superintendent Mark Shoreman. "We claim it's the world's longest freshwater beach."

But the park is also an ideal place to witness the remarkable natural fluctuations that occur in Great Lakes water levels. Thanks to the slight gradient of the sand at Wasaga, when Lake Huron's water level falls by one vertical foot, it can actually change the Wasaga Beach waterline by dozens of feet. In 1986, during historic high water levels on the Great Lakes, Wasaga's visitors only needed to amble a few yards from the tree line to reach the water's edge. But between 1999 and 2014—an unusually long period of historic low water levels—beachgoers were forced to walk 150 yards to the water. And then, by 2017, water levels had rebounded, and people were back to complaining about the lack of beach once again.

Many tourists and property owners find these widely varying lake levels to be alarming—something must be wrong, they assume. But vacillating lake levels are a normal phenomenon on the Great Lakes.

Water levels fluctuate widely—and naturally—on the Great Lakes, particularly on Lakes Huron and Michigan. The top photo shows the US Geological Survey's Hammond Bay Biological Station on Lake Huron during a period of high water in 1986. The second photo shows the same beach during a period of lower water levels in early 2006. (Top photo by USGS Hammond Bay Biological Station; bottom photo by Peter Annin)

They represent what scientists refer to as "natural variability," and that variability plays a key role in the complex Great Lakes ecosystem. "Natural variability is an absolute necessity," says Douglas Wilcox, a wetlands expert with The College at Brockport, State University of New York. "The [Great Lakes] plant and animal communities are not only adapted to that variability, but they absolutely *require* that variability to provide habitat and food, and nesting/spawning [areas] to maintain their populations."

The Great Lakes' interface between land and water is a rich and ecologically productive zone, and different organisms benefit at different water-level stages. During low water, wide beaches and broad expanses of mudflats are created at the lakes' edges. These flats are often actually seed banks that have been harboring the progeny of rare water-level-dependent plants, sometimes for years. When the waters recede, these areas are exposed to the air and the unique plants embark on a robust growth binge, creating all sorts of food, cover, and other habitat for a variety of important wetland species. In essence, these beaches and mudflats imitate a desert after a cloudburst—they bloom. That's precisely what happened in 2000, when lake levels dropped after a long period of high water. "It was incredible. It was just absolutely incredible," says Mr. Wilcox. "These sediments were exposed and just came back like gangbusters [with] the most diverse vegetation you can imagine." This is a cycle that has repeated itself for thousands of years in the Great Lakes Basin.

The extent of these lake-level fluctuations is impressive. The difference between the historic high and historic low water levels on some Great Lakes is more than six vertical feet, and it's not unusual for water levels in the Great Lakes to change by one or two vertical feet from year to year.[1] While fluctuations like that may be invigorating to the ecosystem, they can cause headaches for humans who relish lake-level consistency. Docks can stand awkwardly high and dry one year, and then be under water a decade later.

The Great Lakes region's anxiety about water diversion is ultimately a concern about water quantity. If there was enough extra water to send large amounts out of the Great Lakes Basin, then there likely would be little or no controversy or concern about diversions. But the Aral Sea situation shows that large lakes are vulnerable, and that massive

After an unprecedented period of low water levels on the Great Lakes from 1999 to 2014, the region entered a period of high water that created challenges from Rochester, New York, to Chicago. Water-level variability is a natural process on the Great Lakes, but experts suggest that the region may be entering a period of increasing water-level extremes. (Photo by Baluzek, iStock.com)

bodies of water can be all but eliminated in a matter of decades with the wrong policies in place. A key concern about climate change in the Great Lakes region, however, is that global warming could potentially alter Great Lakes water levels in ways that would make impacts from future diversions look petty—especially during periods of low water. What kind of effect do experts think climate change will have on Great Lakes water levels? That is one of the most intriguing and complex questions facing Great Lakes scientists and policymakers today. The problem is that nobody really knows how climate change will affect water levels, but a number of the brightest minds in the region have expended significant time putting together some projections, and it boils down to a competition between evaporation and precipitation. "The climate's warming, and we think that evaporation rates from the Great Lakes are going to increase with warmer water temperatures," says David Fay, a water-quantity expert with the International Joint

Commission (IJC) in Ottawa. "However, most of the models also suggest that precipitation is going to increase over the Great Lakes, and it's those two factors that are kind of battling it out as to which is going to be dominant. If evaporation wins out, then the lakes are going to drop. If precipitation wins out then the lakes may rise . . . and there's lots of scientific uncertainty about both of those things."

Global surface air temperatures have increased during the last century, and they are expected to increase further during the next hundred years. The same is true for the Great Lakes region. Air and water temperatures are expected to rise, and water levels are expected to be affected by these changing climate conditions. While there is consensus in the scientific community that climate change is happening, and that it will impact the Great Lakes, there is less clarity on how it will affect Great Lakes water levels. The latest evidence suggests, however, that the region may be entering a new era of water-level volatility, which could increase regional water tension as everything from large-scale, in-basin water uses to tiny diversion proposals are met with greater scrutiny.

~

To the average citizen, it's hard to imagine that a temperature change of just a few degrees can have that much influence on an ecosystem. After all, most people can't tell the difference between 55 and 60 degrees Fahrenheit (30.6 and 33.3°C) when they are outdoors. But it's important to realize that during the last ice age more than 20,000 years ago—when much of the Great Lakes region was covered by a mile-thick sheet of glacial ice—the average global temperature was perhaps just 7 or 8 degrees Fahrenheit (3.9 or 4.4°C) cooler than it is today.[2] So when scientists warn that temperatures may rise more than 7 degrees Fahrenheit during the twenty-first century, they are talking about an enormously transformative global temperature rise. "In the next hundred years, we will have the same warming that has occurred since the last ice age, which ended roughly 10,000 years ago," predicts Professor George Kling at the University of Michigan. "That's why people are so worried about a 6- to 10-degree Fahrenheit [3.3–5.6°C] increase in temperature—because it is happening in only 100 years, and not in 10,000 or 20,000 years," he says. "We do not know which of the organisms on earth are going to be able to adapt to such a rapid temperature change."

Signs of global warming are already here. The last decade was the warmest in modern history, and the ten warmest years in recorded history have all been logged just since 1998.[3] The earth's average temperature has already warmed by around 1 degree Celsius (1.8°F) since 1880,[4] and global leaders have set a very challenging goal of keeping that warming below 2 degrees Celsius (3.6°F). But if current global emission trends continue, this century could see average global surface temperatures rise by 3.7 degrees Celsius, (nearly 7°F), according to the Intergovernmental Panel on Climate Change (IPCC), the world's leading climate institution.[5] That would drive transformative environmental change throughout the globe, creating a very different world from what we have today. As scientists have long predicted, sea levels have already begun to rise, global ice cover has decreased, glaciers have receded, storms have become more severe, as have droughts. What's more, the IPCC warned that human-caused climate change has already affected the global water cycle. "In many regions, changing precipitation or melting snow and ice are altering hydrological systems, affecting water resources in terms of quantity and quality."[6] The IPCC has long predicted that tension over water will reach new heights during this century. "Climate change," the organization has said, "will exacerbate water shortages in many water-scarce areas of the world."[7]

Climate change is expected to affect different regions of the earth in different ways. How will the Great Lakes fare? Scientists say that creating climate projections on a local scale is even more difficult than crafting them for the globe, because the closer that they zero in on a particular place, the harder it becomes to predict how the climate will behave. "A lot of the basic understanding of climate change on the global scale is pretty well in hand," says Brent Lofgren, a Great Lakes climate-change expert with the National Oceanic and Atmospheric Administration (NOAA) in Ann Arbor, Michigan. "But a lot of the local impacts of climate change are more uncertain."

One of the most comprehensive recent reports on global warming in the Great Lakes was produced by the Ontario Climate Consortium and the Ontario Ministry of Natural Resources and Forestry. The report analyzed more than 250 regional climate-change studies and synthesized them into a single, comprehensive highlight document. "Climate change is perhaps the greatest environmental challenge facing the ecosystem health of the Great Lakes Basin," the report warned, adding that there is "growing concern by national, provincial, state, and local governments (in addition to key interest groups and stakeholders) that impacts of climate change are already being observed and documented."[8] According to the report, the average annual air temperature in the Great Lakes region has already increased between 0.8 and 2.0 degrees Celsius (1.44 and 3.6°F) during the last sixty years, and the regional growing season has been lengthened by roughly one week during that time.[9] What's more, the report warned that the average annual regional temperature is expected to rise between 1.5 and 7 degrees Celsius (2.7 and 12.6°F) by 2080, but those increases will not be uniform throughout the Basin. The average annual air temperature is expected to increase more in the upper Great Lakes than the lower lakes, and, throughout the region, winters are expected to warm more than summers.[10]

Not surprisingly, these rising air temperatures are expected to be mirrored by rising water temperatures. In the last century, Great Lakes summer surface-water temperatures have already increased by as much as 3.5 degrees Celsius (6.3°F),[11] and Lake Superior—the coldest Great Lake—has become one of the fastest-warming lakes in the world. Professor Jay Austin at the Large Lakes Observatory at the University of Minnesota Duluth was one of more than seventy scientists who participated in a study analyzing 250 lakes around the world. "The vast majority of them are warming, and Superior had one of the highest rates of warming," he says. "It has certainly been warming faster than the landscape around it." These trends are expected to continue. "In the coming century, surface water temperatures are projected to increase by 2.9–6 degrees Celsius (5.2–10.8°F), depending on the climate-change scenario and location in the Great Lakes Basin," the Ontario report said. Lake Superior's water temperature is projected to have the greatest increase, and Lake Ontario's the least.[12] These warmer waters will put pressure on cold water species like lake trout, whitefish, and brook trout and will make it easier for toxins such as mercury and PCBs to be incorporated into fish tissue and absorbed into the food chain.[13]

Precipitation patterns are also expected to change. While it can vary by lake, the region generally receives around thirty-six inches of precipitation per year. The Canadian report projected that the amount would increase by up to 20 percent at the end of this century, with Lake Superior seeing the largest boost.[14] Because of rising temperatures, more precipitation is expected to fall as rain and freezing rain, rather than snow. More important, perhaps, are the expected shifts in when different types of precipitation will fall, with snow being replaced by rain in winter, rainfall increasing in the spring, but decreasing in summer. "Heavier downpours are currently twice as common as they were a century ago, and this trend is expected to continue in the twenty-first century," the report said. "The largest snowfall losses in North America are projected for the Great Lakes Basin, with declines of up to 48.1 percent by the late twenty-first century."[15]

It may seem counterintuitive, but along with more rain, there will also be more drought as precipitation patterns are altered. An increase in the frequency and intensity of storms is expected to lead to more flooding, followed by longer, drier summers that will lead to more droughts. Again, the climate is trending in this direction already. The report said that during the first half of the twentieth century, there were fewer than ten flood disasters per decade in Ontario, but by the 1990s that rate had increased by 500 percent.[16] Large storm events washing nutrients into warmer lakes is expected to increase the incidence of harmful algal blooms, especially in the lower Great Lakes.[17] Of course, dangerous algal blooms have already started occurring in the region, including an algae crisis in August of 2014 that prompted a "do not drink" warning that lasted for days in Toledo, Ohio. The alert created an ironic situation: a metro area of more than 500,000 people, in one of the most water-abundant ecosystems on earth, could not drink the water because toxic algal blooms had overwhelmed the local water-treatment plant.

Ice plays a key role in the Great Lakes evaporation scenario, as ice cover helps cap evaporation from the lakes. "There's a common interpretation that ice cover is a lid to evaporation—that once you get ice cover, evaporation on the lakes stops, which is a true statement," says Keith Kompoltowicz, chief of the Watershed Hydrology Branch at the US Army Corps of Engineers in Detroit. "However, the absence of ice cover doesn't necessarily mean that water levels are going to

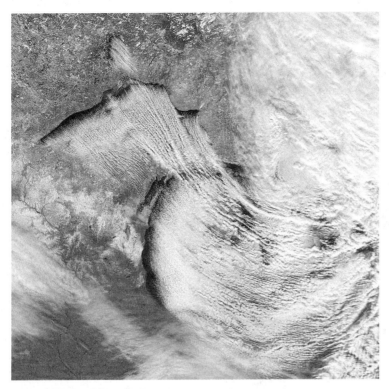

Cold air sweeping over the Great Lakes can create extensive evaporation as well as lake-effect snow. Scientists say the highest evaporation rates often occur when the air temperature is much colder than the water temperature. (NOAA Great Lakes CoastWatch)

drastically decline due to evaporation. . . . We see the biggest evaporation rates when the air temperature is very much colder than the water temperature. So as that [temperature] difference increases, the evaporation rates tend to increase." The duration of Lake Superior's annual ice cover has declined by 45 days during the last 150 years, and from 1973 to 2000 there was an overall decrease in annual ice cover of a whopping 71 percent across the Great Lakes.[18] "Longer ice-off periods can increase water temperature and evaporation," the report said. "This leads to lower water levels and can also have implications for many aspects of aquatic ecosystems." Ice also tends to protect shorelines during winter storms, so a reduction in ice cover could make shorelines more susceptible to winter erosion.[19] The Great Lakes are remarkably

sensitive to winter temperature shifts. "The difference between a high
ice year in Lake Superior . . . and a year when there is essentially no
open lake ice, can be due to differences in winter air temperatures on
the order of 1 to 2 degrees Celsius [1.8–3.6°F]," Professor Austin says.
"If things were consistently 4 or 5 degrees Celsius warmer [7.2–9.0°F],
we would rarely if ever see ice."

Climate scientists have dialed back their earlier predictions that
Great Lakes water levels could drop by several feet by the end of this
century. But the Ontario climate report suggests that while there is
plenty of uncertainty, overall, climate change is still expected to be
a water-level downer.[20] "Most climate-change projections," the study
said, "suggest that there will be an overall decline in water levels from
the combined effects of warming air temperatures, increased evaporation and evapotranspiration, drought, and changes in seasonal precipitation patterns." But some leading scientists say that many of the
studies surveyed by the Ontario report are now out of date, and today
it appears that the competition between precipitation and evaporation
in the Great Lakes region could end up closer to a draw. "I believe
there's a consensus in the scientific community that there is no strong
evidence for either a persistent increase or decrease [in water levels],"
says Drew Gronewold, a hydrologist and leading water-level expert
with NOAA in Ann Arbor. But there is so much uncertainty in the
data that few scientists are willing to make concrete projections. As
Mr. Gronewold puts it, "The truth of the matter is we don't know."

～

An extraordinary period of low water hit the Great Lakes between
1999 and 2014. During that fifteen-year span, the upper lakes repeatedly hovered around record lows for the longest stretch in recorded
history, finally breaking an all-time low-water-level record on Lakes
Michigan and Huron in January of 2013.[21] Docks sat ridiculously high
for years, and some marinas were required to retrofit their operations
completely. The Great Lakes shipping industry declared a dredging
crisis because federal funds were not being released to adequately clear
shallow harbors. The low-water period lasted so long that many scientists, policymakers, and property owners began to wonder: Is this what
climate change looks like on the Great Lakes?

Some of the most alarmed stakeholders were cottage owners on Lake Huron's Georgian Bay, a stunningly beautiful section of the Great Lakes Basin that is home to some 30,000 islands, numerous parks, gin-clear waters, and thousands of venerable off-grid cottages, many of which have been in families for generations. By definition, island properties are only accessible by boat. When low water levels render docks useless, getting to the family cottage with a boatload of summer supplies suddenly becomes a major logistical operation. Many cottagers spent thousands of dollars on dredging to access their docks. But Georgian Bay's geology meant dredging was not an option for everyone; in many areas, the lakebed is solid rock. The result? Some cottagers received permits to hire explosives experts to blast channels into the solid lake bottom, allowing boats to access docks. Bob Duncanson is executive director of the Georgian Bay Association, which represents more than 10,000 regional cottagers. He said one common blasting zone was around Pointe au Baril, north of Parry Sound, where the waters have a shallower profile. "They have had quite a tradition of blasting up there just to create channels in their community and whatnot," Mr. Duncanson said. "They had been doing blasting when the water got down and stayed down because they just felt that maybe that was the only way, long-term, that they were going to live with what they thought was the new low-water regime."

That created an awkward setting in some sections of Georgian Bay. While one cottager might be relaxing on his deck, soaking up the tranquil setting with a cold beer, the neighbor a few islands over could be shattering that serenity with contractors blasting away at the lakebed—at the cost of tens of thousands of dollars. Chilling out at the cottage was becoming more difficult, especially if you had an aversion to snakes. The eastern massasauga rattlesnake frequents Georgian Bay's islands, and while the massasaugas are among the most docile of rattlers, they do get riled when TNT shakes the ground under their bellies. "That brings the snakes out," Mr. Duncanson says. "You get to know how many rattlesnakes you have on your island when blasting is going on." Thanks to the drawn-out low-water period on Georgian Bay, for some, life was becoming more stressful during vacation than it was back in the city. "Stop the Drop" signs were sprinkled from Killarney to Parry Sound, and cottagers wanted something to be done about the low water. "People were shocked," remembers Mary Muter, a long-time Georgian Bay water-level advocate. "People were having to make major changes to docks and intake pipes. People were having trouble getting to their cottages. Municipalities were going ballistic because the government agency that determines property values started reducing property values because of difficult access."

Water-level frustration prompted the GBA Foundation to hire W. F. Baird & Associates, a Canada-based engineering firm, to find out what was going on with Lake Huron. In 2005, Baird's results quickly captured media attention far beyond Georgian Bay. They suggested the low-water problem was not just due to natural variability. Baird said the water-level decline had been exacerbated by human activity on the St. Clair River, at the southern tip of Lake Huron. Starting more than a century ago, and continuing off and on through most of 1900s, dredging projects deepened the navigation channel in the St. Clair River north of Detroit, the main outflow from Lake Huron. Dredging the channel was equivalent to widening the drain in a bathtub. The IJC had long established that dredging on the St. Clair had permanently lowered water levels in Lakes Huron and Michigan by 14–18 inches.[22]

But Baird alleged that as water rushed through the dredged channel it caused the channel to erode even wider, further scouring out the bathtub drain. That was new and very surprising information. Baird said this underwater erosion may have dropped levels on Huron and Michigan (which hydrologically are one lake and have the same water level) by an additional 8–11 inches—for a grand-total drop of 22–31 inches.[23] "Something different was happening on Michigan-Huron," says Rob Nairn who oversaw the Baird study, and owns a cottage on Georgian Bay. "The lakes generally trend up and down with each other, but Michigan-Huron was a lot lower." Baird's conclusions started one of the most emotional Great Lakes water-level controversies in a generation, and prompted many Georgian Bay residents to demand that structures be built on the St. Clair River. They wanted facilities built that would constrict the river to bring water levels back up to make up for the historical dredging and subsequent erosion. Proposals ranged from underwater sills to inflatable dams and even more-elaborate control structures.

The St. Clair River serves as the outlet to Lake Huron and has played a key role in water-level controversies on Lakes Huron and Michigan for decades. (Adapted from US Army Corps of Engineers, Detroit District)

Such proposals landed with a dull thud in some quarters of the Great Lakes. The reason is that Lakes Huron and Michigan are considered to be the last remaining unregulated lakes in the Basin. Lake Superior's water level is manipulated by hydro facilities at the twin cities of Sault Ste. Marie, Michigan, and Sault Ste. Marie, Ontario. Lake Ontario's water level is controlled by a dam on the St. Lawrence River. Even Lake Erie's water is impacted slightly by the Welland Canal bypassing Niagara Falls. But Michigan and Huron are considered to be unregulated, other than the residual effects that reverberate from control works on the other lakes. While some environmentalists were interested in compensating for past dredging on the St. Clair, others were adamantly opposed to regulation structures on the river. "I would expect that the environmental community—and many other communities, like the scientific community—would be quite concerned with any proposal to regulate the levels of Lakes Michigan and Huron," says Andy Buchsbaum, a vice president with the National Wildlife Federation. "I'd rather see proposals to deregulate the other lakes than to regulate the two remaining natural-flow lakes."

The US Army Corps of Engineers raised questions about the Baird report,[24] which started a multiyear dispute about how much the St. Clair River was to blame for the extended period of low water on Lake Huron.[25] The controversy became so intense that the International Joint Commission expanded a study that was already under way to include an examination of the St. Clair and its impacts on Michigan and Huron water levels. To the surprise of many, the IJC study described a situation that was more complex than the Baird report had suggested. Yes, underwater erosion was part of the problem, but the study put more of the blame on climate.[26] "The Baird assumption was that [the water-level drop] was due to erosion," says Frank Quinn, a retired NOAA hydrologist who worked on both the Baird and IJC studies, "and the IJC basically found that it was due to climate."

But there was a third culprit: isostatic rebound. During the ice age, thousands of years ago, kilometer-thick glaciers suppressed the earth's crust in parts of the Great Lakes region. Along several segments of the lakes' northern shore, the crust has been rebounding ever since. Around Georgian Bay, it has been rising faster than many other areas. Meanwhile in Chicago, at the other end of the Michigan-Huron system, the crust is actually falling, which creates an effect similar to tipping up the edge of a gargantuan soup bowl on one side, while pushing it down on the other. This only exacerbated the water-level problem for Georgia Bay residents.[27]

In total, taking all those factors into account, the IJC's International Upper Great Lakes Study estimated that between 1963 and 2006 water levels on Lakes Huron and Michigan had dropped an average of nine inches beyond their natural variability.[28] The IJC's two-phase study, released in 2009 and 2012, examined a number of engineering alternatives to help mitigate that drop, including installing inflatable flap gates, inflatable weirs, dikes, underwater sills, or underwater hydrokinetic turbines, but recommended that these measures "not be

Isostatic Rebound

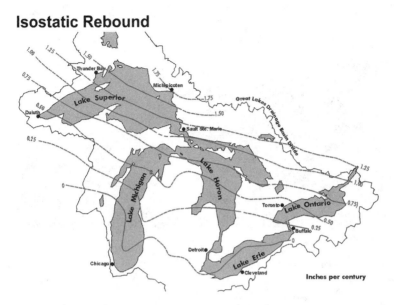

During the ice age thousands of years ago, glaciers suppressed the earth's surface in parts of the Great Lakes region, and the crust has been rebounding ever since. The IJC found that the crust has been rising faster around Georgian Bay than in many other areas, affecting Great Lakes water levels. (US Army Corps of Engineers, Detroit District)

undertaken in the St. Clair River at this time."[29] The 2012 study acknowledged that Georgian Bay residents supported structures on the river, but that many other Great Lakes residents were opposed and that there was also opposition to multi-lake regulation to ameliorate the water level situation."[30] In the end, the study's authors recommended pursuing an "adaptive-management strategy" to deal with extreme water levels and that "further study of multi-lake regulation . . . not be pursued at this time."[31]

The two IJC reports riled Georgian Bay residents who wanted structures built on the St. Clair River. Calls for action reached a fevered pitch when Huron and Michigan broke an all-time low-water level in January of 2013. Four months later, the IJC Commissioners released their formal St. Clair River recommendations to the Canadian and US federal governments. Controversially, they overruled the report's authors and recommended that the federal governments investigate

Lake Huron, including Georgian Bay, experienced an extended period of low water between 1999 and 2014. The all-time low water-level record was broken on Huron and Michigan in January of 2013. This photo was taken on Honey Harbour during 2012. (Photo by Terri Hodgson)

installing engineering structures on the river. But the recommendation was weakened by an influential dissent. The IJC's US co-chair, Lana Pollack, cast doubt on the engineering option, saying the recommendation may "raise false hopes that structures in the St. Clair River, if built, would be sufficient to resolve the suffering from low water levels of Lake Michigan-Huron, while at the same time causing possible disruption downstream in Lake St. Clair and Lake Erie."

Ms. Pollack's dissent rankled many, but thrilled others. Dan Injerd from the Illinois Department of Natural Resources has long maintained that high water creates erosion on Illinois' Lake Michigan shoreline and pushes surplus volume into the reversed Chicago River. Any structural improvements that permanently raise water levels on Lake Michigan would create water headaches in his state. "I would have some pretty significant initial concerns about that," he said. But Roger Gauthier, a retired Corps of Engineers hydrologist, counters that historical dredging and erosion on the bottom of the St. Clair River must be mitigated. "You've got to compensate for the fact that we took off probably twenty inches from Michigan and Huron," Mr. Gauthier says.

But the biggest deterrent to doing something may be cost. Federal officials have estimated that it would take twenty-five years to build structures on the St. Clair and another decade for results to materialize. "Putting in additional dams and dredging the channels further," says the IJC's David Fay, "would cost billions of dollars. . . . So it's a daunting challenge." But there are also costs to doing nothing, warns David Sweetnam, executive director of the nonprofit Georgian Bay Forever, who predicts climate change will eventually force an engineering solution on the river. "At some point, we'll hit a hard bottom and we won't have a choice but to put a plug in somewhere, or some kind of ability to modulate the outflows."

But when the polar vortex hit suddenly in January of 2014, it turned the water-levels story on its head. Wide expanses of the Upper Lakes became encased in ice, dramatically reducing evaporation. Come spring, as the snow melted and the rain fell, water levels rose, and rose. In just two years, Huron and Michigan jumped by more than three feet, and water was up significantly on all five Great Lakes. Reporters were now flocking to places like Mount Pleasant, Wisconsin, where barricaded streets steered people away from eroding bluffs and buildings on the brink of tumbling into Lake Michigan. Many who had been calling for St. Clair River control structures adjusted their talking points. They were no longer lobbying for structures just to combat low water; they now wanted structures to protect people from all "water-level extremes." "We are mindful," says Mr. Duncanson at the Georgian Bay Association, "that there are other stakeholders around the middle lakes that have other issues, like eroding bluffs and things like that. . . . Let's try to find a solution that knocks the high-highs and low-lows."

What frustrates Georgian Bay property owners is how history keeps repeating itself. After low water levels during the 1920s and 1930s, the Corps of Engineers investigated putting sills on the bottom of the St. Clair River, expending enormous time and effort to build a massive model of the river at their Vicksburg, Mississippi, research facility. But Great Lakes water levels bounced back, and the project was mothballed. Then, during low water in the early 1960s, engineers constructed another elaborate 3-D model of the St. Clair River at Vicksburg, only to see those plans shelved once again when water levels rebounded. Frank Quinn participated in that study, and he doubts that St. Clair

Low water levels are a regular occurrence on the Great Lakes. This photo was taken on Georgian Bay's Honey Harbour in 1964. (© Her Majesty the Queen in Right of Canada, as represented by the Minister of the Environment, [1964])

structures will ever be built. "I don't think we'll see anything," he says. "Anytime something is proposed from a physical standpoint, the environmental hue and cry, in addition to the cost . . . [is such that] nobody is going to want anything changed."

~

The Lake Huron water-level controversy stands in sharp contrast to the water-level debate on Lake Ontario. While many Georgian Bay residents are clamoring for some sort of regulation of their lake, over on Lake Ontario water levels have been regulated since 1960, and people seem to have done nothing but complain about it since. Before it was regulated, Lake Ontario used to see nearly seven feet in water level variability—making it historically the most variable lake in the system. Then the Moses-Saunders dam complex was installed on the St. Lawrence River, which turned Lake Ontario into a pseudo-reservoir. For the next half century, the IJC's regulation plan took out the highest highs and the lowest lows, reducing variability down into the four-foot range. Taking out the water-level extremes gave shoreline residents more predictability, but it turned many of Lake Ontario's wetlands into cattail monocultures rather than the thriving nurserylands of biodiversity that they used to be.

This brought about a multiyear push by environmentalists, scientists, and others to put a little more wiggle back into Lake Ontario's water levels, especially on the high-water end. That change would regularly flood out cattail monocultures and restore some of the lost wetland biodiversity. After years of study and debate, in late 2016 the IJC released "Plan 2014," which was designed in part to regenerate wetlands and provide other environmental benefits while keeping the interests of property owners, shippers, and other stakeholders in mind. Plan 2014 was not just focused on Lake Ontario, but also downstream flows on the St. Lawrence River in places like Montréal and Québec City.

As luck would have it, the ink was barely dry on Plan 2014 when it started to snow, and then rain, and rain some more in the Lake Ontario watershed in early 2017. It also snowed and rained heavily in the Lake Erie watershed upstream. And it really snowed and rained in the Ottawa River watershed downstream, which flows into the St. Lawrence near Montréal. The result was more water than people knew what to do with. Lake Ontario's water level rose with unprecedented speed—skyrocketing nearly four feet in just a few months, breaking the high-water-level record in June of 2017. Homeowners on the south shore of Lake Ontario were awash in water. But so were thousands of homeowners in the Montréal metro area downstream. The Moses-Saunders dam was between the two flooded areas, and the IJC was stuck in the middle, with the brand-new Plan 2014 to guide them. New Yorkers on Lake Ontario's south shore were screaming at the IJC to release more water, while the people in Montréal hoped the IJC would hold the water back. The result was a multimillion-dollar flooding imbroglio in both places that quickly became political. Even though it's quite likely that no regulation plan would have been able to adequately handle the record amount of water, anger was immediately targeted at Plan 2014—and the IJC officials behind it—especially in the state of New York. "There's no doubt," Governor Andrew Cuomo famously said during a 2017 press conference, "that the IJC blew it. I

Lake Ontario experienced record high water during the spring of 2017, rising nearly four feet in less than six months. Many homes were damaged by flooding in upstate New York, on Lake Ontario's south shore. (Photo by Steve Orr/ Democrat & Chronicle/USA TODAY Network)

mean, they blew it!"[32] He and other New York residents felt the IJC should have anticipated Lake Ontario's rise by releasing more water earlier in the year.

The IJC pushed back, arguing that the flooding was caused by un-precedented weather and exacerbated by people building structures in flood-prone areas—no matter what regulation plan was in place. While the 2017 flooding did reach low-lying areas farther inland, many homes on Lake Ontario's south shore are so close to the water, that their front "yards" are rimmed with concrete, rebar, and riprap. That's what it takes to keep the lake out of their living rooms. Meanwhile, downstream, many of the people flooded out around Montréal had homes in areas so repeatedly hit by floods that the government prohibited some from rebuilding.

Plan 2014 will continue to be debated of course, but many IJC of-ficials say the bigger problem is local officials in Québec and New York who should not have permitted people to build homes in such vulner-able areas. "I believe flooding will occur again. Erosion is a constant process. They're in susceptible areas, and they are at risk, and that's nothing the Commission controls," warns the IJC's David Fay. "Other levels of government can influence that, and it gets to property rights and all of those issues. Many people have developed in susceptible areas when it comes to fluctuating levels of the Great Lakes." This creates a pattern that is repeating itself throughout coastal zones in North America, where people build close to the water's edge—in flood zones or low-lying areas—only to suffer damage during heavy rains and then demand government assistance to rebuild. In 2017, New York State made $45 million available—up to $50,000 per property owner—to repair flood damage. It also included funding for local governments to conduct flood mitigation and other resiliency measures. "Many of the government bailouts don't require that [property owners] actually increase their resilience," Mr. Fay says. "They're just allowing them to rebuild."

The IJC was created in 1909 to help resolve transboundary water disputes all along the US-Canada border. With unhappy regulated stakeholders on Lake Ontario, and unhappy unregulated stakeholders on Lake Huron, it appears the IJC will have plenty of transboundary water disputes to deal with for some time to come.

～

When water levels were low between 1999 and 2014, people started to wonder if we had reached a new era of permanently low water on the Great Lakes. But today there is a different water-level era that people are wondering about: volatility. Consider these water-level milestones from recent decades confirmed by Keith Kompoltowicz, a water-level expert at the Corps of Engineers:

- Superior, Michigan, Huron, and Erie all struggled with record high water in 1985–86.
- Then in 1998–99, Michigan and Huron plunged three feet in one year. Those lakes had never fallen that far, that fast, in recorded history.
- That drop sent the upper Great Lakes into a record-long period of low water from 1999 to 2014.
- Michigan and Huron set an all-time record low in January of 2013.
- Then Lake Superior experienced a record-breaking rise from January of 2013 to December of 2014. The lake had never before risen so far, so fast.

Great Lakes Water Level Variability

Lake	Year	Level*
Superior		
Record High	1985	603.38 ft
Record Low	1926	599.48 ft
Difference between record high/low		**3.90 ft**
Michigan & Huron**		
Record High	1986	582.35 ft
Record Low	2013	576.02 ft
Difference between record high/low		**6.33 ft**
Erie		
Record High	1986	574.28 ft
Record Low	1936	568.18 ft
Difference between record high/low		**6.10 ft**
Ontario		
Record High	2017	248.72 ft
Record Low	1934	241.93 ft
Difference between record high/low		**6.79 ft**

* Monthly mean water levels in feet above sea level (IGLD 1985).

** Lake Michigan and Lake Huron have the same water level.

Numerous water-level records have been broken on the Great Lakes since 1985, raising questions about whether the region may be entering a period of increasing water-level volatility. (Source: Environment and Climate Change Canada, Great Lakes–St. Lawrence Regulation Office)

- During that same time period, Michigan and Huron experienced the second-fastest rebound on record.
- That was followed in 2017 by the fastest water-level increase on Lake Ontario ever, which also set an all-time high-water-level record in June of that year.

In a thirty-year period from 1986 to 2017, the lakes whipsawed from record highs, to record lows, to record highs. Again, the low-water period of 1999–2014 set a record on the Upper Great Lakes for how long it lasted, only to see Lake Superior rebound to high water at a record pace, which was followed a few years later by Lake Ontario also rising at a record pace—nearly four vertical feet in six months in 2017. What's more, Mr. Kompoltowicz reports that between 1980 and 2017, forty monthly water-level records (as opposed to all-time records) were broken—more than one per year, on average. Of those, only four were low-water-level records. Thirty-six were high-water-level records. Scientists expect to see more monthly water-level records fall as climate change continues to alter historic precipitation and temperature patterns—more rain in winter, spring coming earlier, etc.

With all that extreme water-level action in a thirty-year period, it's no surprise that experts are wondering about a new era of water-level uncertainty. "What it means for the Great Lakes is that we need to be prepared for extremes," says Wendy Leger, co-chair of the IJC's Great Lakes–St. Lawrence River Adaptive Management Committee. "Whether it's extreme weather patterns, whether it's extreme water levels, whether it's extreme droughts and storms . . . we just need to be prepared for extremes." Water levels have always fluctuated, of course, and records are made to be broken. But now the lakes are not only breaking water-level quantity records back to back, but the timescales associated with those milestones are also record-breaking. Is this just a phase, or have we entered a new paradigm of increasing water-level uncertainty and volatility? "It's too soon to tell," says NOAA's Drew Gronewold. "But I think that is the critical hypothesis that we need to be testing right now."

Most experts believe that climate change is already affecting the Great Lakes. The record-shattering water-level activity of recent decades could be yet another sign. Water-level controversies on Lakes Huron and Ontario during the last decade show that people are struggling with lake-level variability as much as ever, resulting in millions in taxpayer-funded studies just to research the problem, even apart from actually doing something about it. Recent climate and water-level trends suggest that those struggles are not going to get any easier in coming years. What's clear is that from Wasaga Beach to Montréal, and from Lake Ontario to Lake Superior, climate change is increasingly going to soak up the resources and attention of Great Lakes government officials, researchers, residents, and the private sector. People

High water levels are also a regular occurrence on the Great Lakes. This photo was taken on the western shore of Lake Michigan during high water in the 1980s. (US Army Corps of Engineers)

will need to learn to expect the unexpected, as the lakes may not always behave as they have in the past. Water-level volatility is bound to increase political tension over water. Low-water periods make Great Lakes residents particularly sensitive about water diversions. Those are the uncertainties. There are also some certainties. People will continue to complain about how Lake Ontario is regulated, and others will complain that Lakes Huron and Michigan are not.

It is natural for humans to want to control Great Lakes water levels. But history has shown that to be a challenge—and that was true before the advent of climate change. Will the region be able to harness the lakes when most signs suggest that living among them could become even more difficult? The public is clearly split between those who think we can engineer our way to a solution, and those who feel it's better to encourage humans to adapt rather than spend large sums trying to re-engineer a system that has so frequently defied control. "To me, the push for structures is one that just refuses to recognize that we need to learn to live with the lakes as opposed to changing them," says John Nevin, who served as a spokesperson for the IJC on the Upper Great

Lakes Study. "The effort to build structures would be better put toward some other use than the kind of fruitless effort to manage the lakes. We manage them enough already. We don't need to manage them any more."

Adaptation is increasingly a regional buzzword. Whatever the future holds for water levels on Lakes Huron and Ontario, given regional climate change projections it seems that adaptation will be a must for the Great Lakes. Officials say that adaptation means installing larger culverts and higher bridges, bigger gutters, larger rain gardens, and floating docks, as well as stronger break-walls and hurricane-force shingles. For some, it means putting more concrete and riprap in the front yard. For others, it means moving people and buildings outside of flood zones—or at least not allowing any new development to occur there. It means creating management plans that are adaptive, flexible, and nimble, and encouraging the officials implementing those plans to be nimble as well. It means creating long-term water-management rules that help reduce tensions over water. It also means thinking more about water—water abundance, water scarcity, and water hazards—when people build, when they decide to rebuild, or when they decide not to rebuild at all.

Chapter 4

Aversion to Diversion

It was one of the boldest engineering schemes ever conceived on the face of the planet, and it called for replumbing much of the natural hydrology of North America. It started in the extreme Northwest—the wilds of Alaska—and marched methodically south through British Columbia before spanning across most of the continent. The plan's western half envisioned harnessing some of the largest and wildest rivers in Alaska, British Columbia, and the Yukon Territory, including the Copper, Susitna, Tanana, and Yukon. The Columbia and Fraser Rivers would have been affected too.[1] The idea was to divert part of the flows of these raging rivers into the mother of all reservoirs: the Rocky Mountain Trench, a giant natural canyon stretching through most of British Columbia. Damming this canyon would create a surreal five-hundred-mile-long inland sea, the waters of which could be sent to the rest of the continent as needed along with up to 70,000 megawatts of surplus hydropower.[2] Of course, the plan called for much of this diverted water to be sent to the American Southwest. The dry Canadian prairies would get a cut too. The system's eastern branch would send water into the Peace River Valley of Alberta and on through Saskatchewan, Manitoba, and western Ontario until it reached Lake Superior. This eastern arm of the system was referred to as the Alberta–Great Lakes Canal and would carry 40 million acre-feet of water to Lake Superior annually.[3] That's enough water to raise the level of all five Great Lakes, double the hydropower output at Niagara Falls, and still have water to spare for the Mississippi River watershed.[4]

Such was the vision of NAWAPA—the North American Water and

Power Alliance—and its cost, in the early 1960s, was estimated at anywhere between $100 billion and $300 billion ($810 billion to $2.43 trillion today).[5] The project would have touched at least seven Canadian provinces or territories, thirty-three US states, and a portion of northern Mexico.[6] Aggressively promoted in the 1960s by the Ralph M. Parsons Company of Pasadena, California, NAWAPA would later be viewed by environmentalists (as well as by most Alaskans and Canadians) as the hydrologic anti-Christ. Though it never came close to being built, the plan was the envy of water engineers who were looking for a way to outdo the massive subsidized water projects that had been built in the 1930s, '40s, and '50s. These "welfare water" schemes came from a generation of men who believed that leaving water in its natural basin was a missed economic opportunity. Water was meant to be moved and used where humans needed it most, rather than foolishly permitted to flow into the sea. Behind their schemes lay a notable disregard for what these projects would do to the natural environment left behind by the displaced water. "NAWAPA, of course, is the granddaddy of them all—the most grandiose and the most ludicrous," says water expert Peter Gleick. "Some people have described it as a water engineer's wet dream—which is sort of a funny joke on all sorts of levels. It's a ridiculous idea. But it was the logical extension of a whole series of somewhat less ridiculous ideas, like . . . the massive plumbing projects that we built in the West." NAWAPA seems bizarrely far-fetched today, but it had a number of influential supporters in the 1960s.[7] Though it merely envisioned the Great Lakes as a connecting channel in a much larger scheme, it struck a chord among regional residents who wondered how long it would take for someone to concoct a similar plan that just happened to send Great Lakes water in the opposite direction. NAWAPA helped inspire a generation of far-flung Great Lakes diversion schemes—none of which made any economic sense.

That history of desire has helped fuel the anti-diversion paranoia that runs rampant throughout the Great Lakes region. The anti-diversion movement hit its stride in the early 1980s, when a string of diversion proposals prompted regional officials to push through a series of policies designed to keep Great Lakes water inside the Great Lakes Basin. Each of these mechanisms heavily emphasized the legal sanctity of the Great Lakes Basin: the squiggly topographic line that rims the Great

The North American Water and Power Alliance Plan

The North American Water and Power Alliance (NAWAPA) was an unrealized scheme hatched during the 1960s to transport massive amounts of water throughout much of the continent. (Geographical Magazine)

Lakes watershed like the edge of a soup bowl. Rain and snow that falls inside that Basin line eventually finds its way to the Great Lakes, but precipitation outside it ends up in the Mississippi, Atlantic, or Arctic watersheds. To the anti-diversion crowd, the edge of the Great Lakes Basin was the all-important line in the sand. Anyone residing outside that natural boundary or divide—even if they lived in a Great Lakes state or province—was not deserving of Great Lakes water.

The GRAND Canal was another water diversion scheme released in the 1960s and was sort of a NAWAPA of the East. While not quite as gargantuan, it was in the same league, with cost estimates between $100 billion and $200 billion ($810 billion to $1.6 trillion today).[8] The Great Recycling and Northern Development (GRAND) Canal was the brainchild of the late Canadian engineer Tom Kierans. During the Dust Bowl years, when he was in his twenties, he took a job in northern Ontario with a mining company. While working there he saw the large rivers flowing into James Bay at the southeast corner of Hudson Bay, and immediately he wondered about the possibility of shipping that water out West. The result, years later, was the GRAND Canal plan that proposed building a massive berm across James Bay as a way to capture all the fresh water flowing into it. Mr. Kierans, who became a successful engineer in Canada, figured it would take about eight years of captured inflow to turn James Bay into a freshwater lake. When that was achieved, the water could be pumped south to the upper reaches of Lake Huron.

Once northern Lake Huron started receiving this enormous inflow of fresh water, Huron's natural water feed from Lake Superior would become superfluous. Mr. Kierans argued that most of the water that normally left the east end of Lake Superior via the St. Marys River could be pumped out of the west end to the Canadian prairies, allowing agricultural fields there to finally attain the bountiful production that Mother Nature's local rainfall never allowed. From the Canadian prairies, surplus water would be directed southward through Montana and Wyoming to the headwaters of the Colorado River system, where it would then feed into the already reworked hydrology of the American Southwest. James Bay water could help grow winter lettuce in Arizona and strawberries in California, while greening up golf courses from Tucson to San Diego.

The Grand Canal Proposed Distribution System

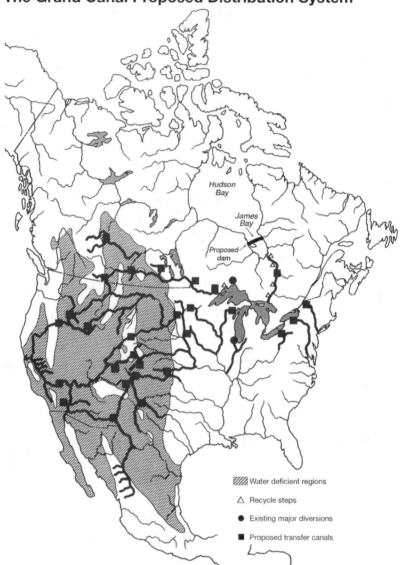

The GRAND Canal proposal envisioned capturing the freshwater inflows to James Bay and transporting them throughout North America. (©Tom Kierans)

In a 2005 interview, Mr. Kierans was still tirelessly promoting the GRAND Canal project. "We have got to realistically count on a billion people living on this continent by the end of this century," he said. "This is the most important project in the world today." According to Mr. Kierans, who died in 2013, the beauty of his GRAND Canal plan—and what made it superior to NAWAPA (which he argued was unrealistic) was that the GRAND Canal was not a diversion. Or so he claimed. A *diversion* takes water from its natural basin and sends it somewhere else, he said, but the GRAND Canal plan waits until the fresh water reaches the sea and then sends it elsewhere, meaning that no freshwater ecosystem is ever robbed of its water. That's a "recycling" plan, not a diversion, he explained.

Semantics aside, Mr. Kierans's plan was unique for a number of reasons. Damming an expansive saltwater bay had never before been proposed in North America.[9] But what was truly unique about the GRAND Canal plan was that it came from a Canadian. Before Mr. Kierans stepped forward, the vast majority of North America's grandiose water plans had come from US engineers—plans that were viewed by many Canadians as hegemonic schemes devised by bullying American watermongers. This time, though, one of their own had drawn up an elaborate blueprint to send Canadian water south, and many of Mr. Kierans's compatriots found his ideas repugnant. "I was branded as a traitor in Canada for even suggesting this!" he complained. "People up here couldn't see the difference between 'diversion' and 'recycling,' no matter what I said."

But unlike NAWAPA, which envisioned sending water *to* the Great Lakes (the lakes were suffering historic low water levels at the time), the GRAND Canal project was a true and massive Great Lakes diversion proposal sending water out of the west end of Lake Superior, the largest such proposal ever to be contemplated in the region. As a point of comparison, the Chicago diversion (chapter 5) currently diverts 2.1 billion gallons per day out of Lake Michigan into the Mississippi River watershed, permanently lowering Lakes Michigan and Huron by 2.5 inches. The GRAND Canal concept proposed diverting 26 billion gallons per day out of Lake Superior to the West—a diversion more than ten times the size of Chicago's. But again, under the GRAND Canal plan, that water would be compensated for by a massive infusion of fresh water into Lake Huron from James Bay. Tom Kierans's son, Michael, continues to promote the GRAND Canal concept, arguing that the recycling plan remains morally superior to NAWAPA, and that the first edition of this book was too harsh on his father's brainchild. "The Great Lakes could be the key to the salvation of Southwest agriculture," he said in a 2018 e-mail. "The GRAND Canal and the Great Lakes would be the centerpiece of a new North American continental water-management system."

The problem for the GRAND Canal idea, however, was that regardless of whether James Bay water was "recycled" or "diverted," Canadians and Americans in the Great Lakes region just didn't like the idea of a massive canal heading west out of Lake Superior. They preferred to see Superior's water remain in the lake. Like NAWAPA, the GRAND Canal has never come close to being built, but not every Canadian has been opposed to it. The elder Mr. Kierans managed to secure support for the GRAND Canal in very high places. Former Canadian prime minister Brian Mulroney viewed the plan "with enthusiasm,"[10] and Robert Bourassa, the former premier of Québec, was so bullish on the canal that he devoted several pages to it in his 1985 book, *Power from the North.*[11]

The NAWAPA and GRAND Canal plans represent outlandish case studies that captured a lot of attention but never materialized. Over the years, however, many smaller diversion schemes *have* made it off the drawing board. In fact, the Great Lakes' diversion history dates back to the early 1800s. According to the International Joint Commission, there have been at least four diversions *into* the Great Lakes since that time and at least four diversions out. There have also been six other "intra-Basin" diversions that artificially diverted water from one lake's sub-basin to another. One of the first diversions came in 1825 when the Erie Canal opened in upstate New York, connecting Buffalo, on the shores of Lake Erie, with Albany, on the Hudson River, thus allowing barges to travel all the way from the Great Lakes to New York City.[12] The largest and most controversial diversion out of the Basin took place in 1900 when the state of Illinois reversed the Chicago River, diverting the river's highly polluted water away from Chicago's Lake Michigan water intake pipes and sending it down the Des Plaines and Illinois Rivers toward St. Louis (see chapter 5). That diversion was later

Existing Diversions in the Great Lakes Basin

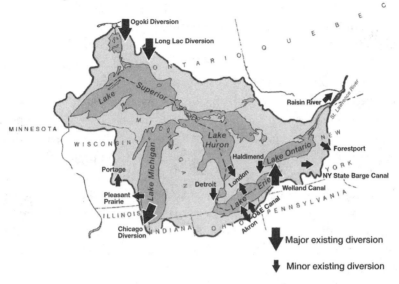

Existing Diversions in the Great Lakes Basin	Operational Date (original project)	Average Annual Flow (cms)*	(cfs)**
Interbasin			
Long Lac (into Lake Superior basin)	1939	45	1,590
Ogoki (into Lake Superior basin)	1943	113	3,990
Chicago (out of Lake Michigan basin)	(1848)1900	91	3,200
Forestport (out of Lake Ontario basin)	1825	1.4	50
Portage Canal (into Lake Michigan basin)	1860	1	40
Ohio & Erie Canal (into Lake Erie basin)	1847	0.3	12
Pleasant Prairie (out of Lake Michigan basin	1990	0.1	5
Akron (out of and into Lake Erie basin)	1998	0.01	0.5
Intrabasin			
Welland Canal	(1829)1932	260	9,200
NY State Barge Canal (Erie Canal)	(1825)1918	20	700
Detroit	1975	4	145
London	1967	3	110
Raisin River	1968	0.7	25
Haldimand	1997	0.1	2

International Joint Commission

*cubic meters per second   **cubic feet per second

There have been more than a dozen Great Lakes diversions since the 1800s—some more celebrated than others. (Adapted from International Joint Commission) challenged in court by other Great Lakes states, resulting in a highly contentious Supreme Court case that dragged on for decades.

The diversion issue erupted again in 1981 when a company announced plans to construct a 1,900-mile coal-slurry pipeline from Wyoming to the Great Lakes. Powder River Pipeline Inc. (PRPI) envisioned grinding coal and mixing it with water to create a slurry that would then be injected into a forty-two-inch pipe buried three feet underground. The pipeline would be able to ship as much as 36 million tons of coal per year to power plants in the Midwest. According to its proponents, the system would be cheaper and more efficient than shipping coal by rail. Published maps showed the pipeline forking as it reached the Great Lakes region, with one terminus near Duluth, Minnesota, on Lake Superior, and a second ending north of Milwaukee on Lake Michigan.[13] The $2.8-billion project (roughly $8-billion today) was the brainchild of energy-industry entrepreneurs based in Oklahoma, Mississippi, and Montana.[14]

But the project got off to a rocky start. PRPI needed water to make the slurry, and taking precious water from dry Western states and piping it to the wet Great Lakes was not the most popular idea. Nevertheless, the investors made headway in securing the necessary water near the Wyoming and Montana coal beds. PRPI was working these Western water leads late in 1981 when William Westhoff, the Mississippi executive charged with promoting the project, gave a speech at a coal export conference in Superior, Wisconsin. During the speech he made the mistake of saying "as an afterthought" that if Western water could not be secured for the project, PRPI was also considering installing a return waterline that would send Lake Superior water westward, where it could be used to create the slurry.[15]

That comment was picked up by the media and transmitted throughout the Great Lakes Basin, provoking outrage. Mr. Westhoff was taken aback by the public reaction and was forced to devote considerable time to damage control. "We have seen the headlines where the [Great Lakes] governors are going to get together and put a surtax on water going to the West," Mr. Westoff said in a meeting with Wisconsin officials a year later. "There was a headline that came out in one of the papers that said we would drain Lake Superior dry.... We don't plan to use Lake Superior water, not now, never did, and I don't think we ever will. I would like to lay that to rest if we could."[16] The following year PRPI abandoned the project completely after essential federal eminent-domain legislation—which would have permitted the pipeline to be built on railroad rights-of-way—failed to pass on Capitol Hill. Despite Mr. Westhoff's attempts to explain away his offhand remark, his project is still known in the Great Lakes region as the pipeline that planned to use Lake Superior water to transport coal slurry from Wyoming to Middle America.

In fairness to Mr. Westhoff, the Great Lakes governors were already on edge when he and his investors came along. The governors had been looking anxiously to the west—not to Wyoming or Montana, but toward the dry High Plains and the infamously overtapped Ogallala Aquifer that lies beneath them. Aquifers are reservoirs of water that, contrary to popular belief, are not large open underground lakes. Instead, the water is housed in cracks, crevices, and holes in underground rock formations or subterranean sand or gravel beds. The Ogallala is huge, stretching from South Dakota through Nebraska, Kansas, eastern Colorado, and Oklahoma to the base of the Texas panhandle; it underlies small sections of Wyoming and New Mexico, too. Despite its enormous size, by the late 1970s the Ogallala had proven vulnerable. Thanks to irrigated agriculture on the arid plains, water levels in the aquifer had plummeted by more than one hundred feet in some areas, even as rainfall replenished the water table at rates of just one to six inches per year.[17] The Ogallala had slowly filled with water over thousands of years, and in less than a hundred years modern irrigated agriculture threatened to suck it dry. "A continuation of existing usage patterns is expected to result in depletion, or near depletion, of this sole major source of water in a large portion of the High Plains," said a federal report in 1982.[18] By the mid-1970s, 20 percent of all the irrigated land in the United States was using Ogallala Aquifer water. The High Plains had also become a major meat supplier, with 40 percent of all the beef cattle in America fattened there using locally grown irrigated grain.[19]

The status quo was clearly not sustainable, but High Plains farmers were counting on their congressmen to fix things. In 1976, High Plains states pushed legislation through Congress asking the US Army Corps of Engineers to conduct a highly controversial $6-million study on the

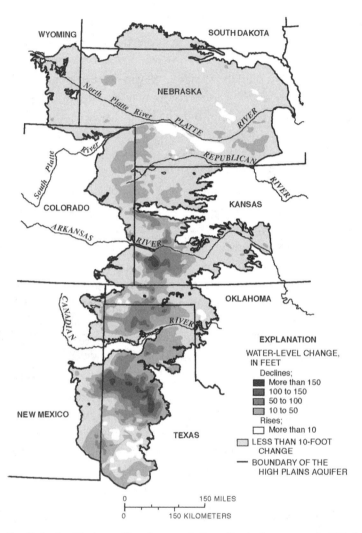

The Ogallala Aquifer has suffered severe declines. In the late 1970s, the US Army Corps of Engineers alarmed Great Lakes officials by studying the transport of water to the Ogallala region from "adjacent areas." (Courtesy of the US Geological Survey)

aquifer's decline. The purpose of the study was to examine the economic and engineering feasibility of transporting water to the Ogallala region from "adjacent areas."[20] The *Six-State High Plains Ogallala Aquifer Regional Resources Study* sent a shock wave of alarm through many neighboring states and made Great Lakes governors furious. One of the eight Great Lakes states (Minnesota) is immediately "adjacent" to one of the Ogallala states (South Dakota). The governors had long worried that a federally subsidized water boondoggle might contemplate shipping Great Lakes water to the Southwest, but the High Plains were much closer and seemed much more threatening.

The Corps ended up interpreting the word "adjacent" quite literally, however, and did not consider studying the prospect of diverting water from any of the Great Lakes states. The controversial study zeroed in on four key diversion concepts that ranged from tapping the Missouri River in South Dakota to diverting water from several streams in Arkansas and/or Texas.[21] The four scenarios varied widely in construction cost—and none of them was cheap—ranging from $3.6 billion to $27.8 billion ($9.6 billion to $74 billion today).[22] A key operating expense was the enormous amount of electricity that would be required to move the water uphill to the High Plains. The Corps estimated that anywhere from sixteen to forty-nine pumping plants would have to be built to move the water. The unit cost of this water—even without the ultimate farmer-delivery expense—rounded out to somewhere between $227 per acre-foot to $569 per acre-foot ($603 to $1,511 today).[23] Those were (and are) unconscionably high water costs. As a point of comparison, nearly three decades of inflation later, Western agricultural water was considered expensive when it cost around $100 per acre-foot.[24] At such high prices, taxpayers would be better off buying out many Ogallala farmers and turning their spreads back into a buffalo commons.[25]

Then the academic community got involved. The extraordinary cost figures unveiled by the Corps's study helped sink any plans to divert water to the Ogallala from adjacent areas, not to mention from the Great Lakes. But to reinforce the point further, University of Michigan professor Jonathan Bulkley examined the additional cost of transferring Lake Superior water to the Missouri River, where—theoretically at least—the Lake Superior water could connect up with two of the

Corps's hypothetical Ogallala diversion schemes. The idea was not to promote Great Lakes diversions, but to demonstrate how ridiculously expensive they would be. Professor Bulkley found that sending Lake Superior water to the Ogallala—not to mention anywhere farther to the southwest—would be laughably expensive. "Anybody that's thinking about pumping Great Lakes water to Arizona is out of their skull," he says.

According to his research, building a 611-mile canal capable of carrying water from Lake Superior to Yankton, South Dakota, at 10,000 cubic feet per second would cost $20 billion ($49 billion today). Additionally, the water would have to be lifted uphill from Lake Superior to the higher elevations at Yankton, which would take a total of eighteen pumping stations requiring the electricity of seven 1,000-megawatt power plants. The power plants alone would cost an additional $7 billion (roughly $17 billion today), not counting annual operating expenses.[26] When Professor Bulkley's steep water-cost calculations ($66 billion today) were added to the extraordinary water-cost estimates in the Corps's Ogallala study ($9.6 billion–$74 billion today), shipping Great Lakes water west sounded more like fiction than science.

While those findings were damning, Great Lakes politicians were still rattled because federal officials had funded the Ogallala diversion study in the first place. The idea that the US government would spend millions of dollars investigating the bulk transfer of water from one basin to another fed right into the heart of Great Lakes residents' worst diversion nightmares. The coal-slurry pipeline proposal and the Ogallala study set off a period of deep insecurity in the Great Lakes region—a situation that only worsened when the US Supreme Court announced its decision in *Sporhase v. Nebraska* at about the same time.

The *Sporhase* case had its roots in a remote section of rural Nebraska, but it resonated throughout the United States. It raised serious doubts about whether a state had the authority to prevent water from being diverted outside its borders. *Sporhase* began with a Nebraska law that prohibited groundwater from being exported to another state—if that other state refused to allow *its* water to be exported to Nebraska. A farmer with property on both sides of the Nebraska–Colorado border challenged the law as a violation of the interstate commerce clause in the US Constitution. In 1982, the Supreme Court ruled in favor of the farmer, declaring that groundwater was an article of commerce and that Nebraska's reciprocity requirement was therefore a barrier to interstate trade under the commerce clause. The justices said that while the federal government gave states great leeway in setting water policy, infringing on interstate commerce crossed a constitutional line.[27]

For the Great Lakes governors, the ruling shattered hopes that they could pass legislation banning diversions of Great Lakes water outside their states' borders. "[*Sporhase* makes] it clear that water 'embargoes' enacted by the Great Lakes States, while serving an important purpose in signaling the region's basic opposition to diversion, will almost certainly be struck down if challenged," predicted a briefing paper prepared for the Great Lakes governors in the wake of the decision. "Once struck down, of course, the [Great Lakes] states would be left scrambling to design and implement defensible legislation."[28] As hard as it was for them to admit, having individual states pass an outright ban on Great Lakes diversions was not an option. The governors would have to come up with some other mechanism for protecting Great Lakes water.

The coal-slurry/Ogallala/*Sporhase* convergence was interpreted ominously in the Great Lakes region as a pro-diversion triple whammy. Though the economics didn't make sense, water—as they say in the West—tends to flow uphill toward money, and Great Lakes politicians worried that none of their existing laws could stop diversions of Great Lakes water. The only thing that came close was the 1909 Boundary Waters Treaty between the United States and Canada, which was designed to help resolve border-water disputes. But the Boundary Waters Treaty had two huge holes in it. First, it only seemed to apply when diversions were large enough to influence the "level or flow" of the Great Lakes. As an example, the proposed coal-slurry pipeline—at 17 cubic feet per second, or 11 million gallons of water per day—would have imperceptibly influenced Lake Superior levels.[29] But if a large number of similar-sized diversions were implemented, their cumulative effects could influence Great Lakes water levels significantly. Yet those impacts would not be covered under the treaty. That meant the Boundary Waters Treaty did not protect the Great Lakes from the most likely diversion problem—death by a thousand straws. Second, because Lake Michigan is the only Great Lake that lies entirely within US borders, it's technically not a "boundary" water and is presumed by many to be excluded from the treaty. This means that diversion proposals relating to Lake Michigan would not be covered.[30]

But there's nothing like a little adversity to captivate the attention of a handful of sleepy governors. The pro-diversion triple whammy helped rally politicians, bureaucrats, and activists from throughout the Great Lakes region. Things got rolling in January of 1982 with the formation of the Council of Great Lakes Governors, which was designed to help coordinate regional responses to all sorts of Great Lakes issues, including the diversion threat.[31] Later that year, Great Lakes governors and premiers met on Michigan's Mackinac Island and declared that no Great Lakes water could be diverted without clearance from all of the Great Lakes governors and premiers as well as from the federal governments in the United States and Canada. The declaration lacked the force of law, but it sent a clear signal. In 1983, federal legislation was introduced in the United States to prevent diversions from the lakes without the consent of the Great Lakes states (though the bill didn't pass). Then the Great Lakes governors adopted a resolution supporting the federal legislation and encouraging Great Lakes governors to adopt anti-diversion laws in each of their states. (Even though those laws would likely be found unconstitutional, they could be used to slow down diversion proposals until a regional anti-diversion policy was implemented.) Then in late 1983, the Council of Great Lakes Governors appointed a special anti-diversion task force that was given one year to draw up an in-depth and authoritative study on Great Lakes diversions, including a recommended action plan.[32]

The task force was a mixture of lawyers and policymakers and included one representative from each Great Lakes state and province. It was led by Peter McAvoy, an aide to Wisconsin governor Tony Earl, a Democrat. Mr. McAvoy says the team quickly decided not to pursue a legally binding regional water compact because it would be too complicated and would take too long to implement. In addition, federal officials told the team that the Great Lakes states and provinces didn't have the right under international law to pen a water treaty with one another. No one was interested in asking the federal governments to beef up the 1909 Boundary Waters Treaty—that would take forever. And given that the US government had just conducted a water-diversion study that sent shudders through the region, the governors were not keen on getting Washington involved at all. They were much more interested in working with the provincial premiers in Ontario and Québec to implement a regional agreement on their own.

After months of deliberation, in late 1984 the task force recommended creating what it called the Great Lakes Charter. A regional agreement between the governors and premiers, the Charter was designed to control Great Lakes diversions outside the Basin as well as consumptive uses inside it. The Charter was the first in what would eventually become a string of water-regulatory systems that would follow in subsequent decades. It was a historic first step that had profound influence on future water-management policy in the region. The Charter's main focus was on large diversions and consumptive uses. If a state or province received a water permit application to divert or consume more than 5 mgd (million gallons per day), roughly the amount used daily by a community of 50,000, it was required to give "prior notice" to all the other states and provinces before the withdrawal could be approved.

After receiving this notice, if the other governors or premiers had concerns about the size, shape, or worthiness of the proposed water use, they could request a "consultation," which was more than just a conference call. "Consultation" meant a face-to-face meeting where the proposed withdrawal would be thoroughly examined, and concerns could be aired. According to the Charter, no governor or premier could approve a large-scale diversion or consumptive use without "the consent and concurrence of all affected Great Lakes States and Provinces." "[The Charter] was designed to be a fence to prevent diversions and [to create] a process and a means to say no," says Richard Bartz, former head of the Division of Water at the Ohio Department of Natural Resources, a key member of the task force. A concern over diversions drove the Charter, but it was also designed to focus new attention on large-scale consumptive use within the Basin, which was a forward-looking idea that forced the Great Lakes states and provinces to come to grips with the sustainability of their own water use. The Charter had one significant drawback, however. It was a nonbinding agreement that any state or province could ignore without penalty.

Everybody liked that agreement except for Michigan. Officials there didn't want the legislative standards included in the Charter. Before one can understand Michigan's opposition, one needs to understand how the state differs from its neighbors on both sides of the border. Michigan is defined by the Great Lakes more than any other state or province because all but a smidgen of its territory lies entirely within the Great Lakes Basin. No other Great Lakes state or province has such a large percentage of land in the watershed. Minnesota may be "the land of 10,000 lakes," but Michigan considers itself to be the "Great Lakes State," and it is the only state to touch four of the five Great Lakes (though the province of Ontario does, too). Because Michigan is so defined by the lakes, arguably no state has more to lose from large-scale diversions of water from the Basin. Or at least that's the way Michiganders look at it. Great Lakes water diversions are an enormous political issue in the state.

Why, then, would a state that's worried about diversions be opposed to including legislative standards in the Charter? In short, because Michigan thought the standards were too lax. Michigan residents are so fervently opposed to diversions that the only agreement that would pass muster in the state was an outright ban—no matter what the Supreme Court said in *Sporhase v. Nebraska*. The other states wouldn't agree to a diversion ban precisely because of the *Sporhase* decision—they assumed the Supreme Court would throw it out. But as Michigan's Charter negotiating team saw it, asking their governor to sign a nonbinding document that permitted diversions under 5 mgd was bad enough. Forcing him to push a bill through the Michigan legislature that made Great Lakes diversions legal would be political suicide. They realized that a ban on diversions was likely to be found unconstitutional—but try explaining that to the average voter. Michigan officials told the task force to take the legislative standards out of the Charter because such standards made it look like Michigan was approving diversions. So the standards were pulled from the Charter and handed out separately at the Charter's signing ceremony. The governors and premiers had a blueprint for the laws they were supposed to pass—it just wasn't integrated into the Charter itself.

Michigan may have held its ground on the legislative standards, but it gave in during another behind-the-scenes dispute. While the task force deliberations were under way, research showed that consumptive uses of water inside the Basin had the same effect on the Great Lakes ecosystem as diversions outside the Basin. Any water taken permanently from the ecosystem was lost, whether it was shipped to the Ogallala by pipeline, left the Basin in a bottle of juice, or evaporated away at a major power plant. In addition, the Canadians pointed out that the majority of the consumptive use was on the US side of the border. "It was interesting because that whole [task force] was set up to look at diversions," remembers Dick Bartz. "And Canada came to the table and said, 'We just got this report here, and [most] of the in-Basin consumptive uses are from the US side. If you want us to talk about diversions, then *we* want to talk about in-Basin consumptive uses, because the impact on the resource is exactly the same.'"

That didn't sit well with Michigan, either. An agreement curbing diversions was easy for Michigan to sign because it can use all the water it wants without its use ever being considered a diversion. Unlike the rest of the states and provinces, Michigan could ship water from one end of the state to the other and it would not break the rules. But a charter that applied to diversions *and* consumptive uses would put Michigan under the same regulatory scrutiny as everyone else, and Michigan didn't like that idea. Diversions were the real threat to the lakes, Michigan argued, not consumptive uses. But the Canadians saw that argument as water hypocrisy—as did many other states—so Michigan eventually backed down. From that point onward, consumptive uses were lumped together on an equal footing with diversions in the Charter. After months of negotiations, by January 1985 the Charter task force had developed a document that was ready for the governors and premiers to sign. A ceremony was set for February 11, 1985, in Milwaukee. In a skyscraper boardroom overlooking Lake Michigan, the majority of the Great Lakes governors and premiers, along with regional water officials and the media, gathered to make the Charter official.[33] The politicians viewed the ceremony as an important milestone. "Some of them delivered these really eloquent speeches," Peter McAvoy recalls. "They were quite moving. They did not just come and do this photo op."

Great Lakes politicians were sending a signal to the rest of the continent—and even the world. Perhaps it was unconstitutional for individual states to ban interstate water transfers, but the governors and premiers were determined to make it difficult for someone to undertake long-range, large-scale diversions from outside the Great Lakes Basin line. Wisconsin and Minnesota moved swiftly to pass laws adopting the Charter's standards. Other states followed later, but for years Michigan remained less than enthusiastic about the Charter's language. On February 28, 2006, more than two decades after the Charter was signed, Michigan finally adopted a comprehensive water-management law, making it the last Great Lakes state to recognize at least some of the Charter's language in its statutes. Meanwhile in Canada, Québec approached the Charter with a laissez-faire attitude as well, taking some fifteen years to integrate Charter-like language into its water laws. And while Ontario was slow to reference the Charter in its statutes, provincial water laws already matched or exceeded the Charter in many areas.

Not long after the signing ceremony, however, the diversion threat returned—and this time it was a lot closer to home than the Ogallala Aquifer. During 1985 and 1986, New York City was going through a serious drought. America's largest city was on a major water alert, and conservation measures were drummed into the heads of people from Staten Island to the Bronx. Officials were under serious pressure to come up with contingency plans for alternate water supplies, and it wasn't long before people started mentioning the Great Lakes. Just seven months after the Charter-signing ceremony, New York State environment commissioner Henry Williams formed a thirteen-member panel to explore a wide variety of water options, and diverting water from Lake Ontario or Lake Erie was one of them. "It's inescapable that the abundant water supply in the Great Lakes will be included in any consideration of water allocation in New York State," he announced during September of 1985. "It's not to say it will happen, but it will be considered."[34]

Because New York City was far outside the Great Lakes Basin, the announcement that the state would consider diverting water there provoked a bitter reaction. Many of New York's Great Lakes neighbors saw it as a hypocritical affront to the spirit of the Charter. The move raised serious regional questions about Governor Mario Cuomo's political credibility—a point that some New York journalists were happy to point out. "The raid on Great Lakes water may be sooner and closer to home than you think," wrote Paul MacClennan, environment reporter for the *Buffalo News*. "What a predicament that poses for the Cuomo administration. The governor on the one hand signed the Great Lakes Charter earlier this year, and a basic premise of the eight-state–two-province agreement is to preserve the lakes' water. . . . But Cuomo also has heavy political debts downstate and a continuing water shortage that threatens the New York City metropolitan area."[35] Like other diversion scares, the New York City option eventually faded away, but it continued to haunt Great Lakes residents, who wondered if New York might resurrect this diversion idea sometime in the future.

The scare from New York only highlighted the Charter's nonbinding nature, and some Great Lakes leaders hungered for something more. A good-faith agreement was a great start, but these officials believed that a legally binding statute was still necessary to throw down a barrier against large-scale Great Lakes diversions—to New York City or anywhere else. Some officials looked to the US Congress for help. They set their eyes on amending the federal Water Resources Development Act (WRDA, pronounced "WORD-uh") by inserting a special section—1109—that referred specifically to Great Lakes diversions. WRDA is federal legislation that is renewed periodically for major public-works projects, and frequently it is rife with pork and other special-interest legislation. Several Great Lakes states saw the 1986 version of WRDA as an opportunity to erect a stronger barrier to Great Lakes diversions, and they managed to slip in the wording without incident.

Section 1109 of WRDA was short (two pages) but powerful. It said that any proposal to divert water outside the Great Lakes Basin needed the unanimous approval of all eight Great Lakes governors. What's more, it covered diversions of all sizes—there was no longer a 5-mgd trigger. Anyone who wanted to divert a single drop of water outside the Great Lakes Basin would have to run the WRDA gauntlet first. While the Charter had targeted diversions *and* in-Basin consumptive uses, WRDA was strictly an anti-diversion document. WRDA went on to say that neither the Army Corps of Engineers nor any other federal agency could even study the feasibility of diverting water from the Great Lakes without the unanimous approval of all eight Great Lakes governors.

WRDA was a dream come true to Michigan. Finally, it had attained a magic veto over diversion proposals in all the other Great Lakes states without the concern of retribution or the burden of regulating its own consumptive water use. That was a power that other states would come to regret, as later chapters in this book will show. But was it constitutional? Many experts didn't think so. The wispy two-page statute lacked any guidance on how diversion applications should be judged—forcing the governors to make up the rules as they went along—and not necessarily requiring them to treat all water applicants by the same standards. In addition, the law provided no opportunity for spurned water applicants to appeal. That left WRDA highly vulnerable to allegations that the law was arbitrary and capricious, if not unconstitutional.

Unlike the Charter, with its clear procedures for "prior notice and consultation," WRDA laid out no such procedure for how governors should go about exercising their newfound water veto powers. Did they have to meet in person? Did the veto have to be in writing? Was a consultation required first, or could a governor just veto the project by making a phone call after reading about it in the newspaper? "For many of us at the time, [WRDA] was viewed as an abomination," said attorney R. Timothy Weston, a former Pennsylvania state official who helped draft the Charter. "It's really one of the worst pieces of legislation created. . . . It provides no due process, it provides no standards, [and] it creates an entirely political and unaccountable arrangement for casting vetoes—which is one of the silliest ways for managing natural resources imaginable."

What a difference a few years of anti-diversion hysteria can make. The governors and premiers had gone from having no regimen for regulating Great Lakes diversions to having two very different and somewhat awkward water-management systems. One was voluntary, but international. The other was binding, but domestic—and of questionable constitutionality. Once WRDA passed, some states lost all enthusiasm for adopting the Charter's legislative standards as law. It certainly helped give Michigan the out it was looking for. "What [WRDA] did was provide us with a framework to approve and deny any diversions," said Jim Bredin, a former official from Michigan's Office of the Great Lakes. "And that's what we were mainly concerned about. We really didn't need to address it through state legislation."

In the wake of the triple whammy, Great Lakes politicians had rallied to the cause of preventing diversions. But the result was a patchwork of policies that few were thrilled with. The Charter and WRDA were both imperfect in their own ways, but a lot of political capital had been spent pulling them together. By the late 1980s, there was little energy to do anything more. Regional officials would have to live with what had been adopted and hope it provided the protections for the Great Lakes they were looking for.

Part II

Battle Lines and Skirmishes

Chapter 5

Reversing a River

In the late 1800s, Chicago was a bustling urban center well on its way to becoming one of world's great cities. Having rebuilt itself after the Chicago Fire of 1871, it was a thriving metropolis of approximately a million people. But it also was a filthy place with wretched sanitation problems, and nothing exemplified that more than the squalid Chicago River. Virtually an open sewer, laced with visible filth, some of the river's worst pollution came from its urbanized tributaries. "Bubbly Creek" was an ecologically dead branch of the river that was filled annually with enough rotting stockyard offal to equal the pollution from a sizable city. Gases from the decaying rot bubbled to the surface, giving the creek its name. "In the summer, when a hard brown scum settled on its surface, cats and chickens could be seen scurrying across it," writes Donald Miller in his book *City of the Century*.[1] There were times, thanks to discharges from the slaughterhouses, when the river ran red with blood.[2] After heavy rains it was not unusual to see the rotting carcasses of dead cats—or even horses—floating in the river's sewage slick as it streamed far out into Lake Michigan. In some cases the polluted plume even neared the city's drinking-water intake structures, two miles from shore.[3] The fear of waterborne illness was constant.[4] "Cholera, and later typhoid, were a problem," says Richard Lanyon, former executive director at the Metropolitan Water Reclamation District of Greater Chicago, the metro region's wastewater treatment agency. "The other problem was just plain old nuisance conditions. The river smelled terrible and, depending on which way the wind was blowing, various parts of the city were 'treated' to this aroma."

During the late 1800s and early 1900s, Bubbly Creek became a notoriously polluted branch of the Chicago River. Thanks to vast quantities of waste dumped into the waterway from nearby stockyards, the creek regularly crusted over with filth. Here a man stands on a section of Bubbly Creek's crust in 1911. (DN-0056839, Chicago Daily News negatives collection, Chicago History Museum)

By 1885, Chicago's leading citizens were fed up with the embarrassingly unhealthy condition of their river. The solution was bold and ambitious: to definitively reverse the river's flow. The primary goal was to flush Chicago's sewage far away from the city's Lake Michigan water-intake pipes, though there was also a desire to use the reversed river for navigation.[5] Reversing the river had been tried before, in 1871, when a less ambitious effort led to limited and very temporary success.[6] This time, city leaders, with the eventual support of the state legislature, were determined to reverse the river's flow decisively and permanently. Their plan was to construct a twenty-eight-mile canal connecting the Chicago River to the Des Plaines River near the village of Lockport southwest of the city, where Chicago's pollution would then flow into the Illinois River and ultimately the Mississippi. Unlike the first attempt to reverse the river, this project was built to divert a large amount of water from the Lake Michigan waterfront: 10,000 cubic feet per second (about 4.5 million gallons per minute). The diversion channel eventually became known as the Chicago Sanitary and Ship Canal, and the diversion itself is called the Lake Michigan diversion at Chicago (also known as the "Illinois diversion," or colloquially as the "Chicago diversion").

Groundbreaking began in 1892. The canal took 8,500 workers eight years to construct; it was 25 feet deep, ranged from 160 to 300 feet in width, and cost $31 million to build (approximately $855 million today). Though much of the canal was dug through flat, soft terrain, roughly fifteen miles were blasted through solid bedrock. The Sanitary and Ship Canal was an unprecedented engineering feat that paved the way for the Panama Canal just a few years later.[7] Chicago would never have grown into the city it is today were it not for the clean, safe, dependable water supply that the Sanitary and Ship Canal ensured by diverting the city's sewage away from Lake Michigan. "Chicago was a city made possible by the largest engineering project undertaken in an American community up to that time, the river reversal and the installation of a new sewage and water system," writes Mr. Miller in *City of the Century*. "[Chicago] was capable of doing big things and doing them well, and this became part of its permanent reputation."[8]

But there was a negative side to the Chicago River's reversal. It was the largest and most controversial project ever to divert water outside

Pollution from the city's sprawling stockyards played a key role in the decision to reverse the Chicago River in 1900. The move sent Chicago's sewage into the Mississippi River watershed instead of Lake Michigan, the primary source of the city's drinking water. (Library of Congress, Prints & Photographs Division, FSA/OWI Collection, LC-USF34-063124-D)

the Great Lakes Basin. Engineering feat or not, it stands as a polarizing example of precisely what water managers and politicians throughout the Great Lakes region are determined to never see happen again. "The Chicago River [reversal] is one of the primary transformations of the Great Lakes ecosystem," says Henry Henderson, director of the Natural Resource Defense Council's Midwest Program. "[It] is the poster child of bad behavior in the Great Lakes."

∼

The canal project was marked by controversy even before it was finished. Despite Chicago's claims that pollution in the reversed river would be harmlessly diluted after a matter of miles, many downstream residents were doubtful. Chief of the skeptics was the City of St. Louis, which worried that the reversed river's sewage would taint the

Mississippi—St. Louis's source of drinking water. As the canal was nearing completion, word spread that Missouri planned to petition the Supreme Court to prevent Chicago from dumping sewage into the waterway. The news prompted Chicago's wily leaders to uncharacteristically take a pass on pomp and circumstance and surreptitiously open the canal during the early morning hours on a cold day in the dead of winter. On the morning of January 2, 1900, ice-clogged water began to flow from the reversed river into the fresh-cut channel of the Sanitary and Ship Canal, and Missouri had lost its opportunity to prevent the canal from opening.

The following day, the *Chicago Tribune* published a detailed and entertaining description of the weather-plagued, Keystone Cop–like effort to get the water flowing before Missouri could file suit.[9] Once word got out that the river had been reversed, it became national news. On January 14, 1900, *The New York Times* trumpeted, in the colorful style of the era, "Water in the Chicago River . . . now resembles liquid. The impossible has now happened! The Chicago River is becoming clear! . . . The stream which for a generation has been the butt of the newspaper paragrapher and the low comedian, which has been known rather as a solid than a liquid, which polluted the city water supply for a quarter of a century, and which twice caught on fire and had to be put out by the Fire Department, is actually approaching translucency and can be seen to move!" The paper went on to say the river had been transformed over several days from a "greasy black" to a "pale green" and "will eventually turn a blue like that of Lake Michigan." "To anyone who has not seen this sink hole of unspeakable filth, and whose nose has not been assailed by the stenches which arose from it, all is wasted. But some idea of the nastiness of it may be had from the fact that the sewage of over a million people flowed into a stagnant stream and then imperceptibly polluted the lake from which those people derived their water supply."[10] Two weeks after the water began to flow in reverse, workers twenty-eight miles downstream put the finishing touches on the southern end of the canal, finally connecting it to the Des Plaines River. That same day word arrived that Missouri had finally gotten around to filing its injunction on behalf of St. Louis, but it was too late—too late, at least, to prevent the reversed river from opening—and the Supreme Court denied Missouri's request.[11]

Construction of the Chicago Sanitary and Ship Canal, circa the late 1890s. (Photo courtesy of the Metropolitan Water Reclamation District of Greater Chicago)

In 1905, the situation heated up again when Missouri filed another Supreme Court challenge against the Sanitary and Ship Canal, blaming the new waterway for an increase in typhoid cases in St. Louis. Illinois's response to Missouri's court filing argued that Chicago's sewage was completely diluted by the time it reached St. Louis and thus there was nothing to worry about. In a comment that exemplified the bitterness of the time, Missouri's attorney general said, "The action of the Chicago authorities in turning their sewage into the Mississippi River for the people of St. Louis to drink is criminal, and Chicago knows it."[12]

Nonetheless, Missouri's tardy and unsuccessful legal challenge made history of sorts. It was the first salvo in what would become an acrimonious, century-long legal dispute involving the Illinois diversion—making the Chicago River one of the most heavily litigated bodies of water in the United States. The litany of lawsuits not only pitted

Illinois against downstream states such as Missouri, but it also eventually prompted legal challenges from the federal government and just about every other Great Lakes state in the Basin. In fact, the Chicago River's burdensome legal legacy is not over. The terms of the diversion continue to be dictated by a highly complicated and much-fought-over Supreme Court decree that controls the water supply for nearly 7 million people in the greater Chicago area. Any effort to change the Illinois diversion in the future would require the approval of a majority of the nation's nine most influential jurists.

~

Fresh from its victory over Missouri in the early 1900s, Chicago was feeling cocky and began taking measures to expand the geographic breadth of its diversion. While other sewage-treatment technologies were available, the city took the regressive approach of embarking on a full-fledged regional effort to use dilution as the solution to its pollution. During the next several years, city officials expanded the Illinois diversion, much to the dismay of the other Great Lake states and provinces. Between 1907 and 1910, on Chicago's North Side, the city dug a canal known as the North Shore Channel, and in 1911 it started another canal, on the South Side, called the Cal-Sag Channel.[13] In just ten years the city had rapidly expanded its diversion of Lake Michigan water at three different points, sending it all into the Sanitary and Ship Canal, and eventually down the Mississippi.

Throughout this period, Chicago kept ramping up the volume of its diversion.[14] In 1900, the flow started out at 4,167 cubic feet per second (cfs); by 1912 it had increased to 6,016 cfs; and by 1922 it had grown to 8,500 cfs. All of these increases came in the absence of a federal permit. As a result, during the early 1900s the US government and Illinois spent a lot of time suing each other in federal court. Then in 1922—the same year the Cal-Sag Channel was completed—Wisconsin filed suit against Illinois, claiming the state was illegally expanding the diversion and blamed Chicago's actions for historically low Great Lakes water levels. Later, Wisconsin amended its complaint by asking the court to halt the diversion altogether. Wisconsin was eventually joined in the suit by Michigan and New York. The City of Big Shoulders was having its way with Lake Michigan water and there was little anyone could do

Development of the Chicago Sanitary and Ship Canal

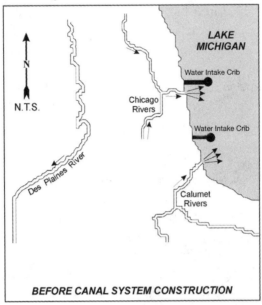

BEFORE CANAL SYSTEM CONSTRUCTION

CHICAGO SANITARY AND SHIP
CANAL SYSTEM COMPLETED

The reversal of the Chicago River reworked much of the natural hydrology of the Chicago metropolitan area. (US Army Corps of Engineers)

Lake Michigan Diversion at Chicago

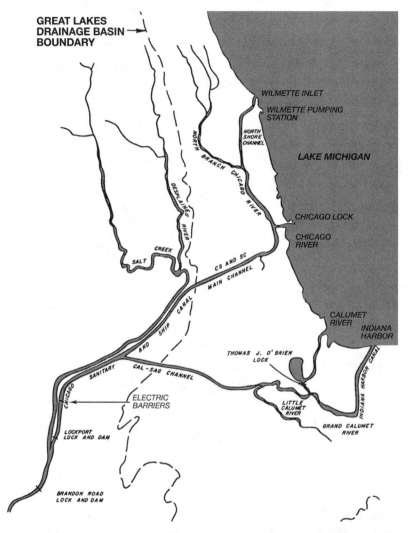

The Chicago Sanitary and Ship Canal in relation to the Great Lakes Basin Boundary. (Adapted from US Army Corps of Engineers)

about it. But Chicago's diversion was also driving a wedge through the heart of the Great Lakes Basin—a situation that would repeat itself time and again in years to come.

While the diversion's volume had nearly doubled in twenty years, Chicago still wanted more water. Illinois congressmen introduced legislation in 1924 to increase the diversion to the maximum the Sanitary and Ship Canal could handle—10,000 cfs—which prompted Canada to file a complaint. Meanwhile, lake levels continued to drop. Then in 1926, in a historically ironic turn of events, downriver states like Missouri, Tennessee, and Louisiana came out in support of Illinois's request to increase the diversion. As time passed, it seems, Missouri and other downstream states had begun to view Chicago's effluent in a more positive light.

Later that year, thanks to all the litigation, the Supreme Court appointed a judge as a "special master" to study the issue intensively and make recommendations. Finally, on April 21, 1930, the Court decided the case of *State of Wisconsin v. State of Illinois*—and Chicago suffered a rare loss. The Court gave the Sanitary District roughly a decade to wean itself from most of the water it had been diverting. The Court forced the district to impose a gradual though radical nine-year reduction from 8,500 cfs to 1,500 cfs by January 1, 1939. During that same period, Chicago was to expand its sewage-treatment program to replace the need for this 7,000 cfs in dilution water that it would lose.

The Court had spoken, but the regional bitterness engendered by the Illinois diversion would linger for years. In the early 1900s, that bitterness was not just about pollution, but was laced with the angry belief that the Illinois diversion was having an enormous effect on water levels in the Great Lakes. Stanley Chagnon, emeritus chief of the Illinois State Water Survey, captures this anger in a comprehensive report he edited and partially wrote for the National Oceanic and Atmospheric Administration in 1994:

> Few would argue that through the late 1800s, Chicago residents faced serious health problems due to the quality of their drinking water. Few would argue that Chicago residents deserve, as much as any other people, clean water for household use. Many, however, have argued that Chicago (through the [Sanitary District] and of-

ten with the blessing of state and federal governments) did not have the right to divert water from Lake Michigan for its own use and then return that water in a contaminated state and to pollute other waters. . . . Especially in the early 1920s, opponents of the diversion also argued that Chicago did not have the right to improve its own navigational interests at the expense of similar interest among the states and Canadian provinces that border the Great Lakes. Newspaper accounts from those years are full of accusations that the diversion was intended to do just that.[15]

Throughout the 1930s, Illinois moved several times to increase the amount of the diversion, even trying a few end-arounds to avoid the Court ruling by seeking legislative action from Congress instead. All of these requests failed except for one in 1940, when another special master recommended that the diversion be increased to 10,000 cfs for just ten days during a period of drought to help remedy deteriorating water quality in the river. This was the first time that Chicago had been permitted to increase the flow of the diversion because of drought conditions. It was not the last time that happened, however. A decade and a half later, in 1956, dry weather prompted another new and unusual precedent. Four years of low rainfall had sapped water flows in the Mississippi and Illinois rivers, and the state of Illinois asked the Court for an emergency increase in the diversion. The Court approved an 8,500 cfs increase that lasted for seventy-six days, starting in December 1956. This was a noteworthy decision with implications for the Great Lakes region in future years. It was the first time that the Illinois diversion had been increased solely to serve the needs of people from outside the Great Lakes Basin.

After World War II, Chicago's metropolitan region expanded rapidly, reaching five million people by 1950. Officials in northern Illinois and southern Wisconsin began noticing an alarming decline in regional wells—up to fifteen feet per year.[16] Chicago's sprawling suburbs were the main reason for this increased load on regional groundwater. Because the 1930 Court decision put no limit on the amount of water that Chicago could use for "domestic pumpage" (mainly drinking water), in 1958 the US Army Corps of Engineers approved a plan to relieve pressure on the aquifer. The suburbs of Elmhurst, Villa Park, and Lombard obtained permission from Illinois, and a permit from the Corps, to tap into Chicago's Lake Michigan drinking water in an effort to slow the rapid groundwater decline. All three of these suburbs were outside the Great Lakes Basin line, a distinction that would have growing political importance in future years.

Wisconsin saw the political significance immediately and challenged this geographic expansion of Chicago's metropolitan water network by filing another lawsuit. Among other things, Wisconsin argued that treated effluent from the Illinois diversion should be returned to Lake Michigan and not be sent down the Mississippi.[17] Illinois then countersued on behalf of the suburbs, specifically denying there was a need for returning treated water effluent to the lake.

For a third time, the Court appointed a special master to study the situation—and the process dragged on for years. Finally, in 1967, the Court issued a decision on the Illinois diversion that was dramatically different, and significantly more complex, than the Court's initial ruling in 1930. First, the Court sided with Chicago by more than doubling the amount of the diversion from 1,500 cfs to 3,200 cfs. That meant that the diversion could total 2.1 billion gallons of water per day. But while the Court upped the amount of the diversion, it also tipped its hat toward Wisconsin by forcing Illinois to count water that it had never been required to keep track of before. For the first time, Chicago drinking water and other "domestic pumpage" (which had been virtually ignored) had to be included in the 3,200 cfs number.

Interestingly, the decree also required Illinois to undertake a seemingly impossible task: calculate the annual amount of rainfall that fell in the 673-square-mile Chicago River watershed. This rain used to end up in Lake Michigan after running off into the once naturally flowing Chicago River. But with the diversion, that rain ended up trickling into a backward-flowing Chicago River and was therefore a hydrologic loss to the Lake Michigan system. The Court (again nodding to Wisconsin) wanted Illinois to include that rainfall amount as part of the new 3,200 cfs number.

But the most important part of the Court's decision was a resounding victory for Illinois. In a key move that had enormous implications for future growth in the greater Chicago area, the Court permitted Chicago's suburbs to tap into the city's Lake Michigan drinking-water system—even if the suburbs were far beyond the Great Lakes Basin boundary. In addition, the Court gave Illinois full authority to decide which communities could be added to the Lake Michigan drinking-water system—again, as long as the state stayed below the 3,200 cfs limit. The Chicago suburbs that were experiencing groundwater problems had suddenly found a new water source that would allow the metropolitan area to expand unhindered for the foreseeable future.

That some of Chicago's western suburbs—located far beyond the Great Lakes Basin line—are drinking Lake Michigan water seems patently unfair to contemporary opponents of Great Lakes diversions. This is a unique and unprecedented right that most Chicago suburbanites don't fully appreciate. There are a number of water-troubled communities in other Great Lakes states that would love to access Great Lakes water, but because these areas lie outside the Basin line their water access has been limited. Residents of these communities look to Chicago's suburbs with envy bordering on anger. One of them, Waukesha, Wisconsin, even approached Illinois to see if it could tap into the Chicago diversion as well, but was told that only Illinois communities qualify under the Supreme Court decree. (Chapters 13 and 15 discuss Waukesha in greater detail.)

A growing number of water-starved communities in the region are discovering just what a cherished privilege the Illinois diversion has turned out to be. "Everybody thinks Chicago gets special treatment," says Richard Lanyon, former executive director at the Metropolitan Water Reclamation District of Greater Chicago. "Well, I guess so. . . . But [other communities] never tried to get what we have. They fought us, and by fighting us have kind of eliminated the opportunity [for themselves]." But many environmentalists and legal scholars see the reversal of the Chicago River as an environmental abomination that should never be repeated. "The Chicago River diversion is an aberration," says Cameron Davis, a long-time Great Lakes environmental advocate and official. "It is certainly an example of something that would never happen today." Lake Superior is the largest lake by surface area in the world, but hydrologically speaking, Michigan and Huron are one lake. Together they are larger than Superior. The International Joint Commission estimates that the Chicago diversion permanently dropped water levels on Michigan and Huron—the largest body of fresh water on earth—by 2.5 inches.[18] That's a lot of water, and it explains why regional officials are committed to preventing a diversion like that from ever happening again.

With the terms of the 1967 Court decree, the purpose of the Illinois diversion changed significantly. In 1900, the bulk of the diversion was used for carrying diluted sewage away from the city. But by the late 1960s, better sewage-treatment technology made it possible to allocate a growing percentage of the diverted water as drinking water for people who lived outside the city. Yes, part of the diversion was still being used to flush dirty water south, but over time that flush water was making up a smaller and smaller proportion of the total diversion allotment. Meanwhile, as Chicago needed less water to dilute its pollution, it needed more water for its collar communities to drink.

Controversy over the Illinois diversion flared again in the 1980s after an Army Corps of Engineers report looked at tripling the diversion's flow. The 1981 study concluded that tripling the diversion was technically possible, but that the increased flow would create a number of hydrologic headaches immediately downstream.[19] Then, in 1988, a drought lowered water levels on the Mississippi River by several feet, hampering the river's billion-dollar commercial barge traffic. Barges, and other vessels, were forced to dodge numerous exposed—and unexposed—sandbars in the low water—if they could move at all. Democratic senator Jim Sasser from Tennessee, speaking for several Mississippi Valley politicians, encouraged President Ronald Reagan to use emergency powers to temporarily divert additional water from the Great Lakes via the Illinois diversion to help alleviate low flows on the Mississippi. Several bills were introduced in Congress to do just that.[20]

While those bills went nowhere, Illinois governor Jim Thompson shocked his Basin neighbors by supporting the call for an increase in the diversion all the way up to 10,000 cfs—the maximum that the Sanitary and Ship Canal could handle. That was an addition of more than 4 billion gallons per day—an enormous, though temporary, boost in the diversion. If the IJC had calculated that the Illinois diversion had already dropped water levels by 2.5 inches, what would this new increase do to Lakes Michigan and Huron? New York had tainted the spirit of the Charter in 1985 by contemplating Great Lakes water for the Big Apple. Now, just three years later, it appeared that Illinois had its own diversion desires.

With this latest idea from Illinois, the situation looked like 1956 all over again: a proposal was on the table to divert water from the Great Lakes to aid people who lived hundreds of miles outside the Basin. This was precisely the kind of out-of-Basin diversion precedent that the Great Lakes Charter and the Water Resources Development Act had tried to prevent. Governor Thompson's decision infuriated his colleagues in the Great Lakes Basin, who immediately labeled him a turncoat. The idea that a fellow Great Lakes governor would come out in favor of such a proposal sparked a political maelstrom—particularly because this governor already ruled over the largest and most controversial diversion ever to send water outside the Great Lakes Basin. Governor Tony Earl of Wisconsin still remembers how angry and incredulous the rest of Great Lakes governors were. "Very early after the Charter was signed . . . Jim Thompson came and said, 'Gee, you guys, we've got to divert more water so we can float the barges [on the Mississippi],'" Governor Earl recalls. "We all said, 'Jim, go powder your ass!'" Governor Thompson's proposal even caught other Illinois officials off guard. "I was in St. Louis when that happened," says Neil Fulton, one of the governor's top water managers at the time. "I never got on a plane so fast in my life." Contacted nearly two decades later, Mr. Fulton was more than happy to distance himself from the governor's diversion idea, saying that he was not consulted before the announcement was made. "That proposal was never staffed," Mr. Fulton says. "We just spent a lot of time picking up the pieces."

More importantly, Governor Thompson's plan didn't make hydrologic sense. Water engineers pointed out that while expanding the diversion would affect water levels in the Illinois River, it would have a nominal impact on the flow regime of the mighty Mississippi—particularly by the time the additional water reached places like Tennessee and Louisiana. "The Mississippi's a huge waterway, and the amount of water you could get from Lake Michigan down there really isn't that significant," says Dan Injerd of the Illinois Department of Natural Resources (DNR). "There probably will never be another suggestion to try to use an increased diversion to alleviate drought conditions on the

Illinois or the Mississippi." Maybe so, but while Governor Thompson's proposal went nowhere, it was the kind of scenario that anti-diversion advocates had worried about for years: that during a period of severe, long-term national drought, panicked politicians from outside the Great Lakes region would come groping for Great Lakes water—only to have one errant Basin governor break ranks and sell out.

In the 1990s the Illinois diversion made headlines yet again, this time for entirely different reasons. High water levels in the Great Lakes were making it difficult for Chicago to stay within the Supreme Court–mandated diversion limits, which further exacerbated regional tensions over water. Officials discovered that more Lake Michigan water was entering the Chicago River than the Court allowed—a lot more. Because water levels can fluctuate, the Court's Chicago River decree permitted Illinois to occasionally exceed the mandated 3,200 cfs limit, as long as Illinois made up for that surplus water in later years. What mattered, the Court said, was that the amount of water diverted over a forty-year time frame should not exceed an average of 3,200 cfs. At no point, however, was Illinois permitted to exceed the 3,200 cfs limit by an average of more than 2,000 cfs per year. But that's exactly what Illinois did for more than a decade. From 1988 through 2000, the diversion exceeded the 2,000 cfs arrearage limit every year. In fact, at the peak of excess diversion in 1993, Illinois was so far out of compliance that its annual water debt was running almost double the maximum ceiling allowed by the Court: 3,725 cfs.[21]

Once again, the other Great Lakes states rallied to challenge Illinois's illegal water behavior, and this time Michigan was leading the charge. Officials in Lansing notified the US Department of Justice that they were planning to file a petition with the Supreme Court asking the justices to reopen the Chicago diversion case because Illinois was so clearly in violation of the Court decree. Illinois said don't blame us, blame Mother Nature. During the late 1980s and early 1990s, lake levels in the Great Lakes were at historic highs. Lake Michigan's water levels were so high that at times the lake was literally pouring over the top of a steel bulkhead that controlled how much Lake Michigan water flowed into the Chicago River. Illinois also admitted that there were a lot of leaks in the system, but said some of them were the responsibility of other entities (like the Corps of Engineers) and that the high water levels were pushing extra water through these holes in the "dike" as well.

Michigan was undeterred by the blame–Mother Nature defense and forged ahead with its legal action. But lawyers with the Clinton administration's Department of Justice intervened and convinced Michigan to take an alternate approach. Rather than asking the Court to reopen the case—which history had shown would take many, many years and cost millions of dollars in legal bills—the Department of Justice talked Michigan and the other Great Lakes states into negotiating an out-of-court settlement with Illinois. The Canadian provinces of Ontario and Québec attended the negotiations as active observers.

The result of these negotiations was something that became known as the Memorandum of Understanding, or MOU, of 1996. Among other things, the MOU required Illinois and the Corps to fix the various leaks in the system. It also required Illinois officials to install a pump so that if notable amounts of extra water ever did leak into the river again—by flowing over the top of the bulkhead, for example—the water could be quickly pumped back into the lake to make up the difference. Most notably, perhaps, the MOU also required Illinois to pay back its illegal water debt under a rigid, multiyear schedule that set specific targets to be met by certain dates. The MOU required Illinois to get back to a zero balance by 2019. Illinois responded with a number of engineering projects and changes that, in combination with extended drought years and much lower lake levels after 2000, helped the state achieve compliance much more quickly than most people (including Illinois officials) had anticipated. By the end of 2005, Illinois had attained a zero balance on its water debt and was on its way to putting water back in the "bank" to draw on in future years.

By the early part of the twenty-first century, roughly 7 million people in 205 communities and water utilities in northeastern Illinois—including Chicago—were getting their drinking water from Lake Michigan. Dan Injerd, the Illinois DNR's diversion supervisor, says that his department is adding an average of one new community every two years to the Lake Michigan drinking-water system. Any community that wants access to Lake Michigan water has to clear some state regulatory hurdles first. To start with, communities are required to show that Lake Michigan is the least expensive water source available—not

Westward view of the mouth of the Chicago River, the flow of which was reversed in 1900. (©Herb Lingl/aerialarchives.com)

the *only* one available, but the *least expensive* one available. Second, if a community is withdrawing water from the deep aquifer, it must agree to cease using groundwater within five years after drawing water from Lake Michigan. "The deep-water aquifer was vastly overutilized in this region, and we want to use Lake Michigan water as a tool to help balance resource use," Mr. Injerd says. "We want to get them off the deep-water aquifer and preserve that for those who are outside whatever will be the ultimate cost-effective Lake Michigan water supply service area."

Many of these suburban water permittees are well beyond the edge of the Great Lakes Basin boundary. "The most distant [Illinois] community that I'm aware of that is in the process of getting Lake Michigan water is the Village of Plainfield," Mr. Injerd says. "It's certainly a lot farther away from the lake than Waukesha [in Wisconsin]." But if Mr. Injerd is adding an average of one suburb every two years to the Lake Michigan water system, it begs the question: How far out from Lake Michigan will he go before telling a suburb or small town that it's just too far away to receive Great Lakes water? Rockford? Springfield? East St. Louis? Carbondale? What *is* the geographic limit of Illinois's Lake Michigan water supply service area? "We don't know," Mr. Injerd says.

When pressed further, he unveils two hypotheses. The first one, which could be called the "rosy scenario," predicts that Illinois will continue to squeeze out enough water from the diversion's 3,200 cfs limit to meet the needs of all the suburbs that ask for it—until finally someone walks through the door from such a faraway place that it's just no longer cost-effective to consider connecting them to the end of the pipe. The other scenario, which is decidedly less rosy, goes like this: domestic water use in northeastern Illinois "becomes so significant that we run out of water—that we don't have enough Lake Michigan water [in the Illinois diversion] to meet the needs," Mr. Injerd says. "We would just have to say, 'No, sorry. We're out of water. We'd like to give you some, you meet the tests, it's cost-effective, but you can't have any because we don't have it.'"

This raises another question, of course. If Mr. Injerd is adding roughly one suburb every two years to the Lake Michigan drinking-water system, isn't he ultimately bringing about scenario number two, the less-rosy scenario? After all, 3,200 cfs is a finite amount of water. How many growing communities can he squeeze into that limit before he runs out? Not to worry, he says. His department is working on long-term water forecasting to 2050, and based on those calculations he's confident that there will be enough water to go around. "I think Illinois will be able to live within its 3,200 cfs limit for a long time to come."

Other water experts don't share Mr. Injerd's confidence. Robert Sasman worked as a hydrologist in northeastern Illinois for the State Water Survey for nearly forty years. He has been around so long that he actually testified before the Supreme Court's special master whose research eventually led to the Court's 1967 decree on the Illinois diversion. Mr. Sasman is troubled by what he sees as serious water problems in the Chicago area's future. "I think it's going to be a major crisis in the years to come," he predicts. "I don't think people realize it at all." The problem, he says, is that the metro area is sandwiched between the limitations of the Court decree on one side, and declining groundwater supplies on the other. In an interview, he suggested sinking new wells inside the Great Lakes Basin to try to tap into Lake Michigan groundwater. He also proposed that the metro area consider tapping the Kankakee, Illinois, and Rock Rivers. But he didn't stop there. He said it's only about a hundred miles from his home in Chicago's western suburbs to the Mississippi River. "There is a tremendous amount of water in the Mississippi, and why not use some of it?" he asks. "The pipelines in the West and Southwest are much more extensive than this kind of proposal." There is something paradoxical, however, in a proposal that suggests that the largest metropolitan area in the water-rich Great Lakes region might someday depend on a pipeline from the Mississippi River to sustain its growth. The fact that credible scientists are even contemplating such measures is telling.

Others argue that there's an easier way to deal with future water problems: ask the other Great Lakes states for permission to increase the Illinois diversion. "This is my personal opinion, [and] I guess it reflects my working out West before I came back to Illinois," says Stephen Burch, a hydrogeologist at the Illinois State Water Survey. "We're going to have to make a deal with the other states to buy water from them ... like, say, Wisconsin, or Michigan, or Indiana, or whoever.

Everybody has a certain claim to the Great Lakes, and if we are the big gorilla, then maybe what we need to do is work out some arrangement institutionally over the next fifty years or hundred years or whatever. And maybe that's how we will go forward."

Why is Dan Injerd so confident about water when some of his colleagues aren't? He's banking on water conservation. Once on the Lake Michigan water system, a suburb must adhere to specific water-conservation measures (water conservation is strongly encouraged in the Supreme Court decree). Water meters are required for all new construction, lawn-watering restrictions are mandated between May 15 and September 15, and communities must set water rates that "discourage excessive water use." Interestingly, for many years, these strict rules only applied to suburban users who were added to the Lake Michigan water network. Chicago, on the other hand, was permitted to waste all the water it wanted without penalty. Prior to 1982, water meters in the city of Chicago were virtually unheard of on private residences. After 1982, meters were required on new homes and rehabs. But existing homes paid a flat fee for unlimited use, which was met with scorn from around the Great Lakes Basin—and from suburban Chicago. While lawns in the 'burbs were turning brown because of mandated lawn-watering restrictions, Chicago residents could lay down water with glee. Then Mayor Richard Daley decided to bring Chicago's paternalistic water system into the twenty-first century. In April 2003, Mayor Daley announced—to the surprise of just about everyone— that Chicago's era of flat-rate water was coming to an end. Residents of roughly 320,000 houses and small apartment buildings were told that in coming years they would have to install water meters. For the first time, all Chicagoans would be expected to pay for water on an as-used basis.[22]

Metering should reduce water use in Chicago as sticker-shocked residents scale back on their spigots. But water use throughout the city has already been on the decline. Trends in water use show why Mr. Injerd is so confident that conservation will give him the wiggle room to continue adding communities to the Lake Michigan water system. State-encouraged changes to Chicago's infrastructure have played an important role, like replacing approximately 900 miles of water mains between 2011 and 2021.[23] But economic changes have influenced water use in Chicago as well. Many of the heavily water-dependent industries—particularly steel—fell on hard times, and with their decline came a notable reduction in regional water use. The statistics speak for themselves. In 1988, Chicago's water use peaked at almost 850 million gallons per day (mgd), but since then it has been cut almost in half, down to 450 mgd. In addition to the decline of heavy industry, Mr. Injerd credits Chicago's efforts to replace aged and leaky water mains, a project that makes him even more secure about the Chicago area's water-quantity future. "Well over half of the population of the entire state is dependent on Lake Michigan water."

During the early part of the twentieth century, Wisconsin served as the lead Illinois-diversion watchdog, quickly challenging anything suspicious. But Michigan has since usurped Wisconsin's long-standing position as the diversion's nemesis. Mike Leffler, who used to run the environment division in the Michigan attorney general's office, worked on the Illinois-diversion file for years. Mr. Leffler says that because Illinois spent years repeatedly adding suburbs to the Lake Michigan water system, the state could have a difficult time convincing the Supreme Court to increase the Illinois diversion in the future. "I would not expect uncontrolled development or bad land-use planning to be adequate justification for increasing the diversion," he says. "You don't build in areas where the resources will not support growth and then complain that you don't have the resources to support growth." When Stanley Chagnon, emeritus chief of the Illinois State Water Survey, was asked if Mr. Injerd's practice of adding one suburb every few years to the diversion's finite water supply was sustainable, his response was brief: "It obviously isn't."

Chapter 6

Carp in the CAWS

Invasive species are nonnative plants and animals that, once introduced to an ecosystem, can spread rapidly in the absence of natural predators, often severely altering local ecosystems and displacing native species in the process. They cause billions of dollars in damage in the United States each year, and cost at least hundreds of millions annually in the Great Lakes, which are now home to more than 180 nonnative plants and animals.

The Chicago diversion, of course, serves as an artificial, human-made link between two of the largest watersheds in North America—the Great Lakes/St. Lawrence and the Mississippi River. That connection, via the Chicago Sanitary and Ship Canal, not only transports water from one watershed to the other, it also serves as a vector for invasive species. Nonnative species in the Great Lakes can work their way into the Mississippi via the canal and vice versa. One way to shut down this pathway, of course, would be to re-reverse the Chicago River, permanently severing the unnatural connection between the two massive watersheds. For that to happen, all the Lake Michigan water used by Chicago and its suburbs would be treated and sent back to the lake where it started, which is what other major Great Lakes cities like Toronto, Milwaukee, Detroit, and Cleveland do.

During the 1990s, any suggestion to re-reverse the Chicago River would have been considered half-baked. But a growing number of influential people are now suggesting that the time has come to seriously revisit the Chicago diversion, including possibly re-separating the Great Lakes and Mississippi watersheds. The reason has nothing to do with water levels, federal statutes, or Supreme Court decrees. It has everything to do with Asian carp. Asian carp are a voracious, fast-growing, homely group of fish that were brought to the United States during the last century (with government approval) to help Southern catfish farmers keep algae, weeds, and mollusks under control in their ponds. Over a period of decades, some of these carp in states like Arkansas escaped and made their way into the Mississippi River as well as several tributaries, where they have proven to be extremely disruptive to the ecosystem.[1]

Four Asian carp species are on the loose in the Mississippi: silvers, bigheads, grass, and black carp, and some grow rapidly to enormous sizes (up to one hundred pounds) and reproduce at a disturbing rate. Grass carp feed on underwater vegetation and black carp prefer snails and mussels. Silvers and bigheads are filter feeders, vacuuming algae out of the water column, and they have been the primary focus of concern in recent years in the Chicago Area Waterway System, or CAWS, which includes the much-maligned Chicago Sanitary and Ship Canal. That's because the fish have proliferated so rapidly, and devoured so much plankton—up to 20 percent of their body weight per day—that they have completely altered the food web in parts of the Mississippi and Illinois Rivers. By 2011, Asian carp had become so prolific that government officials estimated that the invasive fish made up 70 percent of the fish biomass in some sections of those rivers. Silver carp are startled by motors and are known to launch themselves into the air, injuring boaters and making sports like waterskiing all but impossible. YouTube is rife with videos of carp–human collisions. The fish have literally transformed the ecology of the river, as well as the relationship between humans and the river. As the carp have moved closer and closer to Chicago, they have posed one of the greatest challenges to the Chicago diversion in decades, markedly ramping up tensions over the most controversial diversion the Great Lakes have ever seen.

~

Biologists consider the introduction of Asian carp to be an ecological disaster, and they are desperate to keep them from harming the Great Lakes's $7-billion fishery. In 2002, as a means of controlling invasive-species transfers between the two massive watersheds, the US Army

Downstream from the Chicago Sanitary and Ship Canal, Asian carp have transformed the ecology of the Illinois River, as well as the relationship between humans and the river. (Photo by T. Lawrence, Great Lakes Fishery Commission)

Corps of Engineers installed an underwater "demonstration" electric barrier in the Ship Canal near Romeoville (about 35 miles from Lake Michigan) that constantly zapped the waterway with electricity as a species deterrent.[2] That was followed by an additional and more robust underwater electric barrier in 2009. By that time, the Corps was working hard to find the carp-invasion front line in Illinois, and it hired a team of scientists from the University of Notre Dame to help. The team was led by Professor David Lodge, an internationally known invasive-species expert, and included scientists Christopher Jerde and Andrew Mahon, as well as Lindsay Chadderton, who directs The Nature Conservancy's Great Lakes Aquatic Invasive Species Program.[3] They all were aware of a recent study in Europe that had captured DNA-laced water samples to track invasive species. The idea was simple yet brilliant: collect numerous two-liter samples of water, bring them back to the lab, and run genetic testing on particles filtered from the water samples. The filtered particles often included DNA from fish tissue, mucus, feces, or urine. If the critter's DNA was in the water, presumably so was the critter. The Notre Dame team decided to see if this novel approach would help detect the Asian carp front line in the CAWS. The technique eventually became known as "environmental DNA" or "eDNA."

The team started collecting samples during the summer of 2009. To the surprise and alarm of everyone, by November lab results were showing positive carp-DNA hits above the electric barrier, much closer to Lake Michigan than expected. Complicating matters, the news arrived just as the barrier needed to be temporarily shut down for routine maintenance. Officials throughout the region began to panic that Asian carp were on the brink of entering the Great Lakes. Fearing that the maintenance work might allow carp to slip through, federal and state officials drew national attention with their decision to poison six miles of the canal with rotenone, a common piscicide. Media swarmed all over the rotenone moment, which literally killed tons of fish, including one bighead carp forty miles from the lake. Forty miles is a long way, but it was much closer than the Corps believed the leading edge of the carp to be.

Things ramped up a notch when Michigan attorney general Mike Cox filed for an injunction with the US Supreme Court. The injunction demanded that, as an emergency anti-carp measure, key locks on the canal be shut, and that the Court reopen the decree that had ruled over the Chicago diversion for decades. Several other Great Lakes states later signed on to the litigation. Illinois countered that such a move would create flooding mayhem in the city and harm the canal's economically important boat and barge traffic. The federal government quickly dispatched $13 million in emergency anti-carp funding, and the multi-agency Asian Carp Regional Coordinating Committee was formed, putting state, regional, and national carp-control efforts under one umbrella. It had been decades since the waters of the Chicago diversion were this stirred up. "We're at that tipping point right now where the balance is still in our favor to stop Asian carp from getting in," warned Joel Brammeier, president and CEO of the Alliance for the Great Lakes. "But the longer we wait, the more that tips in the other direction."[4]

Notre Dame's eDNA hits kept rolling in, closer and closer to Lake Michigan. By early 2010 they made front-page news with a hit in Lake Michigan itself. The announcement came on the same day that the Supreme Court denied Michigan's emergency request to shut the Chicago locks. People started questioning everything from the efficacy of the electric barrier to the validity of the eDNA process. "Because we don't know for sure that the source of the DNA is live carp, we're taking it as an early warning that it may be a live carp," said Major General John W. Peabody of the Corps of Engineers. "As to how they got there," he added, "the short answer is we don't know, and there's probably no way for us to ever tell."[5] Governors in Michigan and Wisconsin called for a carp summit. Then the Supreme Court rebuffed Michigan's second request for an emergency injunction, much to the relief of the canal's barge industry. "We're obviously very pleased," said Lynn Muench, senior vice president of the American Waterways Operators. "I'm hoping everybody will step back, get out of the courts, and go back to collaborating."[6] The Corps of Engineers announced plans to quickly install a third segment of the electric barrier by October, so the canal wouldn't need to be poisoned every time the barrier was turned off for maintenance.

Questions about eDNA kept mounting. Government teams had spent weeks fanning out with nets and electroshocking boats to try and catch all the carp that the Notre Dame team was detecting. Nets were coming up with no Asian carp. Many field technicians felt they were chasing ghost fish. The eDNA team, meanwhile, was not surprised, as Asian carp are notoriously skittish, and electroshocking can only reach so far down in the water. Still, skepticism about the scientific practice remained widespread. Regardless, the federal government announced $78.5 million in funding for a new Asian carp framework. Congress had long since asked the Corps of Engineers to conduct a Great Lakes and Mississippi River Interbasin Study to prevent invasives from passing through the Chicago canal. That study was now ramping up and would be more focused than ever on Asian carp. In May of 2010, the Corps conducted another rotenone poisoning exercise, this time on the Lake Michigan side of the electric barrier, which netted zero carp, raising deeper questions about eDNA. But the dramatic seesawing continued when, a month later, a large bighead carp was netted in

Lake Calumet, miles above the electric barrier and just six miles from Lake Michigan. That sparked more controversy, and more litigation. Five states, again led by Michigan, filed a new suit—in US District Court this time—to shut down the locks. If an emergency plea to the Supreme Court didn't work, perhaps this more deliberative approach in Federal District Court would. President Barack Obama named John Goss, a soft-spoken official from the Indiana Wildlife Federation, to be the nation's first Asian carp "czar."

In the fall of 2010, the five states' legal challenge landed before a federal judge in Chicago, and it seemed as if eDNA was on trial as much as the Chicago diversion. The hearing featured the Corps's General Peabody and Notre Dame's Professor Lodge making different claims about what a positive eDNA detection meant. Given that two different canal poisonings and months of netting and electroshocking had only turned up two Asian carp, the feds increasingly suggested that many of the DNA hits were the feces of carp-eating birds like gulls or cormorants that were flying (and defecating carp DNA) all over the CAWS. Or, they suggested, the DNA came from fish slime rinsed off boats and barges after silver carp had launched themselves onboard. Professor Lodge and his team acknowledged that alternate eDNA pathways were possible, but they remained convinced that, the vast majority of the time, an eDNA detection represented the recent presence of a live fish. The judge sided with the Corps, however, and once again denied the five states' emergency request to shut the Chicago locks, a decision that the states would again appeal.

In early 2011, carp czar John Goss was armed with an updated control strategy, and Notre Dame's eDNA research was validated after being published in a peer-reviewed journal. The US Fish and Wildlife Service banned the import of bighead carp; silver carp had already been banned in 2007. But the biggest news was a Corps lab study suggesting that the electric barrier might not repel small juvenile fish. "Slightly higher operating parameters than those currently in use may be necessary to immobilize all very small Asian carp, as small as 1.7 to 3.2 inches," the Corps said, adding that juvenile carp were believed to be many miles below the barrier, and therefore were not yet a threat.[7] While there were more than 180 nonnative species in the Great Lakes, and many more in the Mississippi River, the Corps released a report highlighting twenty-nine species in the Great Lakes that posed a particularly serious threat to the Mississippi River, and ten species in the Mississippi that posed a significant threat to the Great Lakes, including bighead and silver carp.[8] The federal government also released a study showing eighteen other pathways—besides the canal—where Asian carp and other invasives could pass from the Mississippi watershed to the Great Lakes and vice versa. These possible transfer points stretched from Minnesota to New York, but none of them appeared as threatening as Chicago's gaping gap in the Basin line.[9] Meanwhile, the five litigating states continued to be spurned when a federal appeals court upheld the lower court's decision against them.

By this point, two sides had emerged on the Asian carp issue. The five litigating states—Michigan, Minnesota, Wisconsin, Ohio, and Pennsylvania—were aligned with environmental groups and other NGOs that doubted the efficacy of the electric barrier, and they wanted the locks shut; they were even arguing for eventual separation of the two watersheds. On the other side, Illinois, the barge industry, other canal industrial interests, the Corps of Engineers, and much of the rest of the federal government had confidence in the electric barrier, arguing that the carp front line was many miles from Lake Michigan, and they did not see lock closure as a realistic option. Besides the disruption to canal commerce, officials were concerned about flooding in Chicago if the locks were closed.

Dan Injerd from the Illinois Department of Natural Resources soberly cautioned that most people who suggest re-reversing the river generally didn't grasp the magnitude of the task, which would require reworking much of the urban plumbing that undergirds the sprawling Chicago metropolitan area. As Mr. Injerd describes it, right now, that plumbing is tilted ever so slightly toward the Mississippi. Re-reversing the Chicago River would require tilting much of that plumbing ever so slightly toward Lake Michigan—not an easy (or cheap) thing to do. "You have to understand [that] this whole region was developed with this plumbing over one hundred and some years," he explains. "You can't just say, 'Oh, let's just shut it off and turn it the other way.' It's not that simple. It's not just a question of: Is the quality of the water good enough to send back to the lake? You're talking phenomenal flood-control issues, storm-water management, navigation. . . . All of these things will be impacted significantly one way or another by any concept that would re-establish some physical separation" between Lake Michigan and the Mississippi River watershed.

In early 2012, two influential Great Lakes organizations released a $2-million report that tried to demystify the whole separation idea. The Great Lakes Commission, which represents all Great Lakes states and provinces, and the binational Great Lakes and St. Lawrence Cities Initiative, representing 130 regional mayors, released the "Restoring the Natural Divide" report highlighting three different options for physically re-separating the two massive basins, while keeping commerce flowing. "Physically separating the Great Lakes and Mississippi River watersheds is the best long-term solution for preventing the movement of Asian carp and other aquatic invasive species," said Tim Eder, Great Lakes Commission executive director, "and our report demonstrates that it can be done."

But as Mr. Injerd had warned, it wouldn't be cheap. The report's three alternatives ranged in cost from $3.26 billion to $9.5 billion. That's a lot of coin, but with a $7-billion *annual* Great Lakes fishery potentially at stake, some saw it as a reasonable one-time investment. Even a few Illinois politicians were warming to the idea. Governor Pat Quinn and Chicago mayor Rahm Emanuel released statements that were mildly supportive of the study. But commercial interests along the canal hated it, arguing the results were predetermined. "Calling this a solution is ludicrous," said Mark Biel, head of Unlock Our Jobs, an Illinois-based business coalition opposed to separation.[10] "It was not a study," complained Lynn Muench, a spokesperson for the barge industry. "It was a propaganda piece."

Down at ground zero in the CAWS, the seesawing continued. The electrical barrier unexpectedly lost power for thirteen minutes when it took longer than expected for backup generators to restore power, continuing to erode confidence in that deterrent. On the other hand, while eDNA hits kept streaming in, no one had caught a live carp above the barrier for two years. By 2013, more than $200 million had been spent on Asian carp control and research. Field studies showed that Asian carp spawning areas were still more than fifty miles from the lake, but moving closer. Environmental DNA was detected in northern Lake Michigan near Sturgeon Bay, Wisconsin, and the Corps reported more potential weaknesses in the barrier. Research showed that fish could slip through the barrier by getting caught up in barge wakes, and small fish (two to four inches) could slip through in schools.[11]

~

In early 2014, the situation took a major step forward when the Corps released its much-anticipated Great Lakes and Mississippi River Inter-basin Study (GLMRIS—pronounced "GLIM-er-iss"). The 210-page report included eight different options for controlling invasive species in the Chicago Area Waterway System—including physical separa-tion—with the most expensive option costing more than $18 billion and requiring a quarter century to implement. The cheapest alternative (other than the status quo) was netting and chemical treatments to control invasives at a cost of $68 million per year. "This report is unique because it identifies a range of options, allows for the incorporation of future technologies, and presents courses of action that may be incor-porated now to reduce short-term risks," said the Corps's Great Lakes and Ohio River division commander, Brigadier General Margaret W. Burcham. General Burcham also urged leaders to vet the options and "build consensus toward a collaborative path forward."[12] Collabora-tion was looking better than litigation, as yet another federal appeals court ruled against the five suing states. Environmentalists accused the Corps's report of exaggerating the costs of separating the basins, and industry representatives continued to be unimpressed. "The GLMRIS report clearly indicates that physical separation is too expensive, too slow, and too uncertain to be a viable solution to the spread of inva-sive species," complained Mark Biel, executive director of the Illinois Chemical Industry Council and a leading voice at Unlock Our Jobs.

Despite the divisiveness, during 2016–17 the region began moving toward implementing at least some of the GLMRIS recommendations. The spot where they planned to showcase the new invasive-species technologies was the Brandon Road Lock and Dam, a "chokepoint" far downstream from Chicago on the Des Plaines River near Joliet. The Corps began working on a GLMRIS follow-up, known as the Brandon Road Report, with its release planned for February 2017. By 2016, the federal government had spent $386 million on carp control and research, which officials credited with continuing to hold the carp

Corps of Engineers' Electric Barrier

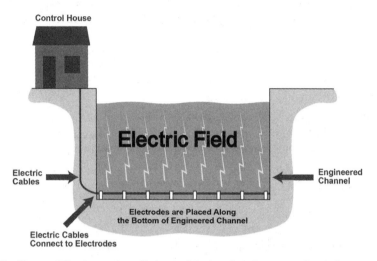

The Corps of Engineers installed a multi-tiered underwater electric barrier on the Chicago Sanitary and Ship Canal near Romeoville, Illinois, in an attempt to prevent the movement of invasive species between the Great Lakes and Mississippi River watersheds. (US Army Corps of Engineers)

front line fifty miles downstream, a claim many still questioned. The US Fish and Wildlife Service had also long since taken over eDNA surveillance, vindicating the scientific importance of the approach. People still debated exactly what an eDNA hit really indicated, but as the government beefed up control efforts, eDNA hits in the Great Lakes region became less frequent. Plans were announced to build a fourth electrical barrier at the original site on the Chicago canal. Meanwhile, a modeling study showed that if Asian carp became established in Lake Erie, over time they could eventually make up a third of the fish biomass in the lake.[13] The study, which acknowledged significant uncertainty, said that losing one-third of the Lake Erie fishery "will not be as great as some had feared." But if the results were borne out, it would transform one of the most important freshwater fisheries in the world. "Who wants a third of the fish biomass in Lake Erie to be Asian carp?" asked Notre Dame's David Lodge, one of several scientists who worked on the study. Mr. Lodge added that the research only looked at the fishery itself. "Impacts like jumping fish hitting people are not included."[14]

For nearly a decade, tremendous attention had been focused on keeping bighead and silver carp out of the Great Lakes. Only one bighead carp had been caught above the electric barrier during that time, although scientists reminded people that three bigheads had mysteriously been caught all the way over in Lake Erie prior to 2004.[15] In early 2017, a Canadian study led by Becky Cudmore, with Canada's Department of Fisheries and Oceans, showed that grass carp, one of the four Asian carp species of concern, had slipped into Lake Erie and Lake Michigan, and that there was a "high" likelihood of their populations becoming established in Lake Erie within five years. What's more, it was "very likely" that they would establish themselves in Lakes Michigan, Huron, and Ontario within ten years. Grass carp feed voraciously on important underwater habitat like shallow weed beds and wetland plants. Like other Asian carp species, grass carp had been intentionally planted in ponds throughout the Mississippi River watershed—as well as ponds in some Great Lakes states—but had escaped and expanded their range.[16]

∼

Then interesting things started to happen with the Corps's Brandon Road Report. Days before the study was to be released, on February 24, 2017, the *Chicago Tribune* printed an op-ed by Illinois's Republican lieutenant governor Evelyn Sanguinetti that criticized the report even before it was made public. She argued that it was an "apparently unnecessary experiment" because control efforts like the electric barrier had successfully kept Asian carp out of the Great Lakes. She was particularly defensive about impacts that the new bells-and-whistles planned for the Brandon Road Lock would have on the barge industry. "Any plan that disrupts commercial navigation with a big-barge bottleneck at the Brandon Road Lock and Dam will face opposition from the state of Illinois," she wrote. "As chair of the Illinois River Coordinating Council, I ask that the federal government delay this project and immediately review whether its costs can justify its purported benefits."

Four days later, the report was put on hold, and word circulated that President Donald Trump's White House wanted it reviewed before release. Reviews of this sort by new administrations are normal, of course, but this review dragged on for months, and things quickly got political. Twelve Democratic senators, representing all eight Great Lakes states, sent a letter imploring the president to release the study. That didn't work. Things suddenly changed on June 22, 2017, however, when another Asian carp was caught above the barrier: for the first time in seven years, a routine net survey had captured a silver carp just nine miles from Lake Michigan. President Trump, who had already proposed cutting Great Lakes Asian carp funding, ran into increasing opposition from the bipartisan Congressional Great Lakes Task Force after the fish was found. Six weeks later the Brandon Road Report hit the street.

The report was considered by many to be a significant step forward in the Asian carp fight. It proposed spending $275 million to design a new lock at Brandon Road that would be very inhospitable to any invasive species. In addition to having its own electric barrier, the lock would feature loud noise blasted through underwater speakers, as well as underwater jets, and a flushing lock system designed to push aquatic species back downstream as boats and barges pass through. The Corps proposed picking up 65 percent of the tab, with the rest to be covered by a "nonfederal partner." There would be millions in annual maintenance costs, too. Illinois officials—who were less than thrilled with the plan to begin with—wondered who that "nonfederal partner" would be, and who would cover the annual maintenance costs. To help appease Illinois's concerns, Michigan, Wisconsin, Ohio, and Ontario formed a financial partnership to commit resources to these additional costs, but Illinois continued to be unimpressed with the whole idea.

Some stakeholders argued that the Brandon Road upgrades would bring only marginal improvements to carp control and thus weren't worth the cost. For example, the report estimated that under the status quo, bighead and silver carp still had a 29 percent chance of getting into the Great Lakes. But with the new Brandon Road carp-deterrent technologies, those chances dropped to 13 percent. Brandon Road opponents didn't think a 16 percent reduction in risk was worth $275 million. (Interestingly, the report said that if the locks were closed, the chances of carp getting into Lake Michigan would plunge to 2 percent.) But when the report was released, cost was starting to become relative—the feds had already spent nearly half a billion dollars on carp control in the CAWS. The Brandon Road Report was just a draft. It would be years before final plans could be approved and funded by Congress, and years after that for any construction to be completed.

Not long after the Brandon Road Report became public, the Asian Carp Regional Coordinating Committee (ACRCC) released an analysis on the silver carp that had been captured nine miles from Lake Michigan earlier that summer. According to the ACRCC, it was a Midwestern fish born in the "Illinois/Middle Mississippi watershed." The four-year-old male carp had spent a quarter of its life in the Des Plaines River watershed, on the other side of the electric barrier, before inexplicably being caught in the Little Calumet River above the barrier. "Analysis shows that the fish spent no more than a few weeks to a few months in the stretch of river where it was found," the ACRCC said. "While we were disappointed to find an Asian carp close to Lake Michigan, we are pleased that we had a successful plan in place that found and removed it so quickly," said Kevin Irons, the Illinois DNR's Aquatic Nuisance Species program manager.[17] But Charlie Wooley, deputy regional director with the US Fish and Wildlife Service was bewildered by the wily carp, telling John Flesher at the Associated Press that he didn't know how it ended up in the Little Calumet. Yes, small fish might slip through, and yes, the barrier had experienced minor power issues, but the feds had always felt that the electric barrier would deter large adult fish. "We're pretty darn confident a fish of this size would be incapacitated going through," he said. "We're baffled and we just don't know how it got there."[18]

∽

History has been kind to the Chicago diversion. A century of legal challenges has altered it, but not stopped it. During the last one hundred years, for the most part, Chicago and surrounding suburbs have received the water they have needed. But will this century be as accommodating to the Illinois diversion as the last? The invasive-species issue is proving to be a formidable adversary. The problem for those arguing for the status quo is that it's not just about Asian carp. The Corps of Engineers has already highlighted twenty-nine particularly invasive species in the Great Lakes that threaten the Mississippi, and another ten invaders already established in the Mississippi that pose a serious environmental threat to the Great Lakes. That means the next century could be a Chinese-water-torture-like drip, drip, drip for commercial interests on the canal as well as for officials in Illinois. The invaders are expected to keep pressing toward the canal, from both directions. Each species will likely make headlines, calling more and more attention to the myriad controversies swirling around the Chicago diversion. If silver carp get through, the drumbeat will just move on to the next threatening invasive.

A classic decades-long war of attrition could ensue, pitting the pro- and anti-Chicago-diversion camps against each other, with each new species transfer representing the next round in the fight. The four dreaded Asian carp species may serve as a metaphor for the CAWS's future. The establishment of grass carp in the middle and lower Great Lakes seems a foregone conclusion, and no one knows what kind of effect they will have on Great Lakes habitats such as shallow weed beds and wetland vegetation. Let's assume that the grass carp are in, so that one is game-over. Silvers and bigheads are knocking on the door. They remain the primary focus of attention and could be next. What about black carp? They appear to be queueing up behind the silvers and bigheads. In 2017, thanks to a $100 bounty on black carp, one was turned in to authorities 110 miles closer to the Great Lakes than previously known. It was caught on the Illinois River around Peoria—still far away from Lake Michigan, but on the march.

Behind the black carp, farther down the Mississippi watershed, is the famed northern snakehead, dubbed a "frankenfish" by the Washington, DC, media after being found in Maryland. The ghoulish nickname comes in part from its looks, but also because of an uncanny ability to survive extended periods out of the water by breathing air. Snakeheads have been in Arkansas since 2008, and some officials believe they have been working their way toward the Mississippi River ever since. In 2017, one was caught in an oxbow lake of the Mississippi River in the state of Mississippi.[19] Will the snakehead be heading north next? Is it already?

And those are just a few examples from the Mississippi side of the electric barrier. At the same time, there are dozens of Great Lakes invaders that could be heading the other way. With more than 180 nonnative species, the lakes are already walking wounded; some of those species, such as the sea lamprey, zebra mussels, and quagga mussels, have significantly altered the food web, which is why regional officials are so sensitive to the threat. The mussels have now spread throughout much of North America, creating serious financial costs to life-blood waterways and hydro systems of the West, making this a continental issue, not just a regional one.[20]

Thanks to this cascade of critters, the Chicago diversion will face continued critical scrutiny for the foreseeable future. In the land of unintended consequences, the diversion deserves a top prize. After a century of litigation over the water-diversion issue, a whole new complicated, costly, and emotional invasive-species controversy has now been layered on top of the water-diversion dispute. Given that two studies have now been published that seriously looked at separating the basins, environmentalists may be feeling momentum on the CAWS issue, but the political forces opposed to separation should not be underestimated. Chicago has been masterful at protecting its cherished diversion, and it is unfazed by the grief it gets from the other Great Lakes states. What's more, the organizations opposed to physical separation are experienced, effective lobbyists with their sights set on killing any proposal that disrupts commerce in the CAWS. As Mark Biel, from the Chemical Industry Council of Illinois confidently put it in an interview with Great Lakes journalist Dan Egan, "I've been lobbying for twenty-five years on behalf of industry," he said. "I'm pretty good at killing bills and ideas that people come up with, and this one has all the elements you'd need."[21]

Because the Chicago diversion has now become a continental issue, calls to re-separate the Great Lakes and Mississippi River watersheds are bound to continue—rising and falling with each new invasive-species headline. Some officials privately suggest that re-reversing the river would make an excellent federal project, bringing Chicago a generation of jobs while also providing significant nationwide environmental benefits. "It really is much bigger than Asian carp," says David Ullrich, former head of the Great Lakes and St. Lawrence Cities Initiative, and chair of the Great Lakes Fishery Commission. "We really have to have a different vision for the Chicago Waterway System." A century ago, that "vision" came through litigation, but litigation has been less successful this time around. Could collaboration bring concrete, long-lasting results? That is the question on the floor, but it's not looking all that promising either. In the meantime, the drip, drip, drip of invasive species will continue to taunt.

Chapter 7

Long Lac and Ogoki

It's a hot July day in the lake country of northwestern Ontario when the DeHavilland Beaver floatplane lifts off from a lake 100 miles north of Thunder Bay. The small craft jostles and jags in a stiff wind as it rises above the rugged and remote terrain that blankets the watershed north of Lake Superior. As the plane climbs into the midafternoon sun, the full extent of the region's expansive boreal forest becomes clear. Lush forests stretch to the horizon, and lakes dimple the landscape, sprinkled like so many watery sequins on the woodlands below. As the miles pass by, the serpentine logging roads, blotchy clear-cuts, and other signs of civilization slowly fade away until there's nothing left but pure, unadulterated Canadian wilderness. Suddenly, after about thirty minutes of flight, an incongruent scene emerges from the forest below. In the middle of nowhere rests a dam. It's not a particularly large or noteworthy structure. Many dams are bigger. What is unusual is where it's located—in a roadless area. This is Ontario's Summit Dam, so named because it sits on the tip of the divide that separates the Lake Superior and Hudson Bay watersheds. As strange as it looks out here in the wilderness, Summit Dam is not alone. Just a few minutes' flight to the north sits the Waboose Dam, and it *is* a noteworthy structure. Spanning 1,700 feet—nearly six football fields—it's much larger than the Summit Dam and is more than 450 feet longer than the Hoover Dam on the Colorado River.[1] The Waboose Dam is so large, yet so remote, that it strikes a surreal pose in the northwestern Ontario bush.

Why are these dams here? They are the primary hydrologic structures behind the giant Ogoki diversion, by far the largest water diversion

The Waboose Dam across the Ogoki River in northwestern Ontario backs up the river's flow over the edge of the Great Lakes Basin divide. The water then flows southward toward Lake Superior. (Photo by Peter Annin)

ever built in the Great Lakes region.[2] The Waboose Dam serves as the diversion's backstop, cutting through the upper reaches of the Ogoki River and blocking off water that would otherwise wind its way to Hudson Bay. Stretching from one bank of the Ogoki to the other, the Waboose Dam steals water from the upper reaches of the river, backing it up into a sprawling man-made reservoir that feeds toward Summit Dam. If Waboose is the plug that creates this giant diversion, Summit is the outlet—and the tap is almost always open—pouring billions of gallons of reversed Ogoki River water daily toward Lake Nipigon and ultimately into Lake Superior. With an average estimated flow of about 4,000 cubic feet per second (cfs), the Ogoki diversion is 25 percent larger than the highly contentious Chicago diversion (at 3,200 cfs). But unlike the Illinois diversion, Ogoki is comparatively devoid of controversy—boring by comparison. Most people don't even know it exists. Its remoteness lends to its obscurity, and so does its age—it was completed in 1943. But the Illinois diversion is four decades older, and it still makes headlines. What is it, then, that makes the Ogoki

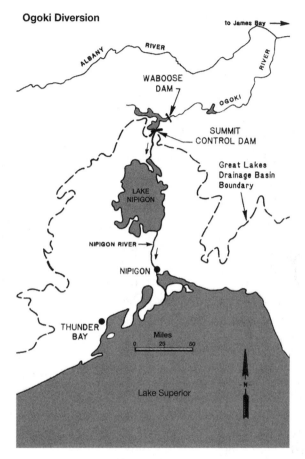

The Ogoki diversion uses the Waboose Dam to back up water from the Albany River watershed and pushes it into Lake Nipigon, and ultimately Lake Superior, in the Great Lakes watershed. (Adapted from International Joint Commission)

diversion so noncontroversial? Perhaps this is because it diverts water *into* the Great Lakes instead of *out* of them. "It's a giver, not a taker," says Ralph Pentland, a Canadian water expert. That, more than anything else, sets it apart from the more controversial diversions in the Great Lakes Basin.

When people do hear about the Ogoki diversion, it's usually lumped together with a neighboring diversion at Long Lac. That diversion, also known by its English name, Long Lake, is approximately eighty miles east of Ogoki and operates on much the same principle—by diverting water from the Hudson Bay watershed into Lake Superior.[3] Long Lake's diversion starts with a dam that blocks off the upper portions of the Kenogami River and pushes that water back over the edge of the Great Lakes Basin divide—or what Canadians often refer to as the "height of land." By damming the Kenogami River on the north side of Long Lake, and blasting and cutting a channel on the south side, engineers managed to funnel the diverted water into the Aguasabon River, which flows into Lake Superior near the town of Terrace Bay.

At roughly 1,500 cfs, Long Lac is no small diversion either. But when Ogoki and Long Lac are lumped together, they become huge— the equivalent of adding a large new river to the Lake Superior ecosystem. They have not only raised water levels on Superior—the largest lake by surface area in the world—they've also raised lake levels on every other Great Lake in the system. According to the International Joint Commission, Long Lac and Ogoki have boosted Lake Superior water levels by 2.4 inches, Lake Michigan and Lake Huron by 4.3 inches, Lake Erie by 3.1 inches, and Lake Ontario by 2.8 inches.[4] Long Lac and Ogoki are so large that they more than offset other diversions, including Chicago's, that have sent Great Lakes water out of the Basin. "There's an accidental balancing," Mr. Pentland says. "It's not good planning. It just happened."

By inadvertently atoning for the sins of others, Long Lac and Ogoki have become more historically palatable. Rightly or wrongly, diversions *into* the Great Lakes Basin are considered to be less newsworthy than diversions *out* of it. Despite the benign reputation of these two water projects, they have had their own social and ecological costs—which helps reinforce the notion that water belongs in its natural watershed and not someplace else. "I don't think there will ever be any more diversions of this magnitude—not without significant political or social change," says Karl Piirik, a water engineer with Ontario Power Generation (OPG), which owns and operates the two diversions. Long Lac and Ogoki are anachronisms, symbols of bygone times when the whims of the drafting table ruled the day, while ecosystems—and people—were expected to adjust accordingly. As Mr. Pentland puts it, "They are dinosaurs from another era."

∼

Long Lac Diversion

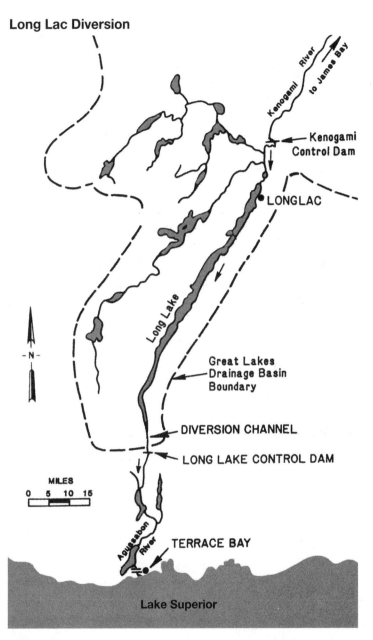

The Long Lac diversion uses the Kenogami Dam to back up water that normally would flow into James Bay. Instead, that water is diverted into Lake Superior near Terrace Bay, Ontario. (Adapted from International Joint Commission)

The tale of these two diversions is rich and historically significant. Long Lac came first, after Ontario made a Depression-era deal with four American paper companies to harvest trees in the surrounding watershed.[5] The companies needed a dependable pulp supply; Ontario needed jobs for its citizens and revenue from natural resources. The timber contract covered a vast and inaccessible area—2,600 square miles—larger than some national forests on the US side of Lake Superior. In return, the companies agreed to pay $300,000 toward diversion construction, build a pulp mill, and employ at least 400 men for the subsequent two decades.

With no economical way to get the timber to market without a diversion, construction began during the summer of 1937. By that time, Canada had started negotiations with the United States to secure hydro rights to water from the Long Lac diversion as the water passed through Great Lakes generating stations. Canada wasn't interested in sending bonus electricity to the United States and wanted to lay claim to this additional water before the diversion came on line. But the Long Lac hydro negotiations bogged down in horse trading that was already under way regarding development of the St. Lawrence Seaway. The Americans wanted the seaway, but many Canadians were opposed, fearing the transportation alternative would compete with Canadian railways, which were already running deficits. Because the United States wouldn't sign over Long Lac's hydro rights until the St. Lawrence Seaway issue was resolved, the Long Lac negotiations stalled.

While the talks bogged down in Ottawa and Washington, the roughnecks continued their arduous chores in the field constructing the diversion works. Northwestern Ontario's bitter winters and mosquito-choked summers were a challenge to the work crews. The remoteness of the Long Lac diversion site made for some extraordinary logistical obstacles as well. During the warmer months, a hundred men and their material were moved by boat from the remote village of Longlac to a work camp at the Kenogami Dam site, ten miles outside of town. Everything they took with them—food, tools, heavy equipment, building supplies—had to be portaged around a sixteen-foot waterfall via a quarter-mile rail track that had been built for the project. After freeze-up, workers used a temporary winter road to access the dam site. They cut lumber with a portable sawmill and hauled gravel from a pit they dug nearby. Most cement pouring was done in subzero temperatures during the winter of 1938. "The quality of the facilities that they made in these remote locations is quite extraordinary," says Karl Piirik. "From an engineering point of view, it's fantastic." Although construction wrapped up by the summer of 1939, the full diversion did not begin until the hydro rights issue was resolved with American negotiators. Finally, in 1940, diplomatic notes (sort of a temporary, quickie version of a treaty) were exchanged between the two countries, and the gates to the Long Lac diversion were thrown open early the following year.

While construction on Long Lac was wrapping up, Canadian officials started talking about adding the larger diversion at Ogoki. The motivation behind Ogoki was very different, and much more urgent. In 1939, Britain and Canada entered World War II, and Canada was desperate to boost its hydro capacity in order to power the war effort. "I remember as a boy, later in the 1940s when lights would go off in the city of Toronto," remembers Frank Quinn, a retired water-policy advisor at Environment Canada.[6] "And this was *after* the war," he says. "With Canada entering the war in 1939, there must have been a lot of pressure," he adds, to find additional energy sources. To resolve the energy crisis, engineers proposed a large diversion eighty miles west of Long Lake to send Ogoki River water south to Lake Superior. From an engineering standpoint, there was a brilliant simplicity in the Canadian plan. Much of Ontario's excess hydro capacity was at Niagara Falls, between Lake Ontario and Lake Erie, near the southern Ontario industrial belt. But the Ogoki's "surplus" water was hundreds of miles away on the north side of Lake Superior. How to get that water to Niagara? By dumping it into Lake Superior and letting it flow downstream, winding its way through the upper Great Lakes until it reached Ontario's generating facilities at the falls. The plan would allow Canada to boost electrical output without building new hydro facilities in remote stretches of northern Ontario or erecting expensive new transmission lines to ship power south. Rather than bring the infrastructure to the water, they brought the water to the infrastructure. Though the diverted water would also generate power at hydro facilities in Sault Ste. Marie, and on the Nipigon River, delivering water to Niagara was what the Canadians were really after.[7]

Building Ogoki's diversion works in the remote Ontario bush was

Based on original from Department of Geography, University of Waterloo

The Long Lac and Ogoki diversions generate power throughout the Great Lakes, but Canada was most interested in capturing the power hundreds of miles away at Niagara Falls. (Based on the original from the Department of Geography, University of Waterloo)

even more challenging than constructing the diversion at Long Lac. Construction began in the middle of winter, in December 1940, and used winter roads and bush planes to transport men and equipment over the edge of the Lake Superior basin divide. A massive 820-man crew built the 50-foot-high, 1,700-foot-long dam at a boiling stretch of the Ogoki River known as Waboose Rapids.[8] Several other smaller earthen dams had to be constructed to round out the edges of the eighty-nine-square-mile reservoir that would hold the backed-up river water. "Ogoki was different," explains Simon Peet, an area supervisor with the Ontario Ministry of Natural Resources, who wrote his thesis on the Long Lac diversion. "It required the construction of a reservoir, whereas Long Lake didn't—there was a lake system already there." At the southern end of the Ogoki Reservoir, the 405-foot-long, 23-foot-high Summit Dam was erected across a channel that had been cut through the "height of land" that divided the Lake Superior and Hudson Bay watersheds. From there, the diverted water would spill through a series of lakes and a river, entering Lake Nipigon and ultimately rushing down the Nipigon River into Lake Superior east of Thunder Bay.

World War II was well under way when the Ogoki diversion finally came on line in July 1943. Because Canadian negotiators had lumped the hydro rights for the Ogoki diversion into the diplomatic note discussions for Long Lac, Ogoki didn't suffer any political delays before the spigot was turned on. Signed in October 1940, the diplomatic notes regarding the hydro rights for Long Lac and Ogoki were highfalutin and unnecessarily obfuscating, but they served their purpose. "There is apprehension in both countries over the possibility of a power shortage," the US note read, stating that the United States would "interpose no objection" to Canada claiming the hydro rights to both diversions.[9] The correspondence emphasized that the notes were meant to be a temporary agreement until more-formal treaties could be signed. That occurred a decade later when the notes were recognized in the Niagara Treaty of 1950, which updated the international hydro rights at Niagara Falls.[10]

The diplomatic notes estimated that the combined size of the two diversions was 5,000 cfs—4,000 for Ogoki and 1,000 for Long Lac—but in reality the diversions have varied widely over time. In a 1985 report, the International Joint Commission found that the combined total of the two diversions had been as low as 2,530 cfs and as high as 8,020 cfs. These wide fluctuations have continued. Between March and August 2004, for example, the two diversions racked up an enormous six-month average of 8,410 cfs.[11] Though the diversion didn't remain at that level for long, this flow was nearly 70 percent higher than officials expected the diversions would be when they signed the diplomatic notes in 1940—and a variance of that magnitude obviously can affect Great Lakes water levels.

Because lake levels fluctuate extensively, even without the help of Long Lac and Ogoki, at times people have suggested using the two diversions to counterbalance the lakes' natural variability. While coastal freshwater ecosystems thrive on fluctuating water levels, humans prefer lake-level stability (see chapter 3). More than once, Canadian officials have been asked to turn off the Long Lac and Ogoki diversions during periods of high water, and in the 1950s and 1970s they even agreed to do so.[12] "We did [shut them down] for some years," says Frank Quinn, the former water-policy advisor at Environment Canada. "But in the more recent period of high water, Ontario Hydro said, 'Well, too bad. We're making so much money from this import, we're just going to keep doing it.'"

Over time, Great Lakes environmentalists, biologists, and water managers have become united in their opposition to using artificial diversions as a means of regulating Great Lakes water levels. "From time to time you get this idea from various people that you can manipulate Great Lakes levels by manipulating diversions—in other words, turning these taps on and off," says Ralph Pentland. "But that was studied by the [International Joint Commission] and was determined to be infeasible."[13] Because diversions like Long Lac and Ogoki are profitable to hydroelectric entities, at times some have suggested that they be expanded. "[There was] a brief period when Ontario and Canada considered increasing diversions—either at Ogoki and Long Lake or [adding] new diversions," Mr. Quinn says. "It became a little controversial there in the early seventies, and we dropped it."

While it's easy to find Great Lakes environmentalists to criticize the Illinois diversion, the same spokespeople are usually perplexed when asked to comment on Long Lac and Ogoki. When contacted for this book, for example, Susan Howatt, the national water campaigner with the Council of Canadians—one of the most vocal groups on water issues north of the border—was stumped when asked about Long Lac and Ogoki. "I don't really have a position on that, to be honest," she said. "I know almost nothing about it." And when Paul Muldoon, executive director of the Canadian Environmental Law Association (CELA) was reached for comment, he passed the question to his colleague Sarah Miller, CELA's project coordinator. Ms. Miller said that while her organization didn't have an official position on the Long Lac and Ogoki diversions, that didn't mean that CELA supports diversions into the Great Lakes Basin. But she admitted that it was inconsistent for environmentalists to be so adamantly opposed to diversions out of the Great Lakes, like the one at Chicago, but comparatively ignorant about major diversions into the lakes, such as those at Long Lac and Ogoki. Did she see any lessons to be learned from the Long Lac and Ogoki diversions? "[Canadians] have manipulated more waterways than just about any other nation," she said. "I think people in power now truly believe that that's harmful—in large-scale degrees—but at the same time, I think that's a reversible position depending on the conditions in the world."

The remoteness of the Long Lake and Ogoki diversions has led to a lack of awareness and has muffled opposition—but not among the indigenous First Nations people who live in the Long Lac and Ogoki watersheds. They have been negatively affected more than anyone, and to them these diversions remain a contentious issue. Their voices just aren't being heard. The Marten Falls Reserve Number 65 tried to change that by having Chief Eli Moonias submit comments to the Great Lakes Compact negotiating team during a meeting in Oak Brook, Illinois, in 2005. Chief Moonias complained that even though the Ogoki diversion's Waboose dam "is in our territory," nevertheless his people were not consulted when it was built. "Ironically, despite the potential for power, to date Marten Falls relies on diesel-fuel generation as our source of power for the community." He complained that the Ogoki diversion dramatically affected whitefish and sturgeon populations in the Albany River, downstream from Waboose Dam. He went on to demand payment to his people for the water lost from the Hudson Bay watershed. "Adequate compensation needs to be provided for the loss of traditional livelihood and loss of economy caused by the loss of water."

Perhaps no community has shouldered the burden of these diversions more than the Long Lake No. 58 First Nation reserve on the north side of Long Lake. Chief Veronica Waboose says that the Long Lac and Ogoki diversions may not be controversial in Toronto, or Ottawa, or Chicago, but they are to her. There are 1,400 members in her Ojibway community, but only 450 live on the 500-acre reserve that the government has given her people, in part because only 200 acres are "usable for community purposes." The other 800 live elsewhere and are waiting for Chief Waboose to come up with more land. That has been difficult, she says, thanks to unsympathetic government officials and the fact that the Long Lac diversion washed away or inundated 142 acres on her tiny reserve—including a large portion of the tribal cemetery. "[Much of] our graveyard has been washed away," she says. "The people who had buried their loved ones there don't have anywhere to go [to pay their respects]." Prior to the diversion, the cemetery was on a hill, but now that hill is an island. The power company surrounded the island with riprap to prevent more graves from washing away, Chief Waboose says, and the hydro company built a one-lane cemetery access road, but she remains concerned about the threat of higher water levels.

Decades ago, hydro officials placed rock along the shore of the reserve in an attempt to remediate shoreline erosion from the diversion. But in recent years, tests confirmed that the rock, which came from mining waste, was contaminated with arsenic. The controversy sparked a decade of negotiations between OPG at the reserve. Mr. Piirik says that OPG wanted to remove the rock completely, but because research suggested that removing the rock might stir up even more arsenic, the reserve members decided to cover it with a membrane, sand, gravel and more rock to bury it in place. The work was done over three years, ending in late 2016. Mr. Piirik says that OPG paid for the remediation work, but that the local community was in charge of the project. "That was a huge leap forward in terms of building trust and working with the First Nation," he said. In a statement, Long Lake No. 58 First Nation officials said the "restoration has been a long time coming," adding that "during an emotional ceremony to mark the completion of the project, members of the First Nation lauded OPG's role in the successful remediation process." Chief Waboose says the main thing her community needs now is more territory—to make up for land lost to the Long Lac diversion and to make up for historical injustices, including the size of her band's small reserve. "We want more land, that's what we're fighting for," she says. "I'm not saying give us money for free, I'm talking about resources for our people so that they could live like other Canadians."

Erosion was a serious problem at the Ogoki diversion as well, in part because soil was washed away when it was exposed to waves, or it sloughed off into the rising diversion waters.[14] This increased turbidity resulted in degraded water quality and fish habitat, particularly in the biologically productive areas near the water's edge. The roaring rapids below the Waboose Dam were tamed, too—nothing but a damp boulder garden remains. Similar changes were seen for several miles below the Kenogami Dam as well. What kind of effect have these diversions had on the Hudson Bay watershed? The limited research that has been done has focused on the effects immediately downstream from these dams and has shown that the loss of diverted water created a decline in fish forage, disrupted spawning and fish migrations, and created declines in species diversity.[15] This research also found that during periods of high water and spring snowmelt, infrequent water releases from these dams mimicked spring flooding, but once the dam's sluices were shut down, fish and other aquatic animals could become stranded in the receding waters.[16]

Canadian officials argue, however, that farther downstream, where the Ogoki and Kenogami Rivers meet up with the Albany, there's so much water roaring through the watershed that the loss of water from the Ogoki and Long Lac diversions becomes imperceptible. That's particularly the case, they say, when you get to the enormous water-rich ecosystems at James Bay or Hudson Bay. While that may be true, there's no evidence that Canadian officials have ever actually studied the ecological ramifications that these two diversions have had downstream in the Albany River drainage basin. "Almost nothing is known of the impacts on the Albany watershed below the points of diversion," Frank Quinn says. "This is, of course, a very sparsely settled region, and aboriginal communities well downstream nearer to James Bay would not have noticed much difference in flow." But it seems hard to imagine that a diversion that could have such a wide-ranging effect on one of the world's largest collections of freshwater lakes has not left the ecosystem wanting on the other side of the watershed divide. In 2005, the Long Lac and Ogoki diversions completed an extensive long-term review process during which officials from the Ontario Ministry of Natural Resources asked Ontario Power Generation to slightly increase the nominal average daily flows from both diversions into the Albany River watershed. (These "flows" are essentially the leakage of a few cubic feet per second that happens to squeeze through the

Waboose and Kenogami diversion dams.) Ontario Power Generation eventually conceded, Mr. Piirik said, and the management plan requiring the releases was revised again in 2015.

What scientists do know is that the diversions caused unexpected water-quality problems in the Long Lake and Ogoki watersheds—particularly with mercury. Chad Day, an emeritus professor at Simon Fraser University in British Columbia who supervised research projects about Long Lac and Ogoki, says that when the diverted waters inundated new land, they washed over ambient mercury in the ground. The mercury eventually made its way into regional fish populations, creating a spike in contamination levels that decreased over time. "The mercury goes into solution and it goes right through the ecosystem," Mr. Day says. "It's in those fish that the Indians have to eat, and they end up with excessive amounts of mercury in their bodies."

The diversions had effects on regional outfitters as well. Fly-in fishing camps are found throughout the area, especially in the Ogoki watershed. During the early years of the diversion, these outfitters were rarely if ever warned about impending water-level changes. So during periods of high water, when hydro officials would release pressure on the ballooning Ogoki Reservoir by opening the floodgates at Waboose Dam, downstream outfitters were often caught off guard. "I don't know if it's any different today, but [these releases] were very insensitively handled because they wouldn't even tell anybody that the water was coming—especially on the Ogoki," Mr. Day says. "Some of the outfitters downstream [would have] their cabins flooded and their materials . . . swept down the river because the water came up and they didn't know it was coming."

From a purely economic perspective, the Long Lac and Ogoki diversions brought solid and tangible benefits to the Canadian economy. People need to remember, Professor Day says, that Britain needed Canada's help in defeating Hitler, and Canada needed help from Long Lac and Ogoki to provide electricity for the war effort. It was an era when governments didn't give much thought to social or environmental impacts of hydro projects—particularly when national security was at stake. "It was a wartime decision. I was alive at the time and I'll tell you people were just terrified about the thought of the Germans and the Japanese coming here and taking North America," Mr. Day says. "People forget about how serious that was." While there were ecological and social impacts in northern Ontario, Mr. Day says the diversions at Ogoki and Long Lac provided a relatively quick fix to a severe wartime energy crisis by delivering hydro capacity right where Canada needed it most—Niagara Falls. Depression-era jobs were created through construction of the diversion works and in harvesting trees in the Long Lake watershed.

Simon Peet, who grew up in northern Ontario, wrote a thesis on the Long Lac diversion and he still works in the region. He is troubled by the negative social and environmental effects that the diversions have created, particularly on native communities, but he says that, from a broad perspective, it's hard to be critical. "My assessment of it overall was that it was positive," Mr. Peet says. "There were some people who were displaced and negatively impacted from erosion and that sort of thing. . . . [But] you have this major project and people don't even know it exists—that must tell you that it has a fairly benign impact." On that point, Mr. Peet and Chief Waboose disagree. But perhaps they can both take comfort knowing that no one envisions diversions like Long Lac and Ogoki ever happening again.

Chapter 8

Pleasing Pleasant Prairie

In the faceless suburbia that sprawls along Interstate 94 north of Chicago, just after crossing into Wisconsin, lies the modest community of Pleasant Prairie. Located in the extreme southeast corner of the state, the town of 21,000 people is bordered by Illinois to the south, the city of Kenosha to the north, and the rich blue waters of Lake Michigan to the east. Pleasant Prairie also straddles the Great Lakes Basin line. The Basin is so narrow in southeast Wisconsin that it cuts right through the middle of the village. Rain that falls on the western side of Pleasant Prairie doesn't find its way to Lake Michigan; it eventually ends up in the Mississippi River instead.

No one in Pleasant Prairie paid much attention to all this watershed business until the early 1980s. That's when officials discovered that some of their groundwater wells were contaminated with radium, a naturally occurring radioactive element that was present in the village's groundwater at four times the federal limit. Fortunately, most people in Pleasant Prairie didn't drink the town's notorious water anyway. The taste was terrible, and the water was so foul that it ruined clothes in the washing machine. Sheets hanging out to dry in the backyard could be stained by an errant lawn sprinkler. Most residents were able to shower in the water after running it through a water softener, but everyone found it useful for at least one thing. "Flushing the toilet," says Michael Pollocoff, the former village administrator. "Most people got their [drinking] water from someplace else."

Whether people drank the water or not, the federal government still considered it a health hazard. The village investigated a wide array of alternative water options, including treatment to remove the radium from the water supply. But that was expensive, and radium concentrations in the sludge would create disposal headaches. Given that the community rests on the shores of Lake Michigan, turning to the Great Lakes seemed like an obvious alternative. The City of Kenosha, just to the north, already pulled its drinking water from Lake Michigan. And as luck would have it, Kenosha's water lines were so close to Pleasant Prairie's that one section of eight-foot pipe was all it would take to connect the two water systems. Kenosha had the capacity and inclination to bring Pleasant Prairie on line; all the two communities needed was clearance from state water officials.

That clearance would have been easy to obtain just a few years earlier, but by the late 1980s diverting water from the Great Lakes had entered a new and more complicated era. In 1985, the Great Lakes governors and premiers signed the Great Lakes Charter, which called for a regional "consultation" before diversions of more than 5 million gallons per day (mgd) could be approved. And in 1986, Congress passed Section 1109 of the Water Resources Development Act (WRDA), which required unanimous approval from all eight Great Lakes governors before a single drop of water could be diverted outside the Great Lakes Basin—at least on the American side of the border (see chapter 4). What did all this mean to the people of Pleasant Prairie? Because their proposed diversion was only 3.2 mgd, they fell well below the Great Lakes Charter's trigger. That meant the Canadians wouldn't have to get involved. WRDA did apply, however, and local officials weren't quite sure what that meant because the federal anti-diversion statute had never been used before. Pleasant Prairie was about to become a test case for the first federal Great Lakes anti-diversion law ever passed in the United States. While the village's water application was minuscule compared with the giant diversions at Chicago, Long Lac, and Ogoki, times had changed. Pleasant Prairie's water application was about to undergo a vetting that most people underestimated at the time. Like any trial run, the road was going to be bumpy. But few, including the Great Lakes governors who would ultimately decide the village's fate, realized what a bizarre test case Pleasant Prairie's diversion application would turn out to be.

~

On March 29, 1989, Wisconsin governor Tommy Thompson sent a letter to the Council of Great Lakes Governors requesting permission to divert 3.2 million gallons per day from Lake Michigan to Pleasant Prairie.[1] On May 15, 1989, Governor Richard Celeste of Ohio, who happened to hold the rotating seat as chairman of the council, sent a letter to all eight governors alerting them to Wisconsin's diversion request. Even though it wasn't required, as a courtesy in the spirit of cooperation exemplified by the Great Lakes Charter, the provinces of Ontario and Québec were also notified about Pleasant Prairie's proposal. Based on the informal feedback that Wisconsin was getting, there was a lot of confidence in the state capitol that Pleasant Prairie's diversion proposal would be approved. "They were saying 'This should be a no-brainer,'" remembers Bruce Baker, deputy administrator of the Water Division at the Wisconsin Department of Natural Resources. "[Pleasant Prairie] doesn't have a water supply, it's a public health issue, it's a very small amount. It's totally insignificant in the realm of Great Lakes water quantity.... The consensus of the group was, 'This is a good one to say yes to.'"

Almost immediately, responses started to arrive from around the Great Lakes. In a letter dated May 30, 1989, Minnesota governor Rudy Perpich consented to the diversion. Good news. Governors from Illinois, Ohio, and Indiana said they had "no objection" to the diversion as well. Because the Great Lakes Charter did not apply, Québec too was in favor of the diversion. But not all the correspondence was affirmative. Ontario officials said they would prefer a solution that did not require a diversion. If a letter like that had come from a governor, under WRDA, Pleasant Prairie's proposal would have been history. But because it came from a Canadian official, who had been notified as a courtesy, it was a disappointment, but not a deal breaker.

Wisconsin still had not received letters from Pennsylvania, Michigan, or New York. Pennsylvania turned out to be remarkably disengaged from the process. "It was hard to get any consistency out of Pennsylvania," remembers Chuck Ledin, former director of the Great Lakes office at the Wisconsin DNR. "This was like a nothing issue for [them]." The situation could not have been more different in Michigan. The governor there didn't send a letter, but one of his staffers requested a meeting to discuss the Pleasant Prairie proposal. That ended up being the first of numerous meetings, phone conversations, and letter exchanges between Wisconsin and Michigan about the proposed diversion. "We were meeting at the Milwaukee airport, we were meeting at the Detroit airport," Bruce Baker says. "They asked for all kinds of information like the land-use plan in the area, [sewer] background, 'What's your water-conservation program in Wisconsin?' Just tons of information." The consultations with Michigan dragged on for months. Meanwhile, Wisconsin officials spent a lot of time on the phone with New York. If Michigan was the proposal's lead scrutinizer, New York was the runner-up. No one else on the US side of the border seemed all that interested. In the end, Mr. Baker says, officials in New York told him, "We're fine with it, but we won't approve it unless Michigan does."

Suddenly the "no-brainer" diversion proposal was hanging in the balance. Mr. Baker heard through back channels that staffers had recommended that Michigan governor James Blanchard approve the Pleasant Prairie diversion, but the recommendation was kicked back. Then, at the insistence of Michigan, Wisconsin offered up what's known in the Great Lakes Basin as a "return-flow" requirement. State officials would require Pleasant Prairie to eventually retrofit its sewage system to return the diverted water back to Lake Michigan after it was used and treated. This would not be required immediately, because Pleasant Prairie had two new wastewater-treatment plants that discharged into the Mississippi River watershed, and the debt load for those plants would be on the books for decades. So Wisconsin floated an offer to have Pleasant Prairie add return-flow by 2010, the year Pleasant Prairie was due to retire its treatment-plant debt. This meant, of course, that the water loss from the diversion would be temporary—a key factor that seemed to break the logjam for Michigan. After yet another face-to-face meeting with Michigan officials in July 1989, Wisconsin's negotiators finally thought an approval letter would be on its way.

But the back-and-forth continued. A key issue for Michigan's negotiators emerged: how was the water going to be used? They had no problem helping the people of Pleasant Prairie out of their drinking-water bind. But Michigan was very suspicious that Pleasant Prairie officials were asking for more water than they really needed. Michigan worried that the diversion would be used to spur future economic growth in the sleepy Wisconsin town. One of Michigan's chief negotiators was J. D. Snyder, then director of the state's Office of the Great Lakes. In a letter dated August 10, 1989, Mr. Snyder said he had a "deep concern regarding the full extent of the proposed diversion, which includes allowances for population and economic growth in addition to addressing current public health needs."[2]

Wisconsin officials provided numbers, letters, tables, facts, and charts to show that the diversion would be primarily used by humans, not corporations. But two people can sometimes read the same information differently, and five months on, Michigan still needed convincing. "You have indicated that the justification for the proposed 3.2 [million gallons per day] temporary diversion is based solely on the need to provide a potable water supply to address public health concerns. Nevertheless, the proposed diversion may provide substantial water for commercial and industrial development," Mr. Snyder said in a letter a month later. "Michigan strongly maintains that any warranted diversion of Great Lakes water must be used to address public health concerns and should not be used for commercial and industrial development."[3]

A few weeks after J. D. Snyder wrote his letter, Governor Thompson broke ground on a new LakeView Corporate Park on Pleasant Prairie's far west side—the end of town that sits outside the Great Lakes Basin. Though this might at first suggest that Wisconsin was negotiating in bad faith, state officials argue that the situation was more complicated. The plan for LakeView was to take water from Kenosha, funnel it through Pleasant Prairie's west side, and then return the water to Lake Michigan. As a new corporate development, this return-flow plumbing could be installed from the start. So the thinking in Wisconsin was that LakeView would use Lake Michigan water, but because it was returning its treated wastewater to Lake Michigan, it would not be a diversion.

Or at least that was Wisconsin's interpretation of WRDA. But since WRDA never defined what a diversion was, it was hard to say if Wisconsin was right. As WRDA's first test case, these kinds of issues had not been worked out by Great Lakes officials. Years later, sending water across the Basin line and then returning it would be seen as a diversion that required a unanimous vote by all eight Great Lakes governors (see chapter 11.) But for the time being, the LakeView project managed to sneak through without further consideration.

Kenosha was used to these kinds of deals. The city had been diverting water outside the Great Lakes Basin since 1964—long before WRDA became law. With roughly 20 percent of the city lying outside the Basin line, the utility continued to add customers (outside the Basin) to the Lake Michigan water system long after WRDA was passed. Each time Kenosha's water service was expanded outside the Basin, the Wisconsin DNR approved the extensions without requiring the city to submit its water application for review by the other governors. "Did we continue to add customers? Absolutely," says Edward St. Peter, general manager of the Kenosha Water Utility, adding that Wisconsin officials didn't consider what he was doing to be a diversion—as long as the treated sewage water came back to Lake Michigan. But he acknowledged that not everyone shared Wisconsin's unique interpretation of WRDA. "Other states, especially Michigan, felt that any water that went out [of the Basin] was a diversion," he says. That led to a debate about the definition of a diversion. "I'd like to see something in writing that says what a diversion is." WRDA didn't answer that question, Mr. St. Peter said, and if a Great Lakes water withdrawal with return-flow constituted a diversion, "then what we were doing was illegal."

Kenosha continued to operate under the radar, but Pleasant Prairie was not so lucky. The village's own consultant worried that the LakeView water deal could derail the diversion's approval. George Loomis was a Lansing lobbyist whom Pleasant Prairie had paid $30,000 to help get its water application approved. In a confidential memo to the village on September 29, 1989, he warned of "significant problems down the road should the future water use of the LakeView Corporate Park ever be claimed to constitute a diversion of water from the Great Lakes Basin."[4]

Meanwhile, Michigan kept requesting more paperwork, and Wisconsin delivered. On October 9, 1989, Bruce Baker sent Michigan a three-page single-spaced letter with numerous attachments. The letter tabulated the costs of all the other water-supply options that Pleasant Prairie had explored but determined to be "infeasible." Mr. Baker also reassured Michigan about Wisconsin's water-conservation statutes. But the bulk of Mr. Baker's letter dwelled on the commercial and industrial water-use issue. It included an estimate that 88.5 percent of Pleasant Prairie's diverted water would go to residential use, and none of the diverted water, he said, would go to LakeView. "Future industrial growth in this portion of the Village of Pleasant Prairie will occur within the LakeView Corporate Park, a development which has an existing water supply connection to the City of Kenosha and thus, will not be served by the proposed diversion." Mr. Baker made it clear that Wisconsin was tired of being strung along. "I again state my earnest hope that all of Michigan's concerns regarding the proposed diversion have been answered by this letter and the preceding correspondence of May 9, June 8, July 20, and August 16, as well as the July 20, 1989, consultation meeting in Milwaukee," Mr. Baker wrote. "Your reticence in approving this proposal has placed the citizens of the Village of Pleasant Prairie and this Department in an untenable position."[5]

~

Michael Pollocoff was irked too. As Pleasant Prairie's administrator, he was supposed to fix the village's water problem, and the locals were getting restless. His neighbors didn't understand why he couldn't access the Lake Michigan water that many could see from their doorsteps. Their water was contaminated with *radiation*—what else did anyone need to know? "We had water that you couldn't stand to smell . . . you didn't like looking at it, and we couldn't clean it up," Mr. Pollocoff says. "To our utility customers we looked like a bunch of knuckleheads." And when you go to bed at night knowing that there's radioactive contamination sitting in your toilet, it's hard for the average citizen to understand why bureaucrats on the other side of Lake Michigan would play hardball.

The situation spawned small-town conspiracy theories. Was Michigan trying to stifle economic development in Wisconsin to gain a regional competitive advantage? Then Mr. Pollocoff's lobbyist told him, "I think your case needs to be made to the public over here." A few weeks later a Michigan paper sent a reporter and photographer over to do a story about Pleasant Prairie's proposed diversion. In the article Mr. Pollocoff reiterated all the details of why his community had submitted its request for Great Lakes water. "There was a picture of me on the front page of the paper holding up a mayonnaise jar of what looks like Kool-Aid but it was water," Mr. Pollocoff says. "Not long after that, we got this kind of begrudging okay [from Michigan]. . . . The governor didn't even sign the letter."

Michigan did finally send a letter, and it was like no other Wisconsin had received. The December 12, 1989, dispatch insinuated approval of the Pleasant Prairie diversion, but it never actually came right out and said it. Instead, the letter said supplying Pleasant Prairie with Lake Michigan water "is not unreasonable. . . . The state of Michigan, however, remains opposed to any diversion of Great Lakes water for purposes of supporting growth and expansion in any area unable to provide its own public water supply."[6] To Wisconsin, the letter was an eerie echo of Michigan's correspondence of the last several months. It suggested that Michigan would support the diversion if Pleasant Prairie's current population remained stagnant. But if the water ended up spurring population growth or economic development, Michigan would be opposed. There was another problem. The letter was not from the governor, which WRDA seemed to require. Instead, it was from David Hales, the director of Michigan's DNR. Critics continue to argue that Michigan's unusual letter doesn't meet the legal requirements of gubernatorial approval under WRDA. For the first time ever, in an interview for this book, an official from the Wisconsin government agreed with that assessment. "Clearly, it's not an approval letter under WRDA," Bruce Baker admits. "They just played games with the letter."

Contacted more than fifteen years later, David Hales's memory of the letter was a bit fuzzy. "My guess is we didn't want to come across as saying, 'Gee, we are incredibly callous about this whole thing.' But at the same time, we wanted to take a clear stand on principle," he said. "We could be reasonable about meeting existing [water] needs, but we didn't think that any capacity to create the ability for growth should be included in any of those plans."

Jack Bails, who works as a consultant in Michigan, was Mr. Hales's deputy at the time. He describes the Pleasant Prairie letter as a "punt" on Michigan's part. While his memory has faded as well, his guess is that Mr. Hales was dispatched to draft the Pleasant Prairie letter in such a way as to give Michigan full deniability that it had ever approved a diversion, while allowing Wisconsin just enough wiggle room to move forward. "I suspect what happened," he says, "is that rather than have the governor respond, this would be responded to by an agency head to provide some political cover." J. D. Snyder says that he drafted the letter to Governor Thompson on behalf of David Hales, and that Michigan officials were genuinely torn. "Indeed, we were inclined to sign off on the request in the interests of the public health of citizens of a neighboring Great Lakes state," he said in an e-mail. "But we were also apprised of the possibility that the request for 3.2 mgd was greater than what was needed for water supply to replace water contaminated by naturally occurring radium."[7] But at least Michigan sent a letter. Officials from Governor Cuomo's administration in New York never ended up putting anything in writing. "After [Governor Blanchard] did what he did, they couldn't figure out what to do," Mr. Baker says. "We never did get a letter from New York." Pennsylvania didn't send one, either.

This put Wisconsin in an awkward position. WRDA seemed to require a strong affirmative vote from all eight Great Lakes governors for a diversion to be approved. But after months of waiting, phone calls, and wrangling, Wisconsin's file on Pleasant Prairie was missing letters from two states and contained a confusing letter from a third— and that letter wasn't even from a governor. In addition, the courtesy notification sent to Ontario had resulted in an objection from that government, even though, technically, Ontario had no standing under the Great Lakes Charter or WRDA to object. It was a tough call, and Bruce Baker and Chuck Ledin sent the final decision upstairs to Governor Tommy Thompson's office. After much deliberation, the decision was made to go ahead. Michigan's letter gave Governor Thompson enough political leeway to move forward with the diversion, while giving Michigan's governor the ability to deny that he had ever approved it. New York and Pennsylvania had been given more than enough time to cast a veto, if that had been their intent. "We went through the process, we did what we had to do," says Mr. Ledin. "We can't make somebody else respond. So in the absence of getting a yes or a no, we went ahead with the project."

 ⌒

Since all it took was one section of eight-foot pipe to bring the Pleasant Prairie diversion online, Mr. Pollocoff decided to forgo hiring a professional construction crew. "We did it ourselves," he says. "We went out there with a crew and said, 'Let's get this pig hooked up.'" After months of delays, making the actual connection to Kenosha's water system took less than a day. "We did make some subsequent other connections so we had a redundant system. [But] the bulk of the problem was solved within a few hours," Mr. Pollocoff says. At first, the water consumption rate in town didn't change much—the original diversion was only 250,000 gallons per day—but once people became convinced that their water was potable, water consumption started ramping up at a steady clip. Today, Pleasant Prairie's diversion averages about 2.44 mgd, still well below the original ceiling of 3.2 mgd. The village had no problem meeting the 2010 deadline for retiring its wastewater-treatment plants that were discharging Lake Michigan water into the Mississippi River watershed. One plant was retired in 2009, the other in 2010. When that happened, Pleasant Prairie residents on the Mississippi River Basin side of town still drank Great Lakes water, but their treated effluent ended up back in Lake Michigan, rather than the Mississippi River watershed.

What about the growth that Michigan was so concerned about? There's no doubt that gaining access to Lake Michigan changed Pleasant Prairie into a sprawling exurb. From 1980 to 1990, when the town's water was undrinkable, the population remained stagnant at 12,000. When Michael Pollocoff arrived at the village in 1985, he says only one home was added that year, and it came on a truck. But after the new water came to town, the village's size increased 50 percent during the next fifteen years. Today 21,000 people live there, and Pleasant Prairie has been transformed from a place people drove through in 1990, to a destination in and of itself today. The village's daytime population swells to 35,000 people, most of them employees of LakeView and other businesses out by I-94—all of which are outside the Great Lakes Basin. Pleasant Prairie's tax base has exploded from $438 million in 1990, shortly after the diversion was approved, to $3.3 billion today. "We're not a bedroom community anymore," Mr. Pollocoff says.

In fact, the village has gone from water beggar to a water broker. In 2014, the California-based Niagara Bottling company announced plans to build a 377,000-square-foot water bottling plant in Pleasant Prairie, on the Mississippi River Basin side of town. The $56 million facility was expected to eventually employ forty people and planned to purchase up to 2 million gallons of diverted Lake Michigan water from the village per day.[8] Statistics provided by the village show that Niagara is currently only consuming around 170,000 gallons per day, but there is something ironic about a California water bottler setting up shop in Wisconsin to bottle diverted Lake Michigan water for its customers. Great Lakes governors have always hoped that companies from California and elsewhere would move to the Great Lakes region for the water. But they have generally assumed that those companies would locate inside the Great Lakes Basin in order to access that Great Lakes water. What's more, Mr. Pollocoff says, Pleasant Prairie is in conversations with neighboring communities to possibly sell water to them too. What kind of governmental approvals such a water deal would need depends on where the community is based, but the fact that the conversations are happening at all is remarkable.

~

Legal doubts have dogged the Pleasant Prairie diversion from the beginning. Environmental groups, as well as officials in other Great Lakes states, have questioned whether the diversion would survive a court challenge. At a minimum, most officials believe Pleasant Prairie falls into a legal gray area. The first legal vulnerability starts with not having approval letters on file from New York and Pennsylvania, and the confusing letter from Michigan makes both Michigan and Wisconsin look bad. Some even say the correspondence from Ohio, Illinois, and Indiana was not worded properly either. Those letters said the governors did "not object" to the diversion, which is not precisely the same as an approval.

"There are some people who still feel that Pleasant Prairie might be illegal. But no one has ever challenged it," says one former Great Lakes official. "It's one of the unspoken issues in the Basin. People accept Pleasant Prairie as being approved, and I can make an argument that it *was* approved. But there are only four letters on file from governors saying that they approved it." More than once over the years, the Michigan attorney general has criticized the Pleasant Prairie diversion, threatening to take legal action to challenge it in court. At one point, those grumblings caused enough of a stir in Wisconsin that a legislative hearing regarding the diversion was held. But as many times as the legality of Pleasant Prairie has been questioned, the situation has always calmed back down without incident.

Pleasant Prairie's case also cast a shadow over WRDA. Many Great Lakes officials believed that the federal law's first test run uncovered many problems with the statute. The two-page law left a lot of key questions unanswered and a lot of details yet to be filled in. Yes, the law said every diversion of Great Lakes water—no matter how small— needed the approval of all Great Lakes governors. But what was a diversion? Was taking water out and returning it after use a diversion? Wisconsin didn't think so. Most others did. The sparsely worded WRDA statute, unfortunately, was no help. And how exactly was a state supposed to go about obtaining approval from the other governors? Were letters on file enough? If so, how should they be worded? Is "not objecting" the same as an approval? Or do the governors have to use the word "approve" in their correspondence? Or was a formal vote in person or by conference call what the law had in mind? These were just some of the questions swirling around the Pleasant Prairie case. Wisconsin, in particular, was interested in filling these WRDA gaps. It had water problems in many other communities that were on or near the edge of the Great Lakes Basin divide. "[Pleasant Prairie] clearly demonstrated to us that the system was a mess," Bruce Baker says. "We asked the Council [of Great Lakes Governors] to get the other states together to try and develop an agreement on how these [proposed diversion cases] would be handled in the future . . . but we could not get all the states to agree."

The Pleasant Prairie experience left a lot of scar tissue in Wisconsin. Yes, the village got its water, and that was a local victory. But the difficulties in the process had a chilling effect on future diversion applications from the state. Chuck Ledin said that in the years after Pleasant Prairie, he regularly counseled water-troubled Wisconsin communities not to submit new diversion requests. The expense, frustration, and uncertainty were just not worth it—especially since he could not guarantee the results. "If somebody wants to get Great Lakes water, they had best be prepared to spend some money and do a good technical justification for the need, and be prepared to defend their request," he said. "Rather than thinking of Great Lakes water as an option, they best be thinking of it as a last resort."

That was a lesson that Lowell, Indiana, was about to learn.

Chapter 9

Sacrificing Lowell

Lowell, Indiana, is a quiet Midwestern town of 9,500 people nestled in the flat, pastoral countryside that lies about an hour's drive south of Chicago. This is corn and soybean country, marked by tree-lined fencerows and creek beds. Lowell's quaint downtown stretches for just a few blocks, with old brick buildings that contain storefront shops with names like "Midtown Hardware" and "Hawkeye's Restaurant." Despite its proximity to Chicago, Lowell is more country than city. It's a place where strangers politely say hello as they pass on the sidewalk, and where store clerks seem genuine when they say, "Have a nice day." Some locals commute to jobs in Chicago; others work in the steel mills just up the road in Gary, but the backbone of the town's culture remains agriculture. "Lowell is a farming community," says David Gard, the gregarious former president of the town council. "It's kind of the best of both worlds. We're rural, but we're on the fringe of the big city."

Throughout its recent history, however, Lowell has been haunted by one thing: water woes. For years its main problem was that its water stunk—literally. A high hydrogen sulfide content gave the water an essence of rotten eggs. Some people didn't notice the taste; others got used to it. But there were those who have never been able to tolerate Lowell's water, even though things have improved. "I've never had any trouble with it, my kids have never had any trouble with it," Mr. Gard says. "But my wife can't drink the stuff."

Lowell's tolerant residents put up more of a fuss, however, when fly larvae started coming out of the tap. Midge flies are tiny mosquito-like insects that some fish love to eat, but that people are not fond

153

of drinking. In the juvenile or larval stage, midge flies live underwater—usually in ponds, lakes, and streams—before emerging to sprout wings and take flight. But in Lowell, the midge fly's thin, quarter-inch larvae seemed to prefer hanging out in toilet tanks on the east side of town.[1] Officials assured local residents that the larvae were harmless, but they couldn't blame people for being disgusted. The problem seemed to be centered in just one of Lowell's water towers, so workers drained, scrubbed, and blasted the inside of the tower with high-pressure hoses. But the larvae returned. "We did everything," remembers Jeffery Hoshaw, former superintendent of the Lowell water utility. But the flies kept coming back. Finally, the town considered using modest chemical treatments, including hydrogen peroxide and other disinfectants, "but by the time we were ready to put something into practice," Mr. Hoshaw says, "they were gone." Neither he nor anyone else was really sure why.

Then the US Environmental Protection Agency (EPA) came to town, and the stoic people of Lowell met their match. In December of 1987, the federal government sent an administrative order to local officials declaring their water a health hazard and demanding that Lowell resolve the issue on a strict timeline. Tests showed that Lowell's problematic groundwater had yet another fault: exceedingly high levels of fluoride. Fluoride in low doses is good for people, especially their teeth. But high fluoride levels can leave teeth stained, and over time it can cause increased bone density, with crippling results.[2] The EPA order required local officials to notify all residents of the health hazard, and the agency gave Lowell six months to find a solution to the problem and two years to implement it. If Lowell failed to meet this deadline, the EPA would either fine the town or take it to federal court, where the penalties could be as high as $25,000 per day.[3] Though Lowell didn't realize it at the time, the EPA's order would end up snatching the town from obscurity and thrusting it to the forefront of the Great Lakes water-diversion debate. The experience would leave the community battered and bruised, and Great Lakes officials would walk away questioning the functionality of the anti-diversion policies they had worked so hard to create.

∽

At first, Lowell's residents took the news from the EPA in stride. After many meetings and public hearings, the town narrowed its choices to two water options. One was to drill new shallow wells on farmland on the outskirts of the town. The other option was to look less than thirty miles north to Gary, Indiana, which lies at the southern tip of Lake Michigan—the largest body of water wholly within US borders. Officials in Gary were willing to ship Lake Michigan water to Lowell, for a fee. The Lake Michigan water was more expensive, but to many residents the money seemed worth it.[4] Lake Michigan water was higher in quality and seemingly as endless as the lake itself, and there was a concern that the shallow-well option could become unreliable during droughts. The town's residents were surveyed and three-fourths of the responding citizens voted for the Lake Michigan option.[5] But that survey was nonbinding, and the final decision was up to the town council. So in early April 1990, Lowell residents packed the council chambers with a capacity crowd that had come to witness the final decision. The tally wasn't even close; the council vote was unanimous— the crowd applauded as council members decided that Lowell would buy Lake Michigan water from the Gary-Hobart Water Corporation, a privately owned utility a half hour up the road.[6]

But in the months that followed, it became clear that Lowell wasn't going to get by that easily. Town residents started reading stories about the Great Lakes Charter of 1985, the Boundary Waters Treaty of 1909, and the Water Resources Development Act of 1986. These stories, and the public meetings that followed, perplexed Lowell's residents. It was becoming clear that the Lowell Town Council didn't have the authority to import water from Lake Michigan. The problem? Lowell lies south of the Great Lakes Basin boundary—though by less than five miles. Water shipped to Lowell and then discharged by its water-treatment plant wouldn't flow back to Lake Michigan but would head south toward the Mississippi and ultimately the Gulf of Mexico, resulting in a net water loss to the Lake Michigan ecosystem. Under federal law (WRDA), and an international agreement (the Great Lakes Charter), this was a very important distinction.

Because Lowell was asking for less than 5 million gallons of water per day (mgd), the Great Lakes Charter did not apply. Lowell wanted to divert 1 mgd from Lake Michigan with the option to increase the flow to 3.8 mgd over time. The problem, however, was that WRDA applied to diversions of any size from the Great Lakes Basin, which meant Lowell's diversion proposal would need the approval of all eight Great Lakes governors. This came as a surprise to the leaders of Lowell and their citizens, who viewed WRDA as a form of water regulation without representation. Snaking through such a convoluted bureaucratic gauntlet appeared daunting, but there was reason for hope. The governor of Indiana would surely vote for it, and the Village of Pleasant Prairie, Wisconsin, had managed to squeak through a similar diversion the year before (see prior chapter). So how could Wisconsin deny Lowell's water request? Despite the bureaucratic challenge, Lowell was quietly confident that ultimately its diversion request would be approved. "We didn't see this as such a big deal," says John Hughes, who was Lowell's town attorney at the time. "We felt it was just a matter of explaining our problem, and, intellectually, people would just agree with us." After all, what was the big deal about sending water just five miles beyond the edge of the watershed? Who would oppose such a proposal when a classic heartland town like Lowell needed help?

The governor of Michigan for one. A year after Lowell's residents applauded their town council's vote to acquire water from the Great Lakes, Michigan governor John Engler issued a press release dashing the town's hopes. "We want to give Indiana a fair hearing," Governor Engler's press secretary was quoted as saying in April 1991. "But a veto is probable."[7] Governor Engler asked for a meeting with Indiana governor Evan Bayh to discuss the issue. The press release put Lowell on notice that Governor Engler was leaning against Lowell's request for Lake Michigan water. Pleasant Prairie, Wisconsin, may have slipped through, the governor seemed to be saying, but that was under a prior Michigan administration. There was a new team of officials in Lansing now, and they were watching Lowell's situation closely.

A meeting to address the Lowell proposal was scheduled in Indianapolis for early June 1991. Michigan and Indiana would be there, of course, and the other Great Lakes states and provinces would be invited to send representatives as well. In essence, the meeting became a "consultation" as envisioned under the Great Lakes Charter. WRDA didn't dictate how water-diversion proposals should be reviewed, so the charter's consultation guidelines were followed instead. And even though the withdrawal request was below the trigger level of the charter, Ontario and Québec were invited to participate. Officials from the Town of Lowell would be making the main presentation, but others would be allowed to speak. Behind the scenes, Indiana was trying to get a sense of where the various states stood on the issue. Who, besides Michigan, needed convincing? After quietly surveying the Basin, Indiana concluded that the only other potential weak link seemed to be New York. Every Great Lakes state and province except Minnesota and Pennsylvania sent representatives to the meeting.[8]

John Hughes, Lowell's attorney, was one of the key presenters. He argued that alternative sources of water had been explored, as had other options, such as treating the contaminated groundwater. Consultants could not assure the town that new wells would produce the quality and quantity of water needed. Based on the town's research, the Lake Michigan option was the most dependable long-term solution. Regarding water conservation, Hughes mentioned that the town had implemented a sprinkler ban and that a weekly news column included tips on how to save water. But he admitted that Lowell didn't have any specific institutional controls. He also said that while the town had originally requested 1 to 3.8 mgd, officials were reducing the maximum request to 1.7 mgd. Hughes expected that 1.1 million gallons would meet the town's daily needs for the next two decades.

Jim Hebenstreit from the Indiana Department of Natural Resources also spoke at the meeting. As the assistant director of the state water division, he had been shepherding Lowell's diversion request from the start. He told the gathering that he didn't think an outright denial of Lowell's request would withstand a court challenge. He pointed out that Indiana—because it diverted water *into* Lake Michigan at other areas—would still be providing a net surplus of water to the lake, even after the Lowell diversion went into effect. And he warned the Great Lakes governors and premiers that they would be facing an "enforcement nightmare" if they attempted to regulate small diversions and consumptive uses in the region.

Some who attended the meeting remember how shocked Lowell officials were at the widespread interest in their proposal. Both Canadian provinces sent representatives, and Ontario made statements questioning Lowell's proposed diversion. John Hughes remembers wondering why the Canadians were even there, given that they had no vote under WRDA and the Charter didn't apply. "Why are they so vocal about this when they don't really have a say in it?" he remembers thinking. Tim McNulty, who was executive director of the Council of Great Lakes Governors at the time, had a different perspective. "I'll never forget the beginning of the formal process, sitting in Indianapolis," he says, "with the Town of Lowell officials—very solid Hoosier people—kind of reflecting the state of Indiana. And then you've got the cultures of all of the other states, including two Canadian provinces present—someone speaking French. I found it heartening because I thought this is really what this is all about—finding a sense of community in this resource that you share."

Dennis Schornack, who went on to become the US co-chair of the International Joint Commission, remembers how unconvinced he was by Lowell's evidence. At the time, he was Governor Engler's point man on the Lowell case and he spoke at the Indiana meeting. "They had some huge, ten-inch-diameter irrigation wells outside of town that were privately held by farmers, so there was a lot of irrigation going on from the same aquifer," he said. "We went through this whole series of questions. They didn't have any kind of best practices in place with the irrigators who were drawing from the same aquifer. . . . It was just sort of pump it at will."

Despite these issues, a number of states tipped their hand at the meeting, making it clear to Lowell, and to the rest of the Indiana delegation, that they wouldn't object to the diversion. Dick Bartz, from the Ohio DNR, suggested that his state would not object. Minnesota and Pennsylvania weren't there but were leaning toward approval, and Illinois had already sent a letter signing off on the diversion. The other three states—Michigan, New York, and Wisconsin—said they needed more information. Nevertheless, having five out of eight votes in hand was movement in the right direction. But because of the way WRDA was written, it only took one state to pull the plug. Mr. Hughes says he wasn't worried about Wisconsin, "but we weren't getting very good signals from Michigan, and we were also concerned about New York."

While Lowell officials were making their case in Indianapolis, the EPA was busy suing them in federal court. On the same day as the Indianapolis meeting, June 7, 1991, the EPA filed a suit arguing that the fluoride-remediation deadline of 1989 had long since passed, and Lowell's residents were still drinking tainted water. The suit asked the judge to force Lowell to clean up its water and requested that the town be slapped with a penalty of up to $25,000 for each day of the violation. One would think that the suit would make Lowell feel even more besieged, but town officials actually had the opposite take on it. They thought the suit might help their case with the governors, making the situation seem even more urgent and possibly creating sympathy for their cause.

The Indianapolis meeting set off an intense round of behind-the-scenes jockeying and negotiations coordinated by the Council of Great Lakes Governors. Indiana put significant pressure on the council to broker some sort of a deal that would get Lowell its water. Michigan and New York were the key skeptics. Ontario was also aligning itself—albeit symbolically—in opposition. Mr. McNulty spent endless hours on the phone trying to forge a deal. He remembers the eight states breaking down into three distinct camps: Wisconsin, Illinois, and Indiana were generally willing to support limited diversions. Ohio, Minnesota, and Pennsylvania tended to be swing states. And New York and Michigan—particularly Michigan—were the most vigilant opponents.

There was the sense, in Michigan and New York, that Lowell hadn't exhausted all its options. More importantly, there was the issue of precedent. The case in Pleasant Prairie, Wisconsin, was arguably different. Pleasant Prairie was on the shore of Lake Michigan, and half the community was inside the Basin. But the entire town of Lowell was clearly and cleanly outside the Basin. Michigan's (and New York's) fear was not that Lowell's puny request would drain Lake Michigan. Hydrologists said that Lowell's proposal was so small that it would be hard to measure in Lake Michigan's massive 1.2-quadrillion-gallon ecosystem (Indiana estimated that Lowell's peak diversion would lower Lake Michigan's water level by 0.000000365 feet).[9]

The issue was that if the Great Lakes governors made an exception for Lowell, how could they prevent dozens, scores, or even hundreds of communities from reaching for Great Lakes water during the next century? In a mere generation, they feared, the million gallons a day in Lowell could become precedent for cumulative diversions that added up to billions of gallons a day from who knows where. In addition, there was the question of where to draw the line once you breach the Basin—if the Great Lakes Basin was not the line, what was? Halfway down the state of Indiana? The borders of each Great Lakes state? Atlanta? Dallas? Phoenix? Los Angeles? There were a lot of unknowns. "We saw it as kind of the tip of the iceberg," Dennis Schornack says. "If one put the straw in at Lowell because it was a health concern for the drinking water, there were a lot of communities that ultimately would be coming to that door with the same kinds of requests. And it would have set, I think, a very bad precedent."

For many of the states, the problem wasn't Lowell's water application, but the lack of direction in the WRDA statute itself. Once again, like Pleasant Prairie, a test case had uncovered problems in the statute. What bothered many governors—including those who supported Lowell's diversion proposal—about the entire Lowell review process was that the Great Lakes governors had no standards or guidelines on what constituted a justifiable diversion. The statute gave the governors a veto, but didn't give them much guidance in how to use it. Tim McNulty couldn't fix WRDA, so he worked the phones for a compromise that everyone could live with, even begrudgingly. What he cobbled together was a compromiser's compromise. The boldest part of the plan was the imposition of a one-year moratorium on future diversions of water from the Great Lakes. The idea was to give the governors and premiers time to come up with a system to gauge and ultimately judge different diversion requests. "So the moratorium was to create the high ground for Michigan and New York," Mr. McNulty says. "They could clearly argue they had taken steps to prevent future actions that might be seriously damaging [until] we have a completely new framework in place."

In return, of course, Michigan and New York would have to approve the diversion, but not without more sacrifices from Lowell. Some officials wanted to require Lowell to return its treated wastewater to Lake Michigan so there was no net loss to the system, as had been required of Pleasant Prairie. Under initial drafts of Mr. McNulty's agreement, the return-flow plan was deemed to be impractical and prohibitively expensive for a town thirty miles from the lake. Lowell resisted the return-flow idea at first, but when this appeared to be a deal-breaker, Lowell gave in: the town agreed to replace the water it was diverting from the lake. While Lowell's return-flow offer was genuine, the details were sketchy and patched together. "As we got closer to the vote, we agreed to replace the diversion with a like amount of water," John Hughes says. "We weren't sure exactly how we were going to do it, but if we had to, we were prepared to sink some wells and pump water into a creek that flows to Lake Michigan."

~

By late spring of 1992, New York had privately agreed to go along with the backroom compromise, and Tim McNulty says he was under the impression that Michigan had, too. "I really felt that we had it," he says. "Dennis [Schornack] was working hard to represent his governor, but also reflect the team spirit of working as a region, and looking back I wonder if I didn't misread how far he could go." With the deal seemingly brokered, a date was set for the governors to take a final vote on Lowell's request—Friday, May 8, 1992. At the time, Lowell officials shared Mr. McNulty's cautious optimism. "We thought we had made a proposal that met all the issues they had raised," John Hughes remembers. "We really thought we had a chance."

The day before the vote, however, Michigan governor John Engler dropped a bombshell by releasing an advance copy of a letter he had written to Indiana governor Evan Bayh. The letter said that Governor Engler planned to veto the Lowell diversion proposal, and the news hit Lowell broadside. "I was shocked," Mr. Hughes says. Now that Michigan had shown its hand, Mr. Hughes had the distinct feeling that Governor Engler had his mind made up from the start, but that the governor's team had kept Lowell—and much of the regional political establishment—needlessly scurrying around for months. Mr. Hughes was particularly offended that Governor Engler announced his veto before the parties even gathered for the vote. "For them to go and upstage the meeting that way—I just thought that was reprehensible," Mr. Hughes says. "I still do, and I'll tell Engler that to his face!" Mr. McNulty was caught off guard, too. So was New York governor Mario Cuomo's aide, Frank Murray, who had spent so much time working with Mr. McNulty on the compromise. "I had long conversations with Frank that day. He was furious," Mr. McNulty says. "He had worked hard."

The next day, the vote went ahead as planned. The tally would be taken by conference call, with the call originating out of the Council of Great Lakes Governors office located on Wacker Drive in downtown Chicago (next to the reversed Chicago River). None of the governors was expected to take part in the call, each deciding instead to pass the vote-casting authority on to senior staffers. Representatives from Ontario and Québec would be allowed to listen in, but not vote. In one of the more perfunctory moments in Great Lakes history, the representatives gathered for the conference call as scheduled, knowing full well that Michigan was going to cast a veto. The Town of Lowell sent a delegation to sit in on the call in Chicago and Mr. Hughes remembers walking into the office fuming with anger. Once the call got under way, the states were asked to cast their votes in alphabetical order. Illinois and Indiana both voted yes. Then Dennis Schornack cast Michigan's no vote and the polling stopped. Mr. Hughes remembers bitterly castigating Mr. Schornack during the call. "I told him off. I thought it was very, very inappropriate for Governor Engler to do that," he says. "If they were never going to approve it, they never should have made us go through the hoops for eighteen months."

In his three-page letter to Governor Bayh, Governor Engler tried to explain the reasoning behind his veto. The letter said that Michigan's attorney general, as well as its natural resources and public health departments, unanimously opposed Lowell's diversion proposal, and that both houses of Michigan's legislature had passed resolutions against it as well. "The issue of diverting Great Lakes water out-of-Basin is an extremely important and sensitive issue to the citizens of Michigan, who clearly have nothing to gain from diversions," the letter read. "While we are sensitive to the needs of the citizens of Lowell to reduce high fluoride levels in their public water supply, we believe that the first priority and obligation of the Great Lakes states and provinces must be to ensure continued protection of this invaluable resource." Governor Engler also highlighted the potential landmark status of Lowell's request. "Perhaps the most important reason that we oppose the Lowell diversion is the precedent-setting nature of the proposal." The letter went on to say that the governor envisioned cases in which a diversion request could be approved, but only when there was a true emergency like "an imminent danger to public health, safety, and welfare." He added that a diversion should only be considered when there were no other feasible water supplies to draw from, and that any diversion proposal should be accompanied by return-flow and strict conservation measures. "The assertion by the Town of Lowell that there are no feasible and prudent alternative water supplies other than Lake Michigan is not persuasive." Governor Engler believed that Lowell, while obviously in a bind, was not facing a water emergency—the town had other options that it was choosing not to pursue.[10]

More than a decade later, Governor Engler's perspective hadn't changed much. In an interview for this book he said he always thought that Lowell looked at the Great Lakes as the first option rather than a last resort. "That would absolutely qualify as the old way of doing things," he said. "I had to marvel at how the proponents of keeping Great Lakes waters in the Great Lakes Basin were strong and righteous, but then could look the other way when suddenly it was time to do something in their own backyard." He also confessed to being "dubious from the beginning" about Lowell's diversion application, saying that he "wanted to defend a point of view" about the Great Lakes being protected from potential precedent-setting diversions. "Since Michigan sits entirely in the Basin, if we don't care, it's hard to imagine that others will."

⌒

Many years have passed since the 1992 Lowell veto, and the case has been nearly forgotten by much of the general public, but not by regional water experts. Lowell marked a turning point in the Great Lakes diversion debate. For the first time since federal water-diversion legislation had been passed, a community that wanted to ship water outside the Great Lakes Basin had been turned down. "Lowell was a key moment in Great Lakes water-management history because somebody finally said no," notes Jeff Edstrom, a former official with the Council of Great Lakes Governors. On the surface, it appeared that WRDA had worked in the Lowell case. A proposal was made, it was evaluated fully for months, and then there was a vote. Some liked the outcome, some didn't, but the system appeared functional— at least to the public. Behind the scenes, however, there was a lot of grumbling. Some were starting to suggest that the water-management system in the Great Lakes Basin was inadequate and needed to be changed. Governor Engler said as much in his veto letter to Governor Bayh. "Reaching a timely decision has been made difficult by the lack of clearly defined procedures and criteria for evaluating diversion requests," he complained. "Neither the [Great Lakes] Charter nor the federal law provide adequate procedures or criteria to evaluate diversion proposals." Governor Engler said he would prefer that the Great Lakes governors establish diversion-review criteria "*before* any new diversions are allowed, not after."[11]

Many governors began to wonder about the effectiveness of WRDA as a piece of water-management law and, in particular, about the infringement it imposed on state sovereignty. What kind of monster had they created? Michigan, the only state almost entirely within the Great Lakes Basin, could simply veto every diversion request that came down the pipe, never having to worry about the political repercussions. The tensions surrounding the Lowell decision had shown what an emotional issue this was, and many wondered if the next diversion application might get uglier. "I thought if we can't . . . work through this on Lowell, the stakes are going to be much higher in other cases and you won't be able to jury-rig something," Tim McNulty says. "To me it wasn't just [about] the merits of the Lowell petition. . . . I could see [similar cases] on the horizon."

~

Whatever happened to Lowell? After some tense times in town, a lot of soul searching, and more than a few contentious public meetings, the community went on to sink new shallow wells outside of town— an option that citizens had rejected a few long years before. They also settled their legal case with the EPA, paying a fine of $65,000 in 1993. But not long after those shallow wells went on line, Lowell started experiencing problems. The wells were so shallow that they proved inadequate and unreliable, particularly in times of drought. Water rates increased markedly. By 2001—ten years after the town council voted to divert water from Lake Michigan—there was growing concern that Lowell would start to suffer economic hardship if a more reliable water source could not be found. A nearby quarry was considered as a water source, so was an expensive reverse-osmosis treatment system.

The town even toyed with the idea of asking for Lake Michigan water again.[12] Finally, in late 2002, a decision was made to drill some new wells in a field about three miles outside of town. "So we punched a well down," says David Gard, former town council president, "and we hit water. Lots, and lots, and lots, and lots, and lots, and lots, and lots, of water." It's not clear why all the water consultants Lowell hired ten years before had been unable to locate this apparent mother lode. Lowell mixed the new well water with old well water to stretch out both resources. "We're pretty confident about our water quantity," Mr. Gard said in 2005. "We're *very* confident about our water quality."

Does that mean Governor Engler was right? Many spurned residents in Lowell would have a hard time admitting it, but Dennis Schornack and Governor Engler think so. Even Mr. Gard admits that he can understand the logic behind Governor Engler's veto. Mr. Gard says he has been to Las Vegas and seen the conspicuous consumption of water that occurs there, with opulent golf courses in the desert and celebrated water fountains on the Strip. To a guy from Lowell, Las Vegas's green desert lawns and unbridled growth don't seem like they can last—unless water is shipped in from someplace else. "This is probably an unpopular opinion [in Lowell], but I almost understand them not giving us the water. You know, obviously, selfishly, at the time I wish they would have. But where do you stop? If the Basin's the barrier, is it one *foot* outside the barrier, or is it one *mile* outside the barrier? Or is it *ten miles* outside the barrier? So now you tell a community three miles out, 'Yeah, you can have it.' Then the guy four miles out says, 'Well what about me? I'm only four miles out.' Then, 'I'm only four hundred miles out.' Then, 'Well, I'm only two states away.' Then, before you know it, we're looking at wrecks at the bottom of Lake Michigan . . . because there's no water there either. People look at Lake Michigan and think it's an unending supply," Mr. Gard says. "It's not. The Great Lakes are very fragile. People think, 'Oh, they're going to be there forever because I can stand on the shore in Indiana and not see [the state of] Michigan. It's an unending supply of water.' That's a fallacy."

Governor Engler couldn't have said it better himself.

A decade later, Mr. Gard's bountiful optimism bumped up against the realities of water-supply management. By 2013, Lowell officials were once again expressing concerns about the quality and the quantity of the town's well water. Lowell's population had grown by 20 percent and the town was pumping 800,000 gallons per day during peak summer months, getting uncomfortably close to its 1.1 mgd capacity.[13] Nevertheless, town officials were contemplating annexing adjacent territory for growth. Lowell's tension between growth and water supply prompted the Alliance for the Great Lakes, a Chicago-based environmental group, to flag the town in a 2013 report as one of eight communities stretching from Wisconsin to Ohio that were most likely to apply for a Great Lakes water diversion in the future. "Lowell has also made known its plans to attract new business development by expanding its town borders, which will put an even greater demand on their water supply," the report warned. "The town may seek water from Lake Michigan in the future if no other reliable and cost-effective option is found."[14]

But Kevin Gray, Lowell's Public Works Director, said that, technically speaking, water quantity hasn't been an issue since the town added a new well in 2016. Rather, he said, once again the problem has been water quality—turbidity in one of the town's particularly productive deep wells. Lowell's attempts to tame the turbidity have brought mixed results. The town violated EPA turbidity health standards in 2014, and officials continue to tweak the chemistry in their water treatment plant in an attempt to maximize the full potential of their deep well water. "The water's here," Mr. Gray says. "We just have to figure out exactly how to get it out of the ground and treat it." The new shallow well in 2016 helped bump up Lowell's capacity to 1.4 mgd, but it continues to consider other water options, including tapping into the Kankakee River several miles away, punching more wells, or even diverting water from the nearby quarry that Mr. Gray says discharges roughly a million gallons per day into a stream.

What about Lake Michigan? Looking long term, Mr. Gray says he can't rule out possibly applying for a Great Lakes water diversion in the distant future. "We may be asking for water from Lake Michigan," he admits. "It's not something that we need tomorrow. But as growth occurs, it's a potential. But we've got a lot of options between now and then." The Great Lakes water-diversion application process has become much more rigorous since Lowell first applied for water in the 1990s. With so many "reasonable" water supply alternatives at its disposal, it's hard to imagine an application from Lowell getting very far. But as the only community ever to have been denied a Great Lakes water diversion, a new request from Lowell would definitely make headlines—especially if the community ended up being denied Great Lakes water a second time.

Chapter 10

Tapping Mud Creek

Gazing at a map of Michigan, it doesn't take long to recognize that the outline of the state's lower peninsula resembles a mitten. Michiganders are very familiar with this unique attribute of course. One of the most geographically recognizable parts of the state is an area that locals refer to as "the Thumb"—a broad peninsula due north of Detroit, bordered by Lake Huron to the east and the shallows of Saginaw Bay to the west. Long ago, Huron County laid claim to the tip of this peninsula— the thumbnail, if you will—and today the area is sparsely populated and highly agrarian, with a town named Bad Axe as its county seat.

Prior to European settlement, this area likely held some of the most impressive old-growth forests in all of the Great Lakes. David Cleland, a landscape ecologist with the US Forest Service, says that the soil conditions and hydrology of the area made it particularly well suited to growing tall, stout white pine and hemlock, some of which could have reached 500 years of age. During the last ice age, the northern Thumb region was scraped pool-table-flat, and the land drained very poorly, leaving the forest floor dented with wetlands and water-filled potholes. The result was classic old-growth Great Lakes forest that only exists in small remnants today. "In that area, white pine would have been as large, old, and as high quality as anywhere," Mr. Cleland says. "This was the perfect white pine / hemlock system."

Nineteenth-century lumber barons dreamed about these kinds of forests. The prized white pines were likely the first trees to be cut. The hemlocks would have been the next to go—their bark being an integral ingredient in the process for tanning leather at the time. Once the hemlocks were gone, lumberjacks would have clear-cut whatever hardwoods were left. The shaded, damp old-growth forests of the Great Lakes were some of the most fire-resistant timber stands in the world. But by removing the old-growth canopy, and leaving behind slash and kindling to dry in the hot sun, the lumber barons of the 1800s created an unnatural tinderbox that would bake and bake, until a lightning strike or some other source set off a conflagration. Two such ground-clearing wildfires swept through the Thumb in the late nineteenth century, the first in the early 1870s and the second a decade later.

With the landscape cleared and torched, a new wave of settlers moved in—the farmers. But before any serious agriculture could get under way, the hydrology of the region had to be altered. The flat, poorly drained land needed to be ditched and/or tiled to dry out the soil for spring planting. Long ago, most farmers in Michigan's Thumb laid drainage tiles three feet underneath the surface of their fields to help gently send water to ditches at the field's edge. "This area was swampland and woods and if it's not tiled, it can't produce. That's the bottom line," proclaims Jim LeCureux, who worked as an agricultural extension agent in Huron County for more than twenty years. Slowly, as farmers laid more and more subsurface tile, the Thumb's wetlands—like the forests before them—disappeared as the hydrology of the entire area was reworked to maximize the suitability of the land for agriculture.

While farmers did everything they could to dewater their fields in the spring, the land was often left wanting during the peak growing season, when the Thumb becomes one of the most arid places in the Great Lakes region. "Historically, there's a four- to six-week window in the summer [when], if we could have some rain, it would make a tremendous difference to the crops," Mr. LeCureux says. The right rain at the right time could help the yields of crops like corn and soybeans, and the well-timed water was precious to high-value cash crops like sugar beets and navy beans. Many farmers made do with what the clouds provided; others irrigated with water from the ground or nearby streams. But in the Thumb many streams were small and intermittent, making them an unreliable water source. And groundwater was spotty—new wells often came up dry or produced water that was too salty for crops or drinking. With the Thumb jutting out into the seemingly endless waters of Lake Huron, it was only a matter of time before local farmers started looking to the Great Lakes for irrigation.

That's exactly what happened in 1983 when three Huron County farmers marched into Jim LeCureux's office, armed with a grand plan. As the local agriculture extension agent, Mr. LeCureux's job was to serve as a conduit of information and expertise between the agricultural researchers at the state's universities and the farmers in the field. He also acted as a sounding board for farmers' ideas. In this case, the farmers had developed an elaborate irrigation scheme that grabbed Mr. LeCureux's attention. They had done their research, starting with an obscure irrigation law passed in the 1960s by the Michigan legislature following a period of low Great Lakes water levels. Under that law, farmers were allowed to form irrigation districts for the sole purpose of withdrawing water from the Great Lakes. But by the time that law had passed, the drought that had prompted it was over, so the statute fell dormant.

Sixteen years later, these farmers were proposing to dust off the law and put it to use in an ambitious way. Their plan was to pump millions of gallons of water from Saginaw Bay and pipe it due south along an abandoned railroad right-of-way, watering communities and farms along the way. It was one of the most enterprising water projects ever proposed in the area. Most intriguing of all, the plan called for subirrigation to deliver water to crops. Subirrigation is an efficient means of water delivery that pumps water into drainage tiles underneath farmers' fields to irrigate from below, avoiding the water waste and evaporation that's often associated with overhead irrigation networks. Mr. LeCureux remembers being impressed by the breadth and scope of the farmers' vision. "I was like 'Wow, this is unique!'" he says. Little did he know, however, that the farmers' plan would morph into an important and controversial case study in the history of the Great Lakes Charter.

∼

Like any good extension agent would, Jim LeCureux passed the irrigation idea along to his superiors. Meanwhile, the farmers approached their local congressman to ask for financial help. Fortunately for them, their congressman was Bob Traxler, a seasoned Democrat in the US House of Representatives who held seats on the appropriations and agriculture committees. Congressman Traxler had a reputation for bringing home the bacon, and in this case he let his constituents know that things were looking good. People in Huron County were getting excited. Then came the stumbling blocks. The first problem was that the 1967 law permitted creating irrigation districts solely for agricultural purposes, meaning that local communities were on their own. The next problem was bureaucratic. Agriculture officials in Michigan, while impressed with the farmers' grand plan, wanted the state's first irrigation district to start off small—a limited pilot project that would draw less negative publicity if it didn't work out. Congressman Traxler managed to shake loose some research funds, and during the next several years a wide array of feasibility studies were conducted in Huron County to determine how and where to set up the irrigation pilot project.

"We analyzed the hell out of that [land]," remembers Mike Gregg, with the Michigan Department of Agriculture. "We went through that whole area with ground-penetrating radar to understand the subsoils, to know where they could subirrigate. There was a lot of money invested." As part of the research, Mr. LeCureux planted a series of irrigation test plots and found that timely application of water during the dry season could increase yields more than 25 percent for cash crops like dry beans and sugar beets. So much research was produced that two hardcover volumes, containing more than 600 pages of detailed information, were published on the project.[1] "There were a whole lot of studies," Mr. LeCureux says. "All this work was funded by money from Traxler." No cost, it seemed, would be spared to make sure that the pilot project was a success.

Finally, officials decided to locate the irrigation district in the northwest corner of the Thumb, on 2,500 acres of land just a few miles south of Caseville, near a straight, mile-long ditch with the unassuming name of Mud Creek. On February 26, 1990, more than a dozen farmers submitted a petition to form the Mud Creek Irrigation District. Under the irrigation plan, the Mud Creek ditch, which naturally flowed into Saginaw Bay, would be deepened so that water would end up flowing in reverse, allowing Great Lakes water to flow far inland where it could be used to irrigate farmers' fields. At the inland terminus of Mud Creek, a series of irrigation pumps would be installed to send the water throughout the 2,500-acre district. In the formal language of the irrigation petition, the farmers pledged that their project would "not materially injure other users of the waters of the Great Lakes" and that it would not "prejudice the state in its relations with other states bordering on the Great Lakes." The Mud Creek pilot project was much smaller than the grand plan that had been hatched seven years before, disappointing many farmers who were turned away. But those who didn't make the cut were buoyed by assurances that if the Mud Creek plan succeeded, irrigation likely would be expanded throughout the area, if not beyond.

Before farmers could contemplate expansion, however, they had to get the initial Mud Creek plan approved. The irrigation petition landed on the desk of David Hamilton, who was then the chief of the Michigan Department of Natural Resources Water Management Section. He recognized its significance immediately. "I pulled together a team within the department," he says, "because it was pretty clear that there were a lot of potential implications of this." The team came up with roughly a dozen significant environmental questions that the farmers would have to answer in order to get an irrigation permit from the DNR. Mr. Hamilton remembers the farmers had a hard time understanding what all the fuss was about. "Their attitude was, 'We just want to grow our corn. This is just water, what's the big deal?'" he says. Finding the answers to many of the DNR's permitting questions was not going to be cheap, and the farmers were unwilling to put up their own money for the research needed to provide the answers. So they went back to Congressman Traxler. "If the federal government hadn't been willing to put money into this," Mr. Hamilton says, "It never would have gotten anywhere."

The farmers used federal funds to hire a team of consultants who put together a polished, thirty-page report outlining the details of the irrigation district, complete with charts, maps, and a thorough hydrologic analysis—all designed to alleviate the DNR's concerns. In the report, the consultants referred to Mud Creek's potential precedent-setting nature by saying that a number of agricultural agencies and farming groups had expressed "widespread interest" in this "first of its kind" project. The report went to great lengths to emphasize that the irrigation district suffered from a dearth of surface and groundwater options, and it reiterated that the irrigation would be seasonal, only taking place for fifty to eighty days per year, starting around early June and continuing through early August. In addition, the report said that the farmers only planned to irrigate 1,800 of the 2,500 acres and that when the pumps were running the farmers would use an average of 8.6 million gallons of water per day (mgd). During a severe drought year, the consultants said, that could potentially increase to 14.4 mgd. The report juxtaposed the Mud Creek withdrawal with the much, much larger Illinois diversion of 2.1 billion gallons per day, stating that Mud Creek was puny by comparison.[2]

While this comparison was certainly valid, a more telling comparison might be with Lowell, Indiana (see chapter 9). That village, which had a population of 7,900 people at the time, was denied a 1-mgd diversion request in 1992 thanks to a veto by Michigan governor John Engler. On an annual basis, Lowell's diversion request would have totaled 365 million gallons per year. By comparison, the consultants were estimating that the Mud Creek Irrigation District was planning to use 430 million gallons of water annually. That's 20 percent more water than Lowell planned to use. It's worth noting that Mud Creek's water would be used by a handful of farmers during just a few weeks, all for the purpose of increasing the farmers' profit margin on crops—and at the time some of those crops were already produced in surplus. Lowell's diversion, by contrast, would have provided water to a village of several thousand people that was under a federal order to improve the safety of its drinking water. The Mud Creek / Lowell comparison is a case study in how much water agricultural irrigation uses compared with "domestic" use in an urban setting. This helps explain why irrigation has often been the single-largest consumer of Great Lakes water in the Basin.[3]

But there was a key difference between Mud Creek and Lowell. Lowell was a diversion outside the Great Lakes Basin, while Mud Creek was a "consumptive use" inside the Basin, meaning that the water withdrawn would not breach the Basin boundary even though some water would be lost to the system. Irrigation water that did not evaporate, or end up in the crops, would eventually trickle down to the local aquifer, or even drain back into Lake Huron. Like Lowell, the Mud Creek project alone would have had an imperceptible effect on

levels and flows in the Great Lakes. Mud Creek's consultants anticipated the project would drop the level of Lake Huron by an infinitesi-
mal 0.0000455 feet.[4] More importantly, however, the project would not
set a diversion precedent.

Dave Hamilton gladly accepted the consultants' report. But his
team was growing increasingly concerned about a new and emerging
environmental issue that the report did little to address—zebra mussels. During the early 1990s, zebra mussels were a major concern in the
Great Lakes, clogging water-intake pipes and costing regional power
companies and municipal water utilities millions of dollars in repairs
and maintenance. The fingernail-sized invasive species had likely been
transported to the Great Lakes in the ballast water of oceangoing ships.
With no natural predators in the Great Lakes, they spread pervasively.
By early 1993, Mr. Hamilton's team was so worried about the spread
of invasive species that they determined the zebra mussel issue to be a
deal-killer. The problem was that the zebra mussels' larvae were practically microscopic and seemed all but impossible to filter out. Pumping
them through a large, twenty-seven-inch pipe was bound to contami-
nate the entire irrigation district and adjoining inland waters with this
unwanted species. Mr. Hamilton told the irrigation district which way
his experts were leaning, and the farmers asked for more time. Eventually they found special filters fine enough to strain the mussel larvae
out, and the irrigation district was back on track for approval.

While Mr. Hamilton was worrying about zebra mussels, he was also
getting political pressure from above. During 1992, Governor Engler's
office was struggling with Lowell's diversion request, and his political
operatives didn't want news of the Mud Creek application to create a
political sideshow to the whole Lowell affair. Aides told Mr. Hamilton
to stall Mud Creek to prevent both Great Lakes water requests from
showing up in newspapers at the same time. "The governor's office
wanted us to slow down," Mr. Hamilton says. "They didn't want [Mud
Creek] to come up right then. So as soon as Lowell was past, Mud
Creek was ready, and so we went forward."

By obtaining the zebra mussel filters, the farmers had gotten closer
to their permit. But there was one more hurdle yet to jump, and it
was not insignificant. With an average usage of 8.6 mgd, the Mud
Creek irrigation plan was large enough to trigger the Great Lakes

Charter, which covered diversions or consumptive-use applications greater than 5 mgd (see chapter 4). That meant Michigan needed to seek the "consent and concurrence" of all the other Great Lakes states and provinces before moving ahead with Mud Creek. (Because Mud Creek was a consumptive use, and not a diversion, the federal Water Resources Development Act did not apply.) Though the Charter was nonbinding, the signatories had pledged to uphold a lofty "spirit of cooperation" regarding water-management issues. Governor Engler would have to send a letter to all the other Great Lakes governors and premiers notifying them of the proposed withdrawal. If just one of those officials requested a "consultation," a public hearing would have to be organized so water experts from throughout the Great Lakes could vet the project.

On November 4, 1992, six months after Governor Engler vetoed the Lowell diversion request, he sent a letter to all the Great Lakes governors and premiers notifying them of the Mud Creek consumptive-use proposal. That letter was followed by a packet that included the consultants' thirty-page report. Those materials set off a burst of activity throughout the Great Lakes Basin, as six governors and premiers sent back a stack of letters all requesting or supporting a consultation on Mud Creek.[5] Michigan responded by scheduling a consultative hearing for April 28, 1993, at a hotel near the Detroit Airport.[6]

Interestingly, a representative from every Great Lakes state and province attended the consultation. But there were very few members of the public. Only twenty-nine people were in attendance; of those, just three were nonbureaucrats—two environmentalists and one Saginaw Bay marina operator. Everyone else was an official of one sort or another. The meeting lasted all day. Every state and province took advantage of its opportunity to ask questions and level concerns about Mud Creek, and some of the discussions were quite stern. Illinois, Indiana, and Québec all accused Michigan of inconsistent water-management policy, arguing that it was hypocritical for Governor Engler to oppose the Lowell diversion while supporting the Mud Creek consumptive-use proposal. Illinois's representative, Dan Injerd from the state's DNR, went so far as to suggest that Michigan either needed to deny the Mud Creek proposal or revisit its veto of the Lowell diversion.

In one of the meeting's more memorable moments, Jim Heben-streit from the Indiana DNR asked the Michigan delegation to explain exactly how the Lowell case differed from Mud Creek. Dennis Schornack, who represented Governor Engler at the meeting, said that Michigan residents considered consumptive uses—where the water use remains within the Great Lakes Basin—to be different from diversions of Great Lakes water outside of the Basin. Michiganders believed that as long as water was applied on the ground within the Basin it would eventually make its way back to the Great Lakes. Diversions, meanwhile, would be lost forever.[7]

Terry Yonkers, the representative from Great Lakes United, a binational environmental group, hammered the project and argued that using a subsidized irrigation system to raise crops that were already in surplus smacked of the "disastrous" federally subsidized water projects of the American Southwest. Like many in the room, he questioned whether such a project was a "reasonable" use of Great Lakes water, arguing that the Mud Creek project would be using Basin water on the "wrong crops, in the wrong place, at the wrong time." By the end of the consultation, both Canadian provinces and the state of Indiana made it clear that they had serious reservations about the Mud Creek plan, and many other states were far from supportive. By the meeting's end, the group had not come close to the consensus that the Great Lakes Charter demanded.

Governor Engler was undeterred. On May 7, 1993—exactly a year to the day after he announced his veto of Lowell's water request—he sent a letter to the governors and premiers alerting them that, despite the concerns raised at the consultation meeting, his staff would recommend that the Mud Creek proposal be approved. His letter made no reference to the fact that regional consensus had not been met. "We feel confident," Governor Engler wrote, "that the rigorous requirements of the Mud Creek proposal will set new standards of excellence for consumptive water use in the region."[8] He gave the other governors and premiers just thirty days to send any final written remarks, as he expected the project would be voted on in coming weeks. Under Michigan law at the time, the governor didn't have final say over the approval of irrigation districts. That approval had to come from the seven gubernatorially appointed members of the state Natural

Resources Commission, which often follows the recommendations of the state DNR. (In this case, because the zebra mussel issue had been resolved, the DNR recommended approval of the Mud Creek project.)

Governor Engler's May 7 letter set off an unprecedented volley of angry, critical, and sarcastic correspondence from his peers around the Great Lakes Basin. Democrats as well as the governor's fellow Republicans were equally critical of the project. The first response came from Governor Jim Edgar, a Republican from Illinois.[9] While Governor Edgar said that Illinois "will not object" to Mud Creek, Illinois remained "concerned with the appearance of inconsistency" on Governor Engler's part. Governor Edgar concluded his letter by saying that Illinois remained unsatisfied with the current system of judging Great Lakes water withdrawals, and he hoped that the Council of Great Lakes Governors might find a way to "restore regional unity" in the Great Lakes Basin.

Ontario premier Bob Rae and Minnesota governor Arne Carlson (a fellow Republican) openly chided Governor Engler for providing subsidized water for the production of surplus commodity crops. Meanwhile, some of the stiffest criticism came from Governor Evan Bayh. Thanks to Governor Engler's Lowell veto, if anyone was going to oppose the Mud Creek water proposal, it would be the governor of Indiana. "The utilization of Great Lakes water for the economic benefit of such a small number of individuals does not represent a prudent water management philosophy for the Great Lakes," Governor Bayh wrote. Then, in a section of the letter dripping with sarcasm, he said that if Governor Engler's support of Mud Creek was a sign that he had changed his position on the use of Great Lakes water, then by all means "we would welcome the opportunity to reopen discussion of the Lowell diversion proposal. Certainly that proposal would reap far more public benefit with less negative impact on the Great Lakes than the Mud Creek proposal." For these reasons, Governor Bayh concluded, he was objecting to the Mud Creek plan under the Great Lakes Charter.

Despite all the criticism, there's no sign that these letters had any effect on Governor Engler. So on June 10, 1993, after a decade of studies, debate, hearings, heated correspondence, and hand-wringing, the Michigan Natural Resources Commission convened to consider the Mud Creek proposal. In a 5–1 decision, the commissioners followed the recommendation of the Michigan DNR and adopted the Mud Creek irrigation plan. But the commissioners were completely unaware of the stream of heated letters that governors and premiers had sent to Governor Engler's office the week before their vote. For reasons that remain a mystery, the letters somehow didn't make it to the DNR nor even to the Michigan Office of the Great Lakes—the two departments charged with briefing the commissioners on any last-minute developments before the vote. Cynics smelled a conspiracy. They accused Governor Engler's staff of burying the letters in his office until after the commissioners voted. But the governor's staff would later blame the snafu on simple incompetence in managing the paper flow in his office. Whatever the case, G. Tracy Mehan, head of the Office of the Great Lakes at the time, was apparently in the dark when he sent a memo to the commissioners on June 9—the day before the Mud Creek vote—stating that no complaints had been received from governors and premiers. "As of this date, we have received no notice or information from the Great Lakes States and Provinces that the Mud Creek project would materially injure other users of the Great Lakes or significantly affect the levels of the Great Lakes," his memo read. He added that the project "does not appear to jeopardize Michigan's relations with other states bordering on the Great Lakes."[10]

That was a surprising claim. Even in the absence of the most recent heated gubernatorial correspondence, it seems bizarre for Mr. Mehan to have assured commissioners that the Mud Creek proposal would not jeopardize relations with other states. Indiana had definitely expressed its disappointment about Mud Creek at the April 28 consultation meeting. It should have been obvious to Mr. Mehan—and everyone else on the commission—that, if nothing else, the Mud Creek proposal would have damaged relations with at least one other Great Lakes state. Why is that important? Above and beyond the consensus approach that the Great Lakes Charter requires, one could argue that Michigan's own laws prohibited an irrigation plan that created friction with its neighbors. Remember the dusty old irrigation law that the farmers were waving about in Jim LeCureux's office back in 1983? That law specifically states that water shall not be withdrawn from the Great Lakes if such a withdrawal will "prejudice the state in its relations with other states bordering on the Great Lakes."[11] A number of officials and environmental advocates appear to have failed to do their homework on that point.

When word of the letter mix-up became public, Governor Engler suffered a severe beating in the newspapers. One commissioner who voted for Mud Creek told *The Grand Rapids Press* that he now felt as if he hadn't properly considered the issue. The same article quoted Kent Lokkesmoe, director of the Minnesota DNR's water division, as saying that there was a "feeling that Michigan is hypocritical" when it comes to Great Lakes water use. An editorial in Michigan's *Bay City Times* said the commissioners had acted "hastily" in approving the Mud Creek project. The *Kalamazoo Gazette* said that Governor Engler had "decreed that Michigan will operate under one standard while applying different standards for others."[12] But the most fervent criticism came from an editorial in *The Grand Rapids Press*, published on July 25, 1993. Under the headline "Diversion by Omission," the editorial said, "Gov. John Engler threw cold water in the face of anyone who thought he was a strong advocate for the Great Lakes. He has shown contempt for the lakes and international agreements in his handling of [Mud Creek]. . . . The governor looks like a hypocrite." The editorial added that obviously the Mud Creek withdrawal would have no physical impact on Lake Huron's water level, but that wasn't the point. "The issue is principle, not quantity. Any removal of water—whether it's to a Great Lakes drainage basin or not—should be allowed only when there's a serious public need and obvious benefit. Neither is the case with the Lake Huron proposal." The controversy prompted environmental groups to ask the Natural Resources Commission to reconsider its vote, but the commissioners refused.

Back in the Thumb, the Mud Creek Irrigation Board was euphoric—most notably because the affirmative decision came just before a $700,000 federal construction grant for the project was due to expire. Once approved, it took three more years for the irrigation district to be completed (the main holdup was convincing the state officials that the zebra mussel filters worked as promised). On August 8, 1996—thirteen years after three farmers walked through Jim LeCureux's door—Michigan released a boosterish press statement marking Mud Creek's completion. "This project is a tribute to those who work the land," Governor Engler cheered in the statement. In a reference to the $2 million in federal subsidies, he added that the Mud Creek project "shows public and private partnerships at their finest." The statement boasted that Mud Creek was the first irrigation project of its kind in the Great Lakes region and that Governor Engler had "led the effort and consulted other regional governors about the consumptive use of Great Lakes waters." Buried toward the end of the press release, officials mentioned the $2-million price tag and added that during the "start-up phase" only five farmers would participate in the district, irrigating just 700 acres. That works out to a federal subsidy of $400,000 per farmer.

How many farmers stayed in the Mud Creek Irrigation District? A total of four. Phil Leipprandt is one of them. Mr. Leipprandt is a solid, broad-shouldered man with a friendly, unassuming demeanor and the strong, callused hands of someone who has spent his life working the land; indeed, his ancestors were some of the first people to settle the area during the late 1800s. He was more than happy to show a stranger around the Mud Creek pump station. Over the years he has used Mud Creek water to raise corn, sugar beets, and alfalfa on 260 acres, which is just one parcel of land that he owns in the area. The irrigated lands have regularly outperformed his other acreage, particularly during droughts. During dry times, he says, "It's sure been helpful to have a few good fields." But in 2003, it was so dry that water levels in Saginaw Bay dropped to a point where water no longer flowed into Mud Creek at all. He and his fellow irrigators were out of luck.

During a long period of low lake levels in the years that followed, things got so bad that everyone stopped using Mud Creek water. The creek was dry, except on days when there was a stiff west wind that would push Saginaw Bay water up the channel, says Gary Osminski, Huron County's deputy drain commissioner. "Quite frankly, it hasn't been used in a number of years," he says. Mr. Osminski's office is supposed to file annual reports on Mud Creek with the state Department of Environmental Quality, even if no one irrigates during the year. "Technically we're supposed to file if there's no usage," he says. "[But] we would typically forget and the DEQ would call, and we'd send them a letter saying there was zero usage. That went on for several years. Well, then they quit calling. So we haven't filed anything in the last three, or four, or five years, or whatever it's been. But it's been zero usage."[13] What's the historical significance of that? The 1967 irrigation law was specifically passed by the Michigan legislature to give farmers a new weapon in combating drought. But ironically, when the first irrigation district created under that law was confronted by drought, lake levels fell to a point where irrigators were unable to deliver Great Lakes water to their fields. The Mud Creek irrigation plan didn't work when farmers needed it most. The zebra mussel filters that caused so much delay—and so much extra expense—are no longer in use because the mussels have become so pervasive that officials have given up trying to prevent their spread to Great Lakes tributaries. As one of the few farmers who experienced some success with the project, Phil Leipprandt's not exactly thrilled with how things have ended up. "If I had to do it over again," he says, "I don't think I'd go through it."

With an endorsement like that, the experiment at Mud Creek can be considered a $2-million flop. But the Great Lakes Charter proved to be a failure as well. The ineffectual Mud Creek consultation was a damning revocation of the spirit of the Charter and an indictment of the document's nonbinding status. The cooperative *esprit de corps* that marked the signing of the Charter in 1985 was shattered by Governor Engler's decision to promote the interests of a tiny political constituency at the expense of Basin-wide consensus. Many of his peers were offended that Michigan would approve a project that seemed so lacking in merit, despite their objections. Others were disappointed that the first consumptive-use test case under the Charter had such a divisive outcome. Sure, there was a healthy airing of views, but what good is that if there's no attempt to forge a consensus? Dick Bartz, who had helped draft the Charter, attended the Mud Creek and Lowell consultations for the Ohio DNR. He says some states and provinces were "incredulous" that Michigan had approved the Mud Creek project. "There's this geopolitical tension," Mr. Bartz says, "[and] some distrust of Michigan that continues today." There aren't many people who think that the Charter worked as planned at Mud Creek, but the few who do are from Michigan.

G. Tracy Mehan says the Mud Creek case brought out some fundamental differences among states and provinces in the Basin about consumptive uses. "People sort of used [Mud Creek] as a forum to vent about consumptive uses, saying, 'Hey, why was Michigan doing this when they opposed Pleasant Prairie or Lowell, Indiana,'" he says. "Of course, the difference was we're residents of the Basin. This is a consumptive use within the Basin, so it's not the same case at all. . . . Maybe there was some failure to dot the i's and cross the t's under the Charter, but this thing was heavily reviewed by technical staff," he says. "At the end of the day the key issue was whether it was within or without the Basin. It was within the Basin. That's Michigan's good fortune, which a lot of people begrudge. But when you have almost your entire state within the watershed, it's a big difference. Watersheds mean something."

Governor Engler is unapologetic about how the Mud Creek case ended up. "We looked at Mud Creek as completely in the Basin. That was simply the distinction," he says. "That [water] wasn't going anywhere." What's more, he says that from the beginning he saw the complaints about Mud Creek as an attempt to seek revenge for his veto of Lowell's water application, especially with regard to Indiana. "I just assumed that it was a little bit of payback time, more than a principled criticism of what water policy ought to be." But he adds that the Mud Creek episode was also a sign that the Charter had already started to deteriorate. Talk had begun about the need to implement a more comprehensive regional water-management paradigm in the Great Lakes region. "I think part of what we did at Mud Creek probably showed that the Charter itself needed to be fixed," he says. "[The charter] represents a statement of intent, but . . . they just never took the next step to turn it into a binding agreement." When he was told about what a multimillion-dollar flop the Mud Creek project had become, Governor Engler declined to call the experiment a mistake. But he didn't defend it either. Instead he suggested that perhaps the best lesson to be learned from the experience is that both the farmers and the environmentalists appear to have exaggerated their claims about the project. "From both sides it probably was an overreaction," he says. "For the proponents [of Mud Creek] there weren't nearly the benefits, and for the opponents there wasn't nearly the impact [on the ecosystem]. It became almost a nonevent."

By the mid-1990s, with the Mud Creek case fading in the Basin's collective memory, many Great Lakes officials were hopeful that the distrust and negative feelings from the project could somehow be channeled into improving the regional water-management system. But it would take a few more years, and a few more controversial test cases, before the collective opinion in the Great Lakes region would reach a point where officials were finally prompted to act.

Chapter 11

Akron Gets the Nod

Back in the early 1900s, Akron, Ohio, had a serious water problem. Between 1900 and 1910, its population had boomed by 60 percent, making the city of 70,000 people so overcrowded that boarding houses were renting beds in shifts.[1] The cramped living conditions were bad, but even more troubling, the local water supply had not kept pace with the robust growth. What water there was ended up becoming so tainted with runoff and pollution that it often made people sick. Summit Lake, the shallow water body that had long been Akron's main water source, was growing increasingly fetid. In desperation, local water officials sank more than seventy wells during the early 1900s, but the overtapped gravel aquifer beneath the city proved to be underwhelming. During a major fire in 1909 there was not enough water to pressurize hydrants. "Many Manufacturing Concerns Wiped Out in Maelstrom of Flames," roared the *Akron Beacon Journal*. "Water Pressure Extremely Low."[2] Months later, state officials, already aware of Akron's water scarcity problem, condemned Akron's entire water supply as a health hazard.[3]

Part of the problem was that the city's water came from a derelict private utility called the Akron Water Works Company, which was either unwilling or unable to resolve the situation, forcing city leaders to step in. "It may be said that the quality of water supplied by the Akron Water Works Company has never been satisfactory for any length of time," proclaimed a city report from 1911. "Conditions surrounding Summit Lake [are] seriously contaminated and vegetable organisms have been present in such quantity as to affect the physical character of the water [and] render it offensive to sight and smell."[4]

Due to the extreme water-quality and -quantity issues, engineers recommended a completely new water source: the Cuyahoga River. They proposed damming the Cuyahoga upstream near the Village of Kent to create a reservoir for up to 350,000 people, from which Akron could pipe water roughly ten miles southwest to its residents. Akron's mayor strongly urged the city council to adopt the engineers' recommendations. "Akron is facing one of the most critical situations in the history of the city. . . . We must act, and act at once."[5] On September 6, 1911, the council adopted the engineers' recommendations, which included buying out the Akron Water Works Company for $815,000.

While the engineers were drafting their plan for the Cuyahoga, Akron politicians were busy working the halls of the statehouse in Columbus. What they wanted was unprecedented legislation granting Akron special water rights. The recent water crisis had given the city a scare, and officials wanted permanent water security—they wanted water they could own, not just use. Water rights like that are pervasive in the western United States, where the prior appropriation doctrine permits people to own water rights, without the burden of having to share them with others. But in the eastern United States, water law is based on what's known as the riparian reasonable use doctrine, which is very different. Riparian reasonable use holds that those who own property along a lake or stream may withdraw all the water they need as long as their water use is "reasonable" and doesn't infringe on other property owners who also have access to the same body of water. In other words, in the East people don't own the water, but they have guaranteed rights to access it, within certain limits. But that wasn't good enough for Akron. Instead, the city was asking the state legislature to take the unusual step of nudging aside the riparian reasonable use doctrine and granting the city special Western-like rights to own the river water. That strategic decision would lay the groundwork for a hundred years of water conflict in the greater Akron area. By the end of the twentieth century, Akron would become one of the most heated water battlegrounds in the entire Great Lakes region.

~

After an extended period of political arm-twisting, the city got the water rights it was looking for. On May 17, 1911, the Ohio legislature passed a bill declaring that Akron "and the inhabitants thereof" had the right to "divert and use forever" the waters of the "Tuscarawas River, the Big Cuyahoga and Little Cuyahoga rivers. . . . The governor, upon behalf of the state, shall execute and deliver to the city of Akron . . . a grant of the right to use forever the waters of such streams, as herein provided."[6] Governor Judson Harmon then drafted what is referred to as the "governor's deed"—a document that mimicked the language in the 1911 legislation and essentially served as the legal title to Akron's water rights. Not long thereafter, Akron broke ground on a reservoir that would later become known as Lake Rockwell, which remains the city's chief water source (see map page 187).

But Akron's plan to grab water from the Cuyahoga upstream and pipe it ten miles south rattled several towns that lined the section of the river between Lake Rockwell and Akron. There were times when the Cuyahoga's flow was low or unpredictable, and officials from these towns worried that Akron's pipeline bypass might leave their communities wanting for water during low-flow times of year. In 1913, the community of Cuyahoga Falls challenged the governor's deed in court. Like other communities sandwiched between Akron and its proposed dam, Cuyahoga Falls worried that the exclusivity of the governor's deed might prompt Akron to someday take all the water in the river. But Akron won that case, and during subsequent years, the city repeatedly won several other court challenges to its unique water right. The Lake Rockwell reservoir was completed in 1915, with a capacity of 2.3 billion gallons. In later years, it was followed by two other reservoirs constructed farther upstream: the 1.5-billion-gallon East Branch Reservoir in 1939, and the 5.9-billion-gallon Wendell R. LaDue Reservoir, in 1962.

This Cuyahoga Valley reservoir system is just one piece of an elaborate puzzle that makes up the complicated water matrix in the greater Akron area. To the northeast of the city lies Lake Rockwell and the rest of the city's 10-billion-gallon reservoir system. To the south is a state-run lake and reservoir system known as "the Portage Lakes." The area was home to a well-known Native American canoe portage path connecting the Great Lakes Basin to the Ohio-Mississippi River

Akron and the Cuyahoga River

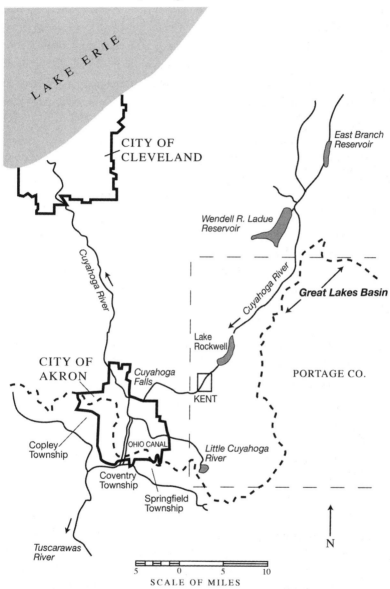

The water of the Cuyahoga River, once so polluted that it caught fire in Cleveland, has become a source of contention in the Akron metropolitan area. (Based on an original from the City of Akron)

watershed. Akron sits on the rim of the Great Lakes Basin, and is where the 250-mile Ohio and Erie Canal, completed in 1832, crossed the watershed line. The canal made it possible to ship cargo by boat from Montréal to New Orleans without ever having to touch the ocean. Canal commerce fueled the economy in Akron and much of northern Ohio. But two centuries of water engineering have blessed Akron with one of the most complex water systems in the Great Lakes region.

Flooding problems and competition from railroads eventually made the canal obsolete, but the Ohio Department of Natural Resources operates a ten-mile remnant in Akron. At the south end of that remnant, water flows toward the Ohio River. At the north end it flows toward Lake Erie. At the middle, behind a nondescript apartment building near Lake Nesmith, you are standing atop the divide that marks the edge of the Great Lakes Basin, where the water seems confused about which direction to flow. "You can see the water come through here and meander and spin," says Josh Garretson, who has the complicated job of managing water in the canal and Portage Lakes for the Ohio DNR. "Supposedly it is one of the very few places in the world where you can see water travel simultaneously in both directions." That remnant section of the canal also flows through Akron's Summit Lake, which lies in Summit County—names that reference the fact that Akron sits on high ground straddling the Great Lakes Basin line.

～

By the 1920s, Akron's water problems were solved and the city boomed. Located in the heart of steel country, and just a few hours' drive from the auto factories of Detroit, Akron used its now-abundant water supply and central location to become the leading supplier of tires for the American auto industry. Akron billed itself as the "Rubber Capital of the World"—and with good reason. Tire companies like Goodyear, General, and Firestone all eventually built headquarters and/or factories there. Akron had become the rubber buckle on the steel belt, and in 1969 the city's water use peaked at 61 million gallons per day (mgd). But as the steel belt began to rust, Akron's rubber economy went flat. Manufacturing plants aged and became less efficient; many tire-producing jobs moved out-of-state or overseas. Akron's unemployment rate climbed, and the once-thriving city center deteriorated as people fled for outlying communities. Water consumption also declined, to roughly 35 mgd, and Akron found itself with a healthy water surplus.

Many surrounding communities discovered that it was cheaper to tap into Akron's water network than to build or expand their own. Akron created a process that allowed its neighbors to swap income tax for water and several communities bought in.[7] Akron may have fallen on hard times, but it had found a way to turn water into cash. "The driving force was economic development," explains Michael McGlinchy, former manager of Akron's Public Utilities Bureau. "What we had, as an asset to share, was our water and sewer service." But selling water to the suburbs can get complicated when you straddle the edge of the Great Lakes Basin. Smitten with its new idea to sell water to surrounding communities, in March of 1992 the City of Akron sent a letter to the Ohio Department of Natural Resources outlining its plan to extend water service of 4 million gallons per day to areas outside the Great Lakes watershed. Akron would pull water from the Cuyahoga River in the Great Lakes Basin and divert it to homes and businesses outside the Basin, where the water would be used, treated, and discharged into the Ohio River watershed.

Knowing that a diversion of this sort was a sensitive issue under Ohio law as well as with the Great Lakes governors, Akron came up with a plan to make up for that lost water. It would send replacement water back to the Cuyahoga (and thus the Great Lakes watershed) just a few miles downstream via the Ohio and Erie Canal. Hence, the city argued in its letter to the Ohio DNR that because the diverted water was replaced with water farther downstream it wasn't really a diversion at all—not under Ohio law nor, the city argued, under the federal Water Resources Development Act. What Akron didn't say, however, was that because of its circuitous return-flow plan, water would be withdrawn above Akron, and returned below Akron, meaning that more than ten miles of river between Lake Rockwell and the city would never see the diverted water.

The letter went on to say that, because the diversion wasn't really a diversion, Ohio needn't bother notifying the rest of the Great Lakes governors about the plan. (Keep in mind that at this time Lowell's diversion request remained active and had not yet been vetoed by

Michigan.) Near the end, the letter said that if the Ohio DNR decided that the department did need to notify the other governors about this non-diversion, Akron requested that "an informal interpretation" of WRDA be solicited "before any formal steps are taken to initiate the notice and consultation process under the Great Lakes Charter." Akron wanted to keep its water request quiet—at least for the time being.

Two months later, attorneys at the Ohio DNR determined that Akron was right, at least in part. Because the water was replaced, the lawyers said that under Ohio law Akron's diversion was not really a diversion. But the federal law was less clear, and the attorneys decided that Akron's diversion request would indeed have to be reviewed by the other Great Lakes governors, just like the proposals by Lowell, Indiana, and Pleasant Prairie, Wisconsin, before it. The next month, Ohio DNR officials met with representatives from Akron to break the news, which sent the city into a cooling-off period for two years. In the meantime, Lowell's water request was vetoed, and the Mud Creek consumptive-use proposal was approved despite the objections of other states and provinces (chapters 9 & 10).

In April of 1994, Akron officials approached the Ohio DNR again, ready to revive their proposal. Although two years had passed, it was as if nothing had changed. Akron stubbornly maintained that its diversion was not a diversion. DNR officials were not so sure whether WRDA applied, so they requested an "informal interpretation" from the Council of Great Lakes Governors. The verdict: a diversion from the Great Lakes Basin is still a diversion even if the water was replaced. Akron's plan would need to be approved by all eight Great Lakes governors.

~

Undeterred, Akron went to work putting together a proposal. The city hired two different consultants (at a cost of $250,000) to prepare a comprehensive report on the proposed diversion, complete with charts, graphs, maps, and a narrative.[8] A video and a color brochure were produced for distribution to the governors as well. Interestingly, neither the title nor the body of the brochure mentioned the word *diversion*. Instead, it was called: *Preserving the Great Lakes through Regional Cooperation, A Proposal by the City of Akron, Ohio.* The brochure was brief and to the point, explaining that Akron was located on the edge of the Great Lakes watershed and that the neighboring townships—with their contaminated wells and failing septic systems—were located "at least in part" in the Ohio-Mississippi River watershed. It emphasized Akron's greatest selling point: that thanks to its return-flow idea involving the Ohio and Erie Canal, there would be "no net loss" to the Great Lakes under this diversion proposal. "This ensures that water used by these townships will either be returned or replaced," the brochure read.[9]

The accompanying video hit that point even harder. In nine minutes of tape, the video mentions the words "no net loss" a total of seven times. The city admitted it had fallen on hard economic times, and that it was hoping to use surplus water as a way to generate badly needed revenue. Just like the brochure, the video managed to describe the Akron water project without once using the word *diversion*. The consultants' report contained less gloss and fluff, and it dove much deeper into detail about the project, estimating that the maximum annual amount for the diversion at 4.8 mgd. At the time the report was written, Akron had a population of 221,000 people and was using 47 mgd, well below the city's record water usage of 61 mgd. The townships had issues with contamination and water availability. They had dug several new wells recently, but had come up dry. The report said that the most promising underground water source near these suburbs had a former "waste disposal site" directly above it containing known carcinogens, and a nearby reservoir had water-quality problems.

On September 30, 1996, the report, video, and brochure were forwarded to all the governors and water managers in the Great Lakes region. At Akron's insistence, Ohio governor George Voinovich requested that the proposal be reviewed informally, and all comments and criticisms be returned to representatives at the Ohio DNR. Any feedback from around the Basin would then be integrated into a final report that would be formally recirculated among the governors and premiers later for their ultimate approval. "Once the technical review is complete," Governor Voinovich wrote, "I will follow up with you again."[10]

It is important to note that by this stage there had yet to be a public hearing about Akron's proposed diversion. There had not even been a public announcement about the diversion plan. At Akron's request, officials had kept its proposal quiet. But once a draft diversion document starts circulating around the Great Lakes Basin, it is almost impossible to keep it under wraps for long. Sooner or later an environmentalist—or a journalist—is going to get wind of it. On February 13, 1997, reporter Bob Downing of the *Akron Beacon Journal* published a story about the diversion, quoting a number of environmental advocates criticizing the proposal as a "precedent-setting end run that numerous other municipalities just beyond the edge of the Great Lakes Basin would use to try to justify diversions." The main critics were two of the leading environmental groups in the Basin at the time: the Canadian Environmental Law Association in Toronto, and Great Lakes United, based in Buffalo and Montréal. The two environmental organizations had just published a comprehensive report on the history of Great Lakes diversions, and they saw the Akron proposal as the latest sign that water management in the Great Lakes was creeping toward more diversions.

An exclusive scoop on the front page of the local paper is not exactly the coming-out party that Akron had planned for its non-diversion diversion. A number of local communities along the Cuyahoga River—especially in the ten-mile bypass stretch between Akron and Lake Rockwell—were shocked to read that Akron was working behind the scenes to cut a special water deal. They were particularly insulted that Akron's deal had been quietly floated to governors in *other states*—without holding a local public hearing first. Many of these upstream communities had grown resentful over the years as they watched Akron hoard the river water during times of drought. "Akron more or less indicated that they owned the river," says Larry Valentine, former head of the Cuyahoga Falls water utility. And thanks to the governor's deed, these streamside communities were powerless to do anything about it.

These towns already felt strongly that there wasn't enough Cuyahoga River water to go around. And now Akron wanted to pump river water outside the Great Lakes Basin? The news sent these communities into a panic. "The more we saw them pumping over the divide," Mr. Valentine says. "The less we saw coming down the river." Officials in Cuyahoga Falls had been unhappy with Akron's special water privileges ever since they filed suit against the governor's deed back in 1913.

But by the 1990s, Cuyahoga Falls had been joined by several other unhappy neighbors who were fed up with living on or near a river that Akron claimed to own. The list included the City of Kent, the Village of Munroe Falls, the Village of Silver Lake, and even the Portage County Board of Commissioners. "How we found out about it is the thing that made everybody upset," says Mr. Valentine. "They knew we were going to get upset. They were trying to get all their ducks in a row before they even approached us."

Dick Bartz says he never saw the controversy coming. Mr. Bartz had been working at the Ohio DNR's water division long enough to have been involved in drafting the Great Lakes Charter. He was also a key point person on the Akron diversion, and as a student of the Charter, his main concern was making sure that Akron's plan satisfied his peers in the Great Lakes Basin. After watching the Pleasant Prairie, Lowell, and Mud Creek cases, his eye was on regional governors' offices, not on a handful of communities in the Cuyahoga Valley. "We walked into a Hatfield-and-McCoy pissing match," Mr. Bartz admits. "We got blindsided by that." He says that he and his DNR colleagues had made a mistake in not informing the communities between Akron and Lake Rockwell about the proposed diversion, but he also says he had no idea that there had been such a longstanding level of antipathy and distrust. "Akron has kind of been the bully, in trying to bully these communities around using water, using sewer, using everything they can," Mr. Bartz says.

∽

After integrating regional feedback into the application, on March 31, 1997, Governor Voinovich circulated the official, public version of Akron's plan to the other Great Lakes governors and premiers. One by one, the various states and provinces sent in their approval letters, signing off on the diversion. Michigan, as usual, was the last state to give the nod. But in an odd way, for political reasons, Michigan needed the Akron diversion to be approved almost as much as Ohio did. Michigan had lost so much credibility in the Basin after the Mud Creek debacle that if it vetoed Akron too, that could have damaged interstate water relations in the Great Lakes region for years. In addition, Michigan had recently confronted Illinois over the Chicago River diversion, prompting new, out-of-court negotiations in that case—negotiations that eventually led to the Chicago River Memorandum of Understanding of 1996 (see chapter 5). So Michigan was picking water fights with many of its neighbors. "I think some hard questions were being put to [Michigan]," says Jack Bails, one of Akron's consultants. "Were they being unreasonable? . . . Were there *any* circumstances where they would approve use of Great Lakes water outside the Basin? Looking back, I think Michigan wanted to get back into the fold, if you will." Michigan officials realized, he says, that if they pushed things too far, the other Great Lakes states might ask for WRDA to be altered or revoked. If support for WRDA were to erode among the Great Lakes states—because of Michigan's intransigence or for some other reason—many observers think Congress would willingly rescind WRDA or at least weaken it.

Akron's no-net-loss return-flow was designed to be politically palatable for the Michigan electorate, so that the governor of Michigan could approve the Akron diversion without suffering political damage at home. "We saw what happened with Lowell, we saw how Pleasant Prairie went," Mr. Bartz says. "And it takes a lot of objections off the table if there's return-flow. . . . It was critical." In April of 1998—exactly six years after Akron had first approached the Ohio DNR about their non-diversion diversion—state officials sent word to Akron mayor Don Plusquellic that the Akron diversion had been approved by all eight Great Lakes governors. "Akron's proposal to extend drinking water service into Springfield, Coventry, and Copley townships has obtained the approval of all the Great Lakes States' Governors as required," the letter read. "The City may now initiate provisions of the drinking water service as proposed."

～

But Akron's water fight was far from over. On April 17, 1998, just two weeks after Michigan gave notice that it had approved Akron's diversion, attorneys representing the disgruntled Cuyahoga River communities sued Akron in state court, challenging a wide array of the city's water practices. "Shipping water across the Basin line to those townships was the straw that broke the camel's back," says Jack Van Kley, the attorney for the disgruntled communities. "That really was what set off the war."The result was that the Cuyahoga—once known the world over as the chronically polluted river that had repeatedly caught fire in downtown Cleveland—had become one of the most conflict-ridden water sources in the Great Lakes region.The heart of the communities' lawsuit was directed squarely at the 1911 governor's deed. They argued that Akron had taken its original water right and broadened it far beyond the deed's intended scope. They wanted the judge to rule that the 1911 deed did not grant Akron ownership to all the water in the Cuyahoga, and asked the judge to force Akron to provide a minimum flow in the river of 10.9 mgd.

Akron was unfazed.The day after the suit was filed, Mayor Plusquellic was quoted in the Cleveland *Plain Dealer* as saying, "They act like we don't have any rights to this water. We have purchased those rights. . . . You're going into issues that were resolved decades ago."[11] In the years following the 1911 deed, Akron had gone up and down the river buying land that had riparian water rights. Some challenged those purchases in court. Some won, some lost. But according to Akron, under Ohio law citizens have twenty-one years to make a claim in such cases, and that statute of limitations had run out long ago. "In a nutshell," said the city's former trial attorney Leslie Jacobs, "Akron's position is, 'You've got to be kidding! Where were you for the last hundred years?'" In its court filing, Akron argued it "has the right, among other things, to possess the water of the Cuyahoga River," and that the governor's deed gave the city the right to use the Cuyahoga "forever, without limitation as to amount . . . and there is no restriction upon Akron's sale of water outside the city limits."

The Ohio media had a field day with the litigation. One mayor from a disgruntled community was quoted by *The Plain Dealer* as saying, "I just can't believe that the state of Ohio can sell a city a river. . . . This to me is ludicrous. I don't care if it's 1911 or 1850. I don't think that can be done."[12] The *Akron Beacon Journal* later predicted that the trial would be moved to another part of the state because the controversy had reached the level of a "regional war for water."[13] Continuing the war analogy, on the eve of the trial in January of 2001, the *Beacon Journal* quoted Mayor Plusquellic, sounding particularly exercised: "If they say we're enemies, then fine. Let's do battle. . . . I didn't start this fight. . . . If I have to shut off water to little old ladies, and churches, and hospitals,

I'm sorry. They're on their own." The same article quoted Bob Brown, manager of the Kent, Ohio, wastewater-treatment facility, who said, "It's ironic [that] we're sitting next to the largest freshwater supply in the world, and we're still fighting about water."[14] As *The Plain Dealer* put it, "This fight sounds like it should be taking place in the water-starved Southwest between Colorado and Arizona."[15]

Before the case even went to trial, Mr. Van Kley filed a pretrial motion challenging Akron's claim that it owned the river under the governor's deed. "We went for the jugular early on by filing that motion," he says. The motion resulted in Akron's first big setback in the case. In a key ruling, on April 20, 2000, the judge found that the governor's deed did not grant Akron unlimited use of the Cuyahoga's water.[16] "We respectfully disagree with the judge's ruling," Leslie Jacobs was quoted as saying, adding that Akron would certainly appeal. "But to put it in context, if he had decided this in our favor—as we think the Ohio Supreme Court will do—the case would effectively be over."[17]

The trial lasted sixteen days and saw testimony that included, among other things, Mayor Plusquellic denying that he was a "bully." A total of twenty-seven witnesses testified, and the stack of legal documents for the case stood eight feet high. The two sides spent a combined $4.3 million preparing for trial.[18] The state judge took eight months to render a verdict, and during the interim both sides made it clear that no matter what the judge decided, the case would be appealed to the Supreme Court. In October 2001, Portage County Common Pleas Judge John A. Enlow released his twenty-eight-page opinion, and while it was a split decision, Akron came out on top.

The judge ruled that while the governor's deed did *not* give Akron the right to sell water to other communities, because Akron had purchased land along the river upstream, the city was a "riparian" landowner. And riparian landowners *can* sell water to their neighbors. So while the governor's deed did not allow them to sell the water, their riparian rights did. "Akron has a right as a riparian owner along the Cuyahoga River to take water for its own use, including the sale of water to others, as long as the amount of that taking is reasonable," he wrote. "This Court concludes that Akron's current taking of water from the Cuyahoga River at Lake Rockwell is not unreasonable."[19] The judge also suggested—but did not require—that the city should continue to release 5 mgd into the river—about half what the river communities had asked for. "We're quite pleased," Leslie Jacobs said after the verdict. "The judge's order sustains our position on all but two points."[20]

Both sides filed appeals the following month, and the longer the case dragged on, the more abrasive the court filings became. The briefs were punctuated with insulting words like *myopic, concocted, fairytale, fable, illogical,* and *revisionist.* When the appeal was finally heard two years later, the jurists seemed unsympathetic to both sides. One appellate judge asked Akron's lawyers whether they felt they had the right to "box up" Cuyahoga River water and "sell it to the people of Biloxi, Mississippi?"[21] On March 31, 2004, Ohio's Eleventh District Court of Appeals handed down its decision, which reversed the lower court's rulings on many counts. Most importantly to the river communities, the court ruled that the city must release a minimum amount of water from the reservoir every day. They declined to say exactly how much water, kicking that decision back to the lower court judge. The opinion, which ran for more than sixty pages, made plain that Akron did not rule the river quite as solidly as it had alleged, arguing that Akron's claim to *all* the water in the river was without merit.

The appeals court verdict was a clear victory for the river communities, and it was time for the plaintiffs to crow. "Akron held that it had an absolute right to the water in the river. We've already won the case because we've disproved that opinion," boasted Chuck Keiper, a Portage County commissioner. "Portage County has for the first time in a century regained its right to that river, which is important to our growth and our future. From that point alone it's worth every penny."[22]

As promised, however, both sides appealed the case to the Ohio Supreme Court. On March 6, 2006, the state's most influential jurists handed down their forty-page opinion, and while the Ohio media declared it a split decision, key segments of the opinion went against Akron. First, the justices agreed with other court decisions that Akron did not come close to owning the whole river or its tributary water as the city had claimed under the 1911 governor's deed. That, obviously, was a major victory for the plaintiffs. What's more, the supreme court decision forced Akron to ensure that a minimum amount of water flow downstream from the Rockwell Reservoir on a daily basis. This too was a coup for the plaintiffs, who worried that Akron might hoard water during droughts. Although the communities didn't get the 10.9 mgd minimum flow that they asked for, they came close, with the court requiring a minimum flow of 8.1–9.5 mgd.[23]

The decision meant that Akron's disgruntled neighbors had finally attained the water security that they had yearned for. It had been a long and bitter struggle. But of all the things that went their way in the courtroom, the communities were happiest to see that Akron's rigid claims under the 1911 governor's deed were thrown out. "The sweetest part," says their attorney Jack Van Kley, "was striking down their interpretation of the 1911 statute."

But Akron did not leave the courtroom empty-handed. The justices pointed out that the city *did* have rights to the river—the rights that Akron had obtained when it purchased the land upstream to create Lake Rockwell. What's more, the justices ruled that Akron's purchase of riparian rights also gave the city the power to legally ship water to other communities. That meant Akron's contested diversion (the one that the Great Lakes governors had approved) would stand.

Given that the state supreme court had finally ruled in the case, there was hope that Akron and its neighbors might finally begin the peace process in their water war. The court suggested as much in its opinion. "We leave the task of resolving future water-allocation issues in this region to appropriate planning authorities."[24] That theme was echoed in an *Akron Beacon Journal* editorial a few days later, "The water war between Akron and its upstream neighbors on the Cuyahoga River is over, hopefully for good."[25]

~

But what happens in an extreme drought? The river communities have spent the last century worrying that Akron would hold back water during a record-breaking dry spell. While the Supreme Court did require Akron to release at least 8.1 mgd, Akron's interpretation of the ruling is that the court was mum about what to do when there is not enough water to go around. "We've always felt that if we had a drought [then] we would be exempt from that release, but that point was never brought up in the ruling," says Ray Flasco, Akron's Water Quality Control coordinator. "We couldn't waste it by letting it go down the river. . . . I think that would negate the ruling or put it on hold for a while. You can't release water you don't have." But that is not how the other river communities see it. When Jack Van Kley, the attorney for the communities, was asked if that was his interpretation of the supreme court decision, his response was definitive: "No, absolutely not. There are not exceptions in the court order for any conditions, so they would still be required to release the same amount during a drought as they do at any other time." And what would happen if they refused? "They would be in contempt of court." Akron's water wars have certainly dissipated since the Supreme Court's ruling in 2006. But the continuing drought disconnect between Akron and its upstream neighbors suggests that the region may be just one drought away from yet another slog back to the legal trenches.

~

What are the lessons to be learned from the Akron case? The city's diversion proposal was approved a decade after the Great Lakes Charter and WRDA had been signed. During that time, three communities and one irrigation district had come forward to ask for Great Lakes water. Pleasant Prairie, Wisconsin, got its water, but questions remained about whether the diversion had been legally approved. Lowell, Indiana, was turned down, leaving at least one state unhappy with the system. Mud Creek, in Michigan, emerged victorious, but hapless. Now Akron was the first community to definitively receive unanimous support from all eight Great Lakes governors for its diversion, only to get bogged down by divisive litigation afterward. The Ohio legal case was a fascinating testament to how bitter water issues can be in a water rich region, but it was Akron's successful vote from the Great Lakes governors that mattered most in terms of Great Lakes water-management history.

Returning water back to the Great Lakes Basin was the crucial ingredient in getting that approval—a factor that would not be lost on future water applicants. While Akron had requested and received permission to divert 4.8 mgd, the diversion continues to be much smaller than that. At its peak, the Akron diversion has only averaged 1.1 mgd. "I've talked to other people around the country, and you don't find many economic development / freshwater agreements like Akron has," says Jeff Bronowski, head of the Akron water utility. "It's pretty dog-gone impressive." The Akron case also showed that a Michigan governor could indeed approve a diversion outside the Great Lakes Basin under certain circumstances. It also showed that after several awkward moments, the governors and premiers were finally formulating a system by which Great Lakes water-diversion requests could be judged. Precedent was being set, which would make it easier for future water applicants to gauge their chances of success.

But the Akron case also serves as a reminder that the governors and premiers are just one piece in the complex water puzzle in the Great Lakes region. Akron got its water, but was then hamstrung by a bitter legal case that cost millions and further soured relations with its neighbors. "Nobody likes the idea of someone else constraining his options," says Leslie Jacobs, Akron's former attorney. "But deep down beneath it all, there is a recognition that, even sitting on the edge of the Great Lakes, water is the principal constraining factor for economic development." In a region that has always taken water for granted, that may be the most important lesson of all.

Part III

New Rules of Engagement

Chapter 12

The Nova Group and Annex 2001

One evening in 1997, John Febbraro was lounging at home in Sault Ste. Marie, Ontario, when a narrator popped up on the television and began pleading for donations on behalf of the world's poor. As dolorous photos of impoverished faces flashed across the screen, the narrator talked about how—with just one dollar a day—viewers could change a person's life in the developing world. As Mr. Febbraro, a Canadian entrepreneur, listened to the sales pitch, he realized that these people didn't just need food—drinking water was a problem for them as well. That's when he came up with a bold and daring idea: to ship Great Lakes water to thirsty people halfway around the world. "They need water," he remembers thinking, "and literally we look in our backyard and we have tons of it!" In the days that followed, Mr. Febbraro huddled with a partner at his diminutive consulting firm, the Nova Group, and they began fleshing out a plan to use oceangoing bulk freighters to ship cool, clean Lake Superior drinking water to Asia. Mr. Febbraro, a former consultant to the Canadian space agency, spent the next several weeks contacting shipping companies, crunching numbers, and developing a business model. The more modeling he did, the more he became convinced of the project's viability. From a business school perspective, however, the model was somewhat unusual—a humanitarian effort on behalf of the world's poor that was also designed to make money. "It was a for-profit," he says unapologetically. "I mean, I'm an entrepreneur, right?"

The plan called for sending an empty bulk freighter out into Lake Superior a few miles northwest of Sault Ste. Marie, where the vessel would pump water into a large disposable liner inside the ship's hold. The water would be purified at a Great Lakes port before the ship continued on to the Far East. The plan was to start with a few shipping runs per year to see how it went and then expand the operation from there. With his strategy mapped out, in early 1998 Mr. Febbraro went down to a government office and was surprised at how easy it was to obtain a permit application. "There was an application that says 'for the withdrawal of bulk water,'" he remembers. "So that is what we filled out." He attached a brief business plan, and on March 31, 1998 (after a quiet, thirty-day comment period that elicited no response from the public), he was granted the permit. The document gave the Nova Group permission to export 158 million gallons of water to Asia per year—one ship at a time.

When news of Mr. Febbraro's water-export scheme hit the papers, it spread rapidly through the Great Lakes Basin, prompting an extraordinary and heated anti-diversion debate. "Sault Company Given OK to Sell Lake Superior Water to Asia," read the headline in the *Sault Star* on April 25, 1998. Congressman Bart Stupak, who represented Michigan's Upper Peninsula at the time, hit the airwaves. "This is Pandora's box," he warned. "We've always worried that somebody will try to divert Great Lakes water to arid regions. . . . My worst fears have been realized."[1] Ever since the Chicago River was reversed nearly a hundred years before, people had worried about additional diversions of Great Lakes water. But never before had someone stepped forward with a plan quite like this. Although most people on both sides of the border agreed that the Nova proposal was a bad idea, it heightened the international water tensions in the Great Lakes region. People were particularly alarmed that the proposal had managed to gain government approval without the public, the press, or politicians even knowing about it. "Nova identified a series of gaps," says Jeff Edstrom, who worked at the Council of Great Lakes Governors at the time. "It was something that wasn't really planned for. Today we think about water exports all the time, but before Nova, people's primary concerns were about pipes."

Mr. Febbraro found himself caught up in controversy and besieged by politicians, media, and average citizens on both sides of the border. "I was on the news almost every day," Mr. Febbraro exclaims. "*Time*

The Nova proposal to ship tankers of Lake Superior water to Asia generated extensive media attention in the United States and Canada, including this editorial cartoon by Tom Toles published on May 13, 1998. (TOLES © 1998 The Washington Post. Reprinted with Permission of ANDREWS MCMEEL SYNDICATION. All Rights Reserved)

magazine, CNN, CTV, ABC—it didn't matter." The controversial nature of his proposal caught him completely off guard. "I was absolutely surprised by the media attention," he says. The most ferocious criticism came from environmentalists. "A lot of environmental groups really got on our case," he remembers. "[They were] saying, 'What the hell are you trying to do here? You're going to set a precedent.'"

As usual, precedent was indeed the chief concern. Once Great Lakes water was turned into an international bulk commodity, how could Great Lakes officials turn off the tap? If the tiny Nova Group was allowed to export Lake Superior water, who could stop some of the largest international shipping conglomerates from lining up to do the same? And if it was okay to ship water to Asia, how could the region say no to the Ogallala or Nevada? While Mr. Febbraro was pummeled in the press, quiet alarm swept through government offices around the Great Lakes region. "It wasn't panic, and it wasn't really dread. At first it was confusion," Mr. Edstrom says. "No one really knew what the proposal was about. Nova had always talked about this water going to an Asian country, but no one could tell if they actually had a buyer. And there were a number of people who were concerned that Nova was a potential front for a big multinational corporation."

After more than a decade of trying to create a system to keep Great Lakes water in the Great Lakes Basin, John Febbraro had stumbled upon an embarrassing exception that left red-faced bureaucrats scrambling. In reality, there were enormous questions about the economic viability of Mr. Febbraro's scheme, but it raised new concerns about whether the Great Lakes were vulnerable to extraction under international trade accords. For years, water use in the Great Lakes had been controlled by an awkward series of agreements and water regulations. The Great Lakes Charter was well-meaning, but nonbinding. The Water Resources Development Act was binding, but only in the United States—and only for diversions, not consumptive uses—and there was worry that WRDA would not withstand a legal challenge. Mr. Febbraro's business plan slipped right through these piecemeal anti-diversion mechanisms. Because the proposal came from Canada, the WRDA legislation didn't apply. And because the diversion was less than 5 million gallons of water per day, it didn't trigger the prior notice and consultation stipulations of the Great Lakes Charter. What's more, at the time, no laws in Ontario prevented the export of Great Lakes water. For years the region had been obsessed about not setting a water-diversion precedent that breached the Basin line, even by just a few miles, for fear that it could set the stage for long-range diversions later on. But here was a diversion proposal that set a precedent for sending Great Lakes water all the way to *Asia*. If people were allowed to ship water to Asia, where couldn't they send it? It was seen as a nightmare precedent. After messy squabbles concerning Pleasant Prairie, Lowell, Mud Creek, and Akron, water officials throughout the region had grown tired of dealing with a system that didn't really work. Nova prompted a rallying cry to do what officials should have done long before: go back to the negotiating table and create a modern, binding, world-class water-management system to regulate Great Lakes withdrawals for the next century and beyond.

~

After lengthy negotiations in late 1998, Canadian officials successfully pressured John Febbraro to withdraw his permit—under one condition: that if things ever changed in the future, the Nova Group would be first in line to export Great Lakes water. In truth, the controversy had an effect on Mr. Febbraro. He realized that he had no interest in becoming a water-diversion pariah. Over time, he came to appreciate where the critics were coming from. "We understood that concern," he says. "So we said 'protect and maintain,' that's fine, and we won't be part of a precedent-setting application."

The following year, Ontario passed a sweeping anti-diversion law that prohibited the bulk removal of water from the Great Lakes, as well as from other major provincial drainage basins. That was followed by the passage of a federal law in Canada that banned diversions from the Great Lakes Basin—at least on the Canadian side of the border. While Canada was strengthening its anti-diversion statutes, the US Congress—at the urging of the Great Lakes delegation—amended WRDA so that diversions *and* exports of water required the unanimous approval of all eight Great Lakes governors on the US side of the border.

The International Joint Commission was also consulted. The Canadian and American federal governments asked the IJC to draw up a blue-ribbon report about Great Lakes water use, including diversions and exports. The IJC was formed by the US-Canadian Boundary Waters Treaty of 1909 to resolve water disputes all along their shared border. After Nova, a lot of alarmist misinformation was flying around, and the public hungered for knowledge and facts that could help put things into perspective. Before the report was released, the IJC held a series of listening sessions on both sides of the border about the Nova proposal, and people turned out in droves to testify against diversions and to pledge their devotion to the lakes. "What struck me," remembers Tom Baldini, who was the US co-chair of the IJC during the Nova dispute, "was the number of people who testified, and the amount of written testimony we received, and the numbers of drawings from little kids, and schools, and the people who commented on not diverting water from the Great Lakes."

In February 2000, the IJC released its comprehensive and well-researched report, which reviewed the lakes' diversion history, touched on international trade issues, and included a number of noteworthy conclusions. One crucial finding was that less than 1 percent of the waters of the Great Lakes was renewed every year through rain, snow, and groundwater recharge. What's more, the report said that if all of the Basin's water uses were considered (including hydropower and the environment), there was no "surplus" water in the system.[2] It also declared that the "era of major diversions and water transfers in the United States and Canada has ended," and that in the short run the greatest diversionary pressures would not come from Texas or Atlanta, but from the "growing communities in the United States just outside the Great Lakes Basin divide."[3] The IJC predicted that, due to climate change and population growth, the region was heading into a period of great water uncertainty, and it urged officials to use a "precautionary approach" and "great caution" regarding Great Lakes water policy. The IJC also said that if diversions were approved, diverters should be required to treat and return 95 percent of the diverted water to the Great Lakes. Finally, the commission argued that new "major" consumptive uses should not be permitted unless strict conservation measures were implemented and the cumulative impacts of subsequent copycat projects considered.[4] While the IJC report was not binding, it was highly influential and helped policymakers hone their arguments as they worked to build a new water-management structure for the Basin.

But the IJC report was not the only post-Nova study commissioned in the region. During the summer of 1998, the Council of Great Lakes Governors met in a closed session in Chicago to discuss what should be done to revamp the regional water-management system. The governors dispatched Russ Van Herik, executive director of the Great Lakes Protection Fund, to round up a team of top-notch national and international legal experts. These lawyers would be asked to pore over state, provincial, federal, and international laws—and water regulations—to determine where all the potential diversion vulnerabilities in the Great

Lakes might be and then to provide "confidential" legal advice about how Great Lakes officials might best go about plugging those holes.

With Canada moving swiftly to pass provincial and federal anti-diversion laws, the northern side of the Basin seemed to be adequately battened down. How the south shore of the Basin would respond hinged on what the governors' legal team turned up regarding laws and regulations on the US side of the border. Mr. Van Herik pulled together a team of twelve attorneys, seven from the United States and five from Canada. The group was asked to engage in a sort of war-game exercise, drawing up scenarios of what legal attacks on Great Lakes water might look like, and then to provide counsel on how the governors should erect the necessary defenses to fend off such attacks. "If you're going to try to keep the money in the bank," Mr. Van Herik explains, "you spend a lot of time thinking about 'How do you rob banks?' Or the same thing software developers use: give me the best hackers in the land and start hacking into the defenses from there."

Several of the legal team's water experts came from "dry" states such as Colorado and Texas, including James Lochhead, a former executive director of the Colorado Department of Natural Resources who had extensive experience dealing with the Colorado River—one of the most contentious waterways in North America. Why would dry-land lawyers be hired to give legal opinions about such a water-rich region? First, because they are experts on fighting for water, and second, according to one source who asked not to be identified, they were hired "to conflict-out the best in the land." In other words, once they were retained to work for regional governors, they couldn't be hired by someone else to file a water lawsuit against the Great Lakes states.

In April 1999, the team presented the Council of Great Lakes Governors with an extensive confidential legal brief and an options paper that has never been publicly disclosed or discussed, although several people were willing to describe it privately. The document laid out five main points:

1. A "just say no" approach to Great Lakes water diversions was likely to be found unconstitutional and probably violated international trade agreements.

2. Current Great Lakes anti-diversion statutes—specifically WRDA —were unlikely to withstand legal challenges.

3. As alarming as all that might sound, the governors did have options, including the pursuit of a Great Lakes water compact, especially if a compact were to be mirrored by similar legislation on the Canadian side of the border.

4. In-Basin consumptive uses of water could be just as damaging to the Great Lakes ecosystem as diversions and should be dealt with as well.

5. Water applicants inside and outside the Great Lakes Basin should be judged evenhandedly.

The legal report also included an example of what a Great Lakes water compact could look like, and it gave the governors a sense of how a cross-border nontreaty anti-diversion agreement with the Canadian provinces might be crafted. The secret briefing paper gave examples of different kinds of water-withdrawal standards and mechanisms, including the benefits and drawbacks of the various options available.

While the brief made for fascinating reading, some officials received it with alarm. "When it came out everyone looked at it and said, 'This is a brief that could be used to challenge the system!'" says one source who asked not to be identified. "It *is* privileged information—but it could get out." In particular, there was confusion about how far the document's attorney-client privilege extended. Technically the governors were the clients, but were governors' aides considered clients as well? What about department heads? The fear was that if this document were disseminated widely enough, the key to the Great Lakes water kingdom might be available to anyone who had the time to file an open-records request. "They're all public agencies, so even though it's stamped 'privileged' if it hits their desk, it's possible people could get it through the Freedom of Information Act," one source said. "There was very real concern about that."

While much of the document needed to remain confidential, there were other parts of it that the governors felt needed to be released to the public, and soon. There was broad consensus in many governors' offices that the public needed to know just how legally inadequate the current anti-diversion system appeared to be, and that the legal team had also determined that a "just say no" approach would be shredded in the courts. Governor John Engler, in particular, was interested in getting that message across, because Michigan voters had traditionally been the most vociferously opposed to diversions. If he was being asked to soften his state's longstanding rigid anti-diversion policy, he wanted his voters to know why. By releasing some of the broader themes of the legal team's research, the governors were starting a slow, methodical public-education campaign to help people realize that a more complicated anti-diversion mechanism was going to be necessary to withstand scrutiny in court.

The governors asked the legal team to produce a boiled-down version of the brief for the public, and James Lochhead, the Denver attorney, was tapped as the lead author. Not only was Mr. Lochhead a former head of the Colorado DNR, and an expert on the Colorado River, he had also represented Denver and New Mexico on water issues and had served as an expert witness in numerous federal and state water-rights cases. The fifty-page background paper that he produced became known throughout the region as the "Lochhead Report," and it did a remarkable job of cutting through the legalese in a way that average citizens could understand. Mr. Lochhead's public report included the same points as the privileged document: WRDA likely would not stand in court; a "just say no" approach was unconstitutional; and he suggested that the best option was to create a regional water compact, with a parallel provincial agreement in Canada. He also argued that both accords should contain a new standard for grading, approving, or rejecting water-withdrawal applications.[5] He also said there was no time to lose. "It has become clear," he wrote, "that there is an immediate need to develop a comprehensive, effective framework among the Great Lakes States and Provinces for regulating future withdrawals of water from the Great Lakes Basin."[6]

The heart of the Lochhead Report highlighted weaknesses in Great Lakes water regulations and then suggested how the governors should go about crafting a new water-management structure. Mr. Lochhead divided the content into several key sections, including federal law, international trade, and WRDA.

Federal law: The report argued that US law, especially the "dormant commerce clause" of the US Constitution, imposes "severe limitations" on individual states that want to ban water diversions on their own. "Some might argue that each Great Lakes State should 'just say no' to the export of water out of the Basin," Mr. Lochhead wrote. "While politically popular, . . . a state law embargo on exports of Great Lakes water would not survive a challenge under the commerce clause."

Among other things, the commerce clause regulates trade among the states, and the basic thrust, Mr. Lochhead said, is that a "state may not discriminate against interstate commerce to advance the economic interest of the state or its citizens." He cited three cases that have resoundingly hammered this point home regarding water: *Sporhase*, *El Paso I*, and *El Paso II*. (*Sporhase*, which involved a Nebraska water statute, was discussed in chapter 4.) "*Sporhase* held that groundwater is an article of commerce, subject to the dormant commerce clause," Mr. Lochhead wrote, adding that the Supreme Court rejected the argument that a state "can discriminate as it wishes between in-state and out-of-state [water] use." However, if a state treats citizens inside and outside its borders "evenhandedly," then impacts on interstate commerce can be tolerated. "Therefore," Mr. Lochhead said, "regulation of water withdrawals by the Great Lakes States must be evenhanded. It must apply equally to in- and out-of-Basin users." The bottom line, he said, is that the commerce clause severely limits an individual state's ability to turn away outsiders seeking Great Lakes water.[7]

International trade: The report's interpretation of international water law was equally disappointing to the governors. Mr. Lochhead argued that international trade agreements (like GATT and the World Trade Organization rules) don't allow the Great Lakes states, the Canadian provinces, or the federal governments of Canada and the United States to "unilaterally" prohibit the export of Great Lakes water. "These international trade agreements, signed by the United States and Canada, severely restrict the ability of the Great Lakes States and Provinces to arbitrarily or unilaterally limit the export of Great Lakes water," he wrote.

The key issue, Mr. Lochhead explained, is whether water—in its natural state—is considered to be a good under international trade agreements or a vital, exhaustible resource held in the public trust. (Preventing exports of a good would be much more difficult under international law.) While acknowledging that this legal issue has been widely debated in academic journals, Mr. Lochhead declared that, in his opinion, water is a good from an international trade perspective and thus any ban on Great Lakes water diversions would violate international trade agreements. (Many Great Lakes lawyers would adamantly disagree with Mr. Lochhead, arguing that the jury is still out on that question.) Mr. Lochhead pointed out that GATT does allow some exceptions for water-export regulations "relating to the conservation of exhaustible natural resources," as long as those water regulations treat domestic and international consumers by the same rules. Thus, he argued, as long as in-Basin and out-of-Basin users are treated the same way, a system could be developed to regulate Great Lakes water withdrawals.[8]

The situation under NAFTA is different, Mr. Lochhead said. On December 2, 1993, Canada, Mexico, and the United States addressed water in a special declaration, saying that NAFTA "creates no rights to the natural water resources of any Party to the Agreement" as long as the water is in a natural state and hasn't entered commerce by becoming a tradable good or product. The statement continued that the accord doesn't "oblige any NAFTA Party to either exploit its water for commercial use or to begin exporting water in any form." The good news, Mr. Lochhead said, is that the NAFTA declaration protected Great Lakes waters from being exported by Mexico, the United States, and Canada. The bad news is that NAFTA only pertained to those three nations, meaning the lakes are arguably open to exploitation by the rest of the world. "The [NAFTA] statement has no force with respect to other countries under GATT or the WTO," Mr. Lochhead wrote, "any one of which could challenge restrictions on the export of Great Lakes water."[9]

WRDA: Then, for the next ten single-spaced pages, Mr. Lochhead picked apart the US Water Resources Development Act, the federal law that the governors had used since 1986 to regulate diversions of Great Lakes water. WRDA requires that all eight Great Lakes governors approve any US proposal to divert water out of the Great Lakes

Basin. It just takes one gubernatorial veto to kill a project. But Mr. Lochhead declared WRDA to be a legal paper tiger. If Lowell, Indiana (see chapter 9), or any other spurned water applicant were to contest WRDA in court, it likely would win. "We believe any challenge to a gubernatorial veto of a proposed out-of-Basin diversion of Great Lakes water under this provision as written may likely prevail," Lochhead said. Because WRDA allowed a governor to dictate water policy to citizens in another jurisdiction, Mr. Lochhead argued that WRDA created "tremendous potential for abuse of power." He continued, "A proposed diverter in one state has absolutely no recourse to the democratic process against the Governor of another state who vetoes the diversion." Not only does such a veto violate the commerce clause, and several other provisions of the US Constitution (including the right to due process), Mr. Lochhead argued, it probably violated international trade laws as well.[10]

That's where the bad news side of the "Lochhead doctrine" ended. Mr. Lochhead spent the next several pages describing what the governors could do to rectify the situation and build a modern, binding, legally sound Great Lakes water-management system. He started by reviewing some basic water-law principles in the Great Lakes region, including the public trust doctrine and the riparian reasonable-use doctrine.

"As a general proposition, the beds of the Great Lakes and all navigable tributary waters are owned by the contiguous Great Lakes states . . . and are held in trust for the benefit of the public," Mr. Lochhead wrote. "The states may adopt regulations to advance substantial public interests, even if such regulations restrict the rights of its citizens." In other words, under the public trust doctrine the rights of individuals don't trump the broader public interest in Great Lakes water.

Second, all Great Lakes states follow riparian law, which generally holds that each shoreline-property owner has a right to "reasonable" water use as long as it doesn't negatively affect other riparian users (see chapter 11 for more on riparian reasonable use). Mr. Lochhead said that while Congress and the courts have repeatedly reaffirmed state authority to regulate water, this kind of jurisdiction is a subauthority often subject to federal oversight. For example, the federal government has primary authority over navigation, and Congress can supersede state law in allocating water between states in order to "serve the national interest."[11] But there are ways around these obstacles, Mr. Lochhead said.

Specifically, he zeroed in on a regional water compact as the ideal model for the Great Lakes governors to pursue. Compacts are cumbersome—because they must be passed by every signatory state's legislature *and* by the US Congress—but the compact model has been used widely throughout the United States. What's more, two Great Lakes states (Pennsylvania and New York) were already parties to other water-use compacts and were intimately familiar with the system. Best of all, Mr. Lochhead noted, once a Great Lakes water compact was adopted by Congress, the compact would be protected against challenges under the commerce clause. Though the states were prevented from signing an international water treaty with the Canadian provinces, the provinces could adopt similar statutes on their side of the border, thereby surrounding the lakes with a parallel water-management structure. The only issue, Mr. Lochhead said, would be international trade agreements—a compact would be vulnerable to a legal attack if it discriminated between domestic and foreign users.[12]

How did Mr. Lochhead suggest the Great Lakes governors make their compact immune to international challenge? By adopting a standard that judged all potential Great Lakes water users—both inside and outside the Basin—evenhandedly. In other words, a proposed consumptive water use within the Great Lakes Basin should be judged by the same standard as a proposal for diverting water outside the Basin. Both in-Basin and out-of-Basin water withdrawals, Mr. Lochhead argued, result in a loss to the ecosystem and hence should be regulated similarly. "A decision over whether or under what conditions to allow an out-of-Basin use of Great Lakes water must be based on a standard closely related to the conservation of the resource, and should apply to both in- and out-of-Basin uses," he wrote. "An out-of-Basin use may be more or less disruptive than an in-Basin use."[13]

What should that water-regulation standard look like? According to Mr. Lochhead, the governors had three choices:

1. A standard that allowed some degradation of the resource—rules so permissive that water withdrawals would slowly deplete the

Great Lakes over time (presumably backed by the argument that the social and economic benefits derived from the water use would justify such resource depletion).

2. A standard of "no net loss" that required diverters, for example, to return their treated wastewater after it was used (a standard similar to the 95 percent return-flow recommended by the IJC in its 2000 report).

3. A standard that would break new legal ground by requiring water users to improve or provide a "benefit" to the Great Lakes ecosystem in exchange for the water that was withdrawn.

Though Mr. Lochhead was notably vague about what he meant by a "benefit," he implied that the governors could require restoration work as a way to pay back the ecosystem for water withdrawals. Regardless, it was obvious that this third option was Mr. Lochhead's first choice. "A benefit standard clearly advances the legitimate state interest of protecting the Great Lakes, an interest compelled by each State's duty to protect the resource pursuant to the public trust doctrine," he wrote. "The most compelling position is one that urges the States, Provinces, and national governments to set a global example of cooperative governance of a shared critical resource. Adopting a standard based on benefit would set this example."[14]

Of everything Mr. Lochhead mentioned in his report, his remarks about the benefit standard were the most newsworthy. His comments about WRDA possibly being unconstitutional and a violation of international trade agreements were serious, but the governors had heard murmurs about that sort of thing for some time. The question was, what could they do about it? The compact model certainly sounded promising, and the benefit standard was an intriguing idea—a whole new way of looking at environmental regulation. The governors were interested; but they weren't quite sure how it would work, so they asked for more detail.

On September 1, 1999, Mr. Lochhead submitted a follow-up memo entirely devoted to the benefit standard. "The new standard ensures that no state or province will approve a new water withdrawal unless there is established benefit to the waters and water-dependent resources of the Great Lakes Basin," Mr. Lochhead wrote. "'Benefit' means incrementally improving upon the present state of impaired ecological health of the Great Lakes."[15] In other words, if a community or business wanted to withdraw water, it would have to compensate for the withdrawal through Great Lakes restoration, or cleanup, to "more than offset the unavoidable damages of the new [water withdrawal]." To Mr. Lochhead, using the benefit standard in a regional water compact was a magic blend of policy that would treat all water users evenhandedly, would withstand legal challenge, and that—in his view—would leave the Great Lakes better off than they were before the water was withdrawn. "A benefit standard means simply this," Mr. Lochhead wrote, "bring me a project with more good stuff than bad stuff."[16]

It was an engaging concept, and several gubernatorial aides—especially in Michigan—embraced the idea immediately. "We were worried that [if WRDA were challenged] we would lose our tenuous authority to say no," says Dennis Schornack, former top aide to Michigan governor John Engler. "[The benefit standard] had kind of a visionary aspect—we're drawing a line in the sand here and from this day forward we are only going to act to improve this resource.... It gave Michigan sufficient justification to back off of the no-diversions stance." But Mr. Schornack says that many US environmentalists were skeptical, at least at first. If a conservative Republican governor like John Engler liked it, how could it be good for the environment? "It took some time," Mr. Schornack says, "for the environmental groups to adopt it as an acceptable or reasonable way to settle these constant disputes over diversions."

Great Lakes environmental groups eventually warmed to the idea, at least on the US side of the border. If the Lochhead doctrine was right, and diversions couldn't be prevented, at least under the benefit standard the diverters could be forced to pay an ecological tax that compensated the regional ecosystem. "This is definitely very forward-thinking," said Cheryl Mendoza, a representative from the Alliance for the Great Lakes, in a newsletter to her members. "This means we will manage our water in a sustainable *and* restorative way so that fifty to a hundred years from now not only will the Lakes still be here for us—they'll be even better."[17]

The Lochhead doctrine certainly generated a lot of chatter in the

Basin—and while Mr. Lochhead had his fans, there were plenty of critics as well. Many Great Lakes water lawyers viewed his report as a Western water-law interpretation of an Eastern water-law issue. Some thought that the public trust and riparian reasonable-use doctrines were treated in a cursory manner, and not everyone agreed with some of his statements of fact—like the idea that water in its natural state is definitely a good under international trade agreements. "This was very much taking the view of Western water-law guys and didn't represent the riparian tradition that we have in this part of the country," says one Great Lakes official, who asked not to be identified. Several gubernatorial officials believed that if more Great Lakes Basin attorneys had been included on the legal team, the report's conclusions and recommendations might have been broader. "There's always been debate about the Lochhead legal study," says David de Launay, from the Ontario Ministry of Natural Resources. "It was one point of view. Whether, at the end of the day, that should be the final policy was a debate right from the beginning."

Despite that healthy discussion, Mr. Lochhead's report helped spur the governors to act. While officials remained years away from releasing a binding regional water-management agreement, there was growing consensus with Mr. Lochhead that a compact was the way to go. But some regional water regulators were having a hard time grasping how the benefit standard would work. And there were other divisions that kept popping up around the negotiating table (such as whether in-Basin consumptive uses should be judged by the same standards as diversions). With many kinks needing to be worked out, gubernatorial aides decided that pushing hard for a compact right away would be unwise. A slower, more methodical approach would have a greater likelihood of success. Under the leadership of governors Tom Ridge of Pennsylvania and John Engler of Michigan (both Republicans), Great Lakes officials went to work drafting a new document that would serve as a plan of action, rather than anything binding on the governors and premiers. It became known as the Great Lakes Charter Annex, or simply Annex 2001, and it was packaged as an amendment to the Great Lakes Charter.[18]

Annex 2001 was remarkably short, sleek, and concise—notably devoid of the obfuscating bureaucratic language that is often stuffed into such documents. Just four single-spaced pages, it wasn't water policy per se, but rather a series of directives that told the public where the governors and premiers were headed, and it hinted at what the ultimate new water-management system would look like. It committed the governors and premiers to developing "an enhanced water-management system that is simple, durable, efficient, retains and respects authority within the Basin, and, most importantly, protects, conserves, restores, and improves the Waters and Water-Dependent Natural Resources of the Great Lakes Basin."

Of the six directives in the document, two were definitely the most important. One commanded the governors and premiers to "immediately" prepare a "binding" Basin-wide agreement "such as an interstate compact," and it gave the governors three years to get the job done. The other key directive committed the governors to establishing a new water-withdrawal "decision-making standard" based on the following principles:

1. that withdrawn water be returned after use and conservation practices be adopted to prevent waste;
2. that a water withdrawal create no significant adverse impacts on the Great Lakes, either individually or cumulatively when considered with other withdrawals;
3. that the withdrawal comply with existing laws and treaties; and
4. that the water applicant conduct an "Improvement to the Waters and Water-Dependent Natural Resources of the Great Lakes Basin" (the benefit standard had officially become an "improvement" standard).

Because it wasn't a binding agreement, compromises over things like the improvement standard were easier to reach. Some people continued to have their doubts, but they didn't mind signing a nonbinding document that kept the momentum going. "Everybody got their piece, and these were—after all—just principles," Dennis Schornack says. "Michigan got the benefit standard, Ohio got the no-significant-adverse-impact, and Ontario got the return-flow." The benefit or "improvement" standard was cutting-edge policy, but the return-flow requirement was extremely important as well. It was seen as *the* greatest deterrent to large-scale, long-range diversions. "It certainly put the kibosh on diversions to the Southwest," Mr. Schornack says. The Annex was signed with much fanfare at Niagara Falls on June 18, 2001, where Republican governor George Pataki of New York played host to several of his peers. "The Annex we signed today is a roadmap for ensuring the continued protection of the Great Lakes," Governor Pataki said. "We want to make sure that . . . our water is used wisely and effectively to the benefit of all our citizens."[19]

It had been three years since the Nova Group's proposal sank in Sault Ste. Marie, spurring an unprecedented movement to revamp the regional water-management system. During that time, the IJC had spoken. The US Congress had amended WRDA. The province of Ontario had banned Great Lakes diversions and so had the federal government of Canada. And Québec had banned diversions outside provincial boundaries. The governors, meanwhile, had merely released their battle plans. The Annex 2001 signing ceremony was marked by a sense of optimism and accomplishment, but in reality it was just the first step toward a solution. Like the Charter to which it was attached, the Annex was not binding. It was a commitment to act, but a document with no real power. As Governor Pataki said, it was a roadmap to a solution, but was far from the final answer that the Basin was looking for. More than thirty-six months had passed, yet the Great Lakes' south shore was no safer than it had been before word of the Nova proposal first spread. So despite all the backslapping and handshakes at Niagara Falls, the signing of the Annex was not the end, but a new beginning. The real work of crafting a binding agreement was yet to come.

Chapter 13

Marching toward a Compact

After the Annex 2001 signing ceremony at Niagara Falls, the governors and premiers dispatched a team of aides to carry Great Lakes water-management negotiations into the next stage. This "working group" of lawyers, policy specialists, and water managers was responsible for turning the Annex principles into comprehensive policy. The team included a few representatives from each jurisdiction—the eight Great Lakes states and two provinces. Some members were fairly new to the water-policy arena, but most had been dealing with Great Lakes water issues for years—in fact, some had even helped draft the Great Lakes Charter back in 1985. The next three years were a grind, marked by an endless string of laborious conference calls and face-to-face negotiations where bureaucrats haggled over enormously important legal language as well as minutiae.

In short order, the working group decided to craft two water-management accords, not one. The first was the Great Lakes–St. Lawrence River Basin Sustainable Water Resources Agreement, sort of an updated version of the nonbinding Great Lakes Charter. It detailed the promises made between the governors and premiers to implement policies to protect regional waters for the foreseeable future. Federal law may have forbidden the states and provinces from signing a water treaty, but nothing prevented them from adopting parallel water regulations on both sides of the international border. The second document was the Great Lakes–St. Lawrence River Basin Water Resources Compact. It was designed to be a binding agreement among the eight Great Lakes states, and it codified precisely how the governors would uphold their side of the International Agreement to be signed with Ontario and Québec. The catch was that, in order to be binding, the Compact would eventually need to be adopted by all eight Great Lakes legislatures and then be approved by the US Congress and the president. Together, the International Agreement and the Compact came to be called the "Annex Implementing Agreements."

From the start, the working group grasped the ambitious nature of its task. If the Lochhead Report represented the initial research phase, and Annex 2001 the road map, then the implementing agreements would end up as the final product. While the International Agreement was the driver during the negotiations, the Compact was arguably the more important of the two documents—not because the United States was more important than Canada, but because the Compact was binding. The Compact was designed as an Iron Curtain of sorts along the US side of the watershed, where most agreed the primary problems lay.[1]

More than once, the talks teetered on the edge of failure. Crafting a new water-management paradigm among ten jurisdictions, across an international boundary, and in the absence of a crisis was not going to be easy. "What we are trying to do is create a system that says people who use water in Milwaukee have an impact on the people who live in Québec City—and that the people in Québec City ought to have a say in that. That's a huge concept," declared Todd Ambs, who was head of the Water Division at the Wisconsin Department of Natural Resources at the time. "Of all the things that I do in my job, this is the only thing that people will still be talking about fifty years from now. It's about the future. It's about having a system in place to deal with problems that we don't have today." The in-person meetings were chaired by Sam Speck, director of the Ohio DNR, the "elder statesman" who was instrumental in crafting compromises and bridging philosophical divides. "He would always be able to pull it back from the brink when one of us was ready to slit the throat of somebody else," says one negotiator. While emotions ran high at times, partisanship did not. The Great Lakes water-diversion debate has always been an extraordinarily bipartisan issue. For example, when the Great Lakes Charter was signed in 1985, the governorships were dominated by Democrats. When Annex 2001 was signed, Republicans were in the majority in the Basin. As the Implementing Agreement negotiations dragged on, the gubernatorial offices in the Basin would eventually end up being evenly split between Democrats and Republicans (the premiers were both provincial Liberals).

Throughout the region's water-management history, it has never been about party; it has always been about place. "As someone who has done public policy work for twenty-five years," Mr. Ambs says, "I'm fascinated by this issue because it has nothing to do with partisan politics and it has everything to do with geography." Nevertheless, all negotiators—including those from Michigan—realized that on the final day, when officials exited the negotiating room for the last time, everyone would have to give up something to get a deal. "Nobody," Sam Speck said, "is going to get everything they want."[2] Some of the most contentious debates—which included raised voices, heated words, and accusatory finger-pointing—were between just a couple of jurisdictions. In some cases, a few negotiators were asked to remove themselves to a separate room until they ironed out their differences and were in a position to present their negotiated sub-settlement to the rest of the group. At regular intervals, the negotiators gave confidential briefings for feedback and input to key stakeholders, including tribes and First Nations as well as industry, agriculture, and environmental groups.

As previous chapters of this book have shown, each state and province has its own "water personality." Michigan is adamantly opposed to diversion, but has often balked at limitations on its own in-Basin consumptive use. New York has major hydropower considerations. Illinois is worried about maintaining its US Supreme Court–mandated water allocation that keeps metropolitan Chicago alive. Ontario shares many of Michigan's anti-diversion sentiments, and Québec, at the tail end of the system, is concerned about what everyone else does upstream. Minnesota has traditionally been the most environmentally progressive water jurisdiction in the Basin—Indiana decidedly less so—with Wisconsin, Ohio, and Pennsylvania somewhere in between.

One of the most emotionally charged issues revolved around how the Compact should treat the Illinois diversion (see chapter 5). At one point, it appeared the Chicago diversion issue might torpedo the entire process. For years the topic had been avoided, but during one late session, just before the first draft of the Compact was released, Pennsylvania suggested that the Illinois diversion be covered under the Compact just like other water withdrawals. Ontario quickly backed up Pennsylvania, and then "it was like a forest fire that starts with a spark," one negotiator said. Several states and provinces—though not all—insisted that if Illinois ever wanted to ask for an increase in its diversion, it should be required to come before the Compact Council for approval—just like any other jurisdiction. Illinois adamantly objected, arguing that the US Supreme Court had ruled over the diversion for more than seventy years, and the state had no interest whatsoever in seeing that change. "There definitely was a desire that there would be more controls over the Illinois diversion through this agreement," says one senior negotiator. "There is absolutely no question that the whole Illinois diversion became a big issue that almost derailed things." But Illinois held firm in the face of stiff opposition, refusing to sign any agreement that changed the way the Illinois diversion was regulated. When the rest of the jurisdictions were faced with no deal, or a special deal for Chicago, they backed down.

～

With the Illinois diversion debate behind them, on July 19, 2004, the first drafts of the Annex Implementing Agreements were released and the public finally got a glimpse of what a new water-management system might look like. In an unusual move, the draft agreements were not consensus documents. Negotiators remained at odds on some key issues, but they had gotten as far as they were going to get for the moment, so they were genuinely interested in the public's feedback. "For all the criticism that the government officials take for being just a bunch of faceless bureaucrats not accountable to the public," one senior negotiator said, "there sure is a lot of time given in these [negotiations] to what the public thinks." In many ways, the documents resembled what James Lochhead had recommended. They were definitely not a "just say no" policy on diversions, but what might best be described as "occasionally saying yes—as long as there's improvement to the Great Lakes ecosystem." While the documents followed Mr. Lochhead's advice by regulating both diversions and in-Basin consumptive uses of water, they ignored his advice by holding diversions to a tougher review process. That meant that regional review of diversions would kick in much sooner than the regional review of in-Basin consumptive uses—and that was not quite as "evenhanded" as Mr. Lochhead had promoted in his report.

The 2004 draft of the Compact included the following key proposals.[3]

Diversions: A new or increased diversion of 1 million gallons per day (mgd) or larger would require regional review by the Great Lakes governors. One gubernatorial veto could kill a proposal. In addition, a diversion proposal would only be approved if the following conditions were met:

- there was no other water alternative;
- the quantity requested was "reasonable";
- water withdrawn would be returned, minus an "allowance" for consumptive use;
- the diversion caused no significant individual or cumulative adverse impacts;
- an "environmentally sound and economically feasible" conservation plan was adopted;
- in exchange for the water, the applicant agreed to do an "improvement" to the Great Lakes ecosystem; and
- the diversion proposal didn't violate any other laws or agreements.[4]

In-Basin withdrawals: A new or increased consumptive use of water inside the Great Lakes Basin of 5 mgd or higher would have to be reviewed by the governors as well, but three gubernatorial "no" votes would be required to kill a proposal, not just one. These withdrawals would only be approved if all or part of the proposed withdrawal could not be avoided through conservation.[5]

Improvement: The document also defined "improvement," which it said included but was not limited to "mitigating adverse effects of existing water withdrawals, restoring environmentally sensitive areas, or implementing ... conservation measures in areas or facilities that are not part of the specific proposal undertaken by or on behalf of the withdrawer."[6]

During the summer of 2004, the Annex Implementing Agreements were opened up to a ninety-day public comment period. Dozens of hearings were held throughout the Great Lakes region and people turned out in large numbers. More than 10,000 comments poured in to the Great Lakes St. Lawrence Governors and Premiers that summer, ranging from citizens' one-line e-mails to polished policy papers submitted by industry and environmental organizations. Individual states and provinces received thousands more comments. The agreements were highly unpopular among industry and agriculture groups, who equated them with a regulatory lovefest and a threat to jobs. "We must be careful not to make this a jobs diversion plan," said Michael Johnston, director of regulatory affairs for the Michigan Manufacturers Association, in a comment representative of the time.[7] US environmentalists were more welcoming, but also critical of several key elements. Many environmentalists argued that all water withdrawals—consumptive uses and diversions—should be judged by the same rules and that the agreements should put a greater emphasis on water conservation.

The response in Canada, however, was even more critical and at times shrill in its condemnation of the documents. Ironically, on the US side of the border, it was industrial and agricultural interests that emerged as the chief critics of the documents, while in Canada much of the opposition came from environmentalists and even Canadian nationalists. *The Toronto Star* ran a number of editorials and news stories that excoriated the Compact as an American pro-diversion Trojan horse. Canadian concern about the Annex Implementing Agreements had been mounting long before the documents were released. Adèle Hurley, director of the Program on Water Issues at the University of Toronto's Munk School was skeptical about the Annex from the start, and her program funded a highly critical position paper on the agreements. The twenty-two-page document was published one month before the draft Compact came out and was written by Andrew Nikiforuk, a Canadian journalist. Mr. Nikiforuk argued that the motive behind the Annex Implementing Agreements was "to supply water to thirsty communities outside of the Basin, and [governors] want to do so without being vetoed by a neighbor such as Michigan, a key anti-diverter state."[8]

He drew a bead on Waukesha, Wisconsin, the water-troubled community on the outskirts of Milwaukee that lies just beyond the Basin boundary (see chapters 14 and 16). Waukesha sits atop depleted and contaminated water wells and made no secret of its desire to tap into Lake Michigan, just fifteen miles to the east. According to Mr. Nikiforuk, the Annex Implementing Agreements were an ingenious and disingenuous scheme designed to get Great Lakes water to Great Lakes communities just beyond the Basin line without creating a precedent that might make more far-flung diversions possible. "Annex 2001," he wrote, "is all about saying 'yes' to communities such as Waukesha without saying 'yes' to Phoenix, Arizona, Singapore, or global water bottlers." Mr. Nikiforuk euphemistically referred to his report as a "critical assessment," and he expressed deep reservations about the motivations behind the Annex process, arguing that it wasn't designed to protect the lakes, but to exploit them. "Annex 2001 appears to be a regional compact dedicated to protecting the Great Lakes Basin," he wrote. "Yet in real terms it is a water-taking permit system designed to minimize conflict among potential water takers." His paper circulated widely on both sides of the border. While many Americans dismissed it as a one-sided anti-Annex editorial, many Canadians embraced it as a muckraking call to action.

As the summer of 2004 passed, Canadian opposition to the agreements mounted, culminating in a public hearing held in Toronto on September 20, 2004. Speaker after speaker rose to lambaste the agreements. "The Annex 2001 agreement is nothing more than a unilateral US water grab," complained Sarah Ehrhardt, with the Council of Canadians. "By putting no limitations on the amount of water that can be withdrawn from the lakes by the US states . . . the Annex 2001 is, simply put, a US permit to drain the Great Lakes dry." At first blush, the Canadian critics seemed to be strafing the Annex agreements, but in truth they were attacking the Lochhead doctrine that lay behind the agreements. What these opponents hated most was that the agreements didn't ban diversions—something Lochhead told the governors they couldn't do. By contrast, in the wake of the Nova proposal,

Canadian officials had moved swiftly to ban Great Lakes diversions under provincial and federal law. Now the Canadian public was asking, Why should their officials sign international agreements that pledged to enact anything less than a ban? Canadian critics couldn't have cared less about the US Constitution's commerce clause or alleged vulnerabilities from complex international trade agreements—what they wanted was a ban on diversions. Any agreement that waffled on that point had to be a complicated American pro-diversion ploy to trick the Canadian public out of Great Lakes water. Canadians were particularly concerned about the improvement standard, which they interpreted as a materialistic bartering system that turned their waters into an international commodity. They weren't comfortable with the apples-and-oranges trade-offs that the improvement standard implied. They didn't see how exchanging water for ecological cleanup would necessarily leave the lakes better off. "Let's not waste the time and energies of the region's best water and environmental experts trying to equate buckets of water with dozens of ducks," complained Ralph Pentland, a former Canadian environmental official and critic of the improvement standard. What bothered Mr. Pentland and many of his compatriots about the improvement standard was that if a diverter withdrew 50 mgd and then cleaned up tons of contaminated sediment as payback, that would create a water-for-restoration bartering system. That, they argued, ran the risk of turning water "in its natural state" into a commodity.

While Canada is not known for being shy about extracting its natural resources, many Great Lakes Canadians look at water exploitation differently—particularly if that water might be headed to the United States. "A reflexive 'aqua-nationalism,' clothed in environmental righteousness, is hostile to any suggestion that Canada's water could ever become a tradable commodity," wrote Chris Wood in *The Walrus*, a Canadian magazine. "The animus is all the more implacable if the discussion involves trading water with Americans—an idea close to treason in some eyes."[9] During the fall of 2004, Canadian criticism over the Annex Implementing Agreements became so heated that Ontario premier Dalton McGuinty had no choice but to distance himself from the documents. On November 15, 2004, the Ontario Ministry of Natural Resources released a statement saying that the citizens of Ontario had spoken and there was no way Mr. McGuinty was signing the latest draft documents until significant changes were made. "Ontarians, and the McGuinty government, clearly want a 'no diversions' agreement, or the position of 'no net loss' as proposed by the International Joint Commission," the statement read. "Ontario is not prepared to ratify the agreement in its current form."[10] A few weeks later, the Canadian edition of *Time* magazine ran a cover story titled, "Are the Great Lakes for Sale? An Inside Look at the Controversial Proposal to Export Water from Our Precious Resource."[11] The keywords there were *proposal to export water*. The Annex Implementing Agreements that had started out as a well-meaning effort to prevent or severely minimize diversions had now been labeled—in Canada at least—as a pro-export initiative. As a result, the Great Lakes St. Lawrence Governors and Premiers was in the middle of an international public-relations nightmare. It had completely lost control of its message, and the Lochhead doctrine was the primary casualty.

～

Few of the negotiators had expected the comment period to go the way it did. The strong Canadian reaction to the documents caught many off guard, and the mood in the negotiation room cooled for a time. Low morale became an issue for some. But that stage was short-lived. "The group settled down and they have really been working well together," said one negotiator in late 2004. "[We're] trying to come up with an agreement we all can acquiesce to." Group chemistry helped overcome the setback. After years of drafting the agreements, many of the negotiators had become friends. "As much yelling as there has been, we always find a way to come back and laugh about it after the twelve-hour negotiations," a senior water official says. He adds that after one marathon session in 2005, "we drank American *and* Canadian beer well into the night and played some music."

As the negotiations dragged into 2005, Wisconsin and Ontario exerted themselves behind the scenes. Wisconsin had its Waukesha problem—a water-troubled suburb just outside the Basin boundary. But several other states, including Ohio and Indiana, had Waukesha-like communities (large and small) that would likely need to apply for a diversion eventually. Ontario, meanwhile, had always shared

Michigan's anti-diversion stance, and after the 2004 public hearings it pushed hard to shunt aside much of the Lochhead doctrine, arguing that what the Basin needed was an anti-diversion agreement with exceptions, as opposed to an agreement that permitted diversions as long as there was an "improvement" to the Great Lakes. Ontario, and others, argued that if the Compact were to be adopted by the US Congress, the commerce clause problem would be nullified (even James Lochhead seemed to agree with that). And there was a growing consensus among working-group negotiators that the only major argument against a no-diversions policy came from the international trade accords—the idea that a foreign entity could argue it was being discriminated against. But Ontario felt that was far too gray a legal area to warrant curbing its anti-diversion stance, and it was gaining converts around the room.

Meanwhile, the improvement standard had become an orphan on the negotiating table. As the months passed, it slowly faded deeper and deeper into the margins. There's no question that Canadian opposition put a dagger in the back of the improvement standard, but American industrialists helped twist the knife. Ultimately, however, the improvement standard died under the weight of its own complexity. By early 2005, most of the negotiators were ready to let the improvement standard go. "Even if you still liked the idea," says David de Launay from the Ontario Ministry of Natural Resources. "No regulator had figured out how you did it."

In June 2005, new drafts of the Annex Implementing Agreements were released for another round of public hearings. While much of the boilerplate remained the same, the new compromise created some markedly different documents at the core. While the 2004 drafts permitted diversions as long as there were improvements, the 2005 documents banned diversions, with limited exceptions. Those limited exceptions fell into three distinct categories: "straddling communities," "straddling counties," and "intra-Basin transfers." Under the straddling-community exception, if a town or city sat right on top of the Great Lakes Basin boundary (like Pleasant Prairie, Wisconsin, or Akron, Ohio), under the 2005 agreements these uniquely positioned municipalities had a right to apply for a diversion. That diversion could send water to the side of town that lay outside the Great Lakes Basin boundary—as long as the diversion request was for the public water supply, the water was returned to the Great Lakes after use, and the community conserved the water and had no other reasonable water-supply alternatives. Perhaps most importantly to these towns, the local governor alone could approve diversions to straddling communities, allowing the towns to bypass the hassle of sending their diversion applications to all eight Great Lakes governors. The same was not true for straddling counties. If a city was outside the Great Lakes Basin, but inside a *county* that straddled the Basin line, it too had a right to apply for a water diversion, but it would have to submit its diversion request to all eight Great Lakes governors—and meet the long list of requirements. Those requirements included adopting a conservation plan, proving there was no reasonable water-supply alternative, and—most important—treating the diverted water and returning it to the Basin after it was used. The one thing these various diversion applicants would not have to do, however, was some kind of ecological improvement project. The improvement standard was dead. But if a community didn't straddle the Basin line, or if it wasn't in a county that straddled the Basin line, then it didn't have a ticket to the dance: it couldn't even ask to divert water from the Great Lakes Basin. Under the new draft agreements, only cities on or near the watershed line could request a diversion. Everyone else was out of luck. And what about the intra-Basin diversion exception? That exception covered diversions that transferred water from one Great Lake watershed to another without the water ever leaving the Great Lakes Basin—for example, a pipeline that withdraws water from the Lake Huron basin and transports it into the Lake Erie basin. Like other diversions, intra-Basin water transfers would have to prove there was no reasonable water-supply alternative, including conservation. If an intra-Basin diversion resulted in a consumptive water loss greater than 5 mgd, the diverter would be required to return the water to the original watershed—and the diversion would need the approval of all eight Great Lakes governors, with one no vote being enough to kill a project.

In the negotiating room, consensus over the 2005 draft agreements remained elusive, but the group was getting closer to a final accord. Wisconsin—with the support of Ohio in particular—had successfully obtained its Waukesha clause in the form of the straddling-county exception. Ontario, to the glee of Michigan and Québec, had come pretty close to obtaining a document that "just said no." Illinois, for its part, managed to reinforce the fact that the US Supreme Court would be the only entity governing the Chicago diversion. But after years of heated debate, the vast majority of the Lochhead doctrine ended up on the cutting-room floor. During the 2005 public hearings, the Great Lakes St. Lawrence Governors and Premiers received three thousand comments and, as in 2004, individual states received thousands more. But the total number was less than half of what had been experienced in the prior round.[12] As a rule, the comments were less combative and more accepting, but there continued to be complaints—and the straddling-county proposal was the most obvious target. "That's been one of our big concerns about the second round of the Great Lakes Annex," said Susan Howatt, national water campaigner with the Council of Canadians. "That is really kind of troubling—when we start using political boundaries rather than environmental boundaries." Even some former governors found the straddling-county clause to be a sellout. "Counties are political institutions . . . watersheds, on the other hand, are natural jurisdictions," complains Tony Earl, former governor of Wisconsin. "The straddling-counties concept [is] really the steep, slippery slope."

But there was also a feeling—particularly in Canada—that things had improved. After years of sifting and winnowing, the right document was beginning to emerge. It was a compromise document that no one was embracing with resounding enthusiasm, but it didn't suffer from the fervent criticism of the year before. "There was a big breakthrough between the 2004 version and the 2005 version," Ralph Pentland said. "[Public reaction] went from almost total condemnation . . . to a fairly broad consensus beginning to form."

⁓

Then bottled water—which had repeatedly been on the negotiators' agenda over the years—emerged as an emotional last-minute issue, particularly for Michigan. In recent years, bottled water had become controversial in much of the Great Lakes region, and it peaked as an issue in Michigan during 2005. Some environmentalists argued that shipping water out of the Great Lakes Basin in bottles was no different than the Nova Group's proposal to export bulk water in tankers. Other constituencies argued that if restraints were placed on bottled water, similar limits would be required for other bottled water-based products like beer or fruit juice. No one was interested in that. The negotiators had widely varying interpretations about how the agreements should deal with the bottled-water controversy. "We have some questions about what bottled water means as it relates to the question of diversion," said Ken DeBeaussaert, director of Michigan's Office of the Great Lakes at the time. But other states didn't see the need to even mention bottled water in the agreements. "[Michigan was] so worried about bottled water," complained Kent Lokkesmoe, former head of the water division at the Minnesota DNR. "It's their political world and I don't understand it all. . . . To me that's a nonissue." For its part, Ontario had already passed a law, in the wake of Nova, that banned bulk water exports but permitted shipments of water out of the Basin in containers of 20 liters or less (roughly 5.7 gallons).

That meant shipping a tanker of bulk water out of the Basin was illegal, but shipping a tanker of bottled water wasn't. The Canadians weren't interested in signing international agreements that weakened those regulations, despite pressure from states to do so. Meanwhile, bottled-water opponents in the United States thought the 20-liter limit went too far, so the issue was tabled again. But because the US federal government considered bottled water to be a product, the National Wildlife Federation (NWF) and the Council of Great Lakes Industries (CGLI)—both of which played an influential role in the Compact negotiations—didn't think bottled water should be considered a diversion under the Compact. Instead, they recommended that states be allowed to impose their own more-restrictive domestic bottled-water rules if they were so inclined. Many negotiators reminded themselves that the Compact was the minimum standard that the states would be required to adopt. While the Compact itself could not be amended, individual legislatures had the option of passing even more stringent water rules in their respective jurisdictions. That, negotiators say, helped them forge an ultimate agreement.

In early November 2005, a final-final compromise was reached. From an overview perspective, the Annex Implementing Agreements remained documents that banned diversions with limited exceptions.

But in the last several months the fine print had changed in several key areas. Regarding bottled water, the Compact ended up following Ontario's lead, banning sales in containers larger than 20 liters or roughly 5.7 gallons, though the Compact made clear that individual governments were welcome to make those rules even more restrictive. Regarding in-Basin consumptive uses, a state would be required to inform all the other jurisdictions about a large consumptive-use proposal greater than 5 mgd—and while those other states could comment on that water use—the other states could not vote it down. This meant that after years of negotiations not much had changed regarding in-Basin consumptive use since the days of Mud Creek in Michigan, with one notable exception: if a state was believed to be approving large consumptive uses that were in violation of the Compact's standard, the state could be taken to court.

The Compact also required each state to create and follow a water-conservation plan. While the specific details of a conservation plan were left up to each state, their plans would have to be submitted to and reviewed by a Compact-created committee on a regular basis.[13] The idea was to keep close track of the conservation leaders and the conservation laggards, using peer pressure to bring the lax into line. Making conservation programs mandatory was a "huge leap," said negotiator Cathy Curran Myers, deputy secretary of the Pennsylvania Office of Water Management and a key negotiator from that state. "It means we will come up with a whole suite of conservation practices. . . . It may be one of the more important things that comes out of [the Compact]."

Perhaps most noteworthy of all was that a new mechanism had been set up, committing the states to work together as a region to manage the Great Lakes resource through a binding compact. A state that violated the rules could be taken to court—not just by other states, but even by citizens or advocacy groups—and a judge would make the final decision. "A compact is essentially a contract," said one Great Lakes official. "If someone doesn't fulfill the contract, that's a breach and they can be sued." The provinces weren't legally bound by the Compact, but the nonbinding International Agreement that mirrored the Compact ensured that the states and provinces would substantially coordinate their water activities with one another, despite being separated by an international boundary. While the provinces would not have the power

Compact Highlights

*The final version of the Compact
included the following key provisions:*

- A ban on new water diversions, with
  limited exceptions.

- A requirement that states regulate
  in-Basin water uses.

- The creation of a uniform regional
  standard for evaluating proposed water
  withdrawals.

- A requirement that each state adopt a
  water-conservation plan.

- Water shipped out of the Basin in bottles
  smaller than 20 liters / 5.7 gallons was not
  classified as a diversion.

- The waters of the Great Lakes were
  defined as including rivers and
  groundwater within the Basin.

- The Chicago diversion was specifically
  exempted.

- The Compact language mirrored that of
  the non-binding International Agreement
  with Ontario and Québec.

to veto diversion proposals on the US side of the border, they would have a voice—just as American officials would not be able to veto Canadian water proposals.

The final documents were released at a major event in Milwaukee, Wisconsin, on December 13, 2005. While the event was billed as a signing ceremony for the Great Lakes governors and premiers, there was a shockingly small turnout—only two governors and one premier showed up: Bob Taft of Ohio, Jim Doyle of Wisconsin, and Dalton McGuinty of Ontario.[14] The no-shows did send stand-ins, and hundreds of other officials, business leaders, and environmentalists filled the ballroom, but it was an embarrassingly low chief-executive turnout for what had been touted as such a major event. Many more governors and premiers had shown up for the signing ceremonies of the Great

The Great Lakes Compact and the companion Sustainable Water Resources Agreement were signed in Milwaukee on December 13, 2005. Seated from left to right are Wisconsin governor Jim Doyle, Ohio governor Bob Taft, and Ontario premier Dalton McGuinty. (Photo by Peter Annin)

Lakes Charter in 1985 and of Annex 2001, raising questions about how much political support really was behind the new agreements. "This is a proud and historic day for the people of the Great Lakes and the St. Lawrence Basin," Governor Taft said after the final documents were released. "These waters are a global treasure that we hold in trust for future generations."[15] It was a proud moment, particularly for the negotiators who managed to forge a deal despite enormous adversity. Releasing comprehensive agreements to manage one of the largest bodies of fresh surface water on the planet was definitely a momentous occasion.

While the signing was an important step, history was still waiting for a binding compact on the US side of the border—home to the largest population in the Great Lakes Basin, and where the greatest increase in water demand would likely be found. The agreements released in Milwaukee, while impressive, were still nonbinding. "The question," said Professor Dan Tarlock at Chicago-Kent College of

Law, "is whether there is sufficient pressure from the governors or [environmental groups] to take the next step and turn this into a compact. . . . Some of these compacts have dragged on for decades. It would only take one spoiler state to put a damper on things." Insiders knew that the arduous legislative task ahead could make the drafting process look easy. "It will be very challenging to get the Compact ratified by each of the eight [Great Lakes] state legislatures, and also consented to by Congress," admitted David Naftzger, executive director of the Great Lakes St. Lawrence Governors and Premiers. "[But] there is momentum. It's building, and our hope is certainly to see quick action."

~

The Compact was released seven years after the Nova Group's controversial water-diversion proposal roused the region to action. Following the Milwaukee signing ceremony, many were predicting that it could take at least that long to move the Compact through the various stages required for it to become binding. Most observers gave the Compact a 50–50 chance of ever becoming law. "There's a fair amount of enthusiasm for [the Compact]," said George Kuper, president of the Council of Great Lakes Industries at the time. "It's going to be tough. There's nothing easy about what has to happen." As the document transitioned from the negotiating room to the legislative floor, skeptics and special interests picked at it from all sides. A key goal of some opponents was to stall until the momentum waned, hoping the Compact would slip into the graveyard of untested ideas. Mr. Kuper's organization even soured somewhat on its prior enthusiasm, thanks to concerns that the Compact could encourage harassing citizen lawsuits. Some environmentalists remained unhappy with the bottled-water exclusion. "This whole thing began with the Nova Group and the concern was about tankers of water going to Asia, and then you end up with an agreement that allows the same or greater amounts of water to go anywhere in the world in bottles?" complained Dave Dempsey, a Great Lakes author. "It just doesn't make sense to me." That's a fair point, but legal experts assured the governors that, as odd as it might seem, if the water was in a bottle it was considered a "product" and would not set a precedent for bulk water diversions by pipe or ship.

One challenge was that some regional legislatures were unfamiliar with compacts in general. In the eastern Great Lakes Basin, states like New York, Pennsylvania, and Ohio were already parties to multiple water compacts, but in the western Great Lakes Basin, states like Minnesota, Wisconsin, and Michigan were much less familiar with the process. The Great Lakes St. Lawrence Governors and Premiers was responsible for helping to fill that knowledge gap, and staff there served a quarterback-like role on outreach and education as the Compact wound its way through sixteen different legislative bodies in the eight Great Lakes states. David Naftzger and Peter Johnson, who hold the top two positions at the Governors and Premiers organization, hit the road to meet with legislators, testify at hearings, and talk in minute detail with supporters and detractors alike about how the Compact would and would not impact Great Lakes water policy.

Illinois was the first state out of the gate, introducing Compact legislation right away in January of 2006. To many, that made sense, given that it was the state that had the least to lose by passing the legislation. "In Illinois, it's a little strange" admitted Dan Injerd from the state's DNR. Because elected officials were being asked to pass legislation that "sort of exempts us out of most of the operative requirements of the agreement." But Illinois legislators failed to pass the bill that year. The Compact was passed by the Ohio House in late 2006 by a vote of 81-5, but it languished in the Senate. As a result, 2006 was a legislative bust for Compact supporters. Andy Buchsbaum, who led the National Wildlife Federation's Great Lakes Office at the time recalls how skeptics started circling. "I remember we were getting called by reporters . . . 'Is the Compact dead? Nobody's passing it.' And we were like, 'Are you guys crazy?'" Mr. Buchsbaum adds that he felt a need to "counsel patience, because there was this kind of rush to say if it's not happening right away, it's not going to happen at all." Regardless, the fact remained that many states were talking about the Compact, but no state had managed to adopt any binding legislation.

The following year was a very different story. Once again, Minnesota lived up to its reputation as a regional environmental leader by not only introducing legislation but getting it passed early in the year, in large part thanks to the leadership of politicians like State Senator Ann Rest from the Democratic Farmer Labor Party. Illinois followed suit by adopting the Compact six months after that, and several other states introduced Compact legislation. Momentum was starting to build again, kind of. Wisconsin formed a special Compact Legislative Council Committee that met with a wide array of stakeholders to draft a bill for the full legislature to consider. Instead, in September of 2007, the special committee disbanded in failure after it "could not reach consensus."[16] Some influential opponents in Wisconsin spoke of killing the Compact, then challenging WRDA in court so that it could be thrown out, thereby allowing communities like Waukesha to pull water from Lake Michigan unhindered. The mixed legislative results in 2007 were followed by an extremely momentous year in 2008. Legislative activity raged in the six remaining states that needed to act. To the surprise of many, Indiana was the third state to adopt the Compact early in 2008. New York adopted the Compact a month later in what would end up being one of the last pieces of legislation that Democratic governor Eliot Spitzer signed before resigning amidst a prostitution scandal.

But a high-stakes drama was occurring in Wisconsin and Ohio. Opponents in those states banded together to either amend the Compact, or kill it. All it took was one state to balk on adopting the Compact and it would be game-over, so the fact that opponents in *two* states were working closely together posed a serious threat. Wisconsin opponents still didn't like the idea that straddling-county water-diversion applications could be dashed by a single gubernatorial veto. They wanted straddling-county applicants to be approved with a simple majority vote from the governors. "Allowing one governor from another state to deny a water diversion to citizens that cannot vote for that governor is a very serious problem," complained Wisconsin state senator Mary Lazich, Republican from New Berlin.[17] Ohio officials, led by State Senator Timothy Grendell, were concerned that the Compact infringed on private-property rights, and they too wanted the Compact amended. "If all the Compact said [was], 'Thou shalt not divert water out of the Great Lakes Basin,' we wouldn't be having this conversation," Senator Grendell said. "But the Compact also has some language that creates at least some uncertainty—if not a certainty—that private water rights in Ohio would be converted to public trust property."[18] Given that half the Great Lakes states had already adopted the Compact as is—by overwhelming majority votes—proposals to amend it were seen as deal-breakers. Legislatures in Minnesota, Illinois, Indiana, and New York would be highly unlikely to revisit the issue again. Compact supporters couldn't tell if the proposed amendments in Ohio and Wisconsin were a genuine effort to change the Compact or just a cynical poison pill. "Either they are intending to blow it up," said Noah Hall, at Wayne State University, "or they are so naïve that they don't know [that] what they are doing is going to blow it up."[19]

After weeks of negotiations, there was finally a breakthrough in Wisconsin. Officials there agreed to address many of the opponents' concerns by tweaking the state's Compact implementing language, rather than amending the Compact itself. But under withering pressure, the Wisconsin opponents caved on the controversial straddling-county one-veto issue. That section remained untouched and could not be softened by implementing language. Wisconsin went on to adopt the Compact overwhelmingly, but only after Governor Jim Doyle, a Democrat, called a special session to get it done. With a deal in Wisconsin, all attention was focused on Ohio. "Wisconsin deserts Grendell on Great Lakes compact," said an editorial headline in the Cleveland *Plain Dealer*, adding that the Ohio House had already adopted the Compact 90–3. The problem was in the Senate.[20] Then Senator Grendell announced a compromise of his own: he proposed amending the Ohio constitution to reinforce the fact that the Compact would not infringe on the state's private-property water rights. If the constitutional referendum was voted down by the public, the Compact would still go into force, but its effective date in Ohio, and therefore everywhere else, would be delayed until after the November election. Senator Grendell's compromise plan worked. Ohio adopted the Compact in late June and as expected, Pennsylvania followed a week later, resulting in the historical irony that Michigan was left as the final state to adopt the Compact. The state that had always been the loudest opponent of water diversions was the last to adopt the Compact—not because passage was ever in doubt, but because the state also overhauled its domestic water regulations at the same time, which just made for a heftier, and slower, legislative lift. Nevertheless, Michigan adopted the Compact on July 9, 2008. After all the drama, the final vote throughout the region wasn't even close. According to the Great Lakes and

St. Lawrence Governors and Premiers, 95 percent of all legislators in the Great Lakes region voted to approve the Compact—a resounding endorsement.

Then it was off to the US Congress in Washington, DC, where numerous senior members of the Great Lakes congressional delegation were eagerly waiting and had already laid the groundwork for quick and uneventful passage. Two weeks after Michigan adopted the Compact, legislation was introduced in the Senate, with Ohio Republican George Voinovich and Michigan Democrat Carl Levin as lead sponsors. "The Hill was totally ready to go. We had a few champions already lined up," remembers Peter Johnson from the Great Lakes St. Lawrence Governors and Premiers. "Senator Voinovich was a big champion and had been a big champion for a long time." Days later, President George W. Bush pledged his support. The week after the bill was introduced in the Senate, it was adopted by unanimous consent. In the House, things went less smoothly, with some of the leading opponents to the Compact coming from the Great Lakes region itself. Bart Stupak, a Democrat from Michigan's Upper Peninsula, announced he would vote against the bill because of the bottled water "loophole" that allowed water to be shipped out of the Great Lakes Basin as long as it was in containers smaller than 20 liters (5.7 gallons). Dennis Kucinich, a colorful Democrat from the Cleveland area, had similar concerns. But these efforts had no impact on the final outcome. The House adopted the Compact by a resounding vote of 390–25 on September 23, 2008.[21]

On Capitol Hill, the Compact's much-feared opposition from the Sunbelt states evaporated, if it was ever there to begin with. Most officials in water-starved states (who tend to be very familiar with water compacts) were surprisingly supportive. "The biggest story was the story that never came to be," said David Naftzger, with the Great Lakes St. Lawrence Governors and Premiers, "which was this expectation that there would be opposition from Western or Southern members of Congress." He said that the Western Congressional officials he met with operated on a principle that regions should be in charge of their own water resources and that, generally speaking, the less federal involvement the better. "The region that had the most 'no' votes was

The Great Lakes Compact and the Sustainable Water Resources Agreement were years in the making and marked a major turning point in Great Lakes water management. (Great Lakes St. Lawrence Governors and Premiers/ Great Lakes Commission)

actually our own," Mr. Naftzger said. "So that was surprising, and support was solid throughout the South and West." President Bush signed the Compact legislation ten days later—on October 3, 2008—which meant that the Compact streaked through DC—start to finish—in less than three months, a huge tribute to the power, influence, and legislative deftness of the Great Lakes congressional delegation.

But the news of the Compact's signing was overwhelmed by the global financial crisis. On the same day, the president also signed the massive $700-billion Wall Street bailout known as the Troubled Asset Relief Program (TARP). The Compact news was completely overshadowed by the Great Recession. On the Canadian side of the border, as expected, Ontario adopted the International Agreement that mirrors the Compact with little drama or fanfare in 2007, and Québec followed in 2009. The Compact may have been signed, but the effective date would have to wait until after the Ohio private-property rights constitutional referendum was voted on, thanks to the unusual stipulation in Ohio's Compact implementing legislation that delayed the Compact's effective date until after that November vote. The combination of the financial crisis and the Ohio referendum meant the Compact's actual effective date was also met with little fanfare or news coverage. But it ultimately became law on December 8, 2008. Ten years after the Nova proposal stirred officials to act, regional water management quietly entered a new and notable era, marked by one of the most ambitious bipartisan Great Lakes legislative feats in history.

Chapter 14

Waukesha Worries

Just before midnight on May 7, 1892, the town fire bell rang out in Waukesha, Wisconsin, but this time the alarm wasn't heralding a fire. The citizens of Waukesha (pronounced WAU-ka-shaw)[1] grabbed their shotguns, pistols, and clubs and headed for the tracks. Rumors had been swirling that a secret train loaded with workmen would arrive from Chicago to steal some of Waukesha's internationally acclaimed spring water. The thieves' plan was to lay a pipeline from Waukesha's Hygeia Spring to some unknown destination outside of town. From there, the water would ultimately be served to thirsty sightseers at the upcoming world's fair in Chicago.[2] The Windy City's water was notoriously bad at the time. One Chicago mayor was even accused of stashing Waukesha water at city hall to avoid the local tap.[3] By contrast, dozens of gurgling Waukesha springs had become premier tourist destinations for moneyed travelers from throughout North America. Some springs were even said to have healing powers, including Hygeia, which was owned by Chicago entrepreneur James McElroy—the man behind the secret train. Given its cachet, Waukesha water was the ideal world's fair beverage, and Mr. McElroy was desperate to serve it to fairgoers.

He had formally asked Waukesha for permission to send spring water south, but he met stiff resistance. Locals worried that piping water to Illinois would curtail Waukesha's prized tourist traffic. If people could get Waukesha water in Chicago, why would they travel to "Spring City"? It was only after being spurned that Mr. McElroy resorted to the midnight train. But rumors arrived long before the locomotive left Chicago, and when that unscheduled train reached the outskirts of town, the surprised workmen were met by hundreds of armed, angry Waukesha citizens who yelled, "Throw them into the river!" After a tense, extended showdown, the work train headed back to Chicago as dry as it had arrived.[4] Waukesha had valiantly defended its famous springs in a standoff that received wide publicity. The *Milwaukee Record* ran an editorial cartoon showing an enormous hog named "Chicago" wallowing in Mr. McElroy's spring, surrounded by armed, stern-faced residents—including one with a revolver trained directly at the pig's head.[5] That kind of media coverage only bolstered Waukesha's national water reputation, cementing its place as a tourist destination for many years to come.

∼

Oh, how the water fortunes have fallen in old Spring City. The water in Waukesha has become famous for entirely different reasons. By the late 1990s, the city had become a parable of water sustainability. With a population of 63,000 at that time, most of the Milwaukee suburb's historic springs were obliterated or abandoned, covered by gas stations, apartment buildings, and parking lots. The last local bottler from the springs era closed in 1997.[6] By 1995, water levels in some municipal wells had dropped by more than 500 feet, and the more deep groundwater the city pumped, the more salts and contaminants emerged. The chief concern was radium, a naturally occurring radioactive element believed to cause cancer after years of exposure; it had been detected in Waukesha's wells at twice the federal limit.[7]

After decades of ominous test results and no corrective action by Waukesha officials, Wisconsin authorities formally pressured the community to take action. In late 2003, Waukesha signed a consent order with the state forcing the suburb to resolve the radium issue in three years. The city would either have to use expensive treatment methods to extract the radium from its water, or find a cleaner, safer alternative water supply. The suburb, which lies just beyond the edge of the Great Lakes Basin, had made no secret of its interest in diverting up to 20 million gallons of water per day from Lake Michigan, a stance that put Waukesha on the front line in the Great Lakes water war. More importantly, it also meant that Waukesha was poised to become one of the first Great Lakes diversion applicants to step forward since the

WAUKESHA FRIGHTENING AWAY THE CHICAGO HOG.
(Printed by courtesy of the Milwaukee Record.)

Waukesha, which once defended its water from outsiders, now plans to divert water from the Great Lakes. (From the collection of John M. Schoenknecht)

Annex Implementing Agreements were signed in Milwaukee in December 2005.

~

By the time Waukesha signed its 2003 consent decree, it had already hired consultants to help find water alternatives. It quickly focused on two main options: spending $77 million to sink new wells in aquifers west of town, or looking east and spending $42 million to pump water from Lake Michigan, just fifteen miles away. The western aquifer option had drawbacks beyond the cost; there were concerns that drawing down those aquifers would eventually lower water levels in nearby streams and lakes. The problem with option two—tapping the Great Lakes—was that Waukesha lies outside the Great Lakes Basin, and thus, under the Water Resources Development Act of 1986 and the Great Lakes Compact released in 2005, a diversion to Waukesha required the unanimous approval of all eight Great Lakes governors. (Waukesha fell under the Compact's "straddling counties" exception; see chapter 13.) By the mid-2000s the Compact had been released, but it hadn't yet been adopted by any of the Great Lakes state legislatures. So if Waukesha did want to pursue Great Lakes water, its application would have to be processed under WRDA, and regional governors would likely use the new standards enumerated in the Compact to evaluate Waukesha's diversion application.

But there was another problem with the Lake Michigan option: the issue of return-flow. Since 1986, no US community had been allowed to divert water outside the Great Lakes Basin without agreeing to return the water to the lakes after it was used. The Compact reiterated the return-flow principle as well. The idea behind that standard was simple: in the rare instances where diversions from the Basin are permitted, the water should be returned (after being treated, of course) to minimize water lost to the Great Lakes system. That's why any Great Lakes diversion application—under WRDA or the Compact—that didn't include return-flow would likely be considered dead on arrival.

This posed a serious problem for Waukesha, which was adamantly opposed to return-flow—primarily because of cost. For decades, the city's treated wastewater has been discharged into the Fox River, a tributary in the Mississippi watershed. This meant that a return-flow requirement would force Waukesha to retrofit its urban water-treatment system to send its wastewater back to Lake Michigan. But the city said the return-flow requirement made Great Lakes water outlandishly expensive. While the Compact was still being negotiated, city officials made it clear that, while they were very interested in diverting Lake Michigan water, they had no interest in returning that water to the lake after it was used.

That rankled environmentalists throughout the region, and they attacked Waukesha from all sides. As usual, the critics' chief concern was not the effect that Waukesha's diversion would have on Lake Michigan water levels (hydrologists said the effect would be imperceptible). As with prior diversion controversies, what Waukesha's critics worried about was precedent. The effect of one Waukesha-like diversion without return-flow would be hard to measure, but a hundred Waukesha diversions would not. In fact, a hundred Waukeshas would nearly equal the Illinois diversion. Critics worried that a Waukesha return-flow exemption could be replicated over time to a damaging degree by communities large and small that lay beyond the Basin line. Many of Waukesha's critics also worried about using Great Lakes water to support sprawl, which they feared could negatively impact urban Milwaukee.

Despite fierce environmental opposition, Waukesha refused to budge on the return-flow issue. As the months passed, positions hardened, and as the criticism mounted, Waukesha started acting like a spurned suitor even before submitting its request for Great Lakes water. Waukesha's attitude didn't play well in newspapers, and seemingly overnight, the suburb became the latest polarizing villain in the eyes of the anti-diversion movement. "They have been quite successful in keeping themselves in the paper to the extent that they showed up in *The New York Times*," remarked Chuck Ledin, former head of the Wisconsin DNR's Great Lakes office. "Every characterization of their posture was one of aggressiveness, and how they had the 'right' to [Great Lakes] water."

Unlike Akron, Lowell, or Pleasant Prairie, Waukesha became an anti-diversion focal point before even submitting a water-diversion application.[8] With each passing decade, it seemed, the Great Lakes water-diversion debate was growing hotter and hotter. "Waukesha is a poster child," admitted Dan Duchniak, the embattled head of the Waukesha Water Utility, adding that the debate over Waukesha was "almost like a cyst that has grown into a cancerous tumor, and we need to figure out a way to treat it."

∽

In many ways, Waukesha brought this image problem upon itself. The city regularly appeared pugnacious, irascible, and unreasonable—particularly in the early years of the debate. When the US Environmental Protection Agency pressured Waukesha to find a safer water source, Waukesha took the EPA to court (and lost). When environmentalists suggested that local leaders adopt water-conservation measures, Waukesha refused (at least at first). When people mentioned that the Great Lakes governors were unlikely to approve a Waukesha diversion without return-flow, Waukesha threatened to sue. Throughout the debate, there was an arrogant undertone from Waukesha's leaders that *they* weren't the ones at fault, *others* were to blame. Hovering in the background was an almost ever-present hint from Waukesha officials that they would resort to litigation if they didn't get Great Lakes water on their own terms.

But Waukesha was also a victim of historical circumstance. It wanted to apply for Great Lakes water while the Annex Implementing Agreements were still being drafted. Yet Great Lakes negotiators had no interest in entertaining a new, highly charged diversion application while the final wording of the agreements remained unresolved. Behind the scenes, Waukesha was told to wait until final drafts of the agreements were released. All Waukesha could do was sit back and dream about the day it could finally apply for Great Lakes water. Even so, while Waukesha hung in an awkward limbo, its name kept coming up in public hearings and news stories about the agreements—often in a critical light. City officials defended their community vociferously. But the more defensive Waukesha became, the more isolated it appeared.

Eventually Waukesha softened its hardball strategy, admitting it was off base. "There was a recognition," Dan Duchniak said, "that if we're looking for future water-supply options, we need to be making friends, not foes. . . . There was a change of tone." There was also a change of strategy. Waukesha started spending $100,000 per year on public relations and water consultants to help the city make its case, burnish its image, and increase the sophistication of its message.[9] The consultants reminded the city that lawsuits aren't cheap and that the governors and premiers whom Waukesha was implicitly criticizing were the ones who controlled the Great Lakes tap.

One of the first things the consultants homed in on was Waukesha's underwhelming water-conservation record. Waukesha residents paid notoriously low water rates—some of the lowest in all of

Wisconsin—and the city had policies that encouraged lawn watering by giving customers a sewer credit for water applied to their grass. "The utility had always prided itself on never having a sprinkling ban," Mr. Duchniak admits, adding that the attitude had always been, "If this was a service that [residents] were requiring, 'Gosh darn it, we're gonna provide it.'" With encouragement from its consultants, however, and to make its eventual Great Lakes diversion application more politically palatable, in 2005 Waukesha embarked on a new conservation strategy designed to raise rates, rein in water use, and—ideally—turn Waukesha into a leading example of water conservation instead of water waste. Mr. Duchniak said his community had gotten the conservation message, and things were going to change. "I think Waukesha could be a role model that could set a good precedent for everyone to follow in the Great Lakes when it comes to conservation," he said back in 2005. Maybe so, but was a Johnny-come-lately water conservationist a viable candidate for a Great Lakes diversion? The city would have to file an application to find out.

The consultants increased the sophistication of the city's message. Waukesha spent a lot of time arguing that it really was *inside* the Great Lakes Basin, not outside as others had claimed. Waukesha does sit in a hydrologically unique geographic position. Yes, it's outside the Great Lakes surface-water divide—rain that falls on Waukesha and runs off into nearby streams eventually finds its way to the Mississippi River. But independent research also showed that Waukesha was inside the Great Lakes deep *groundwater* divide.[10] That means water in the deep aquifer underneath Waukesha eventually discharges into Lake Michigan, because the aquifer is connected to the lake bottom. Waukesha lay quite literally in a hydrogeologic gray area. As the Great Lakes Compact was being negotiated, Mr. Duchniak argued that Waukesha's unique position made it deserving of special consideration.

While that may have helped Waukesha's image, there was still the lingering issue of return-flow. How did Waukesha plan to resolve that? By claiming it deserved special treatment because it was already pulling water away from Lake Michigan underground. The reasoning behind this complex argument emanated directly from the hydrogeologic uniqueness of Waukesha's location. Before European settlement, the deep aquifer under Waukesha fed groundwater into Lake Michigan.

Southeast Wisconsin

While Waukesha lies outside the Great Lakes Basin surface-water divide, it is actually inside the Great Lakes groundwater divide. (Courtesy of the US Geological Survey, modified from D. T. Feinstein et al., "Simulation of Regional Groundwater Flow in Southeastern Wisconsin," Wisconsin Geological and Natural History Survey Open-File Report 2004–01 [2004])

But because of excessive pumping in the region—by Waukesha and others—that groundwater flow had been reversed and water was instead being pulled from Lake Michigan into the aquifer rather than the other way around. One would think this news might hurt Waukesha's case, but Dan Duchniak said it helped. Since Waukesha was already pulling water away from Lake Michigan underground, all it wanted to do, he said, was move that subterranean "diversion" to the surface—and keep its Mississippi River Basin discharge system the same. In other words, his argument goes, because Waukesha's groundwater pumping was already "diverting" water by pulling it away from Lake Michigan *beneath* the surface, why should it have to do return-flow if it diverts water from Lake Michigan *on* the surface?

That kind of reasoning infuriated environmentalists, who saw Waukesha finagling for an undeserved special exception. First, they argued, Waukesha was misrepresenting what was happening underground. Yes, the groundwater flow has been reversed, but because the aquifer was so huge—and the water moved through it so slowly—Lake Michigan water hadn't yet reached Waukesha's wells. Hence, Waukesha couldn't claim that it was already diverting Great Lakes water below the ground. Second, environmentalists said, communities that divert water from the Great Lakes have to send it back—period—no matter what kind of convoluted groundwater situation they might have. Advocates charged that Waukesha was asking for special treatment without precedent in modern times. Every community that had diverted water from the Great Lakes since 1986 has had to return the water to the Basin—a principle that was strongly reiterated in the 2005 Compact. Advocates were particularly adamant that exceptions shouldn't be made for sprawling suburban communities that have grown beyond their ecological means. The Great Lakes, they said, shouldn't be used as a water subsidy for urban sprawl outside the Basin. If Waukesha residents want Great Lakes water, they should move to the water, rather than moving the water to them.

The main point, environmentalists said, is that it's time for people to think about water before they decide where to live—something that, they argued, people moving to Waukesha had failed to do. Environmental advocates argued that if a community has a water problem, people shouldn't just continue moving there and assume the government will bail them out. "We're concerned that Waukesha is the shape of things to come," complained Susan Howatt, national water campaigner for the Council of Canadians. "We can't get into these situations where we make it okay for urban sprawl to [receive] water diversions that aren't sustainable." But under WRDA and the Great Lakes Compact, environmentalists don't have a vote. That responsibility is reserved for the Great Lakes governors. Back in 2005, how did the governors in other parts of the Basin feel about Waukesha's claim to a return-flow exemption? According to one gubernatorial aide intimately involved in drafting the Great Lakes Compact, Waukesha did garner sympathy for many of its claims—but there was zero tolerance for the city's stance regarding return-flow. "There is no sympathy for Waukesha," this person said, "when they say they should be allowed to divert water outside the Basin and then dump it in the Mississippi River watershed—none."

There was another reason for Waukesha to lean toward Lake Michigan. Mr. Duchniak said the aquifers bordering Waukesha had become mired in controversy, too. Conflicts had flared, and lawsuits had been filed by property owners alleging that regional groundwater levels have already been affected by overpumping. "We continue to investigate the western well supply," Mr. Duchniak said. "[But] there's going to be conflicts if we go there [as well].... we're surrounded by water conflict." What if Waukesha was unable to find an alternate long-term water supply before the 2006 state-mandated deadline? The city would have to depend on a combination of water blending and expensive treatment methods to bring its water into regulatory compliance for the short and medium term.

By 2005, Waukesha (or one of its water-troubled neighbors) was expected to be one of the first water-diversion applicants to step forward since the release of the Annex Implementing Agreements. "We would probably make an application that would not include return-flow," Mr. Duchniak said, "and see what happens." But Waukesha would not be able to file a water-diversion application under the Compact until the Compact was adopted by all eight Great Lakes legislatures and the US Congress. That would take years—if it happened at all—and Waukesha couldn't wait that long. Until the Compact was passed, WRDA would remain the primary regulator of Great Lakes water diversions in the United States. What would Waukesha do if its water application wound up being rejected? Possibly sue—either by challenging WRDA or the Compact in court. "I would say the legal option is something that is not off the table," Mr. Duchniak said back in 2005.

～

The talk about litigation confounded Doug Cherkauer, an emeritus hydrogeologist at the University of Wisconsin–Milwaukee. He is an expert on groundwater issues in southeastern Wisconsin and a regular panelist and commentator on the Waukesha issue. He would have liked to see people spend less time battling in the courts and more time sitting around the table thinking about new ways to better utilize the water resources that are available within a watershed. "As a society, the US has historically treated water as a really cheap commodity and as something that is there for the convenience of people. And if we have to move it from one location to another to satisfy the demands of people, so be it—we don't care what happens to the place we took it from," he says. "That worked in the eighteenth century, and it worked in the nineteenth century, and it started to fall apart in the twentieth century, and we ended up with Las Vegas, and Phoenix, and Los Angeles—and places that just shouldn't exist. But now we're seeing that same sort of problem move into the so-called water-rich areas."

Mr. Cherkauer said it was time to move on to a more sustainable way of managing water. Specifically, he wanted to see groundwater-dependent communities like Waukesha take their wastewater, treat it, and then apply it to the ground's surface in ways that allows it to soak into the soil. That way it could recharge regional aquifers, so the water could be withdrawn again and again. It's time to stop the "pump and dump" systems of old that send groundwater wastefully rushing downstream, he said, adding that society needs to start thinking more seriously about water recycling—not just in Waukesha but in all sorts of places.

Whether Waukesha followed his counsel was not the point, he said. What mattered was that the City should spend more time looking beyond the business-as-usual approach and less time drawing up legal strategies with attorneys. "Southeastern Wisconsin is at a crossroads right now," Mr. Cherkauer warned. "We have the opportunity to move forward into the twenty-first century and look for sustainable options, or we have the alternative approach of continuing to do things the way we've always done them—and impacts be damned. I would like to think that we would take this opportunity to sit back and reflect a little bit and do it right, rather than charging off down a path because it's easy."

~

But in early 2006, Waukesha couldn't resist the temptation to slip back into hardball mode. The City hired the law firm of Godfrey & Kahn to help pressure the state one more time to see things Waukesha's way. The law firm sent an unusual letter to the Wisconsin governor, saying Waukesha was entering into "negotiations" with the state regarding the City's desire for Lake Michigan water. "The purpose of these negotiations is to explore a resolution of this dispute as a means to avoid litigation," the letter warned. What's more, since the letter was sent as a part of "settlement negotiations," the law firm maintained that its correspondence should be "protected from disclosure under the Open Record Law."[11] In other words, Waukesha wanted to play tough, but in secret—lest it taint the City's new public relations effort to try to demonstrate a kinder, gentler approach.

Attached to the confidential letter was a document titled "Statement by Waukesha Water Utility Supporting Its Position That Its Request for Lake Michigan Surface Water Is Authorized by the Proposed Annex 2001 Agreement and WRDA." The document reiterated what Waukesha had been claiming for years: all it wanted to do was replace its underground "diversion" with a surface diversion, and since it didn't have to return the diverted underground water to the lake, it shouldn't have to return the diverted surface water either. The city was still pushing to divert Great Lakes water without the expense of return-flow. The situation was straightforward, the law firm said; the City "simply wishes to replace its present withdrawal of water from the deep aquifer with water from the surface of Lake Michigan."

Two months later, the firm sent another confidential letter to the governor, reiterating its claim, but this time it offered up a precedent. Attorneys had dug up a case involving the Town of Dyer in northwest Indiana. It said Dyer had been using groundwater that was tributary to Lake Michigan, just like Waukesha. And just like Waukesha, Dyer was discharging its treated wastewater into the Mississippi River watershed. However, the law firm reported that in 1995 (nine years after WRDA was adopted—and three years after Michigan vetoed Lowell's diversion request), Indiana officials quietly allowed Dyer to stop pumping groundwater and divert water from Lake Michigan instead. Indiana officials allowed this to happen without getting permission from the Great Lakes governors—even though the diverted Lake Michigan water would continue to be discharged into the Mississippi River watershed.[12] How could Dyer's diversion without return-flow be quietly approved and Waukesha's denied? All Waukesha was asking for was to be treated just like Dyer. If not, the correspondence implied, we'll see you in court.

The tactic fell flat, however. Dan Duchniak said that in a follow-up meeting with Bruce Baker at the Wisconsin DNR, Mr. Baker essentially mocked Waukesha's strategy, and was deeply dismissive of the law firm's high-pressure approach. He scolded Waukesha, saying that the no-return-flow idea would never fly, because Michigan, and probably several other states, would surely veto it. "[He] wasn't taking us seriously, and we kinda got pissed off at that, and I actually walked out of his office," Mr. Duchniak said. "Good luck," Mr. Duchniak remembers Mr. Baker saying.

That dramatic meeting was the beginning of the end of Waukesha's opposition to return-flow. Over time, Mr. Duchniak said, officials in the governor's office, the DNR, his consultants, and even contacts in other Great Lakes states convinced him that Mr. Baker was right, there just was no way he would ever get his hands on Lake Michigan water without returning it after it was used. After fervently and controversially fighting return-flow for years, he finally backed down. "It was going to be difficult for us to get Michigan, or any other state, to approve a diversion without return-flow," he said. "We finally came to the realization that it wasn't going to happen." That would prove to be a crucial evolution in Waukesha's thinking about Great Lakes water. Mr. Duchniak describes that as "the day of reckoning," adding, "The table started to turn, and we started to look seriously at return-flow."

The first decade of the new millennium showcased some remarkable backpedaling by Waukesha officials. First, they challenged the EPA's radium rule, and lost. Then they refused to pursue water conservation, before backing down. That was followed by bare-knuckle tactics with the DNR and other officials, before succumbing to a change of heart. And most significantly, after years of opposing return-flow, Waukesha officials finally changed their mind on that, too—just as the Great Lakes Compact looked like it might finally become a reality. Even so, to the surprise of many, it would end up being years before Waukesha finally put together a water-diversion application. In the meantime, another Milwaukee suburb would end up slipping ahead of Waukesha in line to become the first community to test the brand-new Great Lakes Compact.

Chapter 15

New Berlin: The Compact's Forgotten Test Case

When the Council of Great Lakes Governors unveiled the final version of the Compact at a press conference in Milwaukee's regal Pfister Hotel on December 13, 2005, Waukesha was still soaking up most of the water-diversion limelight in the Great Lakes region. At the time, the Compact was just a piece of paper, and people were making wagers as to whether it would ever become law. But if and when it did, Waukesha had been on the front pages so frequently that most people assumed that it would be the first community to apply for a diversion under one of the Compact's controversial exceptions clauses. But Waukesha's judgment day was still years away. Instead, a smaller, lesser-known suburb would be the first community to submit a Compact water-diversion request: New Berlin, Wisconsin, a suburb located between Waukesha and Milwaukee—and sitting atop Waukesha County's famously depleted and naturally contaminated deep aquifer. New Berlin's situation was similar to Waukesha's, including being under state pressure to find a cleaner water source. But in several critical ways, it was also quite different.

Waukesha fell under the Compact's controversial so-called straddling-county exception clause, which allowed communities in a county that straddled the Great Lakes Basin line to apply for a water diversion. But because those communities themselves were clean-and-clear outside the Great Lakes Basin, their diversion proposal would need the approval of all eight Great Lakes governors—a very high bar. New Berlin, on the other hand, fell under the much more liberal "straddling community" exception clause. Because the community itself sat directly on top of the Basin line—partly inside the Great Lakes watershed, partly out of it—its water diversion proposal would be vetted and ruled on solely by the local state's governor, Jim Doyle, a Democrat, who would take it upon himself to determine whether New Berlin met the myriad requirements demanded of a Compact water diversion applicant. No other governor would have the option of vetoing New Berlin's diversion request.

Why? Because the water managers who drafted the Compact wanted to make it easier for water-troubled communities to apply for a water diversion if they were already partly inside the Great Lakes Basin. Managers knew there were numerous communities in the region that literally sat right on top of the Great Lakes Basin line, such as Akron, Pleasant Prairie, and New Berlin, and that managing their water systems had become a plumbing and legal nightmare. In some cases, the side of town inside the Great Lakes Basin was drinking Great Lakes water, while the rest of town was drinking lower-quality or even contaminated groundwater. That meant water managers needed a different water supply depending on which side of the street a person might live on. The primary goal of the Compact's "straddling community" exception clause was to find a way for these water-troubled, uniquely positioned communities to send Great Lakes water to the water-stressed side of town, outside the Great Lakes Basin, without setting a legal precedent that would open the floodgates to long-range, large-scale diversions to far-flung, water-parched areas of the continent.

The straddling-community exception clause was designed to do just that by creating a strict series of requirements for potential water-diversion applicants. First, a straddling community would need to prove that its water-supply problem could not be resolved by water conservation before the community turned to the Great Lakes for help. Then it would need to prove that the amount of water requested was "reasonable" and that there would be no adverse environmental impacts caused by the proposed water diversion. Finally, and most importantly, the water would need to be treated and returned to the Great Lakes after it was used.

Few straddling communities fit the bill better than New Berlin. The suburb of 40,000 people was naturally divided into three different sections. The eastern third of town was predominantly residential,

New Berlin, Wisconsin

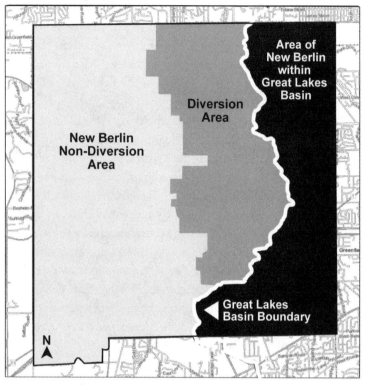

The eastern third of New Berlin lies inside the Great Lakes Basin. In 2006, the city applied for a Lake Michigan water diversion. New Berlin is what the Great Lakes Compact refers to as a "straddling community" because it sits right on top of the Great Lakes Basin line.

and people there were already drinking problem-free Lake Michigan water because that section of town happened to be inside the Basin. The middle third of town had some residential neighborhoods, but also served as the main business district, and was getting by with water from the depleted and naturally contaminated deep aquifer—water that exceeded federal limits for radium. The western third of town was more pastoral, where farms and five-acre farmettes were common, but it was surviving just fine on shallow private wells and thus had no interest or need for Great Lakes water. It was that middle section of town, which sat just outside the Great Lakes watershed line, that the suburb was interested in servicing with a relatively small Lake Michigan water diversion. It seemed like a simple request, but New Berlin's proposal would turn out to be a convoluted and controversial first test of the brand-new Great Lakes Compact.

~

According to New Berlin's voluminous file at the Wisconsin Department of Natural Resources, the suburb's water problems began back in the mid-1980s, when tests showed drinking water exceeded government health limits for carcinogenic radium. Like Waukesha, New Berlin was forced to sign a consent decree promising to resolve the city's water woes by the end of 2006. Consultants convinced city leaders to apply for a Lake Michigan diversion, arguing that it had an advantage over Waukesha or even Akron: returning its diverted water back to Lake Michigan would not be an issue. New Berlin's sewer system was already connected to Milwaukee's wastewater-treatment network, which meant that—even before asking for a diversion—the suburb was already sending its wastewater back to Lake Michigan, and this included the water-troubled middle section of town. History had shown that "return-flow" was *the* biggest issue for diversion applicants, and here New Berlin was sending surplus water back to the Great Lakes before it even asked for a diversion. That might make it the most favorably positioned community ever to request Great Lakes water.

The DNR agreed that New Berlin's case was straightforward, but in the mid-2000s—as with Waukesha—state officials discouraged New Berlin from applying for a diversion because the Great Lakes Compact was still working its way through regional legislatures. Officials feared other Great Lakes states would be reluctant to entertain a diversion application when the Compact's status was in flux. But New Berlin impatiently pushed ahead, arguing that it could meet the Compact's requirements, whether or not it was law. Who would object to that? In April 2006, New Berlin submitted a water-diversion application to the Wisconsin DNR. The application requested 2.48 million gallons per day (mgd) to be diverted to the middle section of town, trumpeting the fact that the suburb's return-flow system was already in place. Rather than make the application public, however, DNR officials—ever worried about water politics—decided to send the water application confidentially to the other Great Lake states and provinces for a quiet peer review.

Quietly circulating a water-diversion application hadn't worked for Akron, and it didn't work for New Berlin either. Just two weeks later, Michigan governor Jennifer Granholm dropped a bombshell press release that spanked down New Berlin's proposal, saying that she would "not consider the application for diversion." Period. The news was splashed across newspapers and television screens the next day. The press release blindsided the Wisconsin DNR, but the agency shouldn't have been surprised. Governor Granholm, a Democrat, was up for re-election against a heavily funded candidate, Republican Dick DeVos. Any water bureaucrat in the Great Lakes region should have known that a diversion application during a Michigan election year would be an extremely tough sell, no matter how strong the application might be. "The political conventional wisdom in Michigan is very straightforward," counseled Noah Hall, a Compact expert at Wayne State University in Detroit. "Don't approve a Great Lakes diversion, especially before an election."[1] That's sage advice, of course—but hold on, Wisconsin officials said. It's not like they sent the application to Michigan unannounced. They had already spoken to representatives from Michigan's Great Lakes office and briefed Dana Debel, Governor Granholm's environmental aide, before sending the document. Ms. Debel seemed receptive to giving the diversion application a closer look, and gave no hint of any knee-jerk opposition that might come from Governor Granholm or other staff. The same was true with staffers in Michigan's Office of the Great Lakes. But once the diversion application arrived, Governor Granholm's campaign officials quickly got wind of it, and that's when things got squirrelly.

"Oh yeah. I remember it well," said Todd Ambs, former head of the Wisconsin DNR's water division. Mr. Ambs said that when the New Berlin application was refined enough that it was ready to be shared with other states, he and his DNR colleague Bruce Baker split up the calls and started contacting water managers and governors' offices throughout the Great Lakes region. The point was to let these officials know that a Wisconsin water-diversion application was ready for regional feedback under WRDA, and to give these officials a quick phone briefing on what to expect in the document. But while

Michigan's natural resource staffers may have been initially receptive to giving the New Berlin application a look, the reaction from Governor Granholm's campaign staff was quite different. "Dana called and said, 'I've just been overruled by the political people,'" Mr. Ambs remembers. "She said something to the effect of, 'They haven't read it. They don't know what's in it. . . . They just made a snap judgment that they were going to say that the governor is opposed."

"Is there anyone I can talk to over there?" Mr. Ambs asked.

No, Ms. Debel said, it was too late. "I'm sorry. The statement is going out in a half hour."

Governor Granholm made no reference to her campaign in the press release, but politics aside, she did make another overall key point in her statement that would end up resonating in the region: no water-diversion proposals should be considered until the Great Lakes Compact becomes law. "The collective regional focus," she said, "now needs to be on all states passing, and Congress ratifying, the [Compact] agreements." Governor Granholm had a point. If water-diversion applications were allowed to be processed before the Compact became law, where would the political pressure be for regional politicians to formally adopt the Compact?

Governor Granholm's bold stroke thrust the Wisconsin DNR on the defensive. Environmentalists reamed the agency for a lack of transparency, and endorsed her suggestion of a diversion moratorium until the Compact was law. They reminded officials that while the Compact was moving through regional legislatures, the federal Water Resources Development Act still gave other Great Lakes states the right to veto diversion proposals of any size. Equally important was the hostile reaction from Milwaukee Mayor Tom Barrett. He was steamed that the DNR had not shared New Berlin's application with him before circulating it with other states—especially since his city was supposedly going to be supplying New Berlin with the diverted water. "It's not the Doyle administration's water to barter," declared Patrick Curley, Mayor Barrett's chief of staff. "We're not about to set a precedent until all the states have [Compact] water laws in place."[2]

But a few weeks later Wisconsin responded to Michigan with a bombshell of its own. In an interview with the *Milwaukee Journal Sentinel*, Bruce Baker, the DNR's deputy water administrator, said that his state had been quietly permitting water diversions *for years*—without seeking the permission of other Great Lakes states—as long as that water was being returned to the Great Lakes Basin. "Our policy," he told reporter Dan Egan, "had always been that if you have return-flow, it's not a diversion."[3] Who needs to consult Michigan if the water is sent back? Mr. Baker admitted that after Congress passed WRDA in 1986, his office had approved water diversions to Kenosha, in the southeast corner of the state, as well as the Milwaukee suburb of Menomonee Falls—without getting permission from other states—because those communities returned the water to Lake Michigan. In Wisconsin, that was not considered to be a diversion, Mr. Baker said, because the water was returned.

Kenosha had been diverting water across the Basin line for decades—long before WRDA was adopted—but Wisconsin had permitted expansions to those diversions, even after WRDA became law, without telling other governors. More noteworthy was the DNR's decision to approve a brand-new diversion to Menomonee Falls starting in 1998. That was different from just allowing an existing diversion to be expanded. The *Journal Sentinel* said the Kenosha and Menomonee Falls diversions totaled 1.4 million unapproved gallons of water per day. The story said the only reason Wisconsin was contacting other states now about New Berlin was not because it was required to, but because Wisconsin "did not want to go it alone at a time when cooperation among the Great Lakes states is so crucial."[4] In other words, when the region was working collectively to pass the Compact in all eight Great Lakes legislatures, Wisconsin was trying to avoid roiling the waters.

So much for that idea. Thanks to Governor Granholm's press release, the waters were now officially roiled. Two key states were locked in a water-diversion battle that could shove the entire Compact approval process off course. Michigan was threatening to veto a controversial water application that Wisconsin said it could approve on its own, apparently as it had been doing for years. The regional comity that had graced the Compact negotiating room was suddenly at risk. "We were pretty pissed off by Michigan's actions," says one former Wisconsin official. "We were trying to play by the Compact's rules here, and [they] just screwed us."

In an interview, more than a decade after the New Berlin application attracted headlines, Bruce Baker was matter-of-fact about Wisconsin's unique WRDA interpretation. "The understanding at the time with WRDA was we're going to not call these things diversions if there's return-flow," he said. But Chuck Ledin, who led Wisconsin's Great Lakes Office for years, had a less nuanced recollection. He said many states engaged in selective interpretations of WRDA—and the Great Lakes Charter—when it served their self-interest. Wisconsin was just doing the same thing. He complained that Michigan had controversially approved the Mud Creek consumptive-use proposal, despite objections from other jurisdictions—a clear violation of the Charter (chapter 10). He denounced Michigan even more vociferously over a larger, but lesser known, consumptive-use case involving the White Pine Mine, near Ontonagon, in 1998. "They did the same thing when they flooded the White Pine copper mine up in the U.P. [Michigan's Upper Peninsula]. They said they were going to take, like, 4 billion gallons to fill the mine. . . . The idea was not a diversion, but a consumptive loss," Mr. Ledin said, which meant that, under the Charter, Michigan officials were supposed to consult other Great Lakes states and provinces before permitting such a massive consumptive use. But Michigan didn't.

What's more, Mr. Ledin said, the state of Indiana had approved a diversion in Dyer (chapter 14) without getting regional review. His point was that a number of Great Lakes states were not following the water-diversion rules that they had set up for themselves, so Wisconsin wasn't either. The system was starting to unravel. "The thing that always irritated people in Wisconsin was that we thought we were doing the right thing by the Great Lakes, and other people were trashing us," Mr. Ledin said. "Sometimes it's better to do something, in the old saying, and then beg forgiveness, rather than trying to beg for approval. . . . Michigan says they're going to do something and they just do it. They tell everyone afterwards they're doing it; they don't solicit comments. Indiana did the same thing," he said. "So the lesson, my lesson, out of all of that was push ahead and do it and don't try to make everyone happy because it ain't gonna happen."

Mr. Ledin also defended the decision to quietly approve a new return-flow diversion to Menomonee Falls in 1998. The approval was part of a decades-long sustainable water-planning effort to help the greater Milwaukee area comply with the federal Clean Water Act. He said that through litigation the DNR had forced Menomonee Falls to abandon its own sewage-treatment system and connect to Milwaukee's. As part of that deal, Menomonee Falls was allowed to connect to Milwaukee's Lake Michigan drinking water system, even though part of the suburb was outside the Great Lakes Basin.

As part of that process, Wisconsin quietly approved the small water diversion to the west side of Menomonee Falls without notifying other Great Lakes states—at least not until Bruce Baker mentioned it during his newspaper interview. But according to an official map provided by Menomonee Falls, that initial 1998 diversion was then followed by two more small diversions to the suburb in 1999, another in 2000, and in 2001, and in 2002, and in 2003—not one of which was reported to other Great Lakes states. Meanwhile, Kenosha officials confirm that the Wisconsin DNR also approved small diversions there, without notifying other Great Lake states, in 1989, 1990, 1995, 1998, and 2003.[5] In total, between 1990 and 2003 Wisconsin approved at least twelve return-flow diversions of Great Lakes water without alerting or consulting other Great Lakes states. All of those diversions may have been illegal under federal law. "WRDA is very straightforward in one respect—it makes diverting water from the Great Lakes outside the Great Lakes watershed, without the approval of all the Great Lakes governors, unlawful," says Noah Hall at Wayne State. "The fact that there is 100 percent return-flow," he adds, "does not make the diversion not a diversion."

Because these historic, incremental diversions are so old, current officials in Menomonee Falls and Kenosha were unable to provide records on their exact sizes. But in all likelihood, they were relatively small. (But keep in mind that WRDA said that diversions of *any* size needed the approval of all Great Lakes governors.) Today, these diversions are on a list of twelve historical Wisconsin diversions that are now grandfathered under the Great Lakes Compact and are published on the Great Lakes St. Lawrence Governors and Premiers website.[6] That means that if those diversions were illegal at one point, they are likely to be legal now. According to an official tally provided by the Wisconsin DNR, Menomonee Falls now diverts 367,000 gallons of surface water from Lake Michigan every day. Meanwhile, according to the DNR, the Kenosha diversion now totals 2.54 mgd—but it's not clear how much of that diversion amount was approved after WRDA was adopted in 1986, though it was probably around a million gallons a day[7]—roughly the amount that Lowell, Indiana, was asking for back in 1991 (chapter 9).

How does it feel to be in a community that received water diversions that some argue may have been illegal? Jeff Nettesheim is Menomonee Falls's director of utilities and is happy to point out that all of the diversions in question went on line before he assumed his current position. That said, and while admitting he is obviously biased, he thinks the DNR made the right decision for his town. "I understood where they were coming from. Well, yeah, physically [the water] went over [the Basin line], but it also returns, so in essence it never left," he said. "It made practical sense to me.... How can Michigan be telling everybody else the way it's supposed to be?"

⁓

Despite the Wisconsin–Michigan spat over the New Berlin application, other states and provinces generally stayed out of the fray, quietly sending Wisconsin the feedback it was seeking about New Berlin. Illinois, Ohio, and New York asked for more details regarding water supply alternatives. Québec and Ontario wanted more information on potential adverse environmental impacts. All in all, pretty soft feedback, which is what the DNR had been expecting. Michigan's opposition still loomed large, however, and Wisconsin kept pushing New Berlin's case, despite Michigan's strong opposition. On September 26, 2006, the Wisconsin DNR announced a sixty-day public comment period about the New Berlin proposal. A press release quoted Bruce Baker saying the state wanted feedback on "how we should handle proposals for Lake Michigan water until the Great Lakes Compact is finalized." In the same press release, Mr. Baker continued to goad Michigan by claiming that "under existing federal law, New Berlin's proposal could be determined to be a non-diversion because no water would be lost from the Lake Michigan Basin."

This time it was Michigan's Republican attorney general Mike Cox who took the bait, spanking down Wisconsin once again. "AG Cox Blocks Wisconsin's Efforts to Divert Water from Great Lakes," screamed a press release from Mr. Cox's office. The release argued that, under WRDA, "New Berlin cannot proceed with the diversion without obtaining approvals from each of the [Great Lakes] governors." In a separate letter, Mr. Cox said he was "troubled" by Mr. Baker's claims, taunting him by wondering why New Berlin kept referring to its proposal as a "diversion" if it was not one. "New Berlin makes clear throughout its application that it is requesting a diversion," the letter said. Perhaps even more damning, Mr. Cox pointed out, Mr. Baker's own boss referred to the proposal as a "diversion" in the cover letter sent to Governor Granholm with the application. What's more, Wisconsin's interpretation of WRDA was starting to attract the attention of other states. Cathy Curran Myers, who was deputy secretary of Pennsylvania's Water Management Office at the time, challenged Wisconsin's interpretation of the federal statute in an e-mail to the DNR: "We believe WRDA applies to the New Berlin proposal." Wisconsin continued to get pushback at home too. Wisconsin environmental organizations aligned themselves with Michigan and Pennsylvania. "The state of Michigan has already indicated that it will invoke its veto authority under the federal legislation, WRDA," wrote Melissa Malott with Clean Wisconsin, a leading environmental group. "The better course for our State to follow at this time is to not move on any applications for diversion until the requisite standards of the Compact are in place."

As 2006 came to a close, in yet another interview with the *Milwaukee Journal Sentinel*, Bruce Baker continued to claim that Wisconsin could proceed unilaterally.[8] But that strategy came to a shuddering halt on December 27, 2006, when Wisconsin's attorney general Peggy Lautenschlager surprised everyone by releasing an official letter saying Wisconsin could do nothing of the sort. As it happens, unbeknownst to the DNR, Wisconsin state senator Robert Wirch had asked Ms. Lautenschlager whether Wisconsin had the right to approve return-flow diversions under WRDA without consulting other Great Lakes governors. Her answer: a resounding "no." Ms. Lautenschlager's seventeen-page, single-spaced letter warned Wisconsin officials that if they approved New Berlin's diversion unilaterally, they ran the risk of marginalizing their state's voice in future water-diversion controversies. Then, after revisiting pages and pages of Great Lakes water-diversion history, she dealt a blow to Wisconsin's unique claim that a return-flow diversion was not really a diversion. "It is my opinion that any new diversions from any portion of the Great Lakes ... for use outside the Great Lake basin, are diversions within the meaning of WRDA regardless of whether the diversions will result in return-flows," she wrote. "Therefore, under the Water Resources Development Act of 1986, such diversions require the approval of all Great Lakes governors."

Suddenly, the Wisconsin DNR found itself in the untenable position of having its own attorney general agreeing with the Michigan attorney general, along with the Commonwealth of Pennsylvania, that unilaterally approving New Berlin would violate federal law. And, presumably, it meant that Wisconsin had been violating federal law for years by quietly approving diversions in Kenosha and Menomonee Falls after WRDA was adopted in 1986. The DNR's Chuck Ledin felt blind-sided. "We reacted to that by asking the City of Kenosha if they were total idiots or whatever prompted them to get Wirch all excited to do that without *any* discussion with DNR ahead of time," Mr. Ledin said. "Somebody got to him from the environmental community, and I don't know who it was, and convinced him that we had to have that answered by the attorney general." To Mr. Ledin's surprise, Ms. Lautenschlager did not share a courtesy copy of the letter with the DNR in advance. "So I was like, 'Oh great, now what are we going to do?'" he said. "How could you counter what the state attorney general said?"

~

As surprising as Ms. Lautenschlager's letter was, it did not prevent the DNR from continuing to vet New Berlin's application. In July of 2007, the DNR gave New Berlin mayor Jack Chiovatero permission to begin water-supply discussions with Milwaukee. The DNR's Todd Ambs released a statement the same day. "We firmly believe that this application meets the standards of the Great Lakes Compact—even though those standards are not yet law," he wrote. "The result, we believe, is the most comprehensive application ever received for the use of Great Lakes water." What's more, because 1,800 homes in the city were on private wells, but returned their sewage to Milwaukee to be treated, the city would be returning 1.3 gallons back to Lake Michigan for every gallon received. "We hope that New Berlin will be able to secure a water source," he said. "Now we must pass the Great Lakes Compact in Wisconsin so that in the future, decisions like these can be made with clear guidelines, direction, and standards."

The following spring, Wisconsin did adopt the Compact. Federal approval soon followed. On December 8, 2008, the Compact became law, and New Berlin's application was tracking perfectly alongside it. Weeks later, New Berlin's consultants asked the DNR to finally make the long-sought diversion a reality. But the DNR said there would be one more delay. Now that the Compact had been passed the agency was required to run New Berlin's application through the Compact process, as frustrating as that might be, before the suburb could get its water. That would require a new water-supply service-area plan, yet another public hearing and comment period, and more examination of the suburb's water-conservation efforts. The latest data suggested that New Berlin's per capita daily water use was roughly 70 gallons per day, which was well under the US average of eighty to one hundred gallons.[9] In addition, under DNR pressure, New Berlin agreed to reduce its per capita water use by an additional 10 percent by the year 2020, a goal it met long before that deadline.[10]

On May 21, 2009, just months after the Compact became law, Governor Jim Doyle finally approved the diversion at 2.142 mgd. For the most part, environmentalists welcomed the decision as a good first Compact test case. "What I am encouraged about is [that] this is the first successful implementation of the Great Lakes Compact," said Jodi Habush Sinykin of the Midwest Environmental Advocates, who had closely followed the New Berlin file. "Their water was a public health issue, and it's important that it will be returned."[11] Andy Buchsbaum, from the National Wildlife Federation's Great Lakes office, called the New Berlin diversion "a good one to start with" because more water was being returned than diverted. "It's like we are getting an import."[12] But Dave Dempsey, a Great Lakes author who served as an environmental adviser to Michigan governor James Blanchard in the 1980s, told the *Great Lakes Echo* he was "very disappointed" by the decision, fearing it would spawn a burst of applications from other straddling communities. He argued WRDA provided stronger Great Lakes protections. "Now we have a system [where] one state can approve [a diversion]," he said. "We had a stronger system before the Compact."[13]

What kind of precedent did New Berlin really set? At the suburb's final public hearing in March 2009, speakers reminded the DNR of the New Berlin diversion's historical significance. But the agency's official written response to those comments downplayed New Berlin's precedent-setting nature, calling it "extremely limited" and adding that it "would depend on the level of similarity between the facts of each request." "The DNR considers New Berlin's situation and diversion request to be unique and not likely to influence DNR's decision on future diversion applications."

That sounds like a bureaucrat's fantasy. History had shown that prior water diversions have always had a huge influence on how pending Great Lakes diversion applications were judged. Now that the Compact was in force, it was extremely likely that New Berlin would not only influence how future straddling-community applications would be handled in Wisconsin, but in other states, too. The bigger question, perhaps, was whether New Berlin's case would have a chilling effect on future straddling-community applications. New Berlin had set a very high bar. For starters, it was returning surplus water to the Great Lakes Basin before it even applied for a diversion. In addition, it promised to continue sending surplus water back to the Basin after the diversion went on line, and that's after allowing for a loss to consumptive use. And finally, even though the community's per capita water use was well below the national average, it still committed to reducing water use by an additional 10 percent. That's a tough act for future straddling-community applicants to follow.

It has been years since New Berlin was approved—so long ago that many Great Lakes residents have forgotten all about it. Fears that the suburb's diversion would prompt a flood of copycat applications have not been borne out. How many potential straddling communities are out there? A 2013 study by the Alliance for the Great Lakes, a Chicago-based environmental group, provided educated guesses as to which Great Lakes cities might be the next water-diversion applicants. It highlighted eight potential diversion hotspots, stretching from suburban Milwaukee to the outskirts of Cleveland. The list was split evenly between potential "straddling community" and "straddling county" applicants. "This report identifies a number of communities," the Alliance wrote, "that may face the need for an alternative water supply soon and could find requesting Great Lakes water a sensible prospect in the coming decade."[14] Of the four potential straddling communities listed, three were in Indiana: Valparaiso (pop. 33,000), St. John (pop. 17,000), and Fort Wayne, which, at 266,000 people, was by far the largest potential applicant. The only other potential straddling community mentioned was Muskego, Wisconsin, which lies directly south of New Berlin and has a population of 25,000. Years later, none of those communities had applied for a diversion. It is unclear how much the high bar that was set by New Berlin has influenced them or any other potential straddling-community applicant.

As drawn out as New Berlin's application was, the Compact definitely made the process easier for straddling communities. Things clearly sped up for New Berlin once the Compact became law. The fact that a straddling community no longer needed to time an application to the Michigan gubernatorial election cycle was an enormous advantage in and of itself. Not requiring regional review, and keeping the decision-making process within the local state, made things much simpler for these uniquely positioned communities. In fact, New Berlin might have found things to be much easier if it has just waited until the Compact was adopted before applying for Great Lakes water. But when the city first applied, it was far from clear that the Compact would ever become law. "Since we were the first test case, I think it took a lot longer because there was a lot of checking and double-checking," says Jack Chiovatero, New Berlin's mayor at the time. "This took up probably six, seven years of my entire mayoral tenure." But if New Berlin felt it had been dragged through the diversion ditch longer than necessary, its experience would pale in comparison with what Waukesha—its "straddling county" neighbor to the West—was about to endure just a few years later.

Chapter 16

Waukesha Takes Its Shot

The Great Lakes watershed is a superlative freshwater basin spanning over 295,000 square miles and harboring 84 percent of all the fresh surface water in North America.[1] When looking at this majestic geographic feature, one can see that on the north side of Lake Huron, the distance between the shoreline and the Basin's edge is substantial. The watershed stretches out into the remote Ontario bush for 100 miles. By contrast, in the urbanized southwest corner of Lake Michigan, between Milwaukee and Chicago, the distance between the shoreline and the Basin boundary is remarkably narrow—less than 5 miles in some stretches.

It is in this slender slice of the watershed—where the shoreline is closest to the Basin line—that regional water tensions are highest. Call it the front line in the Great Lakes Water War. New Berlin lies in this conflict zone, as does Pleasant Prairie, not to mention Chicago—home to the most controversial diversion of the twentieth century, which continues to send 2.1 billion gallons to the Gulf of Mexico daily.[2] The most controversial diversion of the *twenty-first* century lies in this conflict zone too: Waukesha. The amount of water Waukesha desired was a fraction of a fraction of what Chicago pulled out of the Basin every day. Yet, Waukesha has become to this century what Chicago was to the last: the most polarizing Great Lakes water diversion of our time.

Some saw Waukesha as an admirably scrappy suburb that was tirelessly clawing its way toward Great Lakes water, all in the face of misguided and misinformed opponents. To others, Waukesha was a conniving, unctuous, and arrogant water applicant that couldn't qualify

Great Lakes Watershed

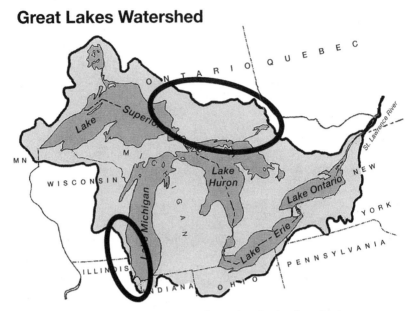

The Great Lakes Basin is approximately one hundred miles wide in some areas, and only a few miles wide in others. The narrow stretch of the watershed passing through southeastern Wisconsin and northeastern Illinois is where water tensions in the Great Lakes region are highest. (Adapted from International Joint Commission)

for Great Lakes water on its merits, so it spent millions on consultants and lobbyists to game the system. To supporters, Waukesha's case was strong and straightforward: the city's depleted groundwater was naturally contaminated with carcinogenic radium and it was under state pressure to resolve its water-supply problems. To opponents, the case was equally straightforward: Waukesha was the victim of its own sprawling, unsustainable water practices and did not deserve Great Lakes water. It had other water options, including increased conservation, radium-treatment technologies, tapping other aquifers, and blending them with its current water supply to meet water-quality standards.

Love 'em or hate 'em, if you followed Great Lakes issues, you were aware of Waukesha. While the Milwaukee suburb was not the official first test case of the Great Lakes Compact, it did set a precedent for the Compact's complicated and controversial "straddling county" exception clause, which permitted a community outside the Great Lakes watershed to apply for a diversion if the town was inside a county that straddled the Great Lakes Basin line (see map on page 251). The straddling-county exception had been stitched into the Compact with Waukesha in mind, because without that clause, the Compact never would have been adopted by Wisconsin (and possibly other states) and thus never would have become law—a political twist that only further steeled the city's adversaries.

Waukesha applied for a diversion in 2010, and the ensuing multiyear drama tested the mettle of elected officials, advocates, and civil servants throughout the region. Millions of dollars and thousands upon thousands of work-hours later, the dispute over Waukesha came to a head in Chicago on June 21, 2016. In the end, the winners were elated, the vanquished crestfallen. But the happiest of all may have been the authors of the Compact itself, because when the Waukesha verdict was handed down, most observers felt that the Compact—one of the most complex water-management tools ever designed—had performed fairly well. No, not everyone was happy with the Waukesha decision, and the case was replete with lessons learned and things that could have been done better. But it was widely believed that, as a water-management tool, the Great Lakes Compact had lived up to the hype and proven to be an effective mechanism for adjudicating water disputes in one of the richest water regions of the world.

~

By the end of 2009, the Great Lakes Compact had been in force for a year, and the New Berlin diversion was up and running. All eyes were now squarely focused on Waukesha. In January of 2010, the Waukesha Water Utility released the first draft of its much-anticipated water-diversion application to the general public and Common Council for comment. The application envisioned a peak water demand of 18.5 million gallons per day (mgd) and an average daily demand of 10.9 mgd. The water would be obtained from one of three Lake Michigan waterfront communities: Milwaukee, Oak Creek, or Racine, with Milwaukee's water being the leading contender—Milwaukee's water was the cheapest, because it was the closest. Similarly, Waukesha had three potential return-flow options. The most expensive option was to build a direct return-flow pipe all the way to Lake Michigan, right through metropolitan Milwaukee. The more financially attractive option was to send the water partway back by pipe to nearby Underwood Creek, where it would flow into the Menomonee River, and eventually Lake Michigan. The third return-flow option was to pipe water southeast to the Root River, which flows into Lake Michigan at Racine. For cost reasons, Underwood Creek was the preferred return-flow alternative. The diversion's estimated total price: $164 million. At the time, water in some Waukesha wells had declined by more than 400 feet and the city was under a new court order to fix its radium problem by 2018.

After the draft proposal was unveiled, some Waukesha officials expressed concern about getting water from Milwaukee. Over the years, Milwaukee—an urban, racially diverse, Democratic power base—had engaged in a number of run-ins with Waukesha—a suburban, mostly white, Republican stalwart. Some Waukesha politicians worried that, once the expensive water-diversion infrastructure was in place, Milwaukee might become Waukesha's water puppeteer, using water to hold sway over the rival suburb. Trust was clearly an issue.

As the application was finalized, Waukesha was in the midst of a colorful mayoral race that pitted the incumbent, Larry Nelson, against Jeff Scrima, a political newcomer with a background in real estate. Mr. Nelson was a gregarious former school teacher prone to wearing colorful Crocs with a sport coat and he had staked much of his political reputation on bringing Great Lakes water to his city. Mr. Scrima, meanwhile, questioned the need for a water diversion, especially if it meant becoming Milwaukee's water pawn. "We, the citizens of Waukesha, don't want to pay for Milwaukee's financial problems," he wrote in an op-ed. "We do have other alternatives to Lake Michigan water, which would better protect Waukesha's identity and independence."[3] The mayoral race became a referendum on Waukesha's water-diversion application.

On April 6, 2010, Mr. Scrima stunned the Waukesha Water Utility by winning the election. Despite those results, two nights later, the Waukesha Common Council voted to approve sending Waukesha's diversion application to the Wisconsin Department of Natural Resources (DNR) by a veto-proof majority of 14–1.[4] With a clear split emerging between the new mayor and the Council, Waukesha's water application was off to a shaky start. Paul Ybarra, Waukesha's council president, increasingly took on a leadership position with the application, filling the void left by Mayor Nelson's dethroning.

There was a sense of postelection chaos in Waukesha. Dan Duchniak, head of the water utility, delivered a copy of the application to the DNR, only to be publicly reprimanded by the mayor afterwards. Mayor Scrima was also publicly investigating ways for Waukesha to resolve its troubled water situation without a diversion. The media was consumed by the idea that the city was divided. After weeks of public discord, DNR officials could no longer ignore the havoc. They sent a letter to Mayor Scrima stating that the chaos in Waukesha had forced the DNR to halt its review after less than three weeks. The letter said a key requirement under the Compact was proving that there was "no reasonable water-supply alternative," but published reports made it clear that Mayor Scrima was still examining other water options. The contradiction was untenable. "The City must confirm that Great Lakes water is in fact the only long-term sustainable water option," the DNR said. The letter listed a host of other deficiencies in Waukesha's application, including the City's neglecting to pay the $5,000 application fee.

In an attempt to get the DNR to resume its review, Mr. Duchniak penned a letter for the mayor to sign in support of the application. Mr. Scrima not only refused, but wrote the DNR saying that he agreed the Waukesha application had a number of deficiencies, especially with regard to alternative water supplies, and he understood the agency's decision to stand down. He said the City needs "to be sure that every reasonable alternative has been thoroughly examined before moving ahead with an application."

Days later, in an interview with Don Behm of the *Milwaukee Journal Sentinel*, he went further. "The City of Waukesha never should have applied for Lake Michigan water to begin with," the mayor said. "I know that's a bold statement. I'm taking a stand here."[5] In a *Journal Sentinel* op-ed, he continued to play the anti-Milwaukee card, and argued that special interests were driving the Waukesha application. "Do the citizens of Waukesha want a railroaded approach to a water solution, which will abdicate their future to the city of Milwaukee?" he asked. "Or do they want a comprehensive solution that allows us to live within our means, protect our environment and pocketbooks, and keep our identity and independence?"[6] That op-ed was met by a scathing response from the *Journal Sentinel* editorial board. "Scrima's objections are based on a hunch—he calls it common sense—and a shadowy conspiracy theory," the editorial said. "We don't buy it."[7] In a sign of Mayor Scrima's increasing political isolation, on July 27, 2010, the Waukesha Common Council voted 13–1 to ask the DNR to resume its review of the city's diversion application. In a letter to the DNR, council president Ybarra tried to paint Mayor Scrima as a politically isolated gadfly who spoke only for himself. "The official position of the city is established by the Common Council.... It is not determined or changed by the comments of an official who may disagree with the policy of the city."

In September of 2010, the DNR agreed to reopen the Waukesha file, but state officials warned Mr. Ybarra that their review would also examine the mayor's claims that the city did not need the diversion and that the application was lacking key information. "You must understand," the letter said, "that the questions that have been raised by the Mayor will be among those that the Department will consider through the review process." Environmentalists pounced on the DNR letter as vindication. They had long complained about the application's deficiencies, but their points were overshadowed by Waukesha's mayhem. "We have been pointing out for many months that the Waukesha application is deficient in a number of important respects and this is reinforced by the department's action," said Cheryl Nenn, the Milwaukee Riverkeeper. Months later, the DNR sent Waukesha an eleven-page, single-spaced letter requesting an extensive amount of additional information.

That started a years-long battle of wills between the agency and the applicant. Eric Ebersberger, who led the DNR's Waukesha application review team, described the period between 2010 and 2015 as a long, wading slog where Waukesha officials spent as much time arguing with the DNR as supplying requested materials. "To me, overwhelmingly, the cause for delay was that Waukesha would continually challenge why we needed the information," he said. "No matter what the topic area was: return-flow, water-supply analysis, water conservation—the reason for so much delay was getting pushback on our requests." Mr. Duchniak admitted challenging the DNR, but said there was plenty of blame to go around. "There was some arm-wrestling through this whole thing," he said. "It was the first time anybody had gone through this, so there really wasn't a standard that was out there."

~

Waukesha supplied the DNR with additional information by the spring of 2011, and the already-voluminous application ballooned to more than 2,400 pages, plus an additional 3,000 pages of supporting material. By July—fourteen months after Waukesha had originally applied—the DNR reached a determination that Waukesha's application was "sufficiently complete."[8] But that was just a start. Now the agency could pivot and actually determine whether it was sufficient to share with other Great Lakes governors and premiers for review. Despite the revisions, the overall details remained the same: a 10.9 mgd diversion, preferably from Milwaukee, with return-flow via Underwood Creek at a cost of $164 million.

As the DNR's evaluation continued, critical public attention zeroed in on what would become the most contentious aspect of the document: the water-supply service area. As part of the application process, Waukesha was required to define the area where the diverted water would be delivered. The City started with its current water-supply service area, but then expanded the area to include sections of four neighboring communities. The reason? State law required that sewer service areas match up geographically with water-supply service areas so that the urban plumbing that delivered clean water to a community matched up with the pipes that took dirty water away. In many instances throughout the state, the sewer service area was much larger than the water-supply service area, which was the case in Waukesha. Its delineated sewer area stretched beyond its municipal boundaries and overlapped with sections of four neighboring communities: Pewaukee, Genesee, Delafield, and the Town of Waukesha (which is a different municipal jurisdiction from the City of Waukesha—see map on page 287). To comply with state law, the DNR ensured that Waukesha included sections of those four adjacent communities in its application.

While such a move might have made sense to state regulators, the "expanded water-supply service area" was hotly opposed by the environmental community. The problem, in their eyes, was that the

Compact required a water-diversion applicant to prove that it had a public water-supply problem with no "reasonable water-supply alternatives." Waukesha had worked hard to make that case in its application, but the four neighboring communities had not. In fact, for a time, some of them even resisted being included in the Waukesha application at all. Environmentalists saw the expanded water-supply service area as a land grab by Waukesha that only increased the amount of diverted water that Waukesha was requesting, and that additional water was going to towns that didn't even need it. They were just being included in the application so the sewer service area mirrored the water service area.

Milwaukee officials remained interested in selling water to Waukesha, but they were adamantly opposed to selling water to the neighboring communities. They felt such a move violated the Compact and would contribute to urban sprawl. Milwaukee's Common Council voted 14–0 to forbid Milwaukee to sell water to the expanded water-supply service area.[9] That vote effectively took Milwaukee out of the running as a water supplier, because neither Waukesha nor the DNR would accept those limiting conditions. With its one-time water-supply front runner now out of the race, Waukesha inked a water-supply deal with Oak Creek. That community's water would cost millions more, but came with no geographic restrictions. But other problems were cropping up. The DNR was becoming increasingly skeptical about the Underwood Creek return-flow plan, due to flooding and other environmental concerns. The agency clearly preferred the Root River option, and instructed Waukesha to "identify a preferred discharge site to the Root River" for its return-flow. Meanwhile, Mayor Scrima was sliding further into the background. He had been effectively marginalized by Waukesha's formidable pro-diversion political forces, and now that Milwaukee had taken itself out of the running as a water supplier, the mayor's anti-Milwaukee political strategy no longer resonated.

Because the water-supply and return-flow scenarios had changed, Waukesha sent a revised application to the DNR in late 2013. The original application had asked for 10.9 mgd, purchased from Milwaukee and returned via Underwood Creek. Cost: $164 million. The revised application lowered the diversion request to 10.1 mgd, listed Oak Creek as the water supplier, and the Root River as return-flow.

Cost: $206 million. The lower 10.1 mgd volume was a direct result of DNR questioning Waukesha's water-demand projections. The DNR felt Waukesha's estimates were too high, so Waukesha cut it back by 800,000 gallons per day. In an effort to boost its chances, Waukesha pledged to return 100 percent of the water to Lake Michigan, even though the Compact allows some loss to consumptive use (generally considered to be 10–15 percent). So, it took fourteen months for the DNR to make sure Waukesha's application was complete, then nearly three years working with the City to get the application to a level worthy of technical review. Now, with a revised application in hand, that technical review could begin.

As the application continued its multiyear crawl through the DNR's cubicle village, Waukesha's water-diversion supporters saw a silver lining in the delays. The review had taken so long that Mayor Jeff Scrima was up for re-election, and diversion supporters fielded a strong candidate to unseat him—Shawn Reilly, a well-known local attorney, Waukesha born and raised. Mr. Reilly campaigned on the slogan "No Drama, Just Work," and repeatedly criticized Mayor Scrima's management style as chaotic and unpredictable. Mayor Scrima responded that he had delivered as the change-agent he was elected to be. "We have shaken up the status quo and that's a good thing," he said.[10] But Mr. Reilly won handily.

On June 24, 2015—more than five years after Waukesha had originally applied for a diversion, and more than a decade after it had first expressed interest in Lake Michigan water—the Wisconsin DNR announced that the application finally met the requirements of the Compact and had reached a point where it was almost ready to be shared with other states and provinces. Environmentalists remained unwavering in opposition. "The importance of this application cannot be overstated," said Marc Smith, policy director with the National Wildlife Federation's Great Lakes office. "The City of Waukesha has not proved conclusively that it really needs to divert Great Lakes water." Mr. Smith released a joint statement with five other environmental groups from Illinois, Minnesota, Ohio, and Michigan enumerating several key complaints. It argued that millions of gallons were available to Waukesha from a combination of deep and shallow aquifers, that the diversion amount was excessive, and the expanded water supply service area was a nonstarter. Environmentalists would spend the next year arguing that if Waukesha reduced its service area, the volume of water needed would drop, making it easier for the suburb to get by on groundwater supplies.

~

By early 2016, the energy surrounding the Waukesha diversion was perceptibly different. People who had followed the case for years could tell that a final decision would be made within months. The countdown started on January 7, when the State of Wisconsin officially shared its Waukesha technical review and environmental impact statement with the other Great Lakes states and provinces, as well as the general public. "The department finds the Applicant is without adequate supplies of potable water due to the presence of radium in its current water supply," the Technical Review said. "[Waukesha] has no reasonable water-supply alternative in the Mississippi River basin (MRB), even considering conservation of existing water supplies."

While the regional review process ramped up the drama, it was arduous and confusing to the general public, in part because it had never been done before. The application would first be picked over by what's called the Regional Body, which includes officials from the eight Great Lakes states as well as the provinces of Ontario and Québec. In order to be inclusive with Canada, the Regional Body would come to a nonbinding determination on Waukesha first. Then, once that was done, the Canadians would head home and the eight Great Lakes governors—keeping the Regional Body's conclusions in mind—would make a final determination on Waukesha with a binding vote. All it took was one gubernatorial veto and Waukesha's application was dead. The Canadians would have a voice, but not a binding vote on this US diversion, just as Americans would not have binding authority over any similar water use in Canada.

The Regional Body's first stop was a private bus tour of Waukesha, where on a sun-splashed February day officials from all ten jurisdictions visited Waukesha's wastewater-treatment facility and its deep and shallow wells, and then they traveled the route (roughly) of the twenty-mile return-flow pipeline, including a stop where Waukesha's discharge pipe would empty into the Root River. Officials were told that Waukesha's deep aquifer had rebounded significantly in recent years, but still was 350 feet below historic levels in some wells and that Waukesha was pumping an average of 6.6 mgd, from a combination of deep and shallow aquifers. The tour ended in Oak Creek on the shores of Lake Michigan, so officials could see firsthand where the flow of water to Waukesha would begin. When the tour ended, it was back to Waukesha for a DNR briefing, followed by questions from the Regional Body. The briefing was given by a number of DNR officials, but Eric Ebersberger, the DNR's Waukesha team leader, spent a lot of time talking about the controversial expanded water-supply service area. The DNR's Shaili Pfeiffer also briefed the group on the fourteen different water-supply options that had been considered, six of which had been examined closely and ruled out, before Waukesha chose to pursue Great Lakes water.

Almost immediately after the briefing ended, questions from regional officials focused on the water-supply service area, starting with Dan Injerd of Illinois, Jennifer Keyes from Ontario, and Kelly Heffner of Pennsylvania. They all politely poked and prodded on the service-area issue. But Michigan's representative, Grant Trigger, was much more direct. He said that his state found the expanded water-supply service area to be "very troubling" and that "we have a problem with" the way Wisconsin went about justifying the service area. "I don't think it works, legally," he warned. Regional Body representatives clearly weren't buying into the idea that Wisconsin law would somehow justify a major expansion in Waukesha's water request.

The next day, the Regional Body met privately to hear concerns about the diversion from Great Lakes tribes and First Nations. That meeting was followed by the Regional Body's only public hearing on the Waukesha diversion. Hundreds of people traveled from all over the Great Lakes Basin to speak. The hearing was so crowded that many who registered to testify ended up leaving before their names were called. Speakers hailed from New York, Ohio, Michigan, Illinois, Indiana, Minnesota, and, of course, Wisconsin. One local, Sandy Hamm, accused Waukesha of being "in the business of growth—they make no secret of it," she said. "When a community doesn't have the resources they currently need, the responsible thing is to stop expanding. . . . The population that needs water should move to the water, not the other way around. . . . God answers all prayers; sometimes the answer is 'no.'"

While that was the only official hearing hosted by the Regional Body, Michigan and Minnesota held their own hearings. The Michigan hearing was surprisingly sparsely attended, but the meeting in Duluth, Minnesota, drew more than 100 people, many of them from out of state. One of the most articulate comments at the Duluth hearing came from Laurie Longtine, from the Waukesha County Environmental Action League. "For decades, Waukesha embraced the annexation of hundreds of acres outside its borders, approved subdivisions large and small, courted commercial sprawl, and permitted multi-unit buildings without asking if it had the means to supply the growth," she said, adding that Waukesha did all this while claiming that it had a "crisis of radium-contaminated water and a dropping groundwater table."

~

While the public hearings were under way, major activity was occurring behind the scenes. Michigan and Ontario both conducted their own technical reviews of the Waukesha application. More importantly, perhaps, there was significant bilateral dealmaking going on. Grant Trigger, Michigan's delegate, who worked closely on the Waukesha file with Jon Allan, head of Michigan's Office of the Great Lakes, was living up to his state's longstanding reputation by playing an enormously influential role in the diversion review process. Mr. Trigger had serious concerns with the application as written, but he thought a compromise might be reachable through a series of amendments. Unlike water-diversion disputes from prior decades, where Michigan was often a leading voice of opposition (or at least resistance) to any diversions, in this case Michigan was working hard behind the scenes to find consensus—assuming the application could be amended enough to get there. The Regional Body had three options: accept Waukesha's application, reject it, or accept it with conditions. Michigan felt that if major revisions were made, there was a chance of building consensus for the latter.

Three key points were driving Michigan down that path. First, the state was heavily influenced by a government study that showed that pumping from Waukesha's deep wells had reversed groundwater that previously flowed into the bottom of Lake Michigan. What's more, Mr. Trigger's team estimated that the reversal of this "tributary" groundwater was robbing Lake Michigan of 1.6 mgd—water that was not being returned to the lake after it was withdrawn. Michigan saw this as an underground diversion, without return-flow, that had been robbing the Lake Michigan Basin of water for years. So, while environmental advocates argued that Waukesha was requesting an unnecessary diversion, Michigan interpreted the application as replacing an underground theft of water that was lost forever, with an aboveground diversion of water that would be returned. Michigan's own calculations showed that Waukesha's application would provide a water net benefit to the lake of more than half a billion gallons per year.

Michigan's second point concerned precedent. Opponents argued that approving Waukesha's diversion would set a precedent for an untold number of potential water-starved communities in straddling counties stretching from Minnesota to New York. Michigan, on the other hand, saw Waukesha's precedent as being much less threatening. Waukesha was already diverting water underground, and the City was using that fact as a key justification for its diversion. How many other potential future water applicants could claim they were already diverting Great Lakes water underground? Probably not many, which is why Michigan saw Waukesha's precedent as being much narrower than environmentalists did. This narrow precedent could actually make future water diversions potentially more difficult, not easier, Michigan thought. And finally, Michigan did not like the idea that Waukesha was removing radioactive material from underground and spreading it in the environment above ground. "It's not environmentally responsible to continue to extract and distribute radium in the environment," as Grant Trigger put it. "We shouldn't be doing that anymore." Where Michigan was in complete agreement with Waukesha's critics, however, was on the service area. "We told Waukesha and Wisconsin that the current service area is unacceptable," Mr. Trigger said in early 2016. "So we are trying to redefine the service area, and if we can't get agreement on that, then it's a 'no.'"

When Regional Body officials gathered for their first round of deliberations on April 21, 2016, the proceedings were open to the public.

Once they started, it was clear that the top issue on everyone's mind was cutting Waukesha's expanded water-supply service area—dramatically. As environmentalists had predicted from the beginning, the Regional Body had no interest whatsoever in sending water to the four adjacent communities. As the Regional Body gathered in a nondescript meeting room at the University of Illinois at Chicago, officials from Michigan, Illinois, and Québec all quickly spoke up on the service-area issue. Michigan and Illinois came armed with proposed language for an amendment on the topic. In the coming weeks, officials would pare back the service area more than once, and with it, they would reduce the diversion size, eventually cutting the original request of 10.1 mgd, to 8.2 mgd, with New York, Ontario, Québec, and Michigan all pushing for the most stringent service-area reductions. In the end, the official map was reduced by nearly 50 percent to Waukesha's existing service area, with the addition of a few small "islands" that were inside the city's boundaries but had not yet been connected to Waukesha's water system.

The Regional Body also added a long list of additional conditions. It required Waukesha to provide an annual water-conservation progress report, establish a prescription-drug collection program to reduce the amount of drugs flushed down the toilet and ending up in the Root River, while also requiring the city to monitor water quality in the Root. More than once, it seemed the Regional Body was ready to vote, but then one jurisdiction or another declared that it was not ready. "I am sort of frustrated sitting here, given how much time and effort I went through to work with our senior leadership to be ready to participate today," complained Jason Travers, from Ontario, suggesting that other jurisdictions were slacking. Dan Injerd from Illinois echoed Ontario's frustrations. "I have told my senior leadership three times now that we were ready to go," he said. "Now it looks like it is going to be a fourth. So somehow we have to figure out how we bring this to a close."

On May 18, the Regional Body voted. The result was a surprising twist: Waukesha's amended application was approved by all parties except Minnesota, which abstained. With the Regional Body's non-binding vote complete, the Compact Council's final binding vote was scheduled for June 21. In the days that followed, as the Compact

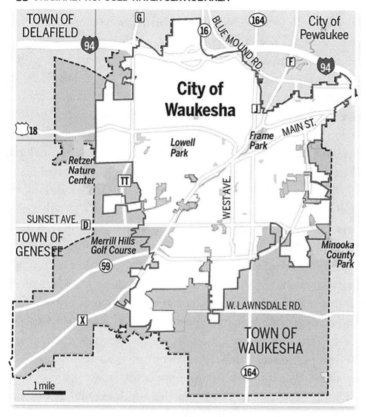

Waukesha Water Supply Service Area

☐ AREAS CURRENTLY SERVED BY THE CITY OF WAUKESHA WATER UTILITY
⊡ ORIGINAL PROPOSED WATER SERVICE AREA

Waukesha's expanded water-supply service area became one of the most contentious aspects of its 2016 water-diversion application. Officials forced the City to cut its service area nearly in half. (June 18, 2016 © Journal Sentinel Inc., reproduced with permission)

Council continued to vet the application, council members said they were working hard to judge the application on the merits, without letting party politics get in the way. But there was always a concern that one of the governors would swoop in at the last minute and politicize the vote. At the time, the Great Lakes states were ruled by five Republican governors (Illinois, Indiana, Michigan, Ohio, and Wisconsin), and three Democrats (Minnesota, Pennsylvania, and New York). No one needed to be reminded that all it took was one governor's veto to kill Waukesha's application. While many of the Compact Council representatives were civil servants, several were political appointees. As Bill McClenahan, Waukesha's lobbyist, put it many months before the vote, "You're asking political people to not act like political people." Some Compact Council members were concerned, too. "If we got consensus on conditions and somebody still voted 'no,' I'd be very disappointed," said Michigan's Grant Trigger in early 2016. "But would I be surprised in this current political climate? No."

The Regional Body's 9–0–1 decision made big news in the Great Lakes region, and Waukesha's critics organized a last-minute push to kill the application. The Great Lakes mayors' association was opposed to Waukesha. Now opposition from other Great Lakes officials came pouring in, especially from Michigan. The state's Republican attorney general opposed Waukesha's application, and a bipartisan supermajority from Michigan's congressional delegation fired off a letter to all Great Lakes governors imploring them to cast a veto against Waukesha. In Lansing, the Republican-controlled state senate passed a resolution opposing Waukesha, and the Great Lakes Fishery Commission's advisory committee voted to oppose the diversion, too. The Compact Implementation Coalition, representing several environmental groups, declared that 98.5 percent of the 11,200 public comments on the Waukesha application opposed the diversion. An even larger group of twenty-one environmental organizations "representing hundreds of thousands of people from throughout the Great Lakes" sent a letter to the Compact Council as well. They asked that the application be vetoed unless a half-dozen additional changes were made, including adding more enforcement measures, reducing Waukesha's allowed average daily demand, and—in a clear deal-breaker so late in the process—insisting that Waukesha's water be returned via the Milwaukee Metropolitan Sewerage District to "avoid adverse impacts on the Root River."

~

It was a crazy month for the Compact Council. From May 18 to June 21, Wisconsin, Michigan, and Minnesota continued to have extensive conversations about the application—conversations that crescendoed the week before the vote. The other states were still uncertain about which way Minnesota was leaning. Environmentalists were convinced that if they could win over Minnesota governor Mark Dayton, a Democrat, he would have the political courage to cast the lone Waukesha veto. "One of the things I really appreciate about Governor Dayton is, if he thinks it's the right thing to do, he'll stand up and do it," said Steve Morse, executive director of the Minnesota Environmental Partnership. E-mails obtained through an open-records request suggest Governor Dayton was still undecided on Waukesha days before the deadline.

Officials from Michigan, Minnesota, and Wisconsin were on the phone throughout the weekend before the Compact Council was scheduled to meet. Then, in an extraordinary move from a historical perspective, on the day before the vote Michigan's Republican governor Rick Snyder placed a confidential call to Governor Dayton, a Democrat, to talk about the Waukesha application. Michigan had spent weeks working toward a unanimous decision from the Compact Council, and if Grant Trigger couldn't get them there, perhaps his boss could. In an interview, Governor Snyder said he called his Minnesota counterpart to tell him that he "thought this was a good application and the reasons why," Governor Snyder said. "It wasn't a controversial call. It was more making sure we were all on the same page . . . which seemed to reinforce where he was at." The idea that a governor from Michigan would place a call to another governor lobbying for a yes vote on a Great Lakes water diversion is a hell-must-be-freezing-over moment in Great Lakes water history. The state that had traditionally been a knee-jerk opponent to Great Lakes water diversions was suddenly showing a more cooperative side. "I think we may have surprised people," Mr. Snyder said. "Because it wasn't just about saying 'no.' It was about, 'Hey, we've done a lot of homework, let's do some more homework together, get the facts out to everyone, and make a fact-based decision.'"

Staffers say that a flurry of activity among Michigan, Minnesota, and Wisconsin followed the call. Michigan officials insist that Governor Snyder's phone conversation with Governor Dayton played an integral role in the final decision. (Governor Dayton declined to comment.) "If Governor Snyder didn't demonstrate the leadership that he did, I don't believe the process would have been successful," Grant Trigger says. Mr. Snyder also called Wisconsin governor Scott Walker, who was intentionally keeping a very low profile on Waukesha for fear of politicizing the vote. "Snyder's concern," says Matt Moroney, an aide to Governor Walker, "was 'let's not make this political. Let's let our experts look at it from the facts of the case.'... I think Michigan really wanted to make sure the Compact worked."

Regardless, even after the call to Governor Dayton, it was still not clear what Minnesota was going to do. Wisconsin's Eric Ebersberger describes a tense scene on the morning of June 21, the day of the vote. In the last hour before the decision, scores of journalists and members of the public were gathered in a meeting room at the University of Illinois at Chicago. Mr. Ebersberger huddled in a lounge—as students napped on couches nearby—with Minnesota's Julie Ekman and Michigan's Grant Trigger to try to resolve final issues. Minnesota didn't like language in the draft decision that seemed dismissive of water quality in the Mississippi watershed and asked for some wordsmithing. More importantly, both she and Grant Trigger wanted to see beefed-up enforcement provisions. Then, with everything seemingly ironed out, the three scurried down to the auditorium, where the video cameras—and the rest of the Compact Council—were waiting. As Eric Ebersberger walked into the room, he was still not sure which way Minnesota's Julie Ekman was leaning. Would she vote yes? No? Abstain (again)?

There was nervous excitement in the room. Compact Council members were decked out in pinstripes and silk blouses when Ohio's James Zehringer opened the meeting by announcing that Minnesota and Michigan had several last-minute amendments. The most important final amendment was rooted in concerns about Wisconsin's capacity to enforce environmental regulations. Just a few weeks before the vote, a damning nonpartisan government report showed that Wisconsin had a pathetic record on enforcing wastewater permits, failing to enforce its own environmental regulations more than 94 percent of the time.[11] That sparked a last-minute flurry of doubt among key Compact Council members regarding Wisconsin's ability to properly monitor any Waukesha decision. The amendment, which passed unanimously, reiterated that any Compact Council state could enforce the terms of

Waukesha's diversion in the event that Wisconsin failed to do so. The Compact Council also added an amendment that allowed any member state to inspect Waukesha's diversion records with just thirty days written notice.

At one point during the last-minute flurry of amendments, Dan Injerd from Illinois became impatient, once again, with what was starting to look like a slapdash ending to an historically significant decision. Mr. Injerd, one of only a few Council graybeards who had actually negotiated the terms of the Compact itself, was growing increasingly uncomfortable with the depth and scope of the eleventh-hour changes to Waukesha's terms. In his view, the time for substantive amendments had long since passed, because Compact Council members were no longer able to clear the final changes with their respective governors. It also increased the likelihood of a last-minute mistake, making the decision more vulnerable to a legal challenge. "We're doing this on the fly," he lectured his colleagues. "We're adding some additional language that, to me, might create some confusion about what that process might be down the road." Michigan's Grant Trigger explained that these eleventh-hour amendments provided extra comfort to Michigan and Minnesota, given the recent late-breaking concerns about Wisconsin's ability to adequately enforce the Waukesha decision. "I do apologize for the lateness," he said. "But it's a reflection of some concerted efforts to try to come to agreement on some things."

After several more minutes of back-and-forth on amendments, the chairman finally called the question. In a tip to the doubts that people had about how Minnesota would vote, Mr. Zehringer reminded everyone that all it took was one "no" vote to kill the proposal but "an abstention will not count as a vote to disapprove." Starting in alphabetical order, Illinois, Indiana and Michigan voted yes. Then all eyes were focused on Julie Ekman from Minnesota.

"Mr. Chair, Minnesota votes to approve," she said.

All the other remaining states voted to approve as well. Waukesha—to the surprise of many—was victorious. It had finally gotten permission to divert 8.2 mgd from the community of Oak Creek and send it back to Lake Michigan via the Root River. Like it or not, the decision was historic. The proceedings quickly adjourned and the media scrum swarmed over to Waukesha mayor Shawn Reilly. "Obviously, I'm very,

very happy," he said. "This is something the City of Waukesha has worked on for a very, very long time."

But mayors come and go. Waukesha had churned through three mayors since it first contemplated a diversion. Dan Duchniak on the other hand, the water utility manager, had been in the trenches for the entire fourteen-year grind and had supervised the production of a 2,499-page application, with a seemingly endless stream of late-night revisions and addendums. While the media surrounded the mayor for a post-vote quote, Mr. Duchniak was alone at the side of the room, choking up. "It's a big relief," he said, tears welling in his eyes. "Fourteen years of work. That's a long time. It's an emotional day, very. It's why I can't talk to people right now. . . . This is really, really a huge relief for us."

Many Wisconsin environmentalists were devastated. "I'm deeply disappointed in the [Compact] Council for ignoring one of the basic tenets of the Great Lakes Compact," said Laurie Longtine, who sits on the board of the Waukesha County Environmental Action League. In an interview months after the decision, she remained convinced that Waukesha had other water-supply options and could have continued to survive on a combination of treatment, conservation, and groundwater. "The city and its water utility," she said, "misled the public, they misled the DNR, and they misled the Great Lakes governors." Regional environmentalists were disappointed, too, but they were more philosophical. Marc Smith with the National Wildlife Federation in Michigan said that while "there are a lot of people who are not happy about it," he felt the vote was a "reasonable and sound decision." The Compact Council, he said, "agreed with NWF and other environmental groups that, as submitted, the application failed to meet the standards of the Compact, so they took it upon themselves to narrow it down, limit it, and put conditions on it that got it into compliance." Some of the most fervent opposition to the Compact Council's decision came from Great Lakes mayors. "We are extremely disappointed in the decision. We think it totally undermines the Compact," said David Ullrich, executive director of the Great Lakes and St. Lawrence Cities Initiative. "We think this is a very bad day for the Great Lakes."

Others saw the situation differently, arguing that as emotional as the decision might be, overall the process by which Waukesha was judged was functional and credible. Eric Marquis, the Québec government's representative in Chicago, attended the June 21 vote and said it showed that "the system works," adding that it was almost like "sustainable development in real time." He said that even though Ontario and Québec were unable to participate in the binding vote, their concerns had been heard and addressed in the Regional Body decision a month earlier. "We definitely had a seat at the table. . . . Our comments and suggestions were taken into account, and many of them were included in the Declaration of Finding," he said. "I think Ontario feels very much the same way."

The Compact negotiations were managed by the Great Lakes St. Lawrence Governors and Premiers. David Naftzger, the organization's executive director, said that, overall, he was happy with how things went. "The decision-making process worked in the sense that it enabled people to thoughtfully come together around something that everyone could agree upon," he said. "Even if they didn't agree necessarily with every single fact of something, as a package, people were prepared to not object and indeed voted in the affirmative." Jon Allan, who directs Michigan's Office of the Great Lakes, agreed that compromise played a crucial role in the final decision. "I know some people had to swallow hard," he says. "You could sort of see—I won't say angst—but you could see people testing where they could go together."

In Minnesota, Governor Dayton released a revealing statement showing the unusually personal attention he had paid to the Waukesha file. "I have given thorough consideration to this important decision," he said, adding that the Waukesha decision will "have virtually no impact on our treasured Great Lakes." The statement from Governor Snyder in Michigan was even more interesting. At first glance, the governor's press release made it sound like he had voted against Waukesha. "Wisconsin will halt Great Lakes diversion," it blared. The news release then immediately reminded Michigan voters that the underground diversion that had been robbing the Lake Michigan Basin of tributary groundwater for years would be halted. The statement minimized the fact that a surface-water diversion had been approved. "The city of Waukesha, Wisconsin, will no longer draw half a billion gallons of water per year from the Lake Michigan Basin and pump it into the Mississippi River Basin," the statement said. "There are a lot of

emotions and politics surrounding this issue but voting yes—in cooperation with our Great Lakes neighbors—is the best way to conserve
one of our greatest natural resources."

Mr. Snyder's staff even produced a short video describing how the
Waukesha vote would halt the underground diversion of water, without
return-flow, and replace it with a surface diversion requiring return-
flow. In an interview, Governor Snyder suggested that his Waukesha
vote might represent a turning point in the way his state evaluates
water diversions. "I hope that if there's future cases," he said, "we'd approach it the same way, in a scientific, fact-based fashion.... Let's do
this in terms of a wise decision-making process, not just an emotional
one." In its post-vote press release, Mr. Snyder's office reminded voters
that Waukesha only set a precedent for other potential straddling-
county applications and did not pave the way for a yellow-brick canal
to Las Vegas. "Any community completely outside of the Great Lakes
Basin, such as those in Arizona or California, are prohibited from
withdrawals."

That nuance, however, was lost on many. Mayor John Paterson of
Leamington, Ontario, reacted to the Waukesha news with an angry
Twitterburst. "This signals the end of the Great Lakes as we know
them. The door has now been opened by irresponsible US govern-
ment officials," he wrote. "Next in line? California??? Heck, let's just
drain the entire basin and pollute the Root River as well. Bad move all
around." He later expanded on those tweets in an interview with CBC
News: "If you open it up to one, how do you then deny it to, let's say, the
State of California, which is in a drought condition?" he asked. "If this
continues, the Great Lakes won't be great anymore. They'll be gone."[12]
Those concerns were echoed by Mayor Richard Harvey of Nipigon,
Ontario. "We all hear about Arizona, we hear about Texas, we hear
about California, where everyone talks about the fact that they want
our Great Lakes water," he said. "Well, this opens up just a small crack
in the door, and they'll be able to get that crowbar into that crack and
start wedging that crack further and further open."[13]

As well-meaning as these comments may have been, Compact
experts say the concerns are unfounded and that the fears expressed
by these two mayors represent one of the most persistent myths surrounding Waukesha. "No decision on Waukesha could open the door

Straddling Counties of the Great Lakes Basin

Waukesha's water-diversion application only sets a precedent for other communities within "straddling counties" in the Great Lakes region. This map highlights those US counties that straddle the Basin line. (Adapted from Nick Ellifson, Waukesha Water Utility)

for water diversions to the Southwest under the Compact," counters Noah Hall, a Compact expert at Wayne State University Law School in Detroit. "The Compact bans water diversions to the Southwest and any other part of the world that's not in a straddling community or a straddling county adjacent to the Great Lakes Basin." Yet the myth persists, especially in Canada.

Given these mayoral concerns, it was perhaps not surprising that two months after the Waukesha decision, the Great Lakes and St. Lawrence Cities Initiative, which represents 130 binational Great Lakes and St. Lawrence mayors, announced it would challenge the Waukesha decision, arguing that it "sets a very bad precedent." Suddenly it looked like the Great Lakes and St. Lawrence Cities Initiative would be squaring off in court with the Great Lakes St. Lawrence Governors and Premiers. Besides the historical and legal significance of Great Lakes mayors battling Great Lakes governors over Waukesha, it also created an awkward situation at the photocopier, given that the two groups share office space on Wacker Drive in Chicago. "Now you really gotta break the ice every morning when you come in," said David Ull-rich from the Cities Initiative, shortly after his legal notice was filed.

The mayors had several specific complaints about the decision. They felt Waukesha still had other water-supply alternatives that had not been seriously considered, and they were concerned about water qual-ity in the Root River. They disagreed with how the so-called town islands within Waukesha's service area were included in the final deci-sion, and they had procedural concerns, complaining that the Compact Council should have held more public hearings throughout the process and in other places than just Waukesha. But there was a key problem for the mayors: while they had moral support behind the scenes, pub-licly they were standing alone before the Compact Council. Despite the resounding opposition to Waukesha's application, not one environ-mental organization signed on to the mayors' complaint. Why? There was a fear in the environmental community that, because the Wauke-sha case was so convoluted, a lawsuit could somehow end up harming or nullifying parts of the Compact itself, a document that had yet to be tested in court. There was a fear that the Compact could become collateral damage in any Waukesha litigation.

The Compact Council heard the mayor's appeal in the spring of 2017, and as expected, after some deliberation, they rejected it. That meant the mayors had to either steel themselves for a long legal battle, drop the case, or find a way to settle. By the summer of 2017 the mayors seemed to have resigned themselves to the legal realities, and with no obvious groundswell of support, the mayors entered into negotiations with the Compact Council. In August of 2017, they announced a settle-ment. The mayors dropped their case after the governors and premiers agreed to revisit the way they processed diversion applications, includ-ing potentially holding more public hearings over a broader geography. While this Compact test case was seen by many as a procedural suc-cess, it was not perfect, and the mayors' settlement served as the first official critique of how the Waukesha case had been handled. "There were some good points in the mayors' appeal that it was reasonable to ask the Compact Council to consider," says Kathryn Buckner, presi-dent of the Council of Great Lakes Industries. "In the end, they weren't persuasive or compelling to the Compact Council, but I think it was worth asking them to take a second look."

Just a few months after the Great Lakes mayors announced their settlement plan, the Waukesha case took another unexpected twist. On October 30, 2017, officials announced that Milwaukee would become Waukesha's water supplier after all. Years before, Milwaukee had balked at selling water to Waukesha when the suburb's diversion application included the expanded water-supply service area. But once the Compact Council stripped the larger service area away, Milwaukee was back in play as a water supplier. The deal was tens of millions of dollars cheaper than obtaining water from Oak Creek, which is ten miles farther away by pipeline. The announcement brought the Waukesha water-supply drama full circle—back to where it had been before Jeff Scrima was elected mayor seven long years before. Milwaukee was back to being Waukesha's preferred supplier of Great Lakes water. The two cities signed a forty-year contract on December 20, 2017.

~

Waukesha eventually became the most controversial Great Lakes diversion since Chicago. But Chicago's diversion totals 2.1 *billion* gallons per day, none of which is returned to Lake Michigan. At 8.2 *million* gallons per day, Waukesha's diversion is tiny by comparison, and 100 percent of its diverted water will be returned. Yet Waukesha now practically rivals the Chicago diversion in name recognition. In fact, when it comes to water diversion in general, Wisconsin is starting to overshadow Illinois as a water-tension hotspot. If Illinois was the water diversion front line of the last century, Wisconsin has been coming on strong with at least six water-diversion flashpoints in recent years,[14] and others rumored to be on the way. There are many reasons for Waukesha's polarizing place in Great Lakes water-management history. Chief among them: the city exemplifies one of the most fractious sections of the Great Lakes Compact, the straddling-county exception clause. Many regional residents have never been able to stomach the idea that a community completely outside the Basin can apply for Great Lakes water, even if it is returned. The Waukesha debate shows just how exceedingly protective the Great Lakes region has become about its namesake natural resource. *Diversion* remains a dirty word.

Waukesha also dredged up a slew of other polarizing topics, including suburban sprawl, racial inequality, environmental sustainability, party politics, and legal precedent—all of which compounded the tension. Waukesha's often arrogant and entitled approach, especially in the early years, created enmity that never really dissipated. The city churned through three mayors and spent $5 million over more than fourteen years—just to get permission to access Great Lakes water. The city's original dream of 20 mgd (see chapter 14) was slashed by more than half to 8.2 mgd. Waukesha now faces additional expenditures of at least $286 million to get its new water system up and running. That cost will primarily be borne by the water bills of Waukesha's 70,000 residents, or roughly $4,000 per person / $10,000 per household.[15]

While many environmental advocates worry about the precedent that has been set, some regional water managers openly wonder whether any more straddling-county applications will follow Waukesha, given the extensive time and money that was required to extract a unanimous Compact Council vote. "We are setting a precedent that might make it almost impossible for someone else to go through," said Dan Injerd, Illinois' Compact Council representative. "Is that good government? A decade-long process that will cost you millions of dollars for an uncertain answer?" He was taken aback by the anti-Waukesha hostility, especially given that it is a community in a Great Lakes state that pledged to return 100 percent of the water. At times, he said, it seemed like people were talking about "Waukesha, Arizona, rather than Waukesha, Wisconsin." There still may be more legal challenges in Waukesha's future, especially over water quality in the Root River. Cory Mason, the Mayor of Racine—which is where the Root empties into Lake Michigan—has been a vocal opponent of Waukesha's effluent being discharged into the Root. Many of his constituents have been vocal opponents, too.

As usual, the State of Michigan played an outsized role in influencing the deliberations, albeit in an uncharacteristically collaborative way. Wisconsin's Eric Ebersberger called Grant Trigger "an alpha dog" on the Compact Council, saying he played a crucial leadership role in bringing the group to a final unanimous decision. Michigan's governor Rick Snyder, whose twitter handle is "@onetoughnerd," also played a role in reaching consensus, despite heavy bipartisan opposition from his state's congressional delegation and from the Republican-controlled state senate. Minnesota kept everyone in suspense until the last minute, which was a new role for the state. As a liberal Democrat, it would have been easy for Minnesota governor Mark Dayton to veto a water-diversion application that came from a state led by Scott Walker, a conservative Republican. The Compact was designed to take politics out of Great Lakes water decisions, and since the Waukesha application came from a Republican-controlled state, Governor Dayton's vote—along with votes from his fellow Democrats, Andrew Cuomo in New York and Tom Wolf in Pennsylvania—showed that a water-diversion decision devoid of politics was possible. In a highly partisan era, officials in the Great Lakes region continued to showcase their ability to cross party lines to reach consensus on highly divisive policy issues.

As shattered as some environmentalists were about the outcome, they played an enormously important role in reducing the size of Waukesha's diversion and in adding a long list of conditions that could end up looming large after the Waukesha diversion goes on line. Despite comments by some Compact Council members that the time and money that Waukesha expended could have a chilling effect on future water-diversion applications, sooner or later another community is bound to apply for its own straddling-county diversion. The magnetism of Great Lakes water is just too strong. Environmental groups see this as inevitable. "The region has set a high bar for future diversions," warned Molly Flanagan from the Alliance for the Great Lakes. "We've sent a shot across the bow for other communities that may want to divert Great Lakes water." Waukesha officials certainly feel the time and effort were worth it to bring world-class water back to the old "Spring City."

Now, the question is: Who, if anyone, might be next?

Chapter 17

Who Will Win the War?

Water is the foundation of life, a key driver of ecosystems and econo-
mies. From wetlands to Wall Street, water availability is often the de-
termining factor between prosperity and deprivation. Citizens in the
Great Lakes Basin learned that lesson late, but they learned it just as
emotionally as anywhere else. Since the mid-twentieth century, water
quality and invasive species have been the chief ecological concerns
in the Great Lakes. But in recent years water *quantity* has emerged as
an important environmental flashpoint as well. Prior chapters in this
book have shown that the Great Lakes region is blessed with water
abundance but is surprisingly cursed by water conflict. The era of water
tension began with the reversal of the Chicago River in 1900, and it
reached a new and especially contentious stage as the twentieth century came to a close.

Many experts believe that water conflict has become a permanent
fixture of life in the Great Lakes region. Polluted tributaries that once
caught fire now play host to water battles resembling those of drier
regions. Along the southern rim of the Great Lakes Basin, water skir-
mishes are expected to be a regular feature of the future—and that
will be particularly true in places like the southwest shore of Lake
Michigan, where the edge of the Basin lies closest to the shoreline. The
effects of climate change on the Great Lakes could exacerbate these
tensions further. "If the Great Lakes are going through this struggle,
imagine what more arid parts of the world are going through," says
Cameron Davis, former Great Lakes advisor to President Barack

Obama. "Nobody's immune from this tension. The entire world is struggling with it."

Are the Great Lakes ready for their acrimonious water future? Thanks to the passage of the Great Lakes Compact and International Agreement, they are more prepared than they have ever been. Negotiators of the two agreements persevered despite a merry-go-round of governors and premiers, divisive regional differences, conflicting water philosophies, and debilitating mission fatigue. Completing the process was an impressive collaborative feat that wove together ten jurisdictions across an international boundary stretching from the Iron Range of northern Minnesota to the rushing waters of the St. Lawrence River in Québec. "Even back then, we always thought we were doing something for the future," says Kate Bartter, a former aide to Ohio governor Bob Taft, and a key Compact negotiator. "We really felt this was our legacy project. . . . It was really a privilege to be able to think long-term."

The Compact became law ten years after the Nova Group's controversial water-diversion proposal roused the region to action. The document cruised through eight Great Lakes legislatures in less than three years, and then raced through DC in just three months—a remarkable achievement. The adoption of the International Agreement in Ontario and Québec was similarly impressive. The Compact was tested immediately by the straddling-community application from New Berlin in 2009 and Waukesha's embattled straddling-county application in 2016. The document's complex water-diversion exception clauses increase the likelihood that portions of the popular law will continue to be shadowed by confusion and consternation for years to come. Water policy is complicated, but as the world exits the century of oil and dives deeper into the century of water, it will be incumbent upon citizens of the Great Lakes region to embrace those complexities, understand them, and make their voices heard.

As this book has shown, the Great Lakes' extensive water-diversion history has been defined by a series of controversial case studies, starting with the most controversial of them all in Chicago in 1900. The massive Canadian diversions at Long Lac and Ogoki followed in the 1930s and '40s. During the late 1980s, in what might best be called the

"WRDA era," Pleasant Prairie initiated the modern period of Great Lakes water-diversion disputes. That paved the way for Lowell, which remains the only community ever to have been denied a Great Lakes water diversion. Mud Creek showed Michigan's Great Lakes water hubris at its peak, and it marked the beginning of a transition in how that state approached the whole water-use debate. As emotional as the Akron diversion turned out to be, it showed that Michigan could indeed approve a water diversion with return-flow, which other states considered a major turning point. New Berlin and Waukesha marked the transition from the WRDA era to the Compact era, with each community testing different exception clauses in the new agreement.

The Compact has now been on the street long enough to acquire some crucial first test cases. Most observers feel that the landmark law has worked as designed. Yes, Waukesha's opponents remain disappointed, and the Great Lakes mayors, governors, and premiers have worked together to make the next major diversion application go more smoothly than the last. But the overall feeling in the Great Lakes region is that the first few test runs of this complicated legal system have been colorful, but serviceable. "I think the Compact's authors have largely been successful in tamping down the broader conversation about sending Great Lakes water to far-flung places," says Molly Flanagan at the Alliance for the Great Lakes. "We've put protections in place to keep water here for these communities and I think that's an important thing." The private sector gives the Compact high marks as well. "Industry was interested in making sure we didn't lock up the resource in the interest of protecting it," says Kathryn Buckner, president of the Council of Great Lakes Industries. "We think it's working great, and we don't see, so far, that there are any significant changes that need to be made."

∽

Thanks in part to the invasive-species issue, Chicago will likely continue to be the most complicated and controversial diversion of this century, just as it was during the last. But southeastern Wisconsin is coming on strong, with more contemporary water-diversion hotspots than all other Great Lakes states and provinces combined: Pleasant

Prairie, New Berlin, Waukesha, and to a lesser extent, Menomonee Falls and Kenosha. Following that trend is Mount Pleasant, the most recent southeastern Wisconsin community to consider a Great Lakes water diversion under the Compact's straddling-community exception clause. Mount Pleasant is a uniquely shaped village of 26,000 people that wraps around Racine's west and south sides. The village stretches from the shore of Lake Michigan westward, past the Great Lakes Basin line, ending at Interstate 94. Mount Pleasant's interest in Great Lakes water was triggered by the proposal by Foxconn Technology Group to build an enormous, $10-billion liquid-crystal-display (LCD) manufacturing facility that promises to eventually employ 13,000 people. The Taiwan-based company came to Wisconsin for the water, as well as $3 billion in state incentives that helped lure the company away from Michigan and Ohio, which were also in the running. The stakes over Foxconn are high: a study by the Metropolitan Milwaukee Association of Commerce estimated that the facility could add more than $51 billion to Wisconsin's gross domestic product over fifteen years.[1]

Foxconn scoured southeastern Wisconsin for a place to site its massive campus, which eventually is expected to cover 20 million square feet, roughly the size of three Pentagons. The company wanted to be close to ground transportation corridors, major airports, potential employees from either side of the Illinois border . . . and the abundant waters of Lake Michigan. Ideally, from a water standpoint, Foxconn would have landed completely inside the Great Lakes Basin (which would have been much easier in Michigan, of course), but due in part to the narrow width of the Basin in southeastern Wisconsin, Foxconn landed in a straddling community instead, prompting Mount Pleasant to pursue a water-diversion application to support the facility.

Foxconn brings a whole new twist to the straddling-community conversation. In an irony of ironies, its corporate campus will straddle the basin line—a characteristic that it is hard to imagine the drafters of the Compact ever envisioning. As one Wisconsin official describes it, the flat screens may end up starting the assembly process in the Mississippi River watershed, with the finished product exiting the other end of the sprawling campus in the Great Lakes Basin. The facility's geographic position raises intriguing questions for the Great Lakes

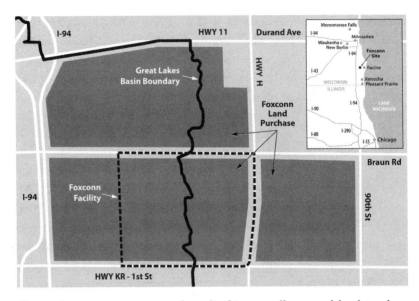

Foxconn's corporate campus, and much of its overall proposed land purchase, straddles the Great Lakes Basin line—a situation that has tested the Great Lakes Compact in unexpected ways. Officials say the $10-billion project will be the size of three Pentagons and eventually employ up to 13,000 people.

Compact. "I don't think anybody envisioned something like this happening," says one Wisconsin official. "So I think we're in kind of uncharted territory here."

So the straddling corporate campus is part of a straddling-community application. Mount Pleasant doesn't have its own public water-supply system. The vast majority of the village is already in the Great Lakes Basin and municipal customers get Lake Michigan water from Racine. It's just the far southwest corner of Mount Pleasant that happens to slightly jut out across the Basin line, and that's where Foxconn has decided to build its multifaceted facility. Because the Compact says that a water diversion can only be used for public water-supply purposes, and since Mount Pleasant does not have its own public water-supply utility, Racine submitted the water-diversion application on behalf of Mount Pleasant, which in turn applied on behalf of Foxconn. The application requested 7 million gallons of water per day (mgd)— 5.8 mgd for the Foxconn facility—roughly 40 percent of which (2.7

mgd) will be lost to consumptive use. The rest will be returned to Lake Michigan, as required under the Compact. By comparison, the highly controversial Waukesha water diversion will pull 8.2 mgd from Lake Michigan and return 100 percent of the water. As usual, the amount of water isn't really the issue—it is a pittance compared to the 1.2 quadrillion gallons of water in Lake Michigan. What matters is whether the Foxconn diversion meets the letter of the law under the Compact, and if it is setting any unintended precedent that the region might regret later.

A key question in the Foxconn debate is whether the Compact's water-diversion exception clauses were designed to encourage corporations like Foxconn to develop large industrial facilities at the edge of the Great Lakes Basin. Or were the exception clauses designed to help water-strapped communities in need? Or both? Local officials say that Mount Pleasant was not having any water issues until the Foxconn facility was proposed. "The question was never really fully answered in the negotiations with the Compact about when exactly did we think these exemptions were okay for straddling communities," one Wisconsin official says. "Is industrial use okay, or not okay? Is it something we want to be encouraging or discouraging as much as possible? . . . I think what we are seeing with the Waukesha case, and then with this case, is some of those things are going to begin to get defined just by practice and precedents that get set." Certainly, a key driving force behind the Compact was to bring jobs to the water, rather than send water to jobs someplace else. That's the "blue economy" that the Great Lakes governors and other boosters have been talking about for years. Foxconn is a global corporate force of nature, lured to Wisconsin personally by Governor Scott Walker. Hon Hai / Foxconn Technology Group is one of the largest multinational corporations in the world, ranking high on *Fortune* magazine's "Global 500" list, and it has more employees (worldwide) than Milwaukee has people. But the overriding philosophy behind the Great Lakes Compact's approach was that, ideally, any blue-economy jobs would land completely inside the Great Lakes Basin. Foxconn came close.

But, deep in the bowels of the Compact's fine print, there may be a hurdle for the company, and it has to do with the Compact clause that limits new diversions to "public water supply purposes." As the document puts it: "Public Water Supply Purposes means water distributed to the public through a physically connected system of treatment, storage, and distribution facilities *serving a group of largely residential customers* that may also serve industrial, commercial, and other institutional operators" (emphasis added). Mount Pleasant is a community of 26,000 people, most of whom live in the Basin and don't need a diversion. The diversion is for the small section of town that lies outside the Basin, which is expected to host 13,000 new workers. Does that mean the diversion will be serving "a group of largely residential customers"? That's the multibillion-dollar question in Madison and Taipei. "It will be interesting if this brings up a private right-of-action, or if another state sues," says one Wisconsin official. "That would certainly put a wrench in the whole project."

At a packed public hearing in March of 2018, speakers zeroed in on the "largely residential customer" issue. "Here's the rub," said Jodi Habush Sinykin of Midwest Environmental Advocates. "A 'group of largely residential customers' will not be the ones served by the 7 million gallons. . . . Rather, the complete opposite is true. Racine will use the majority, if not the entirety, of the diverted Great Lakes water to serve the industrial needs of a single, private, foreign, industrial entity, Foxconn."

Remember that under a straddling-community application like Racine's, the local state alone decides whether a water-diversion application can be approved. There is no requirement for regional review, and no threat of a veto from other Great Lakes states.[2] (Think of New Berlin, not Waukesha.) But the other Great Lakes jurisdictions could make their views known in other ways. "Even though it may be a decision exclusively of Wisconsin under the straddling-community clause," said Jon Allan, director of Michigan's Office of the Great Lakes, "it's still incumbent upon every state and province to understand the nuances and the specifics of that arrangement so we can make sure that it fully and adequately conforms to the Compact, because protection of the Compact is paramount."

As the Racine water-diversion application moved through the approval process, the threat of environmental litigation hovered in the background. Large-scale, long-term capital investment tends to shy away from uncertainty, and Foxconn may not attain a final position of certainty in its multibillion-dollar investment until after the water diversion's potential legal issues are resolved. "It is going to be an issue," admits one Wisconsin official in reference to Foxconn's straddling circumstance. "Look, this Foxconn thing was competitive in the region, and if you're another state who lost out to Wisconsin, as Michigan and Ohio did, wouldn't you say, 'Hey, here's an opportunity for me to raise all kinds of trouble?'" Experts agree that the Foxconn proposal could be interpreted as pushing the limits of what was intended by the Compact's authors. "It's definitely not what was anticipated for the limited purpose of the straddling community and straddling county," says Noah Hall, the Wayne State Compact expert. "I'm not so sure it will be a deal-breaker.... We were concerned about limiting the exceptions to public water supplies," he says. "But that's not to say that we will have done a good job.... The thread of money in water is real."

The Foxconn debate has prompted a legal discussion behind the scenes about the "intent" of those who authored the Compact and International Agreement. Does the Foxconn deal sound like the kind of diversion that the straddling-community exception clause envisioned? "No—it was much more aimed at residential," says one senior Canadian official who spent years in the discussions. "It wasn't meant that you were going to have a Tesla factory farm . . . put one toe into the Basin and that will allow them to get a pipe that would then provide them with the water that they needed.... For some of the environmentalists, this would be exactly the horror story." It's called the "straddling community" exception clause for a reason, these officials say, not the "straddling factory" exception clause. But Todd Ambs, who negotiated the Compact under Wisconsin's Democratic governor Jim Doyle, disagrees. He says the language referring to predominantly residential customers does not refer to the community that *wants* the water, but rather the community *supplying* the water. Under that line of thought, as long as Racine has plenty of water to share, and most of its customers are residential, it can supply water to Foxconn and the company can use it for whatever it wants. Mr. Ambs doesn't see a problem with a Foxconn straddling-community application "as long as they're getting the water through a public utility that still has room under their cap," which Racine definitely does.[3]

Wisconsin officials certainly realize that they have the final say on

Foxconn, but also that a controversial decision could stress the Compact in new and unique ways. "I do think we have a credible argument that this is copacetic under the Compact," says one Wisconsin official. "But I am curious about how much of an issue it's going to be. . . . Is somebody going to sue?" Business leaders dread the thought of one state suing another over water. "I would like to believe that the region will act more regionally," said Kathryn Buckner, president of the Council of Great Lakes Industries. "This is a program designed to be protective of the region as a whole, and hopefully we aren't as short sighted as to see that one facility can break that down and create a fracture in that regional program."

Three states submitted official comments raising questions about the Racine diversion: Illinois, Michigan, and New York. "It is unclear that the proposed diversion is largely for residential customers," the New York letter said. "The water is intended to facilitate the construction and operation of the future industrial site of the Foxconn facility." Regional mayors raised questions about the application, too. The Great Lakes and St. Lawrence Cities Initiative complained that "the City of Racine is not the straddling community requesting the water; Mount Pleasant is. And in fact, Mount Pleasant isn't the entity with the water need; Foxconn, a private business, is."

Despite these complaints, on April 25, 2018, as expected, Wisconsin approved Racine's 7 mgd water-diversion application. The decision allowed the city "to extend public water service to the 8 percent of [Mount Pleasant] that is in the Mississippi River Basin, partially including the Foxconn facility site," a DNR press release said. The agency added that the annual consumptive use from the diversion would lower Lake Michigan's water level by 0.0025 inches, or the thickness of a "lightweight" sheet of paper. "We received approximately 800 comments on the Racine application, which shows the public's strong interest in this topic," said Adam Freihoefer, from the DNR's Bureau of Drinking Water and Groundwater. "We appreciate the public's involvement and I thank those who took the time to comment." The key quote from the agency's Findings of Fact also focused on the language about residential use, saying Racine delivered water to more than 5,500 homes in Mount Pleasant already. "The proposed additional industrial and commercial customers within the diversion area will not significantly change the fact that the [Racine water] utility's distribution of water to the public in the Village of Mount Pleasant will serve a group of largely residential customers."

Environmentalists were disappointed by the Foxconn proposal, almost from the start—primarily because Wisconsin waived key non-Compact-related environmental requirements in order to fast-track construction of the giant LCD factory. Approval of the water diversion only made things worse. Environmentalists challenged the Racine/Foxconn diversion on May 25, 2018—the first litigation ever filed under the Great Lakes Compact. Midwest Environmental Advocates, which filed the petition, said diversions can only serve "a group of largely residential customers," yet 83 percent of the 7 mgd requested by Racine "will be used to supply Lake Michigan water to one single private industrial customer, Foxconn," and the rest of the water would be used by "industrial and commercial facilities surrounding the Foxconn facilities." The legal challenge remained unresolved as this book went to press.

Foxconn declined an interview request for this book, and because the company's situation could remain dynamic for some time, few experts were willing to speak on the record about it. But all were fascinated by the geographic uniqueness of the company's situation, and the challenges that it could pose to the next phase of Great Lakes water discussions, disputes, and debates. As one senior Wisconsin official put it, "This particular site is just fascinating from the [Great Lakes] divide standpoint. . . . I just can't get over it." However things end up, the Racine / Mount Pleasant / Foxconn water diversion has landed in a familiar neighborhood for Great Lakes water disputes. It is just up the road from Pleasant Prairie, and just down the road from Waukesha and New Berlin. Southeastern Wisconsin is becoming water-diversion row.

～

The Pleasant Prairie diversion reemerged as an issue in recent years as well, after the Wisconsin Department of Natural Resources reported in 2010 that the total maximum amount of the town's diversion had been markedly increased from 3.2 mgd to 10.69 mgd. However, permission for that significant increase was not granted by the Compact

Council. Instead, Wisconsin appears to have unilaterally increased the maximum amount of Pleasant Prairie's diversion, a step that Wisconsin says it was permitted to take on its own as part of the state's Compact implementation process.

Like all states under the new Compact, Wisconsin was allowed to "grandfather" diversions that already existed, like Kenosha or Menomonee Falls. Pleasant Prairie was grandfathered, too. As part of that process, states were required to declare the official maximum permitted amount of the diversion as well; these are known as "baselines." As was mentioned in the Waukesha chapter (16), Wisconsin statute requires that water-supply service areas match up with sewage service areas so that the plumbing that delivers clean water parallels the plumbing that takes dirty water away. State officials say that since Pleasant Prairie's sewer area was larger than the water-supply service area, they expanded the water-supply service area to match, and they added more water to Pleasant Prairie's diversion in the process—to the tune of an *additional* 7.49 million gallons per day. That's close to the entire amount the Compact Council gave Waukesha—8.2 mgd—and more than the Foxconn diversion's 7 mgd. "The Compact provides for states to establish baselines for existing diversions," explained Shaili Pfeiffer from the Wisconsin DNR in an e-mail. "Under the process used to determine baselines for existing diversions, Pleasant Prairie's authorized diversion amount was set at 10.69 mgd (this volume included the 3.2 mgd approved under WRDA)."[4]

How can Wisconsin officials unilaterally grant millions of gallons of extra diverted water to a community without the approval of the Compact Council? Not everyone is certain that they can, including a former head of the Water Division at the Wisconsin DNR. "I see no way that that could be done legally," says Todd Ambs. "Did it follow the appropriate process? Unless I'm really missing something, I don't see how it could."

Of course, Wisconsin tried this before, during the Waukesha water diversion case. The DNR ensured that Waukesha expanded its application so the water-supply area matched the sewer area, as state law required. But that was quickly nixed by the Compact Council, which pared back Waukesha's service area by almost 50 percent, and its diversion volume by nearly 20 percent, down to 8.2 mgd. But in July of

2010, with a bureaucratic stroke, Pleasant Prairie was cleared to divert an additional 7.49 mgd without so much as a public hearing, not to mention a vote from the Compact Council. DNR officials say don't blame us, blame Wisconsin's legislators—they are the ones who passed Wisconsin's Compact-implementing legislation, which required the agency to match up water-supply areas with sewer areas. One senior DNR official admitted that the Pleasant Prairie diversion increase was "startling," but said, "Our hands were tied by statute."

The move seems to have gone unnoticed by environmentalists, other states, and the media. Wisconsin officials said that they listed the larger Pleasant Prairie diversion amount in reports they were required to file with the Compact Council and Regional Body, "And we didn't get any questions about it," said one DNR representative. "Frankly, I'm surprised it hasn't come up before."

~

The water unease swirling around Foxconn and Pleasant Prairie is just the latest sign that the diversion issue is here to stay, as are the tensions that accompany it. "There's no doubt about it, there will be increasing water tension in the region and it's not going away," predicts Andy Buchsbaum with the National Wildlife Federation. While many experts see an era of increased conflict on the horizon, there is debate about how those water tensions will be borne out. "There are a lot of people who feel that once you fire one shot it will be all-out war—it will be scorched earth," says Dan Tarlock, emeritus professor at the Chicago-Kent College of Law. "I'm in the camp that believes there will be an endless series of small guerilla acts. . . . There are going to be more conflicts. They just aren't going to be big ones." Large or small, some of those battles are expected to end up in court, a scenario that regional water managers have expected from the beginning. "Everything gets refined by litigation," says Chuck Ledin, former head of the Great Lakes office at the Wisconsin DNR. "That's just the way the system works. So I'd say somewhere along the line it will happen [to the Compact]."

Many have wondered whether litigation challenging a particular water-diversion case could jeopardize the Compact itself. Could the Compact become collateral damage in a water-diversion lawsuit? "It would be next to impossible to challenge the Compact itself," says Peter Johnson, with the Great Lakes St. Lawrence Governors and Premiers. Mr. Johnson says there might be challenges to the way the Compact is interpreted, but not to the validity of the document itself. "Compacts are exceedingly difficult to challenge on their face." Even critics of the Compact, like Patricia Mulroy, the former general manager of the Southern Nevada Water Authority, agree that challenging the Compact would not be worth the effort. "Taking on the Great Lakes Compact is a foolish exercise," she said, "because it was such a heavy political lift to get it across the finish line."

What about Congress? Could it unwind the Great Lakes Compact on its own? Michael McCabe, an expert on interstate compacts with the Council of State Governments, says that this question remains unresolved, but he seems to be leaning toward a no. "It used to be generally assumed that congressional consent was always revocable by Congress," he says. But recent federal court decisions have suggested that an unlimited power to repeal congressional consent would damage the entire concept of a compact. Why should states go to the trouble of creating compacts if Congress can unilaterally toss them out? Many states pursue compacts precisely because they are difficult to undo. "That's why I'm saying it's not clear that an effort by Congress to revoke consent, and essentially pull the rug out from under the states, would survive judicial scrutiny. It's just that the question hasn't been finally resolved at the US Supreme Court level." Other experts said that if Congress started unilaterally nullifying compacts, it could rattle a foundational pillar of the US legal system. "I mean, you've got literally hundreds of compacts out there," said Peter Johnson, adding that if Congress began tossing out compacts "that would throw a whole system of governance . . . into question."

As regional leaders position themselves for the next stage in the Great Lakes water war, in many ways it is the unknowns that could end up posing the greatest challenges. Think back to the time of the Chicago diversion (chapter 5) and the mindset of civic leaders more than a century ago. At the time the diversion was launched, its primary purpose was to solve Chicago's abysmal sewage-disposal problem. Local officials never imagined that, decades later, the Illinois diversion would be transformed into a water-supply crutch for one of the world's greatest metropolitan areas. They never imagined that fears would one day arise that the waters of the Great Lakes might be siphoned off to the Ogallala Aquifer or the city of Las Vegas. And they certainly never imagined that a foreign fish, prone to leaping high in the air, would prompt influential people to contemplate re-reversing the Chicago River.

This long view raises an obvious question for regional leaders in the twenty-first century: What is in the Great Lakes' water future that we are not envisioning today? What unknown water crises—local, regional, national, international, or climatological—lie ahead? What undiscovered technologies might make large-scale, long-range water diversions more cost-effective—or, on the other hand, even completely obsolete? "You don't really worry much when the fight is playing out the way you expected the fight to play out," says Noah Hall, at Wayne State. "What concerns me is what I don't know. [What] are the fights and the issues that we don't anticipate, and the loopholes and the ways of manipulating Compact language that we did not even remotely foresee?" Predicting the future is not an option, but planning for it is. Officials can implement the most comprehensive, adaptable, binding water-management system imaginable and hope it helps the region navigate through the insecurities of an unpredictable world. Regional leaders spent years attempting to craft such a mechanism. As imperfect as it may be, the Compact is the best they have been able to put forth. It will continue to be tested and refined, with each new test case serving as the next precedent-setting building block.

Throughout Great Lakes history, the people of the region have risen to the challenge of ensuring that the lakes are protected. During the heavy pollution years of the early and mid-1900s, the public roused late, but brought about historically significant changes in water policy that—generations later—made the lakes cleaner and healthier, although much more work definitely needs to be done, especially in Lake Erie. In fact, the success of the Great Lakes Compact has led some to suggest that water-quantity concerns could slide to the back burner in the Great Lakes because the lakes are now protected. The lead-contamination water crisis in Flint, Michigan, in 2015 and the toxic algal bloom contamination in Toledo, Ohio, in 2014 both raised a serious question for Great Lakes residents: What's the benefit of all that water, if you can't drink it? "It doesn't do any good to protect one of the greatest natural reserves in the world," says Molly Flanagan at the Alliance for the Great Lakes, "if communities can't actually make use of that water."

The job of sustainably managing the Great lakes will always be a work in progress. The region has a long-standing reputation in Congress and throughout the nation for working across party lines for the greater good of the lakes. That cooperation has brought transformative legislative victories, like the Compact and the Great Lakes Restoration Initiative. In recent decades, the Great Lakes states and provinces have matured markedly as a region, often thinking of themselves more as a group than a collection of individual jurisdictions. Local fidelity and a sense of place are important, but many officials see the largest future Great Lakes challenges transcending jurisdictional boundaries—including the US-Canada border—more than they have in the past. "This isn't just about water. This isn't just about the Great Lakes," says Jon Allan, who leads Michigan's Office of the Great Lakes. "This is about shared governance, and resources that matter, and how do you do that collectively and thoughtfully?" Many others agree. "The Compact was a huge win," says Molly Flanagan. "It's worth taking a moment to reflect on the victory and what we are capable of doing as a region when we decide something is worth protecting."

The adoption of the Compact clearly represented a resounding legislative feat—a bipartisan, multi-jurisdictional, multi-year, cerebral, forward-looking legislative effort adopted in the absence of a crisis and written for future generations. Those are words that one rarely has an opportunity to string together in reference to public policy. Many who worked on the Compact openly wonder if it could be replicated today. Looking forward, the Compact will only be as strong as those who enforce it. The question now is whether future generations of stewards will prove capable of the task at hand, and whether the Compact itself, and those shepherding it, will foster management decisions that match the unforeseeable challenges that lie in wait.

Epilogue

Is the era of long-range, large-scale water diversions over? The first chapter of this book features North American water experts debating that question. On one side are the experts who believe that the financial costs and environmental permitting hurdles required to build massive new water-diversion projects are simply insurmountable today. These experts argue that water technologies such as desalination and toilet-to-tap water treatment are cheaper, easier, and less controversial than building far-flung pipes and canals to transport water across the landscape. But other water experts maintain that long-range, large-scale diversions have not gone away; they've just gone dormant. These experts argue that in the future, major water-diversion proposals will emerge as climate change and regional scarcity drive up the commercial value of clean, reliable fresh water, thereby making such projects financially ponderable, especially in places like the American Southwest. As for permitting, if companies are still managing to get permits to build oil and gas pipelines that transect the continent, then water pipeline permits are likely to be even easier to obtain.

Water diversion certainly remains popular overseas. As was mentioned in chapter 1, the Chinese have spent years constructing the massive $63-billion South-to-North Water Diversion Project to ship bulk water hundreds of miles from the Yangtze River in the south to heavily populated areas like Beijing farther north. In the Persian Gulf, Abu Dhabi has combined desalination and water diversion to create its own globally unique water project. The emirate has built a 124-mile diversion pipeline to transport desalinated water to the Liwa desert, where it is then pumped underground into an aquifer for future use. "We do believe that this could be a blueprint that can be replicated," said Razan Al Mubarak, secretary general of Abu Dhabi's Environment Agency.[1] Known as the largest desalination water reserve in the world, the $435-million project holds 6.7 billion gallons and can supply up to 100 million gallons of drinking water per day if needed.

The water-diversion era doesn't seem to be over in the United States yet, either. The Southern Nevada Water Authority (SNWA) has long proposed tapping billions of gallons in groundwater reserves per year in eastern Nevada, and diverting that water hundreds of miles south to Sin City. The multibillion-dollar proposal, which has been tied up in the courts for years, has pitted rural ranchers and environmentalists against one of the world's shrewdest water agencies. Today the SNWA is pursuing a multipronged water-diversion approach designed to ensure that Vegas has a reliable supply despite only getting four inches of rain per year. While the agency continues to battle in court for rights to the eastern Nevada groundwater, it is also building a large, $817-million, three-mile tunnel to the bottom of Lake Mead, the giant reservoir behind Hoover Dam. Mead serves as the Southwest's water bank, and it supplies the vast majority of Vegas's water—300,000 acre-feet per year. Vegas already has a pipe to Lake Mead, but because an extended drought continues to suppress the reservoir's level, officials worried the first pipe wasn't deep enough. So in 2000 they built a second one. Now, as Lake Mead water levels continue to trend downward, they worry the second pipe may not be deep enough either, so they are building a third pipe—the so-called Third Straw—that will access the very bottom of Lake Mead. This means that even if Lake Mead drops to a level referred to as "dead pool"—when Hoover Dam's turbines will have long since stopped spinning—Vegas will still be able to access the reservoir's dregs. As the water author Charles Fishman put it, "Las Vegas doesn't have water challenges or water troubles. Las Vegas has a water emergency."[2]

California has its own controversial water-diversion proposal that has been making headlines for two decades.[3] The Cadiz Water Project wants to extract 16.3 billion gallons of groundwater per year from under the Mojave Desert and pipe it 43 miles to the Colorado River Aqueduct. There, the desert groundwater would merge with Colorado River water already on its way to millions of Southern Californians.[4] The Cadiz pipeline ran into stiff resistance from the Obama Administration. But it quickly received a green light from the Trump Administration in 2017, before getting hung up by an environmental legal challenge.[5] Cadiz has received support from dozens of local, state, and federal elected officials. But it's unclear how the litigation will impact its plans.[6]

Senior water officials in Arizona are very familiar with long-range, large-scale water diversions. The state already depends on one of the largest federal water-diversion projects in US history, the Central Arizona Project, or CAP. The 336-mile water-delivery system was finished in 1993 and carries 1.5 million acre-feet of water per year to major cities like Phoenix and Tucson, as well as to farmers and tribes throughout much of the state. Theodore (Ted) Cooke serves as CAP's general manager, and he says that while water-diversion projects are a good idea "in principle," these days desalination usually makes more sense. "We get two or three letters from concerned citizens every year that say, 'Why don't we just build a pipeline and transfer water from the Arkansas River or from the Missouri River?'" he says. "Great ideas, [but there's] no money to do that . . . and all the water that exists belongs to somebody else." He sees the Pacific Ocean or the Sea of Cortez as more-viable options. "It would make a lot more sense, because of proximity, to do desalination there, than build a $15- or $20-billion pipeline to the Missouri River and pipe it across six states to get it here."

Tapping the Missouri is not a new idea. The US Bureau of Reclamation created a stir in 2012 when news organizations reported that the agency was considering a plan to divert water hundreds of miles from the Upper Missouri River to Denver. As one news report put it at the time, "Water would be doled out as needed along the route," the story said, "with the rest ultimately stored in reservoirs in the Denver area."[7] The purpose was to deliver federally subsidized water to Denver, thereby relieving pressure on the Colorado River, which would benefit water-troubled downstream states. The Missouri River diversion proposal resulted from a Bureau of Reclamation projection suggesting the Colorado River Basin could face a 3.5-million-acre-foot annual shortfall by mid-century.[8] Rose Davis, a Bureau of Reclamation spokeswoman, said that her agency interpreted those projections as a "wake-up call." "We threw open the doors and said 'Bring it on,'" she said. "Nothing is too silly."[9]

The Mississippi River has recently been contemplated as a water-diversion source as well. Thomas Buschatzke, who directs Arizona's

Department of Water Resources, says the Southern Nevada Water Authority, the Metropolitan Water District of Southern California, and the Central Arizona Water Conservation District jointly commissioned a study that examined diverting water from the Mississippi River. The results? "There's plenty of water, it's technically feasible," he said, "but across the United States, states are in a 'you're not taking our water' mode, [and] the Great Lakes states put together a Compact to make sure no one took their water." Consequently, he says, "sharing water between states is highly unlikely." Many other experts believe that cities will continue to do what they have always done when water times get tough: purchase some of the extensive senior water rights that farmers have throughout the Southwest, especially in California. While the cost of that water can be extremely expensive, it is usually cheaper than building a desalination plant, and more politically palatable than a water diversion.

Patricia Mulroy, the former head of the Southern Nevada Water Authority, supports diverting floodwaters from the Mississippi River to other areas. What does Arizona's Mr. Buschatzke think of that idea? "I think that in some point in time, the need and the politics will change to a point where that might actually happen. But that's not happening in my tenure as a director, because I think, rightly so, there are other options—squeezing more out of conservation . . . we have in-state supplies, we have reclaimed water, treated effluent—that can close some of our gaps. There are cheaper options. Before you go to that level, and build political support for that kind of project, you're going to have to show that you did everything else that you possibly can."

The Great Lakes Compact may not have received much opposition from Western politicians on Capitol Hill (see chapter 13), but that does not mean it is popular in the West. Nevada's Pat Mulroy has particularly strong words about the Great Lakes Compact, suggesting it smacks of provincial selfishness. In an interview with Charles Fishman, author of *The Big Thirst*, she put it this way: "We take gold, we take oil, we take uranium, we take natural gas from Texas to the rest of the country. . . . We move oil from Alaska to Mexico, but they [Great Lakes officials] say, 'I will not give you one drop of water!' They've got 14 percent of the population of the United States and 20 percent of the fresh water in the world—and no one can use it but them? 'I might not need it. But I'm not sharing it!' When did it become *their* water anyway? It's nuts!"[10]

But many people in the Great Lakes region argue that water is different from oil. Ecosystems depend on water for their survival. The same cannot be said for oil, natural gas, or uranium. So diverting water somewhere else can rob a local ecosystem of its lifeblood, with the Colorado River delta and the Aral Sea being the most notable examples. In an interview for this book, Ms. Mulroy said the Great Lakes Compact was "born of fear" and "became too restrictive." "I think it was a great effort to try to have a binational management of a shared resource," she said. "I don't take issue with that at all, but I think in setting the parameters, and setting the restraints on that, they went too far." She predicted that eventually the Great Lakes Compact's tight reins will need to be loosened. "Anything that is born of fear and paranoia, in essence, has some issues with it," she said. "There is going to come a day when somebody, somewhere, in a loud enough voice, starts talking about hoarding, saying, 'Wait a minute, folks, you've got 20 percent of the world's fresh water? . . . Why would you be able to contain and restrict it in the manner that you have?"

~

Popular or not, the Great Lakes Compact has been effective in stifling those who might otherwise add the Great Lakes to the list of water-diversion options for the American Southwest (or anywhere else). While the Mississippi and Missouri Rivers continue to be invoked as water-diversion alternatives, for the most part, the Great Lakes have fallen to the sidelines in those conversations. Residents of the Great Lakes region remain insecure and protective about their signature bodies of water. But thanks to the Compact, it is hard to imagine a long-range, large-scale water diversion coming anywhere close to the Great Lakes region for decades to come, if ever. The era of long-range, large-scale water diversions may not be over, but most regional officials believe it is over for the Great Lakes Basin—at least as long as the Compact remains in force.

Water diversions within a state are one thing, but water transfers that cross state boundaries have always been the biggest hurdle for water-diversion proponents. The fact that Nevada's in-state groundwater diversion project—which was first proposed in the 1990s—still has not come to fruition should be a comfort to those concerned about even more geographically ambitious water-diversion proposals. California's Cadiz Water Project finds itself in a similar position.

While the Great Lakes Compact has increasingly helped to rebuff water speculation from outside interests, it has not reduced water tensions in the Great Lakes Basin itself. If anything, water tensions have increased since the Compact was adopted in 2008, as communities continue to test the document's controversial straddling-county and straddling-community exception clauses. As a result, Great Lakes residents who were once so worried about outsiders taking their water, are now fighting among themselves instead. Vigilance about Great Lakes water use is paramount in order to ensure sustainable use of the region's bountiful water resources. But keeping a big-picture perspective is important, too. There are regional leaders who worry that some environmental advocates are pushing "strident" interpretations of the Compact that could run the risk of confusing the public and might also make it more difficult to have a thoughtful evaluation of whether a specific diversion request makes sense. "I worry about a deadening effect," says Elizabeth Cisar, senior program officer for the environment at the Joyce Foundation in Chicago. "If people kind of pop off every time there's a conversation about a potential diversion, eventually the public will just tune that out." For the foreseeable future, however, it seems that Great Lakes water battles will continue to pit regional residents against each other rather than against some other outside force. Perhaps that is an unintended consequence of the Great Lakes Compact. But if recent history is any guide, that seems to be the current course the region has charted for itself. Some find that to be singularly ironic. Others argue that it is far better than having to worry about outsiders coming to call.

Acknowledgments

Writing this book has been a collaborative process. Hundreds of interviews were conducted to build the reportorial foundation for the manuscript. I would like to thank the scores of people who agreed to be interviewed—some of them countless times for countless hours—and more than a few of them anonymously. I am especially grateful for those who tirelessly answered my repeated calls, e-mails, and requests for facts, figures, details, documentation, confirmations, and reconfirmations.

There are a few people who played a crucial role behind the scenes to help make this second edition a reality. First, I would like to thank Michael Miller, former president of Northland College, for his singular vision and steadfast support. I am particularly grateful to Kellie Pederson, who worked overtime in the closing months to help round up the myriad photos, charts, and figures that make the book more informative, engaging, and pleasing to the eye. I would also like to thank the friends who provided frank and salient feedback on the manuscript, including Lynn Broaddus, Julie Buckles, Debbie Cervenka, Mike Kohlman, Michael McAdoo, Ron Seely, Erik Streed, Theron O'Connor, Dave Ullman, and Kate Ullman. The manuscript is a stronger read, thanks to their perceptive counsel. Debbie Cervenka has long been a singular advocate for this book, and has given away more copies of the first edition than any other person, by far. I am fortunate to have had her support and contributions to the second edition as well. I would also like to thank the Institute for Journalism and Natural Resources and the Robert W. and Susan T. Brown Family Foundation for their assistance with reporting and research, as well as my colleagues at the Mary Griggs Burke Center for Freshwater Innovation for their help as we continue to wed the disciplines of science and communication on behalf of a better-informed and ecologically engaged populace.

Finally, and most importantly, all authors lean heavily on their families during the writing process—this author more than most. My wife Meri played an enormously important role in helping to compile this manuscript, serving as the deft frontline editor of all 107,000 words. She also created many of the figures in the book, and ran quality control on the entire package. It's hard to imagine the book coming together without her, and the gratitude I feel for her support leaves me humbled. My two grown sons, Nicholas and Reid, made major contributions to the manuscript as well. Both are excellent writers in their own right, which makes them great editors too. I remain eternally grateful to all three family members, for their unwavering feedback, love, and support throughout the multiyear reporting and writing process.

www.greatlakeswaterwars.com

Notes

Chapter 1

1. US Geological Survey, US Department of the Interior, "The World's Water," December 2, 2016, https://water.usgs.gov/edu/earthwherewater.html, accessed November 2, 2017.

2. United Nations, "Water," http://www.un.org/en/sections/issues-depth/water/ accessed November 2, 2017.

3. United Nations Department of Economic and Social Affairs, International Decade for Action 'WATER FOR LIFE' 2005–2015, "Water Scarcity," November 24, 2014, http://www.un.org/waterforlifedecade/scarcity.shtml, accessed November 2, 2017.

4. United Nations, "Water," http://www.un.org/en/sections/issues-depth/water/, accessed November 2, 2017.

5. Cheryl Colopy, "How No-Flush Toilets Can Help Make a Healthier World," *YaleEnvironment360*, October 11, 2012.

6. United Nations, "Water for a Sustainable World," United Nations World Water Development Report 2015, 2.

7. United Nations Educational, Scientific, and Cultural Organization, World Water Assessment Program (WWAP), "Facts and Figures," http://www.unesco.org/new/en/natural-sciences/environment/water/wwap/facts-and-figures/all-facts-wwdr3/fact2-agricultural-use/, accessed May 12, 2017.

8. Peter H. Gleick, "Water, Drought, Climate Change, and Conflict in Syria," *Weather, Climate and Society*, American Meteorological Society, July 1, 2014, 3.

9. Throughout, quotations that appear without text or endnote citations are from interviews conducted by the author.

10. Pacific Institute, "Water Conflict Chronology List," http://www2.worldwater.org/conflict/list/, accessed November 4, 2017.

11. Paul Harrison and Fred Pearce, "Population and Natural Resources: Freshwater," *Atlas of Population and the Environment*, American Association for the Advancement of Science, 2000, http://atlas.aaas.org/index.php?part=2&sec=natres&sub=water, accessed November 4, 2017.

12. Jonathan Kaiman, "China's Water Diversion Project Starts to Flow to Beijing," *The Guardian*, December 12, 2014.

13. Ezra Fieser, "Suriname Will Tow a Giant Bag of Water to Fight the Caribbean Drought," Bloomberg, November 22, 2016.

14. Juan Forero, "Latin America Fails to Deliver on Basic Needs," *The New York Times*, February 22, 2005.

15. For a detailed recap of the Klamath River situation see the documentary "A River Between Us," http://www.ariverbetweenus.com, accessed January 5, 2016.

16. Ellen Hanak, Jeffrey Mount, and Caitrin Chappelle, Water Policy Center, Public Policy Institute of California, "California's Latest Drought," July, 2016, http://www.ppic.org/publication/californias-latest-drought/, accessed November 7, 2017.

17. Dean Murphy, "Pact in West Will Send Farms' Water to Cities," *The New York Times*, October 17, 2003.

18. Interview and field visit with Michael Carpenter, research hydrologist, US Geological Survey, Tucson, AZ, April 2004.

19. Sally Spencer, US Embassy and Consulates in Mexico, "Mexico Pays Rio Grande Water Debt in Full," February 26, 2016, https://mx.usembassy.gov/mexico -pays-rio-grande-water-debt-in-full/, accessed November 7, 2017.

20. Bruce Ritchie, "River Basin at Center of Fight among States Listed as Most 'Endangered,'" *Politico*, April 12, 2016.

21. Kathy Lohr, "In Drought-Stricken Georgia, a Prayer for Rain," National Public Radio, November 14, 2007.

22. Sharon Terlep, "P&G Caught in a 400-Year-Old Feud Over Potomac River Rights," *The Wall Street Journal,* November 24, 2016.

23. Olivia Quintana, "After Drought, Water Again Flowing through Ipswich River," *The Boston Globe*, November 7, 2016.

24. Robert Glennon, "Water Scarcity, Marketing, and Privatization," *Texas Law Review* 83, no. 7 (June 2005): 1873.

25. United Nations Food and Agricultural Organization, Aquastat, http://www.fao .org/nr/water/aquastat/water_use/index.stm, accessed November 7, 2017.

26. US Environmental Protection Agency, "Saving Water in Nevada," Fact Sheet, May 2016.

27. "America's 25 Fastest Growing Cities," Forbes.com, https://www.forbes.com /pictures/ffgh45femlk/americas-fastest-growin/#75b2f4e42907, accessed November 7, 2017; see also: Henry Brean, "Court Upholds Plan to Pipe Groundwater to Las Vegas Valley," *Las Vegas Review-Journal*, August 24, 2017.

28. Report by Peter Jennings in "Las Vegas Shows Strains of Population Boom, Learning Lessons from One of the Country's Fastest-Growing Cities," *ABC World News Tonight*, November 30, 2004.

29. Marc Reisner, *Cadillac Desert: The American West and Its Disappearing Water* (New York: Viking Press, 1986), 121.

30. US Geological Survey, US Department of the Interior, "Colorado River Basin Focus Study Area," December 9, 2016, https://water.usgs.gov/watercensus/colorado .html, accessed November 8, 2017.

31. United Nations, "Water for a Sustainable World," United Nations World Water Development Report 2015, 12.

32. International Joint Commission, "Protection of the Waters of the Great Lakes, 2015 Review of the Recommendations from the February 2000 Report," December 2015, 16.

33. Michael J. Mishak, "Sharing Water Is Key to Richardson's Plan," *Las Vegas Sun*, October 4, 2007.

34. Montréal Economic Institute, "Exporting Water: A Source of Wealth for Québec," undated press release. Media reports suggest it was released on or about August 27, 2008.

35. Tony Ganzer, "NASA Scientist: Undoing Great Lakes Progress Would Take Generations to Recover," Ideastream Public Radio, April 4, 2017.

36. IJC, "Protection of the Waters of the Great Lakes," 8.

37. "Great Lakes Factsheet No. 1," in *The Great Lakes: An Environmental Atlas and*

Resource Book, 3rd ed., ed. Kent Fuller and Harvey Sheer (Chicago and Toronto: US Environmental Protection Agency Great Lakes National Program Office and the Government of Canada, 1995), http://www.epa.gov/glnpo/atlas/gl-fact1.html.

38. IJC, Protection of the Waters of the Great Lakes, 6, 43.

39. Kent Fuller and Harvey Sheer, eds., *The Great Lakes: An Environmental Atlas and Resource Book*, 3rd ed. (Chicago and Toronto: US Environmental Protection Agency Great Lakes National Program Office and the Government of Canada, 1995), 3.

40. Marwa Eltagouri, "Chicago Area Sees Greatest Population Loss of Any Major US City, Region in 2015," *Chicago Tribune*, March 25, 2016.

41. Great Lakes statistics are from Fuller and Sheer, 3, 4.

42. IJC, "Protection of the Waters of the Great Lakes," 10.

Chapter 2

1. Philip Micklin, "The Future Aral Sea: Hope and Despair," *Environmental Earth Science* 75, no. 9 (2016): 8.

2. Ibid., 4.

3. Ibid. The average depth was 10.8 meters in 2009 and had dropped to 6.9 meters by 2014.

4. Médecins Sans Frontières, *Karakalpakstan: A Population in Danger* (Tashkent, Uzbekistan, 2002), 6.

5. Ibid., 14.

6. Micklin, "The Future Aral Sea," 8.

7. Smaller versions of a dike existed in the same area since the early 1990s, but they experienced repeated structural problems including complete failure in 1999. See: Micklin, "The Future Aral Sea," 6.

8. Ibid., 11.

9. Ibid.

Chapter 3

1. Peter J. Sousounis and Jeanne M. Bisanz, eds., *Preparing for a Changing Climate: The Potential Consequences of Climate Variability and Change, Great Lakes Overview*, a report for the U.S. Global Change Research Program (Ann Arbor, MI: Great Lakes Regional Assessment Group, October 2000), 2.

2. J. D. Annan and J. C. Hargreaves, "A New Global Reconstruction of Temperature Changes at the Last Glacial Maximum," *Climate of the Past* 9 (2013): 367–76.

3. Climate Central, "The 10 Hottest Global Years on Record," http://www.climatecentral.org/gallery/graphics/the-10-hottest-global-years-on-record/, accessed May 30, 2018

4. Earth Science Communications Team, NASA Jet Propulsion Laboratory, California Institute of Technology, "Global Temperature," https://climate.nasa.gov/vital-signs/global-temperature/, accessed December 20, 2017.

5. Intergovernmental Panel on Climate Change (IPCC), "Summary for Policymakers," in *Climate Change 2013: The Physical Science Basis*, Contribution of Working Group I to the Fifth Assessment Report of the Intergovernmental Panel on Climate Change, Geneva, Switzerland (2013), 23.

6. IPCC, *Climate Change 2014 Synthesis Report*, Contribution of Working Groups I, II, and III to the Fifth Assessment, Geneva, Switzerland (2014), 6.

7. IPCC, "Summary for Policymakers," in *Climate Change 2001: Synthesis Report*, Geneva, Switzerland (2001), 12.

8. J. L. McDermid et al., *State of Climate Change Science in the Great Lakes Basin: A Focus on Climatological, Hydrological and Ecological Effects*, report of the Ontario Climate Consortium and the Ontario Ministry of Natural Resources and Forestry (October 2015), 2.

9. Ibid., 28.

10. Ibid.

11. Ibid., 33.

12. Ibid.

13. Ibid., 51, 49.

14. Ibid., 29.

15. Ibid., 29, 30.

16. Ibid., 42.

17. Ibid., 66.

18. Ibid., 40.

19. Ibid.

20. Ibid., 36.

21. Hydrologically, Lakes Michigan and Huron are considered to be one lake, and their water levels are the same.

22. W. F. Baird & Associates, *Regime Change (Man-Made Intervention) and Ongoing Erosion in the St. Clair River and Impacts on Lake Michigan–Huron Lake Levels* (January 2005), i.

23. Ibid.

24. US Army Corps of Engineers, "Corps Responds to Recent Lake-Level Study," press release, February 4, 2005.

25. For more about the fascinating history of dredging and erosion on the bottom of the St. Clair River, see: Dan Egan, *The Death and Life of the Great Lakes* (New York: W. W. Norton & Co., 2017), 286–96.

26. "International Joint Commission's Advice to Governments on the Recommendations of the International Upper Great Lakes Study, A Report to the Governments of Canada and the United States," April 15, 2013, 3.

27. International Upper Great Lakes Study Board, "International Upper Great Lakes Study, Impacts on Upper Great Lakes Water Levels: St. Clair River, Final Report to the International Joint Commission," December 2009, 31.

28. Ibid. (2009 summary report), i.

29. Ibid., 18. The 2012 report also recommended pursuing a more robust Lake Superior water-regulation plan as well as a new adaptive-management plan to help the region prepare for the uncertainties of climate. But it said an enormously expensive multi-lake regulation plan to deal with extreme water levels and climate would not be worthwhile.

30. International Upper Great Lakes Study Board, "International Upper Great Lakes Study, Impacts on Upper Great Lakes Water Levels: St. Clair River, Final Report to the International Joint Commission," March 2012, 13.

31. Ibid., 14. The 2012 report also recommended pursuing a more robust Lake Superior water-regulation plan as well.

32. *Watertown* (New York) *Daily Times*, press conference with New York governor Andrew M. Cuomo, "Cuomo: IJC 'Blew It' with Plan 2014," May 30, 2017, https://www.youtube.com/watch?v=xJnY9IQ5wLg, accessed October 1, 2017.

Chapter 4

1. Marc Reisner, *Cadillac Desert: The American West and Its Disappearing Water* (New York: Viking, 1986), 487–88.

2. Ralph M. Parsons Co., *North American Water and Power Alliance: NAWAPA*, undated promotional video, circa early 1960s.

3. Ibid. An acre-foot equals 325,851 gallons—the amount that would cover one acre to a depth of one foot.

4. Reisner, *Cadillac Desert*, 488.

5. Ibid., 487; Parsons video.

6. "A Question of Birthright," *Time*, October 1, 1965; Parsons video.

7. Reisner, *Cadillac Desert*, 489.

8. Interview with Tom Kierans, creator of the GRAND Canal proposal, March 2005.

9. The Dutch did successfully complete a project similar to the GRAND canal on the IJsselmeer (a now-closed-off bay of the North Sea, fed by the IJssel River), which Kierans holds up as a model.

10. Reisner, *Cadillac Desert*, 495.

11. Robert Bourassa, *Power from the North*, 146–55.

12. "The Erie Canal: A Brief History," New York State Canal System, http://www.canals.state.ny.us/cculture/history/index.html.

13. One map of the pipeline was printed on the cover of *The Proposed Powder River–Midwest Coal Slurry Pipeline*, transcript of an October 27, 1982, meeting between William Westhoff of Powder River Pipeline Inc. and representatives of Wisconsin state agencies (Wisconsin Coastal Management Program, February 1983). The second map was printed in the *Oil & Gas Journal* (January 19, 1981): 41.

14. *Proposed Powder River–Midwest Coal Slurry Pipeline*, 1, 2, 6.

15. Ibid., 6, 7.

16. Ibid., 7.

17. Wisconsin Coastal Management Council, *The Interbasin Transfer of Water . . . The Great Lakes Connection* (May 1982), 53.

18. US Army Corps of Engineers, *Six-State High Plains Ogallala Aquifer Regional Resources Study, Summary Report* (1982), 3.

19. Ibid.

20. Ibid., 4.

21. Ibid., 20.

22. Interestingly, the Corps's findings on cost mirrored those of a similar study conducted by the US Bureau of Reclamation in 1973. The West Texas and Eastern New Mexico Import Project envisioned diverting water from the Mississippi River via a canal stretching from Louisiana to the High Plains. But after studying the idea, the Bureau declared the plan "economically infeasible." See: "Not a Drop to Drink," *Wisconsin Magazine*, Wisconsin Educational Television Network, March 1, 1985.

23. Ibid., 61, 90–94.

24. Interview with Peter Gleick, president, Pacific Institute, May 2005.

25. For more background on the buffalo commons idea, see: Anne Matthews, "The Poppers and the Plains," *The New York Times*, June 24, 1990.

26. J. W. Bulkley, S. J. Wright, and D. Wright, "Preliminary Study of the Diversion of 283m3 s-1 (10,000 cfs) from Lake Superior to the Missouri River Basin," *Journal of Hydrology* 68 (1984): 461–72.

27. *Sporhase v. Nebraska*, 458 US 941 (1982).

28. *Final Report and Recommendations: Great Lakes Governors Task Force on Water Diversions and Great Lakes Institutions; A Report to the Governors and Premiers of the Great Lakes States and Provinces Prepared at the Request of the Council of Great Lakes Governors* (January 1985), 15.

29. Ibid., 4.

30. The idea of excluding Lake Michigan from the Boundary Waters Treaty seems particularly outdated given that scientists have pointed out that, hydrologically speaking, Lakes Michigan and Huron are considered to be one lake, thanks to their massive connecting channel at the Straits of Mackinac.

31. When the council was originally formed in January 1982 it was called the Council of North Central Governors Inc. and only included the states of Wisconsin, Minnesota, and Michigan. Eventually all eight Great Lakes governors joined the organization and in March 1984 its name was changed to the Council of Great Lakes Governors.

32. Information in this paragraph on the council and its resolutions is from *Water Diversion and Great Lakes Institutions*, 4, 5.

33. Pennsylvania and Indiana were the only states not to send a governor to the Charter's signing ceremony, although Indiana sent an official to sign on the governor's behalf. No provincial premiers were in attendance, but representatives did serve as stand-ins.

34. Quoted in Paul MacClennan, "State to Weigh Using Great Lakes to Ease N.Y. City Water Crisis," *The Buffalo News*, September 12, 1985.

35. Paul MacClennan, *The Buffalo News*, September 8, 1985.

Chapter 5

1. Donald L. Miller, *City of the Century: The Epic of Chicago and the Making of America* (New York: Simon and Schuster, 1996), 218–19 (the quote is from p. 219).

2. Ibid., 123.

3. Erik Larson, *The Devil in the White City: Murder, Magic, and Madness at the Fair That Changed America* (New York: Vintage Books, 2004), 138, 175.

4. A long-held Chicago legend says that thousands of city residents died in a cholera and typhoid epidemic after a massive rainstorm in 1885. Though many people, including public officials, regularly repeat the story, Libby Hill debunked the myth with her well-researched book, *The Chicago River: A Natural and Unnatural History* (Chicago: Lake Claremont Press, 2000). See p. 117.

5. Hill, *Chicago River*, 119.

6. Miller, *City of the Century*, 130–31.

7. Hill, *Chicago River*, 122–27.

8. Miller, *City of the Century*, 131.

9. See Hill, *Chicago River*, 128–30.

10. *The New York Times*, "Water in Chicago River, Since the Canal Was Opened, the Stream Begins to Move. Now Resembles Liquid," January 14, 1900.

11. Hill, *Chicago River*, 132.

12. Quoted in Stanley Chagnon, "Lake Michigan Diversion at Chicago," National Oceanic and Atmospheric Administration, 22.

13. Hill, *Chicago River*, 139, 184.

14. Unless otherwise cited, information about the diversion's flows and the associated history of suits and countersuits comes from Stanley Chagnon's "Lake Michigan Diversion at Chicago." See especially pp. 23, 26, 28, 30–31, and the diversion history timeline toward the end of the report.

15. Chagnon, "Lake Michigan Diversion at Chicago," 29.

16. Ibid., 31. Research would later show that, by the late 1970s, water levels in deep aquifer wells in northeastern Illinois had plummeted by a jaw-dropping 900 feet, revealing one of the worst examples of groundwater overuse in the nation. See: International Joint Commission (IJC), "Protection of the Waters of the Great Lakes: Final Report to the Governments of Canada and the United States" (February 22, 2000), 27.

17. Just as in the 1922 lawsuit charging illegal expansion of the Illinois diversion, Wisconsin was later joined in this 1957–58 suit by other Great Lakes states.

18. International Joint Commission (IJC), Great Lakes Diversions and Consumptive Uses (January 1985), 15.

19. The Corps's study was titled "Increased Lake Michigan Diversion at Chicago: Demonstration and Study Program Information Report to the Congress," and it helped influence the adoption of the Great Lakes Charter, discussed in chapter 4. The study and its initial ramifications are covered in "Not a Drop to Drink," *Wisconsin Magazine*, Wisconsin Educational Television Network, March 1, 1985.

20. Douglas Turner, "Battle Looms as Reagan Gets Plea to OK Diversion of Lakes Water," *The Buffalo News*, July 9, 1988.

21. The US Army Corps of Engineers is responsible for monitoring the diversion, but it can take years for the agency to produce certified results, which helps explain why it took other states so long to discover that Illinois was so far out of compliance.

22. Gary Washburn and Rudolph Bush, "Drink Up, City, but Meter Will Be Running; Chicago Will Measure All Water Use, Drop Flat Fee Charge," *Chicago Tribune*, April 9, 2003.

23. City of Chicago press release, "Mayor Emanuel and Department of Water Management Commissioner Tom Powers Highlight the Need for Investments in Chicago's Infrastructure," October 14, 2011.

Chapter 6

1. For a complete history on how Asian carp entered the Mississippi River watershed, see Dan Egan's excellent book *The Death and Life of the Great Lakes* (New York: W. W. Norton & Co., 2017), 154–57.

2. The barrier was originally installed to keep the invasive round goby from moving from the Great Lakes to the Mississippi, but the goby got through before the barrier was completed.

3. The author of this book worked as managing director for the Environmental Change Initiative at the University of Notre Dame from 2010 to 2015, and worked closely with Professor Lodge and his team during that time.

4. Joel Hood, David G. Savage, and Cynthia Dizikes, "DNA of Asian Carp Discovered in Lake, High Court Won't Force Illinois to Shut Waterways," *The Chicago Tribune,* January 20, 2010.

5. Susan Saulny, "Carp DNA Is Found in Lake Michigan," *The New York Times,* January 19, 2010.

6. Michael Tarm, "Court Refuses 2nd Asian Carp Injunction Request," Associated Press, March 22, 2010.

7. US Army Corps of Engineers Press Release, "Corps Releases Operational Parameters Report," March 25, 2011.

8. Great Lakes and Mississippi River Interbasin Study Natural Resources Team (Veraldi et al.), "Non-Native Species of Concern and Dispersal Risk for the Great Lakes and Mississippi River Interbasin Study," Appendix III, September 16, 2011.

9. US Army Corps of Engineers, Great Lakes and Mississippi River Interbasin Study, "Focus Area 2, Aquatic Pathways Assessment Summary Report," September 14, 2012.

10. John Flesher, "Great Lakes Groups Ramp Up Pressure to Separate Mississippi River from Great Lakes," Associated Press, January 31, 2012.

11. US Army Corps of Engineers, "Summary of Fish–Barge Interaction Research and Fixed Dual-Frequency Identification Sonar (DIDSON) Sampling at the Electric Dispersal Barrier in Chicago Sanitary and Ship Canal," report, December 20, 2013.

12. US Army Corps of Engineers, "Corps Submits Report to Congress with Alternatives to Prevent Asian Carp and Other Species' Transfer Between the Great Lakes and Mississippi River Basins," press release, January 6, 2014.

13. Hongyan Zhang et al., "Forecasting the Impacts of Silver and Bighead Carp on the Lake Erie Food Web," *Transactions of the American Fisheries Society*, December 30, 2015.

14. University of Notre Dame, "Asian Carp Could Cause Some Lake Erie Fish Species to Decline, Others to Increase," press release, January 4, 2016.

15. Zhang et al., "Forecasting the Impacts of Silver and Bighead Carp."

16. Canada Department of Fisheries and Oceans, "Ecological Risk Assessment of Grass Carp (*Ctenopharyngodon idella*) for the Great Lakes Basin," Science Advisory Report 2016/057, last modified July 10, 2017.

17. Asian Carp Regional Coordinating Committee, "Autopsy Complete of Silver Carp Captured 9 Miles from Lake Michigan," press release, August 18, 2017.

18. John Flesher, "Asian Carp Found in Little Calumet River Had Evaded Three Electric Barriers," Associated Press, August 18, 2017.

19. Mississippi Wildlife, Fisheries and Parks, "First Confirmed Snakehead Caught in Mississippi Lake," press release, June 8, 2017.

20. Dan Egan, *The Death and Life of the Great Lakes,* 187–211.

21. Ibid., 183.

Chapter 7

1. Unless otherwise cited, specifications of the Waboose Dam and the associated Ogoki Reservoir are from Keith Charles Bridger, "The Ogoki River Diversion: Reservoir, Downstream, Diversion Channel, and Receiving Water-Body Effects" (master's thesis, University of Waterloo, Ontario, 1978), especially pp. 11 and 12. The crest length

on Hoover Dam is 1,244 feet, according to the US Bureau of Reclamation; see: http://www.usbr.gov/lc/region/pao/hoover.html.

2. According to the International Joint Commission, the largest diversion in the Great Lakes Basin is the Welland Canal, which bypasses Niagara Falls. At 9,200 cfs, it greatly exceeds the Ogoki diversion in size. However, because the Welland Canal transfers water from one Great Lake to another, it is considered an *intra-Basin* diversion within the Great Lakes watershed. The Long Lac and Ogoki diversions are *interbasin* water transfers, withdrawing water from the Albany River drainage basin in the Hudson Bay watershed and sending it to the Great Lakes.

3. According to officials at Ontario Power Generation, which owns and operates the Long Lac diversion, "Long Lake" is the name of the diversion (and the lake), while "Longlac" (one word) is the name of the town nearest the diversion. However, the diplomatic notes exchanged between the United States and Canada refer to the diversion as "Long Lac." All official references by the International Joint Commission also use the name "Long Lac." Consequently Long Lake and Long Lac are used interchangeably by officials when referring to this diversion. These names are used interchangeably in this chapter as well.

4. International Joint Commission (IJC), *Protection of the Waters of the Great Lakes: Final Report to the Governments of Canada and the United States* (February 22, 2000), 12.

5. The history of the Long Lac diversion is told by Simon Edward Peet in "The Long Lake Diversion: An Environmental Evaluation" (master's thesis, University of Waterloo, Ontario, 1978). Unless otherwise cited, details about the diversion's impetus, negotiations surrounding implementation, hydro rights, and construction logistics are from this source, especially pp. 18, 22, 24–29.

6. This Frank Quinn is not the same person as the American Frank Quinn, formerly of the US National Oceanic and Atmospheric Administration, cited in chapter 3.

7. Ogoki construction details, unless otherwise noted, are from Bridger, "The Ogoki River Diversion," 11. As subsequent diplomatic notes would make clear, the Canadians decided to build a new generating plant on the Welland Canal to capture the Long Lac and Ogoki waters, rather than capturing the waters at Niagara Falls. See: Glenys Big-gar, *Ontario Hydro's History and Description of Hydro-Electric Generating Stations* (Ontario Hydro, 1991), 84. See also: International Joint Commission (IJC), "Great Lakes Diversions and Consumptive Uses" (January 1985), 78.

8. According to Chief Veronica Waboose of Long Lake No. 58 First Nation, *waboose* is the local Ojibway term for "rapids." Interview with Chief Waboose, October 2005.

9. Quoted in IJC, *Great Lakes Diversions*, 77.

10. Ibid., 78.

11. International Joint Commission, International Lake Superior Board of Control, minutes of the September 22, 2004 meeting, http:// www.ijc.org/php/publications/html /September222004-e.htm.

12. Canada agreed to have the diversions "reduced or stopped" in 1952 and 1973. See IJC, *Great Lakes Diversions*, 13.

13. Mr. Pentland is referring to the IJC study, *Great Lakes Diversions*. See p. 23.

14. J. C. [Chad] Day and Frank Quinn, *Water Diversion and Export: Learning from Canadian Experience* (Waterloo, ON: University of Waterloo Press, 1992), 78.

15. See: Bridger, *Ogoki River Diversion*, 136.

16. See: Peet, *Long Lake Diversion*, 58.

Chapter 8

1. Copies of all of the letters quoted from or referred to in this chapter were provided upon request by the agencies or individuals involved.

2. Letter from J. D. Snyder, director, Michigan's Office of the Great Lakes, to Bruce Baker, Wisconsin Department of Natural Resources, August 10, 1989.

3. Letter from J. D. Snyder, director, Michigan's Office of the Great Lakes, to Bruce Baker, Wisconsin Department of Natural Resources, September 7, 1989.

4. Memorandum from consultant George Loomis to Michael Pollocoff, Pleasant Prairie village administrator, September 29, 1989.

5. Letter from Bruce Baker, Wisconsin Department of Natural Resources, to J. D. Snyder, director, Michigan's Office of the Great Lakes, October 9, 1989.

6. Letter from David Hales, director, Michigan Department of Natural Resources, to Wisconsin governor Tommy Thompson, December 12, 1989.

7. E-mail from J. D. Snyder to the author of this book, September 10, 2007.

8. Sean Ryan, "Niagara Bottling to Buy up to 2 Million Gallons of Water a Day in Pleasant Prairie," *Milwaukee Business Journal*, April 2, 2014.

Chapter 9

1. Kevin Voigt, "The Larvae Are Back in Lowell's Water," *Northwest Indiana Times*, September 14, 1990.

2. Letter from US Environmental Protection Agency, Region 5, to Lowell Water Department, December 30, 1987, provided upon request by the EPA.

3. Ibid.

4. Melanie Csepiga, "Water Woes Put Lowell in Scramble," *Northwest Indiana Times*, March 15, 1990.

5. Melanie Csepiga, "Lowell Opts for Lake Michigan Water," *Northwest Indiana Times*, April 3, 1990.

6. Ibid.

7. Melanie Csepiga, "Michigan Governor May Leave Lowell Thirsting for Water," *Northwest Indiana Times*, April 26, 1991.

8. All information about this initial meeting concerning Lowell's diversion request is from: State of New York, Department of Environmental Conservation, Hearing Report and Interviews, Appendix B, *Summary, June 7, 1991, Indiana Consultation Meeting Regarding the Lowell Water Diversion Project*, January 10, 1992. See especially pp. B35–B38.

9. Letter from Patrick R. Ralston, director, Indiana Department of Natural Resources, to Thomas C. Jorling, commissioner, New York Department of Environmental Conservation, March 4, 1992, provided by John Hughes, Lowell's attorney.

10. Letter from Michigan governor John Engler to Indiana governor Evan Bayh, May 8, 1992, provided by John Hughes, Lowell's attorney, and other sources.

11. Ibid.

12. "Lowell Optimistic about Chances for Lake Water, Officials Believe Town Should Qualify under New Guidelines for Tapping into Great Lakes," *Northwest Indiana Times*, June 19, 2001.

13. Melanie Csepiga, "Lowell Eyes New Concept for Water Plant," *Northwest Indiana Times*, June 10, 2013.

14. Jared Teutsch, "On Track? Ensuring the Resilience of the Great Lakes Compact," Alliance for the Great Lakes, September 26, 2013, 7.

Chapter 10

1. The two volumes of research were *The Saginaw Bay, Michigan, Subirrigation / Drainage Project: 1987–1988*, and *The Saginaw Bay, Michigan, Subirrigation / Drainage Project: 1989–1990*. Both were edited by Frank M. D'Itri and Jody A. Kubitz and were published by the Institute of Water Research at Michigan State University.

2. Williams, Ominski and Associates, and Fishbeck, Thompson, Carr & Huber Inc., "Great Lakes Water Use Proposal, Mud Creek Irrigation District," public information document, presented to the Office of the Governor, State of Michigan, the Natural Resources Commission, and the Michigan Department of Natural Resources (January 1993).

3. International Joint Commission (IJC), "Protection of the Waters of the Great Lakes: Final Report to the Governments of Canada and the United States," February 22, 2000, 10.

4. Williams, Ominski et al., "Great Lakes Water Use Proposal, Mud Creek Irrigation District," 26.

5. Letters requesting or supporting a consultation were received from governors in Illinois, Pennsylvania, Minnesota, Ohio, and New York, and from the premier of Ontario.

6. The description of the April 28, 1993, Mud Creek consultative hearing is from handwritten notes taken by David Hamilton, then chief of the Water Management Division at the Michigan Department of Natural Resources, and "Charter Consultations: Mud Creek Irrigation District—Summary of Key Issues," both of which are on file at the Michigan Department of Environmental Quality. Several meeting attendees were interviewed as well.

7. As has been pointed out in prior chapters, consumptive use can result in a loss of water to the system through evaporation or integration into a product. Such losses would occur in Mud Creek, but the water lost would be much less than if Mud Creek were a diversion.

8. Draft of letter from Michigan governor John Engler to the governors of Ohio, Wisconsin, Indiana, Pennsylvania, New York, and Minnesota, and the premiers of Ontario and Québec, May 7, 1993, on file at Michigan Department of Environmental Quality.

9. The response letters to Governor Engler's May 7, 1993, letters are all on file at the Michigan Department of Environmental Quality.

10. Michigan Department of Natural Resources, interoffice communication, from G. Tracy Mehan, director, Michigan's Office of the Great Lakes, to Larry DeVuyst, chairman, Natural Resources Commission, June 9, 1993.

11. State of Michigan Irrigation Districts Act, Act No. 205, Public Policy Acts of 1967, as amended by Act No. 221, Public Acts of 1978.

12. David Poulson, "Word about Water Diversion Bottled Up by Engler Staff," *Grand Rapids Press*, July 16, 1993; "Huron Irrigation Risks Too Much," *Bay City Times*, July 22, 1993; and Peter Luke, "Irrigation OK Hurts Engler," *Kalamazoo Gazette*, July 18, 1993.

13. According to the Michigan Department of Environmental Quality, while Huron County often did not file annual reports between 2005 and 2016, it did send letters confirming zero usage during those years, except for 2013, for which there is no correspondence.

Chapter 11

1. *Portage County Board of Commissioners, et al. v. City of Akron et al.*, Case No. 98 CV 0325, "Akron's Motion for Summary Judgment as to Akron's Rights Under the 1911 Grant," filed January 31, 2000, in Portage County [Ohio] Common Pleas Court, Appendix Tab 8 at 343.

2. *Akron Beacon Journal*, May 18, 1909, 1.

3. City of Akron, "Report of the Board of Control Transmitting to the City Council the Report of the Engineers on an Improved Water Supply for the City of Akron, Ohio, 1911," August 12, 1911, 14.

4. Ibid.

5. Ibid., 5–12.

6. Ibid., 2.

7. In some cases Akron annexed neighboring communities, but annexation proved bitterly controversial as towns despised losing their identities to the bigger city. In the face of this annexation opposition, Akron created something known as JEDDs—Joint Economic Development Districts. The JEDDs were a political compromise between Akron and its neighbors: the JEDDs allowed surrounding towns and suburbs to tap into the city's water system without the pain of annexation. In exchange, the employees and businesses in those communities agreed to pay Akron's 2 percent income tax.

8. Black & Veatch and Public Sector Consultants, "A Report on the Proposed Expansion of the City of Akron Water System," prepared for the City of Akron (July 1996).

9. City of Akron, "Preserving the Great Lakes Through Regional Cooperation, A Proposal by the City of Akron, Ohio," brochure (circa 1996).

10. Letter from Ohio governor George Voinovich to all eight Great Lakes governors, September 30, 1996, provided upon request by the Division of Water at the Ohio Department of Natural Resources.

11. Patrick O'Donnell, "Suit Asks Court to Stop Sale of Water," (Cleveland) *The Plain Dealer*, April 18, 1998.

12. Patrick O'Donnell, "Akron Sued over Control of River's Flow," (Cleveland) *The Plain Dealer*, May 11, 1998.

13. Gregory Korte, "1911 Deed Rejected in Court; Akron Loses First Round in Fight for River Water," *Akron Beacon Journal*, April 21, 2000.

14. Gregory Korte and Julie Wallace "Courts to Decide Who Owns Cuyahoga River," *Akron Beacon Journal*, January 8, 2001, 1.

15. John C. Kuehner, "Akron Lands in Court in Fight about Water," (Cleveland) *The Plain Dealer*, January 9, 2001.

16. *Portage County Board of Commissioners et al. v. City of Akron et al.*, Case No. 98 CV 0325 appeals court summary, 667.

17. Gregory Korte, "1911 Deed Rejected in Court; Akron Loses First Round in Fight for River Water," *Akron Beacon Journal*, April 21, 2000.

18. Paula Schleis, "Akron Case Holds Water, Judge Says; City Keeps Control of Lake Rockwell Dam, Though Recreation Will Be Allowed," *Akron Beacon Journal*, October 10, 2001.

19. Judge John A. Enlow, "Findings of Fact and Conclusions of Law," *Portage County Board of Commissioners et al. v. City of Akron et al.*, Case No. 98 CV 0325, Portage County Court of Common Pleas, Portage County, Ohio, 17–19.

20. John C. Kuehner, "Court Backs Akron Claim on River Water," (Cleveland) *The Plain Dealer*, October 10, 2001.

21. Mike Sever, "Rights to Cuyhahoga Water Argued; Portage County, Ravenna, Akron in Appeals Court," (Ravenna, Ohio) *Record-Courier*, December 12, 2003.

22. Mike Sever, "Court: Set Rockwell Flow; Deny Public Access to Lake," (Ravenna, Ohio) *Record-Courier*, April 1, 2004.

23. According to the court, that flow was meant to consist of 5 mgd that Akron would release from the reservoir daily as well as an additional amount of leakage (through the dam) and seepage (from the ground underneath the reservoir).

24. *Portage County Board of Commissioners v. Akron, Ohio*, St.3d, 2006-Ohio-954, 33.

25. "Ruling Regionally, the Ohio Supreme Court Declares an End to the Water War. The Winners? Akron and Its Neighbors," *Akron Beacon Journal*, March 8, 2006.

Chapter 12

1. Associated Press, "Lake Superior Heads to Asia," May 1, 1998.

2. International Joint Commission (IJC), "Protection of the Waters of the Great Lakes: Final Report to the Governments of Canada and the United States," February 22, 2000, 6, 43.

3. Ibid., 16, 17.

4. Ibid., 22, 46–48.

5. James S. Lochhead et al., "Report to the Council of the Great Lakes Governors, Governing the Withdrawal of Water from the Great Lakes," May 18, 1999, 44.

6. Ibid., 2.

7. Quotations and arguments from ibid., 15–19.

8. Quotations and arguments from ibid., 19–20.

9. Quotations and arguments from ibid., 20.

10. Quotations and arguments from ibid., 22, 21.

11. For Lochhead's discussion of the public trust and riparian reasonable-use doctrines, see ibid., 34, 37.

12. Ibid., 42, 43.

13. Ibid., 44.

14. Ibid., 47–49.

15. James S. Lochhead, "The Benefit Standard," memo to the Council of Great Lakes Governors, September 1, 1999, 1–2.

16. Ibid., 2, 10.

17. Cheryl Mendoza, quoted in Lake Michigan Federation [now called the Alliance for the Great Lakes], "Act Now to Protect Great Lakes Water," *The Lake Effect* (Fall 2004), 1.

18. For all Annex 2001 quotations and directives, see Council of Great Lakes Governors, *The Great Lakes Charter Annex: A Supplementary Agreement to the Great Lakes Charter* (June 18, 2001).

19. Council of Great Lakes Governors, "Great Lakes Governors and Premiers Sign Charter Annex," press release, June 18, 2001.

Chapter 13

1. By the time of the post–Annex 2001 negotiations, the Canadians had already passed their federal and provincial anti-diversion laws, rendering Great Lakes protections more stringent on the Canadian side of the border. WRDA existed on the US side of the border, but it was considered by most to be legally vulnerable, and thus inferior.

2. Quoted in: Dan Egan, "Diversion Rules Face Rough Waters to Gain Approval, Great Lakes Hearing Draws 100 in Chicago," *Milwaukee Journal Sentinel*, September 8, 2004.

3. The companion, nonbinding International Agreement was released at the same time.

4. Great Lakes St. Lawrence Governors and Premiers, "Great Lakes Basin Water Resources Compact," draft, July 19, 2004, 7, 14.

5. Ibid., 7, 14, 15.

6. Ibid., 3.

7. "Great Lakes Pact Opposed," Associated Press, September 15, 2004.

8. For quotations from the Munk Centre paper, see Andrew Nikiforuk, "Political Diversions: Annex 2001 and the Future of the Great Lakes," Munk Centre for International Studies, Program on Water Issues, University of Toronto, June 2004, 3, 4, 6.

9. Chris Wood, "Melting Point, How Global Warming Will Melt Our Glaciers, Empty the Great Lakes, Force Canada to Divert Rivers, Build Dams, and Yes, Sell Water to the United States," *The Walrus*, October 2005, 44.

10. Ontario Ministry of Natural Resources, "Level of Protection in Draft Great Lakes Charter Annex Agreements Not High Enough; Changes Needed before Ontario Will Sign," press release, November 15, 2004.

11. "Are the Great Lakes for Sale? An Inside Look at the Controversial Proposal to Export Water from Our Precious Resource," *Time*, Canadian edition, December 6, 2004.

12. Michigan was a notable exception to this trend, receiving more comments during 2005 than in 2004.

13. The Compact stipulated the formation of the Compact Council, a committee responsible for reviewing regional water decisions. Technically, the eight Basin governors should sit on the council, but the Compact conceded that governors could assign their seats to staff members or agency officials.

14. Governors Doyle and Taft were co-chairs of the Great Lakes St. Lawrence Governors and Premiers at the time and arguably had to be at the signing ceremony, so to his credit Premier McGuinty was the only top official to make a statement simply by attending.

15. Governor Bob Taft, statement read at a press conference following the Annex Implementing Agreements signing ceremony, Milwaukee, Wisconsin, December 13, 2005.

16. Wisconsin Legislative Council Proposed Report to the Legislature, Special Committee on Great Lakes Water Resources Compact, October 5, 2007, 7.

17. Mary Lazich, "Counterpoint: The Compact Is Flawed," (Milwaukee) *BizTimes*, March 21, 2008.

18. Paul Cox, "Grendell Offers Compromise on Great Lakes Compact," WCPN Ideastream Radio, April 9, 2008.

19. Dan Egan, "Great Lakes Compact Hits Rough Waters," *Milwaukee Journal Sentinel*, February 17, 2008.

20. "Wisconsin Deserts Grendell on Great Lakes Compact," unsigned editorial, (Cleveland) *Plain Dealer*, April 13, 2008.

21. Technically speaking, Congress was "consenting" to the Compact.

Chapter 14

1. Some Wisconsin residents also pronounce the city's name as "WAU- kee-shaw."

2. Unless otherwise noted, details about Waukesha's midnight standoff in 1892 are from David P. McDaniel, "Spring City and the Water War of 1892," *Wisconsin Magazine of History*, Autumn 2005, 28–39.

3. Libby Hill, *The Chicago River: A Natural and Unnatural History* (Chicago: Lake Claremont Press, 2000), 116.

4. McDaniel, "Spring City," 28–39. Chicago entrepreneurs did eventually serve "Waukesha water" at the world's fair. It just happened to come from Waukesha County, not the city itself.

5. John M. Schoenknecht, *The Great Waukesha Springs Era, 1868–1918* (Waukesha, WI: John M. Schoenknecht), 156.

6. These details on the downfall of Waukesha's springs are from an interview with John M. Schoenknecht, author of *The Great Waukesha Springs Era*, September 2005.

7. Radium contamination was also an issue in Pleasant Prairie, Wisconsin; see chapter 7.

8. While Waukesha had not submitted a formal Great Lakes diversion application, Mayor Carol Lombardi did send a letter to Wisconsin governor Jim Doyle on August 18, 2003, saying that the city was "beginning a process to obtain permission to withdraw 20 million gallons of water per day from Lake Michigan."

9. One consultant was a former official with the Council of Great Lakes Governors. Another served as a consultant for the City of Akron on its diversion case.

10. Aquifers have underground watershed divides similar to those on the surface, although, as Waukesha's case shows, the surface-water divide and the groundwater divide don't always line up vertically in the same place. Research has shown that groundwater pumping in Waukesha County and other parts of southeastern Wisconsin has moved the groundwater divide to the west, away from Lake Michigan. However, the city of Waukesha lies between the surface-water divide and the "presettlement" groundwater divide—that is, the groundwater divide before it was affected by excessive pumping. For more information on the groundwater flow system in Waukesha County, see the US Geological Survey, "Water Resources of Wisconsin," http://wi.water.usgs.gov/glpf/.

11. The City of Waukesha provided the legal documents to the author of this book with the understanding that they would be cited.

12. Officials in Indiana confirmed the law firm's description of the Town of Dyer's water diversion.

Chapter 15

1. Dan Egan and Darryl Enriquez, "Michigan Shuts Tap to Lake, New Berlin Blocked in Request to Divert Water," *Milwaukee Journal Sentinel*, June 30, 2006.

2. Ibid.

3. Dan Egan, "Who Should Be Able to Tap the Great Lakes?" *Milwaukee Journal Sentinel*, July 17, 2006.

4. Ibid.

5. According to Kenosha officials, these dates are approximate.

6. Great Lakes–St. Lawrence River Basin Water Resources Council, 2009, http://www.glslcompactcouncil.org/ViewWithdrawals.aspx, accessed May 16, 2017.

7. In the July 17, 2006, *Milwaukee Journal Sentinel* article Bruce Baker of the Wisconsin DNR said that, combined, the Menonomee Falls and Kenosha diversions that occurred between 1986 and 2003 totaled 1.4 mgd. If Menomonee Falls total is 367,000 gallons per day, then that leaves roughly a million gallons per day left over for Kenosha.

8. Dan Egan, "DNR Could OK Water Diversion, Despite Opposition There's Precedent for Using Lake Michigan to Supply New Berlin," *Milwaukee Journal Sentinel*, December 10, 2006.

9. US Geological Survey, US Department of the Interior, "Water Questions & Answers: How Much Water Does the Average Person Use at Home per Day?" December 2, 2016, https://water.usgs.gov/edu/qa-home-percapita.html, accessed May 20, 2017.

10. According to annual reports that New Berlin is required to file with the Wisconsin DNR, it had reduced its per capita water use by 10 percent by 2013, seven years before the 2020 deadline. http://dnr.wi.gov/topic/WaterUse/documents/NewBerlin/DNRResponse2014.pdf, accessed May 15, 2017.

11. Darryl Enriquez, "New Berlin's Request for Lake Water Approved—A First under Great Lakes Compact," *Milwaukee Journal Sentinel*, May 21, 2009.

12. Sarah Coefield, "Landmark Wisconsin Diversion of Great Lakes Water Is Both Praised and Blasted," *Great Lakes Echo*, May 22, 2009.

13. Ibid.

14. Jared Teutsch, "On Track? Ensuring the Resilience of the Great Lakes Compact," Alliance for the Great Lakes, September 26, 2013, www.greatlakes.org.

Chapter 16

1. Great Lakes Information Network, "Great Lakes Facts and Figures," http://www.great-lakes.net/lakes/ref/lakefact.html, accessed September 1, 2017.

2. International Joint Commission, "Great Lakes Diversions and Consumptive Uses," January 1985, 15.

3. Jeff Scrima, "Is Water from Milwaukee Really Necessary?" *Waukesha Freeman*, March 2, 2010.

4. Letter from Paul Ybarra, Waukesha Common Council president, to Matthew Frank, secretary of Wisconsin Department of Natural Resources, August 6, 2010.

5. Don Behm, "Waukesha Mayor Continues Opposition to Lake Water," *Milwaukee Journal Sentinel*, July 5, 2010.

6. Jeff Scrima, "Let's Trust Waukesha's Citizens," *Milwaukee Journal Sentinel*, July 10, 2010.

7. "Who Speaks for City," *Milwaukee Journal Sentinel*, July 14, 2010.

8. Don Behm, "Waukesha's Water Application to DNR Clears Hurdle," *Milwaukee Journal Sentinel*, July 1, 2011.

9. Don Behm, "Milwaukee Vote Puts Waukesha Water Talks at Impasse," *Milwaukee Journal Sentinel*, July 6, 2012.

10. Christopher Kuhagen, "Waukesha Mayoral Election Entering Home Stretch," *Milwaukee Journal Sentinel*, March 19, 2014.

11. State of Wisconsin Legislative Audit Bureau, "Wastewater Permitting and Enforcement, Department of Natural Resources," Report 16-6, June 2016.

12. Greg Layson, "Waukesha, Wis., Plan to Tap into Lake Michigan Called 'Wrong Decision,'" CBC News, June 22, 2016.

13. CBC News, "Nipigon, Ontario, Mayor Says Waukesha Water Decision Sets Worrying Precedent," June 23, 2016.

14. Waukesha, Pleasant Prairie, New Berlin, Menomonee Falls, Kenosha, and Foxconn/Racine.

15. City-data.com estimates Waukesha has 2.4 people per household,. http://www .city-data.com/city/Waukesha-Wisconsin.html, accessed September 1, 2017.

Chapter 17

1. Metropolitan Milwaukee Association of Commerce, "State Gross Domestic Product Leveraged by Tax Credit Investment at Various Jobs/Capital Expenditure Performance Levels," March 22, 2018, http://www.mmac.org/uploads/1/1/3/5/113552797 /mmac_foxconn_roi_release_and_tables.pdf, accessed March 24, 2018.

2. If a straddling-community diversion *consumes* 5 mgd or more—averaged over any 90-day period—the application is subject to regional review by other Great Lakes states and provinces. Even so, the other jurisdictions do not have the authority to veto a straddling-community application.

3. Racine's water permit allows the city to withdraw more than 60 million gallons of water from Lake Michigan per day. In 2017, the year before Racine's application was approved, it withdrew an average of approximately 17 million gallons per day, giving the city more than 40 million gallons of buffer to accommodate the 7 mgd requested in the Racine / Mount Pleasant / Foxconn diversion application.

4. While Pleasant Prairie is permitted to divert up to 10.69 mgd, the Wisconsin DNR says it is currently only diverting 2.44 mgd.

Epilogue

1. Zaharaa Alkhalisi, "This Desert Reservoir Could Fill 10,000 Olympic Swimming Pools," *CNNMoney*, January 15, 2018.

2. Charles Fishman, "The Big Thirst," *Free Press*, 2011, 55.

3. The Pacific Institute, "The Cadiz Valley Groundwater Storage Project," http:// pacinst.org/publication/cadiz-valley-groundwater/, accessed March 11, 2018.

4. Cadiz Inc., http://www.cadizinc.com/faq-on-hold/, accessed March 11, 2018.

5. Sammy Roth, "Environmental Groups Sue Trump Administration over California Desert Groundwater Project," *The Desert Sun*, November 28, 2017.

6. Cadiz Water Project, http://www.cadizwaterproject.com/project-support/, accessed March 11, 2018.

7. Felicity Barringer, "Water Piped to Denver Could Ease Stress on River," *The New York Times*, December 9, 2012.

8. Bruce Finley, "Missouri River Pipeline Mulled to Ease Front Range's Water Woes," *Denver Post*, December 4, 2012.

9. Ibid.

10. Fishman, "The Big Thirst," 85.

About the Author

A veteran conflict and environmental journalist, Peter Annin spent more than a decade reporting on a wide variety of issues for *Newsweek*. For many years he specialized in coverage of domestic terrorism and other conflicts, including the bombing of the federal building in Oklahoma City and the Branch Davidian standoff outside Waco, Texas. He has also spent many years writing about the environment, including droughts in the Southwest, hurricanes in the Southeast, wind power on the Great Plains, forest fires in the mountain West, recovery efforts on the Great Lakes, and the causes and consequences of the "dead zone" in the Gulf of Mexico.

After his time at *Newsweek*, Annin became associate director of the Institute for Journalism and Natural Resources, a nonpartisan national nonprofit that organizes educational fellowships for midcareer environmental journalists. In September 2006, he published his first book, *The Great Lakes Water Wars*, which has been called the definitive work on the Great Lakes water-diversion controversy, and received the Great Lakes Book Award for nonfiction. From 2010 to 2015, Annin served as managing director of the University of Notre Dame's Environmental Change Initiative, which targets the interrelated problems of invasive species, land use, and climate change, focusing on their synergistic impacts on water resources.

He currently serves as codirector of the Mary Griggs Burke Center for Freshwater Innovation at Northland College in Ashland, Wisconsin. He has a bachelor's degree in journalism from the University of Wisconsin and a master's in international affairs from Columbia University in New York.

Index

Note: page numbers followed by "f" and "t" refer to figures and tables, respectively.